The Genius of
GARDENING

The History of Gardens in
Britain and Ireland

The Genius of
GARDENING

The History of Gardens in
Britain and Ireland

Christopher Thacker

Weidenfeld and Nicolson
London

Overleaf *The long avenue of woodland, water, steps and sculpture at Buscot, designed by Harold Peto. A genial combination of restraint-with-variety.*
Frontispiece *Around 1975 Russell Page created this small, discreet yet memorable garden in a courtyard at West Wycombe Park – a masterpiece in green, grey and silver.*

First published 1994
Text and illustrations © Christopher Thacker, 1994

Filmset by Selwood Systems, Midsomer Norton

Printed in Great Britain by Butler & Tanner Ltd, Frome and London

George Weidenfeld and Nicolson Ltd
The Orion Publishing Group
Orion House
5 Upper St Martin's Lane
London WC2H 9EA

British Library Cataloguing-in-Publication Data
A catalogue record for this book is available from the British Library

ISBN 0-297-83354-5

For Thomasina

CONTENTS

Introduction
'The Genius of Gardening'

That restless but creative quality, 'the genius of gardening', it was said in *The World* on Thursday, 12 April 1753, was one which was special to the inhabitants of Britain and Ireland; they kept changing their gardens:

> They are usually new-created once in twenty or thirty years, and no traces left of their former condition. Nor is this to be wondered at ... Were any man of taste not to lay out his ground in the style which prevailed less than half a century ago, it would occasion as much astonishment and laughter, as if a modern beau should appear in the drawing-room in red stockings ...

Perfectly true – and this history tells of the ever-changing styles of British and Irish gardens from the year dot to the present day. What that journalist in 1753 didn't say, however, was that, fashion or no fashion, the gardens themselves grow, flourish, spread, encroach, recede, collapse and grow again, always different from before.

Thus the inborn 'genius of gardening' changes them, and they themselves will not stand still. The recording of them, whether with a camera, or in watercolours, or with 'level and line' and a drawing board, or with pen and paper to write a book like this, is always of something already different from what it was when the process began.

Over some 2,000 years, Britain and Ireland have seen all sorts of gardens, with a host of uses. Work came with most of them. In 1587 William Harrison wrote:

> I comprehend, therefore, under the word 'garden' all such grounds as are wrought with the spade by man's hand.

A few years later, George Wither's book of *Emblemes* (1635) included the picture of a spade, with the motto 'The *Spade*, for *Labour* stands'.

But it all took time. When Bacon wrote in 1625, in 'Of Riches', that 'the *Improvement of the Ground* is the most natural obtaining of Riches', he added 'but it is slow'. Even so, we should take delight in gardens. In 'Of Gardens' Bacon confirmed that 'it is the purest of Humane pleasures', and long before, in 1506, the poet Stephen Hawes had rightly and proudly celebrated 'the gardyn gloryous' of his native land.

Large or small, vanished or fearlessly flourishing, these gardens reflect a long and glorious history – the subject of this book.

My warmest thanks to Rowena Foster, who typed the lot; to Elain Harwood, my colleague and loyal helper in the 1980s at English Heritage; to the staff of the London Library; and to Candide, whose final advice led me, 30 years ago, to wonder about it all.

1

Druids, Romans and Anglo-Saxons

'Holy Groves'

The raw materials of gardens – stone, water, grass, trees and other plants – have been present in Britain and Ireland for many thousands of years. Native trees, familiar to the ancient Celts, included one or more forms of alder, (crab) apple, ash, beech, birch, (gean) cherry, elder, elm, hawthorn, hazel, holly, (small leaf) lime, oak, poplar or aspen (*Populus tremula*), rowan, service, sloe or blackthorn, whitebeam, willow and yew. Shrubs and flowers included mistletoe, dog rose, probably woad (*Isatis tinctoria*), columbine, wild daffodil (*Narcissus pseudonarcissus*), bluebell and a host of other, to us, 'wild' flowers.[1]

But, and this history has many a 'but', the early Britons did not make gardens. Their agriculture was far from primitive, and archaeologists have found ample evidence of farming activity round many pre-Roman sites, yet these did not, apparently, include any distinctively 'garden' areas.[2] While the desperately vague references in Celtic mythology talk of 'sacred waters', the 'magic quicken-tree' (the rowan), the 'apple-tree of Ailinn' and the 'yew-tree of Baile',[3] they leave us gardenless, both in date and in place. The Isle of the Blessed – Avalon, the apple-island of forgetfulness – reappears in late-medieval and subsequent descriptions, but no one has ever told us how it was first laid out, or, in truth, where it was.

We are left with the Druids, yet even here our knowledge remains slight and often oblique. What they may have done at Stonehenge – if they did – is still subject for speculation. The first written record tells of their presence in Gaul around 50 BC, with the comment that their doc-

A part of the first-century Roman garden at Fishbourne in Sussex. Excavations in the 1960s revealed accurate bedding patterns, which would have been planted with trimmed box hedges like these.

A modern stone circle – echoing the prehistoric circle at Avebury – in the garden at Hazelbury in Wiltshire.

trine had come to Gaul from Britain, and that those who wished to study Druidism generally went to Britain to do so.[4]

Well over a century later, around AD 70, Pliny the Elder in his *Natural History* commented at length on the Druids 'in the Gallic provinces', who revere the mistletoe, when growing on the oak trees in their sacred groves. 'A priest arrayed in white vestments climbs the tree and with a golden sickle cuts down the mistletoe, which is caught in a white cloak.'[5]

Druids had been specifically mentioned in Britain itself a decade or so before Pliny wrote, when in AD 61 a revolt of the Britons led the Roman forces to strike across Wales to the Druid sanctuary on the island of Anglesey.[6] The Roman troops were faced both by the Druids and British soldiers, and by the British women, stained with woad,[7] 'their hair loose to the wind . . . resembling the frantic rage of the Furies'. The Britons were defeated, the Druids were killed, and their 'religious groves, dedicated to superstition and barbarous rites, were levelled to the ground'.

This is virtually all that we know of the Druids in Britain, of their 'holy groves', and of *any* kind of garden in the British Isles before the Romans. Much, much later, in 1723, the antiquarian Henry Rowlands built on these and other slight scraps, to make Anglesey into the type and origin of 'a wish'd *Elyzium*', which became one of the sources of the hermitage in eighteenth-century landscape gardens. But it is not in any other way an auspicious beginning for the history of British gardening. A little is known of early British agriculture from the evidence of the early field-systems, and Roman writers commented briefly on the produce of the island. Julius Caesar claimed that the inhabitants of Kent were the most advanced, while the rest, in the 'interior', 'do not grow corn, but live on milk and meat'.[8] Around AD 10, or a little earlier, the Greek geographer Strabo stated dismissively that Britain produced corn and cattle, but that the inhabitants knew 'nothing of planting or of any sort of husbandry'.[9] By about AD 60 (i.e. after the Roman Conquest) Tacitus could write more accurately 'the soil does not afford either the vine, the olive, or the fruits of warmer climates; but it is otherwise fertile, and yields corn in great plenty'.[10]

Britain has never been able to 'afford the olive'. But the Romans brought the vine, and they brought gardens.

Gardens in Roman Britain

The Roman conquest of Britain began in AD 43, and within four or five years much of England was under Roman control. Wales was overcome between AD 70 and 80, and northern England and a part of southern Scotland were subjugated in the next decade. Though the whole of Scotland was never ruled by the Romans, and most of the country remained independent, the territory south of Hadrian's Wall (built east-west from the Tyne to the Solway around 122) was fairly firmly a part of the Roman Empire until 367, and was still ruled intermittently by one or another Roman leader until early in the fifth century.

England and Wales, therefore, and a part of southern Scotland, were exposed to three centuries or more of Roman rule and Roman culture; and it is with us still in countless ways, large or small: a network of roads, the names of many of our towns, and architectural relics scattered throughout the land, with lesser artefacts, such as sculpture, mosaics, pottery, tools, jewellery and coins, still to be found in or beside these buildings. Roman gardens were also introduced to Britain, though until the late 1960s none had been clearly discerned or perceptively excavated. The discovery and excavation in 1961-9 of the Roman palace (or if a villa, then a palatial one) at Fishbourne in West Sussex gave sudden and wholly convincing proof that the lavish and sophisticated gardens made by the Romans in Italy and many parts of the Empire were made in England too. The existence of partly or wholly enclosed courtyards in Roman villas at Brading in the Isle of Wight, at Sudeley in Gloucestershire and at Apethorpe in Northamptonshire, for example,[11] had led to sugges-tions that these were garden areas, but enquiry into this was not followed up. At Fishbourne, the extensive remains have been dated around AD 75, and include a large enclosed formal garden within the main quadrangular buildings of the palace, and a less formal terraced garden extending from the south side of the palace down towards the sea.[12]

It is possible that the palace at Fishbourne was built for the British ruler Cogidumnus or Cogidubnus, King of the Regni of West Sussex, who came to peaceable terms with the Romans and was confirmed in his possessions as their client-king.[13] The large formal garden there is vast – around 80 by 100 yards. It was surrounded with a colonnade (like the many surviving, but smaller, peristyle gardens in Pompeii and Herculaneum), and was crossed from east to west (the narrower dimen-sion, a mere 80 yards) by a broad path, dividing the garden in two. Lesser paths ran round the edge, and beside all these paths a regular pattern of trenches was dug into the basic gravel and clay and filled with soil. The symmetry of the trench pattern (to each side of the central path, it comprised lines of alternating semicircular and rectangular recesses, with long straight trenches on either side) implies symmetrical planting, and it is most likely that it was of low box hedging, clipped to a uniform height. It is not too fanciful to consider this as the first evidence of *topiary*, the art or craft of clipping bushes into artificial shapes, in Britain. Pliny the Elder, writing around the time the garden at Fishbourne was created, claimed that *nemora tonsilia* (clipped arbours) had first been devised some 80 years before, about 4 BC,[14] and the letters of his nephew Pliny the Younger have references to several topiary features of extreme sophistication in the gardens he had made around AD 100.

While there is no particular doubt that box was used for the main pattern of the bedding, other planting at Fishbourne is less sure, since pollen analysis has been unsuccessful. Post-holes beside the east colonnade have encouraged the suggestion that some kind of pergola was erected, possibly for roses and fruit trees.

Excavations at Fishbourne have also proved that at least two sides of the large formal garden were fitted with a line of pipes, supplying water by gravity feed to basins or small fountains set at intervals beside the colonnade. That the Romans had by this period the desire and the competence to execute such refinements is clear both from the letters of Pliny the Younger, written around AD 100, and from the engineering treatise *De Aquis urbis Romae*, written at about the same time by Frontinus, who had by curious coincidence been provincial governor of Britain from AD 74 until 77 or 78.

North-west of the palace buildings there may have been a kitchen or vegetable garden, and to the south, as I have said, was a terraced and, apparently, less formal garden, which might have been similar in style to the *imitatio ruris* (the imitation or semblance of the countryside) mentioned by the Younger Pliny as a part of his Tuscan garden-estate.[15]

As I write in the 1990s, the garden at Fishbourne is the only example of a Roman garden known to have survived – after excavation – in the British Isles. Were its dimensions modest, we might question its importance. But its not less than princely size is proof that the idea of the Roman garden, recently formulated in Italy, had been promptly, fully and successfully transplanted to England. Fishbourne is an inspiring yet perplexing statement that the great tradition of formal garden design, which was to reappear in the late sixteenth century (inspired by the gardens of Renaissance Italy), was already there, fully-fledged, in the first century AD.

Knowing little of Roman gardens in Britain, we know somewhat more of the plants grown in them. Box (*Buxus suffruticosus sempervirens*) was most likely used for the edging of formal garden designs, and this may have survived, fortuitously, at Box Hill in Surrey, though a later reintroduction has been suggested. Certainly the opium poppy (*Papaver somniferum*) was brought to Britain by the Romans, and also sweet cherries (in contrast to the native wild or gean cherries), which came from

Greece, via Italy, by about AD 100. Sweet chestnut (*Castanea sativa*) is one of the more noticeable of Roman introductions, since it has become so widely naturalised. In contrast the vine is a matter of argument. Tacitus had said, that vines would not grow in Britain, while the Emperor Domitian issued an edict towards the end of the first century restricting the planting of new vineyards outside Italy. Yet seeds of cultivated grapes *have* been found at numerous Roman villa sites in Britain, as far north as York and Doncaster. At North Thoresby in Lincolnshire, a site of some 12 acres may have been developed as a vineyard around 280–5.[16] Several writers on the history of gardening in Britain cite the permission given by the Emperor Probus around 280 to the inhabitants of Gaul and Spain and to the 'Britanni' to cultivate vineyards, but, as André Simon pointed out long ago,[17] these 'Britanni' were 'a people settled on the banks of the lower Rhine', and not the native inhabitants of the British Isles.

Early in the fifth century Rome lost control of Britain, and the gardens which had been made there to Roman patterns were destroyed or abandoned. For several centuries, during the early Middle Ages, gardens were to remain a little-known part of British history.

One garden episode in the twilight of Roman-British history, however, must be added. Fairly early in the fifth century the newly consecrated Bishop of Angers, named Maurilius (in French, Maurille), was overwhelmed with the sense of his unworthiness. Escaping from his bishopric, he crossed to Britain, where he was employed as a gardener by a British ruler (the Latin calls him *rex* and *princeps*, but without naming him), who knew nothing of Maurilius' rank or importance. Later, a party from Angers, who had travelled far and wide to find Maurilius reached Britain, 'and, with angelic help, were led directly to the mansion of the prince where Maurilius was living. They entered, and heard Maurilius being summoned, to come along quickly with the vegetables with which the king was accustomed to be provided. Then, turning towards the voices, they perceived Maurilius hurrying up with the vegetables.'[18] Maurilius was persuaded to return to Angers, where he died and was made a saint. He is remembered on 13 September. A part of his story – or legend – is shown in a fifteenth-century tapestry fragment at Angers, where he appears in two linked scenes. In one he digs his garden with a long-handled, iron-shod spade. Round him are fruit trees (including gooseberries) and a small bed with flowers. In the adjacent scene he presents a bowl of fruit to the Queen, who sits with the King in a sumptuous garden pavilion.

We may wonder who the King was – King Arthur perhaps? We may smile too at the gooseberries – Maurilius might indeed have cultivated them in France, but not in Britain – they were not introduced until 1275, when new plants, from France, were acquired for the gardens at the Tower of London.

The Dark Ages

While it is not difficult to describe the main aspects of garden activity in continental Europe from the fifth until the eleventh century – their purpose, techniques, tools, plants and design[19] – little can be said about this period in Britain until the later tenth and eleventh centuries.

We may consult Anglo-Saxon documents – medical and herbal texts, and a glossary[20] – and learn that their vocabulary included many names of herbs, shrubs and trees. The *Vocabulary of Archbishop Alfric* (c. 995) gives Latin plant names with their Anglo-Saxon equivalents, but we cannot be at all sure that the plants were actually grown in Britain. Among the plants, however, occur three items which are more suggestive: *botanicum vel viridarium* (herb garden or place for plants) is rendered as *wyrt tun* (a place for plants); the next line reads *cucumerarium* (a place for cucumbers, i.e. a hot-bed), also rendered as *wyrt tun*; and *amenus locus* (a pleasing place, one of the Latin synonyms for a garden) is translated as *luffendlic stede* (a lovely place). The first two terms are clearly cruder in the Anglo-Saxon. In contrast, the third is exact, and might suggest the reality of the *luffendlic stede* in Aelfric's time.[21]

We may also consider the evidence of charters, in which the *perambulations* defining the extent and boundaries of property name a great number of trees, singly or in groups, which served as markers (as of course did other features such as roads, streams, ditches and rocks). A list of these trees, drawn from the charters, comprises: thorn, oak, apple, willow, pear, elder, maple, lime, ash, birch, aspen or poplar (*Populus tremula*), holly and service. Of these, only the pear was not indigenous, and may have been introduced either by the Romans or the Anglo-Saxons. To these we may add vines, the *winestreow* mentioned several times as marking a boundary.[22]

Alicia Amherst in *A History of Gardening in England* (1895) remarks that these vines 'might have been survivals of Roman vineyards'. This remains uncertain, though some vineyards are known, or implied, in Saxon times, beginning with the statements by the Venerable Bede in the geographical preamble to his *Ecclesiastical History* (finished in 731), that 'Britain . . . also produces vines in some places', while Ireland 'abounds in milk and honey, nor is there any lack of vines'.[23] Again, a law of King

Alfred (d.901) stipulates that anyone who had 'damaged the vineyard or field of another must pay compensation',[24] and gifts of vineyards are recorded in the mid- and later tenth century – one, at Wycet in Wiltshire, 'together with the vine-dressers on the estate'.[25]

However important vines and vineyards may have been for the Anglo-Saxons (their name for our October was *Wynmoneth*), we cannot truthfully say that vineyards are gardens. A part, maybe, and to be valued, but often more accurately a part of agriculture, a part of the farm. An eleventh-century Anglo-Saxon miniature of 'vine-dressers'[26] is useful corroboration that vines were cultivated in England, and fascinating as an illustration of their tools – a kind of slasher, and a doubled-sided bill-hook. But it is not a *garden* scene.

There is indeed little directly to do with gardens in this period, and what there is is bleak and undetailed. Near the abbey of St Albans around 940, a Danish refugee named Wulfa lived for a long while as a hermit, and 'cultivated gardens, with herbs, vegetables and water'. His example persuaded Eadfrith, the somewhat worldly abbot of St Albans, to reform and lead a better life.[27] At the monastery at Ely, which was restored in 963, the new abbot, Brihtnoth (d.981) planted 'gardens . . . and orchards broadly round the church' which became famous for their beauty.[28]

Likely enough, the gardens of Wulfa and Brihtnoth would have been firmly utilitarian, cultivated to produce herbs and roots for the pot, herbs for medicine and vegetables and fruit for eating. Flowers had medicinal virtues as well as their usefulness in adorning the church; and they were essential for the work of the bees, which produced both honey and wax. Beehives would have been as certainly a part of an early medieval garden as they were in later periods, until the seventeenth and eighteenth centuries. We might note that the English words 'bee', 'hive', 'honey' and 'mead' all go back to the Anglo-Saxon.

The features of gardens in this period are hardly mentioned, though we must assume that whatever gardens there were had some kind of enclosure – a wattle fence, a quickset hedge of thorn, a ditch or moat, or some combination of these. One brief but lurid snippet concerns the powerful (and treacherous) Alderman Edric of Mercia who, at Oxford in 1015, 'betrayed Sigferth and Morcar . . . He allured them into his bower, where they were shamefully slain'.[29] The original Anglo-Saxon reads *into his bure*, and would normally mean 'into his garden arbour' (i.e. a shelter or roofed seat in a garden or orchard) though it *might* mean his 'private room'.

Some gardens may have had a 'mount' or hillock, useful in this period as a look-out post to see over the garden enclosure and out into the countryside. At Rydal Mount in Cumbria, the small rounded knoll

Prompted by Henry Rowlands' writings on the Druids' 'holy groves' in Anglesey, Thomas Wright's Louthiana *(1748) recorded similar features in Ireland – like these 'remains of a Druidical grove'.*

St Maurilius at work in the garden of an English king – a tapestry made in the 1490s illustrating his brief visit to England in the fifth century.
© *F. LASA, Inventaire Général, S.P.A.D.E.M.*

westward from the house has been claimed as a pre-Norman construction, and the early medieval Welsh tales in the *Mabinogion* and the comparable tales from Irish mythology both have references to woodland clearings or glades within which rises a mound, mount or *sidh* of more than natural significance.[30] Nonetheless, the incorporation of 'magic glades' into the realm of imaginative and poetic gardens does not have any place in our garden history until much later in the Middle Ages, in allegoric and chivalric literature (see Chapter 3). If indeed the mount at Rydal Mount is of pre-Norman origin, its first purpose is most likely to have been defensive, with little or no sense of garden pleasure or adornment.

One pleasurable feature may however be dated tentatively from the eleventh or even the tenth century – the Miz-maze at Breamore in Hampshire. This *turf maze* (i.e. with its gravel path cut into the surrounding turf; it is hedgeless) is sited on the line of a section of Grim's Dyke (probably pre-Roman) on a ridge a mile north-west of Breamore church, a building which retains portions of Saxon masonry, and some 200 yards south of the site of a deserted Saxon village. The maze itself is now surrounded by trees planted in the later nineteenth century, but was previously on open ground. While most turf mazes in the country are thought to be of late medieval or even of sixteenth-century origin (see Chapter 3), the Breamore maze may have a fair claim to be a pre-Norman survival, from its proximity to the abandoned Saxon village, and without other later buildings nearby.

2

FROM THE CONQUEST TO 1200

The Early Normans

Between the Conquest in 1066 and the early twelfth century we do not hear a great deal about gardens, but what there is, directly or implicitly, is worth reporting. The main source is the material of the Domesday Book (*Liber de Wintonia*), compiled by direction of William I in 1085–6. The aim was fiscal, to find out 'what, or how much, each man had, who was an occupier of land in England, either in land or in stock, and how much money it were worth'.[1]

While King William's commissioners recorded their assessments in most counties in a fairly consistent way, gardens – under the terms *horti*, *orti* or *hortuli* – only occur in a scattering of instances, normally in conditions which suggest they were small and utilitarian, probably to provide what we would now call market-garden produce. In Middlesex, close to the capital, there were in Fulham '8 cottagers [*cotarii*] with their gardens', and elsewhere in the land of St Peter's, Westminster, there were '41 cottagers, who pay 40s. a year for their gardens'. At Holywell, outside Oxford, there were '23 men having small gardens [*hortulos*]', and together with some pasture, the 'gardens in Dover' brought in 9s.4d. Elsewhere, in Hertford 'two houses with one garden' are recorded, another garden is at Barnstaple in Devon, yielding 3d., others are at Warwick, and at Clopton in Cambridgeshire there is one more. Apart from one orchard (*pomerium*) in Nottingham, that is about all. In some counties cottagers are absorbed into broader categories of land-holders, in others – Berkshire and Surrey, for example – they are often mentioned, though without reference to gardens.

There is little else to do with gardens. Several fishponds (*vivaria*) are mentioned, as distinct from fisheries along the big rivers, and 40-odd vineyards,[2] several 'new' or 'newly planted'. Like gardens, vineyards are not listed consistently throughout the Domesday Book, their financial yield possibly being absorbed in the revenue of larger areas. While fishponds and vineyards are not all that convincingly to do with gardens, another matter, referred to even less regularly, may well be considered a part of this history – bees, honey and beehives. These appear sporadically – not at all, for example, in Berkshire, Buckinghamshire, Hertfordshire, Kent, Middlesex or Surrey, but occasionally or often in Essex, Gloucestershire, Hampshire, Oxfordshire, Wiltshire and East Anglia generally. The references are either to payments of honey (in *sesters* or *sextaries*), to the number of beehives, or to the beekeepers (*melitarii*), and there can be no doubt that while some honey came from bees which were based in forest and woodland, some, if not most, would have been from hives centred in orchards and gardens – as was the case in Roman times, with Virgil's 'Old Corycian' in the *Georgics*, and as it continued in Britain until well on in the seventeenth and eighteenth centuries.

Last, literally on the very outskirts of gardens, come parks and woodland enclosures (sites of immense importance in the later parts of this history, providing much of the ground which was to be 'landscaped' in the eighteenth century). Forest and woodland are principal elements in the Domesday survey, but there is generally nothing to suggest that these are 'designed'. Within areas of forest, however, parks or enclosures (*haiae*) are not uncommon, and these are sometimes qualified as *ferarum silva* ('a wood for wild beasts', i.e. places for hunting); less often, they are eyries, for hawks. Most important are the King's *Nova Foresta* in Hampshire, begun in 1079, and the forest of Old Windsor, which was enclosed by 1086 (there had already been a hunting lodge at Old Windsor in Anglo-Saxon times). A comment in the Domesday Book for Berkshire, to do with Battersea, adds that 'King William gave this manor to St Peter's in exchange for Windsor'. This should be noted, since the park, garden and forest at Windsor will be of interest for many centuries. William's castle at Windsor was sited two miles away from Old Windsor, and his wooden fortification was rebuilt in stone by Henry II, around 1165–79.

Let romance close this section. In 1092 or thereabouts, the Conqueror's son William Rufus wished to inspect a 12-year-old maiden, Eadgyth, who was then kept in Romsey Abbey in Hampshire. He made his way into the cloister with the excuse that he wished to inspect 'the roses and other flowering plants'.[3] The girl was, however, wearing a veil, in common with her companions, and was not identified. To our point, the chronicler wrote that William Rufus 'went into our cloister' (*claustrum*) to view these plants. We may argue, whether *claustrum* means the whole of the abbey, or the particular 'cloister'. If the latter, it is an encouragingly early sign that monastic cloisters could be planted with flowers; if merely the former, it remains a vivid proof that gardens with 'roses and other flowering plants' did indeed exist in that remote age.

The Twelfth Century – an Age of Expansion

After the scanty facts which tell of gardens just after the Norman Conquest, the picture of twelfth-century gardens seems suddenly to expand. From early in the reign of Henry I (1100–35), sites of gardens are named, sometimes with novel and intriguing features, and in the reign of Henry II (1154–89), we are made aware of a variety of gardens, large and small, spread broadly over the country, and belonging to different categories of people. From the middle of the century, we learn a little more of the plants and trees they had acquired, and much more of the tools used to cultivate them.

Of the different kinds of garden, the royal gardens and parks are the most ambitious, ecclesiastical gardens are often extensive and carefully managed (though they include some of truly diminutive size), and private gardens extend from the grand properties of noblemen close to the crown to the plots of well-to-do citizens. In 1174, the chronicler William Fitzstephen records that those citizens of London who live on the outskirts have 'gardens . . . which are well furnished with trees, spacious and beautiful'. Having claimed that London was founded by the Trojans, he describes the games of the Londoners, notably the warlike manoeuvres of young men on horseback, riding in the fields just outside the city.[4] Though he does not use the word 'labyrinth', it is clear from his Latin that he is adapting phrases from Virgil's description in the *Aeneid* of the *Lusus Troiae*, the 'Troy game' of maze-like evolutions performed by Aeneas' young soldiers.[5] Taken on its own, this passage has no garden connection, but the Virgilian references become significant in the context of 'Daedaline work' at Woodstock constructed at about this time (see page 26), and of the many turf-cut mazes of supposedly medieval origin in England, with names referring to Troy (see Chapter 3).

During the twelfth century the kings of England had gardens attached to many of their residences, and hunting parks were usually set nearby, though not, of course, immediately beside the Tower of London or

Westminster Palace. The gardens are recorded at residences in widely separated areas: at Winchester in Hampshire, at Nottingham Castle, at Arundel Castle in Sussex, at Havering in Essex and at Kingsbury, near Dunstable in Bedfordshire. In Dublin, a temporary garden-palace was made for Henry II in 1171, in wickerwork 'in the fashion of the country',[6] an early and curious example of an elaborate summerhouse or arbour in 'carpenter's work'. The King may however have had little choice if he wanted prompt accommodation, as building of a solid kind was then far less common in Ireland than in England. Some 20 years later, Giraldus Cambrensis was to say as much of his countrymen in Wales, that they 'content themselves with small huts made of the boughs of trees twisted together'. He goes on to say 'they have neither orchards nor gardens, but gladly eat of the fruit of both when given to them ... little is cultivated, a very small quantity is ornamented with flowers, and a still smaller is sown'.[7] For lack of evidence to the contrary, I believe as much may be said of gardens in both Scotland and in Ireland until the close of the Middle Ages, though large noble or ecclesiastical establishments can hardly have been gardenless. In his remarks on Wales, Giraldus refers only to two gardens: one, 'an orchard with a delightful garden ... on a small plot of ground' beside the church of St Ludoc on the River Teivy, and the other, that of his birthplace, the Castle of Manorbier in Pembrokeshire. Here – for Giraldus, 'the pleasantest spot in Wales' – the castle had 'a fine fish-pond under its walls ... and a beautiful orchard on the same side, inclosed on one part by a vineyard, and on the other by a wood, remarkable for the projection of its rocks, and the height of its hazel trees'.[8]

Most medieval references to gardens are in Latin, and explanation of the commonest terms is needed. *Gardinus* is related to the French *jardin* and the English and Germanic 'Garten'/'garden'/'garth'/'yard', and meant (approximately) an open space or enclosure, most often with plants. The word *claustrum* (an enclosure, hence a cloister) could mean either the institution as a whole (an enclosed society), or a particular enclosure within the whole, i.e. a cloister. When the latter was meant, its interior arrangement could vary considerably, from an open patch of ground to a graveyard, or grass, or a variety of garden forms, for herbs, or vegetables, or fruit or flowers.

Frequently, a garden is called a *herbarium*, appearing in English and French as 'herber', and meaning (approximately) a place for plants, and so, often enough, a garden with herbs (a herb garden) or vegetables. It comes also to mean simply an enclosed garden area, possibly with no more than grass and with emphasis on the *enclosed* aspect of the place. Hence the related word 'arbour' comes to mean a garden enclosure with a hedge or trellis-work, within which there may be grass or a more elaborate scheme. Gradually, by about 1400, the word 'arbour' is limited to the hedge or trellis structure alone, meaning (approximately) a hedge or trellis-work garden structure, ranging in size from a small partly covered seat to a summerhouse (called also a bower) or a lengthy pergola with a 'roof' of wooden poles or overgrowing branches. The hedges were at first made simply from cuttings of hawthorn or privet (often called quickset), but again became more varied, with the addition of other plants, for example, eglantine or briar rose.

Royal Gardens

Three royal gardens from the twelfth century should be singled out, both for their details, and because they continue to be mentioned for several centuries. They are at Windsor Castle in Berkshire, at Clarendon Palace in Wiltshire and at Woodstock in Oxfordshire. At Windsor, where William I had already acquired land for a hunting park near to his new castle (see page 21), Henry I, in about 1110, bought additional ground beside the castle, which was later developed as one of the castle garden areas. The first clear reference to a garden appears to have been in 1156–7, when 11 shillings was spent 'in Operatione Vinee et Gardini' ('for work on the vineyard and garden');[9] further payments for vineyard work are recorded in 1158–9.[10] The vineyard (or vineyards) at Windsor are noted until the late fifteenth century. In 1184–5, hedges round the kitchens are noted, and in 1195–6, we hear of payments for the King's cloister (*pro claustro*) and for the King's garden (*herbarium*). In the first half of the twelfth century, a further group of references tells of payments and work on the King's *herbarium* (1235–6), and of a fence and palings for enclosing the King's *gardinum* (1239–40) and a quickset hedge (*viva haga*). Between various royal apartments and a chapel, room enough is to be allowed for a lawn (*pratellam*). It is apparent that by 1239–40, there were at least two gardens, one within and one outside the walls. The outer one is to be enclosed with a ditch.[11] By 1245–6, we hear of a stone seat set in the castle wall, beside the lawn near the King's lodging (*juxta pratellam*), and there is a separate reference to the garden hedge (*haiam gardini*) and a fair orchard (*unum pulcrum virgultum* – the Latin *virgultum* is the source of the French *verger*) in the same garden. The lawn was probably laid with turf, renewed from time to time, cut fresh from the fields, while the orchard was most probably set out with fruit trees in an orderly pattern. In this year begin references to one or more gardener's houses, and in 1256–7, there is a reference to a trellis round the King's cloister.[12]

For the vineyards, we may conjecture that a part of at least one vineyard at Windsor (there were several) was ornamental, possibly with vine-covered walks, since two centuries later, in 1387, King Richard II gave 'the garden called the vineyard' to his wife, Queen Anne,[13] and in 1472, King Edward IV showed 'his garden and vineyard of pleasure' to a French guest after hunting with him in the park.

At Clarendon, near to Salisbury, there had been a military gathering place in the 1070s (William I was there briefly in 1072), and work on a royal residence began by 1130 or a little before. In Henry II's reign, there was further work on a hunting lodge, rapidly becoming a 'palace' in 1158–9. A church council was held there in 1164, at which Thomas à Becket was a member, and in 1167–8 payments were made for turfing (*turbando*) in the enclosed space beside the royal apartment.[14] This may indeed be the first reference to turfing, and hence to anything resembling a lawn, in British gardens. Lacking both weedkiller and lawn mowers, medieval gardens could have open grassy spaces only by laying new turf, cut from downland pasture, and beating it down firmly with mallets. The process, which had to be repeated every few years, is first described, so far as I know, by Albertus Magnus around 1260, and seems to have been followed until at least the seventeenth century.[15]

At Clarendon surviving documents mention the gardens repeatedly in the middle years of the thirteenth century. In 1247, work in the Queen's *herber*; in 1249, work in the King's *herber*; and by 1250 it is clear that there was a 'great herber' for the King (in which a bench was made) and a lesser *herber*. In 1252, the Queen's *herbarium* was 'repaired and altered', and a year or so later the paling fence round the garden was resited.

Woodstock, north of Oxford, has the most varied and intriguing history of any British garden in this period. There was already a royal residence at Woodstock around 1000, used by King Æthelred, and a royal forest there is referred to in the Domesday Book. By about 1110, Henry I may have had a wall built round a large area of woodland, and kept a menagerie in a part of it. Later, Henry of Huntingdon claims as much, and William of Malmesbury includes among the inmates a porcupine, lions, leopards, lynxes and camels.[16]

The main area of the emparked woodland was simply the King's hunting park (in the *Anglo-Saxon Chronicle* for the year 1123, it is referred to as 'his deer-fold'). While the walled hunting park at Woodstock continues to this day, much of its area corresponding to the parkland round Blenheim Palace, there was further garden development at Woodstock in the reign of Henry II. Not only was there work at the main residence, but from around 1165 a secondary site, some 250 yards to the south-west, adjoining a branch of the River Glyme and with a spring or well at its centre, was developed as a lesser or 'private' residence. This spot, known as Everswell, was rapidly identified from the early thirteenth century as the place where Henry II kept his mistress, Rosamund Clifford, the 'fair Rosamund' of later legend. The *factual* references, gathered together by H. M. Colvin and others in *The History of the King's Works*,[17] indicate that in the thirteenth century the Everswell site included two or more separate gardens with paved walks, adjacent chambers for the King and the Queen, an extensive enclosed orchard, and two or three pools, one surrounded by a cloister and one by a bench. The Everswell gardens and buildings were virtually obliterated by Capability Brown's landscaping in the mid-eighteenth century, but by then – and indeed since the fourteenth century – references of a *fanciful* kind to Henry II's accomodation for 'fair Rosamund' had accumulated, revolving round the theme of the 'bower' as a retreat of utmost complexity, designed to protect the lady from Henry's jealous wife, Queen Eleanor. To this end, Henry was said to have constructed 'a chamber of marvellous architecture, similar to "Daedaline work"', i.e. resembling a labyrinth.[18]

Some later accounts make this 'Daedaline work' into a sequence of underground tunnels, others into a 'bower':

> Of stone and timber strong,
> An hundred and fifty doors,
> Did to this bower belong.

This word 'bower' led many to think that the house was within a garden labyrinth.[19]

While the garden maze was unlikely at Woodstock, the connection with the classical maze made by Daedalus is to be noted, coming as it does in the same period as the labyrinthine manoeuvres of London boys at play, referred to by William Fitzstephen (see page 22), and as the building of another maze-like residence in Flanders, described around 1195 by Lambert of Ardres. This was designed by Arnold, Count of Ardres, 'with a skill little different from that of Daedalus', and was like 'a virtually inextricable labyrinth ... leading from inner room to inner room, chamber to chamber, passage to passage.'[20]

Ecclesiastical Gardens

Beside the royal extravagances of Woodstock most ecclesiastical and private gardens of the twelfth century were strictly utilitarian, providing fruit, vegetables, herbs for flavour and for physic, and, of course, honey and beeswax. Sugar, as distinct from honey, remained a rarity; in 1176 an exceptional payment was made from the King's funds 'pro xxxiiii libris zuccare' ('for 34 pounds of sugar') at 9d. a pound.[21]

Yet flowers, and delight, can be a part of this, as in 1108 when the then Archbishop of York died in a garden (*viridarium*), which he had visited to enjoy the fresh air and the refreshing perfume of the flowers.[22] Eighty-odd years later, the gardens of Lanthony Priory at Gloucester were praised for their *pleasing* qualities, linked with vineyards and orchards.[23]

One ecclesiastical garden, that of the priory at West Tarring in Sussex, has a little-sung but exceptional importance. Here, in the 1140s, Thomas à Becket is thought to have planted the first fig tree to have survived in England, having brought it back from Italy after a pilgrimage to Rome. The half-acre fig orchard remains in part within the old flint and brick walls, and the existence of these trees and their connection with Becket is attested from the mid-thirteenth century, when the Bishop of Chichester, Richard de la Wych (*c*.1198–1253) cared for the garden.[24]

Figs, like the hazel, for example, grow and prosper when cut back to the main root or stool, and those at West Tarring, which I have seen with astonishment and admiration, still form a leafy grove, some ten feet high, throughout the walled enclosure. This must be the oldest surviving garden, with original walls and with plants, in the British Isles.

Only one other introduction in this period need be noted – the sweet or Spanish chestnut. Grown by King Richard at Avranches in Normandy about 1190, it was claimed to have been planted in England, at Tortworth in Gloucestershire, in the reign of King John (1199–1216). The two instances add up to a reasonable probability.[25]

Among the tiniest gardens of the Middle Ages are those of the monks of the Carthusian order, who established themselves in Britain from the late twelfth century onward. Each monk in the small community lived a solitary life within his individual cell and its garden, leaving this private enclosure only for services in the church and on a few rare occasions of celebration in the Christian year. The first Carthusian foundation in Britain was at Witham in Somerset in 1178, and the second at Hinton in Avon in 1227. While no garden areas remain to be seen at either of these sites, the ruins of Mount Grace in North Yorkshire, founded around 1397, still retain considerable sections of the sequence of small individual cell-plus-garden enclosures running round the cloister. Most of the gardens measure about 60 by 40 feet, sometimes a little more. Each monk was free to cultivate the ground as he thought best, though not necessarily for food, since each monastery also possessed farmland, which was cultivated by lay brothers for the upkeep of the monastery.

While we have no details of the gardening of these Carthusian monks, a variety of records touching on garden matters survives from the later twelfth century in connection with Christ Church cathedral priory at Canterbury. Around 1165, a detailed plan was drawn up to show the arrangement of the water supply, marking the course of underground pipes, the well, fountain heads and fishpond. Each of the priory buildings is named, as are several open areas. East of the big cloister and north of the church is a rectangular area marked 'herbarium', apparently arcaded, like the cloister, on three sides, and with trellis-work structures along the fourth (eastern) side and across the middle of the enclosure. I think that 'herbarium' may in this instance mean herb garden, rather than lawn or ornamental garden. Westwards from the church lies the fishpond, with trees roughly sketched by the wall, and some distance to the north, outside the town wall, stretch three small diagrammatic pictures labelled 'pomerium' (orchard), 'vinea' (vineyard) and 'campus'. The last, meaning field, is illustrated with standing corn, and indicates as well as any other argument that here, at least, orchard and vineyard are not part of a garden but part of a farm.

In the following decade, two separate writers commented on the luxurious living of the monks of Canterbury, in ways related to garden matters. In the 1160s, Giraldus Cambrensis passed through Canterbury, and was shocked by the monks' worldly and gluttonous behaviour, as they consumed copious fermented liquids, claret, mead and mulberry juice[26]. He provides us with one of the earliest confirmations that the red mulberry was then cultivated in Britain, and it is likely that the tree under which the knights left their cloaks, before the murder of Thomas à Becket in 1170, was also a mulberry. Then, in 1176, Peter of Blois accused Richard Dover, the Archbishop of Canterbury, of vainglory in making fishponds and a hunting park, while doing harm to the clergy.[27] These references to the garden, agricultural and hunting aspects of the priory may, with caution, be taken as valid for other large ecclesiastical institutions of the period.

Tools

One further detail from Canterbury at this time (c.1178) must also be mentioned, the rare and beautiful section of stained glass in the west window, which shows Adam digging with a spade. Beside him, hung on a branch, is a mattock. These are indeed wildly anachronistic, but a splendid introduction to the matter of gardening tools, which are several times referred to, and occasionally illustrated, in the twelfth century.

Adam may drive the spade into the ground with his bare foot, as he might have done long, long ago. But the iron tip to the spade, and the curved iron blade of his mattock, tell not of the Old Testament, but of medieval blacksmiths. By the twelfth century iron-shod spades were common. One is shown in an illustration to Henry I's dream (c.1135) where peasants line up to threaten him, the labourer's spade having an iron rim all round the sides and lower edge.[28]

Tools are listed for the first time in Alexander Neckam's (or Necham's) *De Utensilibus* ('Concerning Tools'), a treatise written in the 1190s.[29] The list is given as what the *rusticus* (the peasant, or country labourer) needs, and we may reasonably see this as covering both farm and garden work:

> Let him also have a broad-bladed knife, a spade or shovel, a long knife, a threshing-sledge ... a seed-box for preserving seed, a wheelbarrow [*cenevectorium*], a basket, a little basket, a mousetrap to deal with the armies of mice. Let him have a snare or trap to catch wolves.
>
> Let him also have stakes and sticks, well-tried and hardened in the fire. Let him also have a two-sided billhook [*bisacutam*] for tearing out brambles, thorns, prickly plants and butcher's broom, and for setting and restoring cuttings ... and a big knife for making cuttings, and grafting them into trees ... and mattocks to rip out undergrowth, weeds, nettles ... thistles, and wild barley. These are also easily pulled out with a hooked grub-axe.

In all this, we should note especially the reference to the barrow – *cenevectorium* – which is as early as we may find in Britain, and the general, and more important, point that these tools cover much of what will be used until the nineteenth century. Yet in some parts of Britain they were not known – Giraldus complains, at this same time, that the Welsh, who 'have neither orchards nor gardens', do not use sickles in mowing, and that their way of ploughing is clumsy.[30]

3

'Hortulus Angliae'

When Leo of Rozmital visited England in 1446, his impression of the country as a whole was that it was 'like a small garden, surrounded by the sea on all sides'.[1] Though his travels were only in the south, he could indeed have found a diversity of gardens, large and small, up and down the land, with a rich variety of trees and plants, cultivated with skill, and joyously described in imaginative literature.

In London, Rozmital saw 'elegant gardens, planted with various trees and flowers, which are not found in other countries'. Such 'elegant gardens' could have been royal, ecclesiastical, or belonging to private citizens, as they did in William Fitzstephen's account of 1174 (see page 22). But they had come on mightily since then. Already in 1295–96, the London garden of the Earl of Lincoln, in Holborn, was so productive that many herbs and vegetables were sold, as well as roses, apples, pears, cherries, 'great nuts' (possibly walnuts, recently introduced) and many gallons of verjuice (unripe grape juice); all this apart from the choice fruits which were sent to the Earl himself.

London's need for vegetables was incessant. Remembering the small gardens of the *cotarii* (cottagers) in the Domesday survey of 1086, we may note the dispute in 1345 to do with the market for garden produce established near and around St Paul's churchyard. By this time, the gardeners and their servants, selling 'pulse, cherries, vegetables, and other wares to their trade pertaining' had become a nuisance, and a source of scurrility and clamour. In the end, an English compromise was achieved – the market continued, but in a better-defined area.[2]

In contrast were the grand gardens of the King and of the great ecclesiastics. At the Palace of Westminster, for example, continuing records from the mid-thirteenth century tell of royal gardeners, employed with no notable break from 1262 until 1366, and employed at the same time at the Tower of London,[3] with crucial details for this history in 1259. In

A rare English miniature of a garden scene, c. 1400. In their enclosure, the king and queen play at chess. They sit on turf seats. The gardener holds a serrated bill-hook.
Bodleian Library, Oxford, MS Bodley 264, f. 258.

The 'Heraldic Beasts' which ornamented royal gardens at Richmond and Hampton Court have gone. But they reappear at Kew in the 1960s, outside the Palm House – and of course in Alice Through the Looking Glass.

This glorious scene, embroidered on a valance in the 1590s, shows a great deal of the Renaissance garden – banqueting (and a beggar), sporting gods and goddesses, and a serious game of chess.
Courtesy Christie's, London

that year, a *roller* was used in the gardens, and turf was laid down and mown. While we have known about turfing since 1167–8 (see page 25), this is the first reference to a garden roller, probably, since this is what was used later, a stone cylinder held by iron axles.[4]

Not all royal gardens were large, and could therefore be made quickly. At Caernarvon Castle, a garden with a lawn was made for Queen Eleanor of Castile in 1283. In 1295, five years after her death, this area, now called the 'King's garden', was dug and hedged for 24 shillings.[5] Ecclesiastical gardens are often mentioned, in London and elsewhere. At Lambeth Palace (then in Surrey, on the south bank of the Thames) turves were laid in the new *herbarium* in 1234.[6] There had been a monastic garden on this site since before the Conquest, and it was to attain high fame in later centuries, both for itself and on account of those who frequented it (see Chapter 13). By 1322, there were several areas in the garden, totalling 19 acres in all, including a 'great garden', vineyard, rabbit garden (or warren), herb garden and two fishponds. Among the plants grown there at that time were 'olearum [colewort], fletrocilii [parsley], shervil, clarey, littuse, spynhach, toncressis [cress], caboche, concomber and gourds, isope, bourage, and centurrage [possibly centuary]'.[7]

Ecclesiastical property, like that of the King, spread over much of the country, and in many instances an outlying property might be of value as farmland, but not have a garden. Again, often enough the garden was firmly for fruit, vines, vegetables and herbs, and not distinguishable from a farm, unless by its modest area and its proximity to the main part of the establishment. In the Close at Ely, where gardens had been noted around 970, the areas of vineyard and garden were stated to be 16 and 6 acres respectively in 1229,[8] while in the far north of England, the Bishop of Durham's palace at Bishop Auckland had had a hunting park since the eleventh century, and a garden beside the palace was noted in 1241, for repair to the hedges.[9] By the 1330s, the park extended to about 1,000 acres, and it was walled round in 1350.[10] While the garden area beside the palace has today no convincing echoes of the thirteenth century, the wide parkland has survived and evolved as a notable landscape, extensively modified in the eighteenth century.

Another great ecclesiastical property was at Highclere in Hampshire, part of the bishopric of Winchester. In 1210–11, the park was enclosed with planks, running for 111 perches, for 20s. 1d.,[11] and in 1218, the Bishop's Register notes the purchase of 61 fruit trees for the garden. In the late fourteenth century, William of Wykeham had a new episcopal palace built, on the site of the present castle, now set in parkland whose layout was reshaped in the eighteenth century.

To 'Delve and Sette'

Records from other church sources may tell of tools, which might be used as well in the garden as on the farm. At Beaulieu Abbey in 1269–70, the accounts refer to the production of honey and cider, and to the making of 'civeria' (hand barrows, cf. French *civière*) and a 'cenovector' (wheelbarrow), first mentioned by Alexander Neckam nearly a century before (see page 29). By 1388–89, the tools held by the *gardinarius* at Abingdon Abbey are far more numerous than in Neckam's list, but not much different in kind. There is a distinction between a long-handled scythe – 'j falx pro prato' ('one scythe for the field') – and 'ij parve falces pro autumpno' ('two small scythes [or sickles] for harvesting'), a distinction gardeners will remember until the introduction of lawn mowers in the nineteenth century. We should note also 'ij cissorie' ('two [pairs of] shears'), which are newcomers in British garden documents though invented in Roman times, and 'j dungpot' ('one dungpot').[12]

To complete this outline of medieval garden tools, it is appropriate to mention the short English verse-treatise on gardening by Jon Gardener, called by some *The Feate of Gardeninge*, and written most probably in the later part of the fourteenth century.[13] While Alicia Amherst, who first published the poem, showed that the dialect is probably Kentish, and the author himself claims to show how to cultivate 'al the herbys of yrlonde', so that he might have been writing for a patron based near Dublin (most likely an English nobleman), the poem itself tells nothing of the author, or of anything except how to succeed in the garden: digging, sowing, planting, grafting, with detailed sections on matters which are important. Few tools are mentioned, only those to 'delve and sette' (dig and plant), together with a saw, a knife and a wedge for grafting and, right at the end of the poem, a dibble, for 'setting' (planting) saffron bulbs:

> With a dybbyll thou schalt ham [them] sette
> That the dybbyl before be blunt and grete
> Three ynchys depe they most sette be
> And thus seyde mayster Jon Gardener to me.

The poet divides his 196 lines into eight sections, according to topic. He begins with the growing of vegetables – colewort, leeks, onions, garlic and a few herbs. Then he covers the grafting of trees (he mentions only apple and pear); setting vine cuttings; setting and harvesting garlic, leeks and onions; planting out colewort to have them all through the year;

growing parsley; and then (lines 149–184) 'Of other maner herbys', where he proposes 'a row of all the herbs of Ireland', setting off on line 159 with a breathless list of 88 herbal plants, mostly four to a line:

Pelyter [pellitory] dytawnder [dittany] rewe and sage
Clarey tyme ysope and orage
Myntys saverey tuncarse [town cress] and spynage
Letows calamynte avans [avens] and borage . . .

After this list, there is one last brief section on saffron. Having advised that, using a broad blunt dibble, you should set them 3 inches deep, he stops. But a gardener would know what to do.

Not only is this the earliest mention in English of a dibble or dibber. It is one of the first references to saffron (*Crocus sativus*), whose introduction from the Levant is said by Hakluyt to have been achieved by a pilgrim to the Holy Land who 'stole an head of Saffron, and hid the same in his Palmers staffe, which he had made hollow before of purpose, and so he brought this root into this realme, with venture of his life'.[14] This pilgrim was said to have brought his illegal import to Saffron Walden, where the town later took its name from the extensive and successful cultivation of saffron. Two dates for the first mention of saffron in the region are around 1330 and 1359,[15] both of which would explain Jon Gardener's giving the final lines to saffron in his poem, as an intriguing 'novelty'.

Thirteenth- and fourteenth-century introductions of trees and shrubs include the peach in the early 1200s or a little before (we should remember that King John is said to have died in 1216 after a surfeit of peaches[16]), the almond by the mid-thirteenth century, and the walnut by 1295. It is possible that gooseberries were meant by *gresiller*, when bought for the King in 1275,[17] though these may not have been introduced until 1509 from Flanders.[18] Among the scented shrubs, lavender was known in England by about 1265, and rosemary a century later (1360–62). Carnations, or gilliflowers also arrived in the mid-fourteenth century.[19]

The 'Pleasance' and Poetry

In all this, and indeed since the time of the Roman palace at Fishbourne, there is precious little of garden *design*. Terms such as *herbarium*, *virgultum* and *hortulus* may imply order, and thus a plan, but only the Canterbury plan of around 1165 actually shows the *herbarium* within a walled enclosure. This is somewhat remedied in the late thirteenth century, when garden moats are clearly referred to. At Alvechurch in Worcestershire, the Bishop's palace is known to have had a 2-acre garden with *double* moats, and a few years later, in 1302, something equally ambitious was laid out for the Abbot of Peterborough – 'a beautiful herber ... surrounded with double moats, with bridges and pear trees and most delicate plants' – a feature of around 2 acres which lay between other parts of the abbey grounds, the Derby yard, and the fishponds.[20]

Moated garden areas, sometimes some distance away from the house, were in fact not uncommon in the Middle Ages, often, it is thought, to give security to crops and also to cattle in uncertain times. While most are familiar only to archaeologists,[21] one outstanding and indeed most beautiful example survives at Helmingham in Suffolk. Here the Hall stands in a square moat, with a separate rectangular moat to the side containing the walled garden. Though the present Helmingham Hall was not begun until 1487, it stands on the site of an earlier moated building. The moated garden enclosure is thought to have been made in Saxon times as a defence for cattle, and was probably used for garden purposes from the twelfth or early thirteenth century. Until 1745, when it was walled, the boundary within the moat was lined with a wooden fence, to keep out deer from the surrounding park.

After Alvechurch, Peterborough and Helmingham comes Kenilworth in Warwickshire. Though the castle was begun around 1125, little is known of garden work at Kenilworth until 1414–17, when King Henry V had a 'pleasance' or pleasure garden laid out half a mile to the west of the castle, on the far side of the Mere or Great Pool (an artificial lake which until 1649 stretched round three sides of the castle). This 'pleasance' involved a square, double-moated enclosure of some 10 acres, round a square central area of about $2\frac{1}{2}$ acres. Here there was a banqueting-house and gardens. A metrical life of Henry V, written by Thomas Elmham, relates that in 1414 the King 'kept Lent at Kenilworth Castle, and in the marsh, where foxes lurked among the brambles and thorns, built for his entertainment a pleasure garden [*viridarium*] ... a delicious place which he caused to be called Plesant Mareys'.[22]

Little else is known of the 'pleasance' in the marsh except its end, mentioned by John Leland around 1540. Referring to Henry VIII's repairs to the castle, he added: 'Among these reparations, the praty banketynge house of tymbre, that stood thereby in the mere, and bare the name of pleasaunce, was taken downe, and parte of it sete up in the base courte at Killingworthe castle.'[23] Alas, all gone except for earthworks, just like the garden made by the Earl of Leicester close beside the castle in 1575 (see Chapter 5). A 'banketynge' or banqueting-house was normally used for a small part of a meal, not the entire function (see page

49). The name 'pleasance' reappears in the early 1500s, when the royal palace and gardens at Greenwich were called *Placentia*.

In this period other royal gardens received much attention – at Eltham in Kent, for example – but comment on Windsor must suffice. The first garden works there have already been mentioned (see page 24), to which more must now be added. In the 1240s, the large garden area north of the Castle was embellished, and the hedge repaired; this was repeated in 1253, and in 1261 the hedge was replaced by a wall. John Harvey has painstakingly established the identity and often the wages of royal gardeners in this period; his list for Windsor Castle begins in 1256, with Emo or Edmund the Gardener, paid $2\frac{1}{2}$d a day and employed until 1277. In 1268, he was joined by Fulk le Provincial, also employed until 1277. With few gaps, Harvey's list continues well into the sixteenth century.[24]

In 1311, a detail concerning turf confirms the practice recommended by Albertus Magnus half a century before – the use of turf for seats or 'benches'. At Windsor in 1311, 1,300 turves were supplied for the 'benches' in one of the inner gardens.[25] While references in imaginative literature and illustrations in paintings show 'turf benches' again and again (see page 38), the sizeable order for Windsor Castle is a reassuring confirmation that this garden feature was in fact a reality, and not just poetic and artistic fancy.

Reality and fantasy come together at Windsor in 1413, or a little later, during the imprisonment there of King James I of Scotland. Held by the English from 1404 to 1424, he was moved to Windsor Castle in 1413, where he was kept for most of the next 11 years. From his prison-tower he looked out over an extensive garden, in the corner of which was an arbour; and there he spied, walking up and down, a maiden of great beauty. Falling in love with her at once, he described his feelings in his poem *The Kingis Quair*, and most helpfully for this history included two stanzas (31 and 32) describing the arbour:

> Now was there made fast by the tower's wall
> A garden fair, and in the corners set
> A herber green, with wandis [wands or withies] long and small
> Railed about; and so with trees set
> Was all the place, and hawthorn hedges knit,
> That not a one was walking there forby [past],
> That might within scarce any wight espy.
>
> So thick the boughs and the leaves green
> Beshaded all the alleys that there were,
> And midst every herber might be seen

> The sharp, green, sweet juniper,
>   Growing so fair with branches here and there,
> That, as it seemed to anyone without,
> The boughs spread the herber all about.[26]

While the 'true' strand of this episode relates to the garden at Windsor and to Lady Jane Beaufort, whom James was to marry in 1424 at the end of his captivity, the imaginative strand relates to two poetic themes telling somewhat similar stories, both highly likely to have been known to King James. First is that of the 'two noble kinsmen', Palamon and Arcite, who are imprisoned after defeat in battle, and who look from their prison window into the garden outside, spy the fair Emilia, and, simultaneously, fall in love with her. This was told in Boccaccio's epic poem *La Teseide* in the 1340s, and adopted by Chaucer around 1385 in *The Knight's Tale*. The theme continues well after its adaptation by King James, with a superb French miniature, *c*.1465, showing Emilia in her walled garden, with a lawn, turf benches, trellis-work grown over with vines and roses and carnations and columbines in the foreground.[27] It then surfaces in dramatic form in John Fletcher's tragedy *The Two Noble Kinsmen*, written around 1610.

Parallel to this is the broader theme, equally well-known, of the poet-dreamer-lover, who comes to a shady arbour, muses there, and is roused by a vision, quite often just outside the concealing branches of the garden retreat. The first example in this vein is the 'Prologue' to *Lancelot of the Laik*, a Scots poem of around 1380–5, where the poet, in misery, comes to 'a gardinge',

> Of which the field was all depaynt with green.
> The tender and the lusty flowers new
> Up through the green upon their stalkis grew
> Against the sun, and their leaves spread,
> Wherewith that all the garden was y-clad.[28]

Falling into 'an extasy or sleep', the poet then dreams of a green bird, who gives him helpful advice.

A while later, around 1385, comes Chaucer's *Legend of Good Women*, in which the poet goes to 'the flowry mede' in the 'joly month of May',

> For nothyng else, and I shal not lye,
> But for to loke upon the dayesye . . .
> The emperice and flour of floures alle.

Night falling, he hurries home, thinking to rise early and gaze again on the 'dayesye', so,

> . . . in a litel herber that I have,
> That benched was on turves fresshe y-grave,
> I bad men sholde me my couche make . . .
> I bad hem strawen flowers on my bed.[29]

The poet sleeps and dreams, and the vision proceeds. A few years after Chaucer, and under his influence, a woman poet wrote *The Flower and the Leaf*. Here the poet wakes, as did Chaucer in the early hours, and follows a grassy path 'till it me brought To right a pleasaunt herber, well y-wrought'. The 'herber' or arbour was indeed a good one.

> That benched was, and with turves new
> Freshly turved, wherof the grene gras,
> So small, so thik, so short, so fresh of hew,
> That most lyk to grene wol, wot I, it was.

> And shapen was this herber, roof and al,
> As a prety parlour, and also
> The hegge as thik as a castle-wal,
> That, who that list without to stond or go . . .
> He shuld not see if there were any wight
> Within or no.

This fine hedge 'with sicamour was set and eglantere' (eglantine, the briar rose), and though outsiders could not see in, the lady could peep out, marvelling at 'the fairest medler tree That ever yet in al my lyf I sy'; then comes 'a goldfinch leping pretily Fro bough to bough', and anon a nightingale, sitting 'in a fresh green laurer-tree'. The fragrance of the laurel (i.e. the bay, *Laurus nobilis*) matches that of the eglantine, and the song of the nightingale that of the goldfinch so perfectly that the poet 'surely ravished was Into Paradyse'.[30] Concealed in the herber, the poet watches as a gallant assembly of men and ladies arrive to do honour to the daisy – some to the flower, some to the leaf – the meaning of which is then explained.

One other imaginative work from the thirteenth and fourteenth centuries must be mentioned, however briefly – the first part of the *Roman de la Rose* or *Romaunt of the Rose* – since, although it was originally written in French in the 1220s, it was accurately translated into English by Chaucer in the 1380s, well over a century and a half later. While the original French text, together with the illustrations to manuscripts from around 1300 onwards and to early printed versions in the 1480s and 1490s, give a fascinating insight into the interpretation of the garden scenes over several centuries,[31] it remains a garden seen by a French author, and illustrated by French or Flemish artists. By Chaucer's time, the garden in Guillaume de Lorris' original poem was old-fashioned, and Chaucer's faithful translation does not bring it up to date in any way.

'The Gardyn Gloryous'

While students of allegorical poetry may find much that is derivative in Stephen Hawes' *Passetyme of Pleasure, or the History of Grande Amour and la Bel Pucel* (completed by 1506, first printed 1509), tracing it back to the *Roman de la Rose*, the poet's description of 'the gardyn gloryous' in which la Bel Pucel was sitting, making a chaplet or garland of flowers is astonishingly up to date, and replete with novel features.

As in the past, the garden is enclosed, with a wall, and seems to have been square or rectangular in plan. But the detail is new. The garden was adorned with *knots* – geometrical beds lined with low hedges of clipped evergreens, and with a variety of patterns or designs (a fuller definition is given on page 41):

> With Flora paynted and wrought curyously,
> In dyvers knottes of mervaylous gretenes;
> Rampande lyons stode up wondersly,
> Made all of herbes with dulcet swetenes,
> Wyth many dragons of marvaylous lykenes,
> Of dyvers flowers made full craftely,
> By Flora couloured wyth colours sundry.

It might also be suggested that the lions and dragons are, to some extent, three-dimensional, since they 'stode up wondersly', and are an early form of *topiary* – bushes and trees clipped and trained into artificial shapes. By the 1530s John Leland would refer to several gardens with topiary work (see page 48), and it had been executed in most extravagant form in Florence since the 1460s.

In Hawes' poem, these knots with lions and dragons are set round 'an herber fayre and quadrante, To Paradyse ryght well comparable,' in whose centre,

> ... there was resplendyshaunte
> A dulcet sprynge and mervaylous fountayne,
> Of golde and asure made all certayne.

For an arbour or a cloister to have a source of water at its centre is not uncommon, but in this poem, the water comes from a *fountain*, of an elaborate kind:

> In wonderfull and curyous symylytude
> There stode a dragon of fyne gold so pure
> Upon his tayle of myghty fortytude
> Wrethed and scaled all with asure
> Havyng thre hedes, divers in fygure
> Whiche in a bath of the sylver grette
> Spouted the water that was so dulcette.[32]

The key word in this stanza is 'spouted', for it implies that the water came from the dragon's three heads *with some force*, that the water came out *under pressure*. This is an achievement of Renaissance technology, unknown in the Middle Ages, when 'fountain' meant no more than 'fount' or 'source of water'. With some hesitation, I would suggest that this might be the earliest reference in English to a 'fountain' in the present, accepted sense of the word.

In comment on Stephen Hawes, C. S. Lewis remarked that 'he describes nothing that he has not seen, whether with the inner or the outer eye'.[33] In garden terms, this is entirely correct. Hawes had been appointed Groom of the Chamber to King Henry VII in 1502, and would have known well the King's favourite palace at Richmond in Surrey, recently rebuilt after the old palace, then called Sheen, had been burnt down in 1497. There had been a garden attached to Sheen since at least the 1360s, including fishponds, vineyard and herber, and in the 1380s a small island in the Thames, the 'Nayght', was adorned with a pavilion.[34] Henry renamed Sheen 'Richmond Palace' after his own title, Earl of Richmond, and in 1501 it was the setting for the lavish reception and wedding of Catherine of Aragon and the King's older son, Arthur, Prince of Wales (the Prince died in the following year, and his widow, Catherine, was married again in 1509 to his brother, who had just become King Henry VIII).

A contemporary account of this event includes this passage on the gardens, which has a singular closeness to Hawes' description of knots:

[There were] under the King's wyndowes ... moost faire and pleasunt gardeyns, with ryall knotts aleyed and herbid; many a marvelous beast, as lyons, dragons, and such other of dyvers kynde, properly fachyoned and carvyd in the grounde, right well sondid [sanded], and compassid in with lede; with many vynys, sedis, and straunge frute, right goodly besett, kept, and noryshid, with much labor and diligens.[35]

Knots

While the obvious similarity of the real palace gardens and the garden in the poem brings gardens of fact and gardens of fantasy together for the first time in this history, it is, I think, just as important to note that the 1501 account is the earliest detailed reference in English to knots, which were to be the central and defining feature of sixteenth-century gardens. They appeared suddenly on the British garden scene, and without any extended ancestry on the Continent. The earliest illustrations are in the first printing (1499) of Francesco Colonna's *Hypnerotomachia Poliphili* ('The Dream of Poliphilus'), though his Italian text was written earlier, around 1470. In his text, the word *tapeti* (carpet) is used, which has no helpful connection either with the French terms *carré* (a square), *parquet* (a little enclosure or subdivision) or *entrelacs* (an interlaced pattern), or the English 'knot'.

In gardens, knots are normally beds with geometrical patterns, usually square, with the borders and main lines laid out in contrasting strips of low-growing evergreens, for example, thyme, lavender, santolina and box. Flowers were often planted in the gaps between these lines of evergreens, though not always. Sometimes the spaces were filled with sand ('right well sanded' at Richmond Palace), or other inert materials. The outer edge of the entire pattern might be lined with bricks, or planks (thereby raising the bed above the level of the surrounding path or alley), tiles, bones or even with strips of lead, as at Richmond. The design might be purely geometrical – a circle within a square, or something more elaborate – and its lines might cross each other, 'under' and 'over' as in embroidery, thus giving the appearance of entwined or interlacing threads – a 'knot'. Often these abstract designs were given a pictorial interest by incorporating the shapes of animals or other objects, such as a crown, a sword or a shield, either in three dimensions, like the lions' which 'stode up wondersly' in Stephen Hawes' poem, or in a low almost two-dimensional form with the outlines in tightly clipped evergreens. Another related theme was the representation of heraldic motifs, like the 'ryall knotts' of the Richmond gardens, with a part or the whole of the royal or the owner's coat of arms, or the interlaced initials of the owner and his wife.

These knots, at Richmond and in Hawes' poem, are early and uncommon examples, but will become widespread later in the century, particularly in complex geometrical forms.[36]

Pageants

At Richmond there were also 'heraldic beasts' – carved wooden representations of lions, unicorns, tigers or other animals, set up on posts in the gardens. They are referred to in George Cavendish's *Life of Cardinal Wolsey*, written after Wolsey's death in 1530. After his fall in 1529, Wolsey stayed for a while in a lodge within the park at Richmond. Cavendish accompanied him, and remarked on 'certain images of beasts conterfeit in timber' standing in the 'pleasant walks and alleys' of the garden. The most carefully carved was one of a 'dun cow', and Wolsey explained to Cavendish that it was related to the King's title, 'appertaining of antiquity unto his earldom of Richmond', and had therefore a heraldic significance.[37]

The description of the Richmond Palace garden in 1501 concludes with matters which must, unlike the knots, have been relatively frequent in courtly gardens – matters of entertainment:

> In the lougher ende of this gardeyn beth pleasaunt gallerys, and housis of pleasure to disporte inn, at chesse, tables, dise, cardes, bylys ['bills' or skittles]; bowlyng aleys, butts for archers, and goodly tenes plays.

As the sixteenth century progressed the use of gardens for grand entertainment become more frequent and more elaborate. Not only were gardens themselves places where numbers of people could be amused – as at Richmond – but 'the garden' was seen as a place to be represented in entertainments of a theatrical kind, as being a scene from which pleasure could be derived. So at Richmond Palace in 1511, the second year of Henry VIII's reign, the entertainment for Twelfth Night involved

> ... a pageant devised like a mountayne ... on the top of the which mountayne was a tree of golde, the braunches and bowes frysed [edged] with gold, spredynge on every side over the mountayne, with Roses and Pomegarnettes.[38]

Not long after, in mid-February, a series of elaborate jousts at the Palace of Westminster began with another 'pageant' (i.e. a scene or setting, often on wheels, where an entertainment or dances are performed), 'made like a forest with rockes, hilles and dales, with divers sundrie trees, floures, ha[w]thornes, ferne and grasse'.[39]

On the next evening, when the day's jousts were over, there was supper, and then chapel, and songs, music and dancing, and, after a while,

> Then was there a device or a pageant upon wheles brought in, [out of which stepped a gentleman who showed] howe in a garden of pleasure there was an arber of golde ... therein were trees of Hawthorne, Eglantynes, Rosiers [rose bushes], Vines and other pleasaunt floures of divers colours, with Gillofers [gillyflowers or carnations] and other herbes all made of Satyn, damaske, silke, silver and gold, according as the natural trees, herbes, or floures ought to be.[40]

We might note that this entertainment went amiss – after the performance, the 'pageant' was rolled back to the far end of the hall, to wait until the lords and ladies had finished dancing,

> ... but sodanly the rude people ranne to the pagent, and rent, tare, and spoyled the pagent, so that the Lord Stuard nor the head officers could not cause them to abstaine, excepte they should have foughten and drawen bloude, and so was this pagent broken.

Such is the fragility of gardens. Nine years later, in 1520, Henry VIII of England and François I of France met on 'neutral ground' at the 'Field of the Cloth of Gold' in northern France (set 'within the Englishe pale', and so within this history). Their alliance was hardly permanent, no more than the artificial garden background to their meeting. Here Henry had set up a 'mountain' on which were two trees, the Hawthorn/Aubépine for Henry, and the Framboisier/Raspberry for François. The trees were artfully intertwined, with leaves and fruit, 'in compasse about an hundred twentie and nyne foote ... their beautie shewed farre'. And beneath and beside these glorious and artificial trees, 'on the montaigne was a place herber wise, where the Herauldes were'.[41] The trees, the 'mountain' and the 'place herber wise' soon disappeared, just like the heraldic beasts which contemporary drawings show on the tops of the tent poles, rising above Henry's grandiose encampment. But the idea of these creatures, first seen in a British garden at Richmond Palace, was to survive and thrive in later royal gardens, particularly at Hampton Court and Nonsuch.

In 1523, an equally extravagant sequence of pageants was staged for the King in London. Many of the scenes had no garden connection, but one at least should be noted, set up near to Cornhill, beside the 'Stockes',

> ... where was a quadrant stage where on was an Herber full of Roses, Lyllies and all other flowers curiously wrought, and byrdes, beastes and all other thynges of plea-sure. And aboute the Herber was made the water full of Fyshe, and about it was the Elementes, the Planettes and Starres in their places and every thing moved ...[42]

One more pageant in Henry's reign must be mentioned, at Greenwich in May 1528. Another of the King's favourite palaces, and often referred to as 'Placentia' or 'the Pleasance' (like Henry V's 'pleasance' in the marsh at Kenilworth – see page 35), the establishment at Greenwich had begun as a hunting park for Humphrey, Duke of Gloucester in 1433. In the 1450s, the property was held by Queen Margaret, and contained an arbour with a hedge round it. The residence was later rebuilt by Henry VII, and again by Henry VIII. Quite apart from its political and architectural importance, the site at Greenwich, rising up southwards from the Thames towards Blackheath and Shooter's Hill, was to be of growing interest for its park and gardens until the present day. In May 1528, Henry VIII was entertaining ambassadors from France, with the view to his daughter Mary marrying the Duke of Orleans. Beside the tilt-yard (the area for jousting) at Greenwich, he had a temporary banqueting house set up, 100 feet long by 30 feet wide, 'the roof was purple cloth ful of roses and Pomgarnettes', and in this space the evening entertainments took place. Letting down a curtain, there was revealed

> ... a goodly mount, walled in with towers ... and all the mount was set full of Christal coralles, and rich rockes of rubie ... and full of roses and pomgranates as though they grewe: on this rocke sat eight Lordes ...
>
> Then out of a cave issued out the lady Mary doughter to the Kyng and with her seven ladies ...[43]

The fate of this fragile 'mountain', with its flowers, its cave and its 'rich rockes of rubie' was less abrupt than some. The king commanded that the pageants 'should stand still, for thre or foure daies, that al honest persones might see and beholde the houses and riches'.

The several 'mounts' or 'mountains' in these pageants were already known in Continental entertainments of this kind, and were related to the hillocks or viewing platforms which were raised within some medieval properties, to enable those inside the walls to see over the neighbouring countryside. By the 1530s, they were not uncommon in British gardens (see pp 17–18). The 'cave' in the last pageant, with 'Christal coralles', is of interest as the earliest reference to a grotto in England – a feature which had been recommended in Italy by Alberti in the previous century,[44] but which was not to become common in the British Isles until the early seventeenth century, though a few examples are to be found before.

Hampton Court

In 1529, Henry VIII entered into possession of the palace, gardens and park at Hampton Court. There had been a house with gardens on the site of the palace since the thirteenth century, belonging to the Knights of the Order of St John, and in 1514, this property was taken over by Thomas Wolsey, Archbishop of York (1514) and Cardinal (1515). Garden activity is recorded in detail in 1515, with accounts for garden tools – repairs and acquisitions – provided by John Chapman of Kingston, 'my Lordes gardyner'. The lists are hardly different from Alexander Neckam's in the 1190s (see page 29), and would serve us today fairly well:

> 3 spades . . . 2 iron rakes . . . 2 lines . . . 4 dibbles . . . 1 hand bill [i.e. a bill-hook] . . .
> a wheel barrow . . . 2 hatchets . . . a pick . . . a tubb to watter therbes.[45]

By the 1560s, the watering can appeared, to replace the 'tubb', but there was to be little further development until the seventeenth century.

Two other items in John Chapman's accounts must be noted – 'twigs to bind the arbour', and 'twystes' for the same purpose. These would have been thin strips of pliant wood – hazel or willow most probably – for tying or strapping together the main poles of an arbour, and for attaching to the main structure the branches and shoots of the plants intended to grow up and over the framework – vines, honeysuckle, roses, and the sturdy hawthorn.

Such arbours were indeed made in Wolsey's garden. In the late 1520s, Wolsey's loyal servant George Cavendish began a verse biography of his master, in which he gave Wolsey these lines describing the garden works at Hampton Court:

> My gardens sweet, enclosed with walles strong,
> Embanked with benches to sytt and take my rest;
> The knotts so enknotted, it cannot be exprest,
> With arbors and alys so plesaunt and so dulce,
> The pestylent ayers with flavors to repulse.[46]

As in the past, the gardens were enclosed, with arbours as described. We should note also that the walls were 'embanked with benches' – with *turf seats*, which had been common for several centuries. In 1516, Thomas More finished his *Utopia*, the account of which was recounted to him – so he claimed – when he was in Antwerp in the service of Henry VIII. He had met the seafarer Raphael Hythloday, and related that,

> when we . . . hadde spoken these comen wordes, that be customably spoken at the fyrste metynge . . . of straungers, we wente thens to my house, and there in my gardeyne, upon a benche coveryd with grene torves (*considentes in scamno cespitibus herbeis constrato*), we satte downe talking togethers.[47]

The whole description of the government and ways of 'Utopia' was therefore narrated and noted by Hythloday and by More as they sat on a turf seat. Not, I think, of importance in the scheme of More's ideal state, but of interest in the history of British gardens, since the references by Cavendish and More are among the last. 'Grassy slopes' where one might recline remained popular, like Titania's 'bank whereon the wild thyme grows' or the grassed and flowery tree-trunk against which Isaac Oliver's young man reclines, but turf *benches* did not reappear.

Knots, however – 'so enknotted, it cannot be exprest' – were in the ascendant. Beside Cavendish's phrase there is a detail, from 1520, relating to the Duke of Buckingham's garden at Thornbury in Gloucestershire, when 'John Wynde, gardener, for diligence in making knottes in the Duke's garden' was paid 3s. 4d.[48] Edward Stafford, the Duke of Buckingham, had laid out most elaborate gardens at Thornbury before his disgrace and execution in 1521. Park, orchard and gardens were given walled enclosures and elaborate walks and alleys – some of the alleys 'with roosting places' covered with hawthorn and hazel.[49] These 'roosting places' were a form of screened or private garden room, anticipating the 'banqueting houses' which appeared at Hampton Court a few years later, then at Nonsuch (see page 48).

At Hampton Court such knots were admired for the rest of the century. As at Thornbury, the knots were within enclosed garden areas – the Pond Garden, the Privy Garden and the Mount Garden, together with the Privy Orchard, all on the south and south-eastern side of the palace – and connected with covered walks. But unlike Thornbury, Hampton Court was to be lavishly decorated with the insignia of the Tudor monarchy – with 'heraldic beasts' and with lines of wooden posts and rails surrounding the garden beds, and painted in green and white, the Tudor colours. 'Heraldic beasts' had already been set up in the gardens of Richmond Palace in Henry VII's time (see page 42), but it is clear that Henry VIII had far more. Their making, painting, gilding and setting up on posts dates from the early 1530s, and they included lions, tigers, dragons, bulls, griffins, leopards, horses, antelopes, harts, hinds, rams, greyhounds, badgers and 'yallys' or 'jalls'. Most were carved in wood, some were in stone, and it appears from the craftsmen's accounts that around 200 of them were set up in the garden and orchard areas.[50] Beside the many 'beasts', there was a copious allowance of brass sundials – around 30 of them – and various representations of the King's and the Queen's coats of arms, some on separate posts, some on shields held by the 'beasts' and some on 'vanes' – like weathervanes – held up by the 'beasts' over their heads or on separate poles. From the few illustrations which survive, it would seem that each 'beast' with its post was 8 feet or so tall, and those with 'vanes' above must have reached 10 or 12 feet, standing high over the railed garden beds, and often visible from outside the palace walls.[51]

One painting, of the King with his family in the palace at Whitehall, has glimpses on either side into the garden, where the features I have mentioned – rails and beasts – appear in brief and tantalising form. Painted around 1545, it demonstrates both the characteristics of these features, and their use in other royal gardens. Later in the century, Queen Elizabeth was to display heraldic beasts in her gardens (or at least to continue to keep them in place – see page 84), but they were uncommon after her reign until at least the later twentieth century, when a dozen of the creatures reappeared beside the Palm House in the Royal Botanic Gardens at Kew. In the sixteenth century, such flaunting devices were rare and almost exclusively royal. As exceptions, I can think only of the Earl of Leicester's 'Bear and ragged staff' motifs at Kenilworth in 1575, which were both ephemeral and exceptional (see page 85), and the 'popinjay' motifs (the emblem of Lord Lumley) displayed in the gardens at Nonsuch, at Cheam in Surrey, from around 1579. These were, however, matched or outdone by Leicester's display of emblems in honour of Queen Elizabeth.[52]

Hampton Court in the 1530s had two other features we should note – the mount and the two arbours. The mount, in the Mount Garden, between the old Water Gate and the palace, was much larger than the raised hillocks of some medieval gardens, and had a brick foundation, earthed over and planted round with 'quicksets' (probably hawthorn), railed in with ash poles and withy strips. At the top was the 'South Arbour', a building with two storeys, each having 48 glazed windows, and with a dome above surmounted by a lion holding a vane.[53] The 'West arbour' seems to have been of similar size, though not raised on a mount. Both buildings were obviously far grander and more elaborate than the modest 'herbers' described by poets around 1400, and were early and notable examples of the 'banqueting-houses' which were referred to in gardens from the 1550s onwards.

At Hampton Court the mount itself, planted round with thousands of 'quicksets' trained with poles and withies, could be matched in the late 1530s or early 1540s at Wressle Castle in the East Riding of Yorkshire, described by the topographer John Leland. Within the castle moat were gardens, and outside were orchards – like the 'Privy Orchard' at Hampton Court. Leland wrote 'And yn the orchardes were mountes *opere topiario* ('with topiary work'), writhen about with degrees ('steps') like turnings of cokilshilles, to cum to the top without payn'.[54] It is worth noting that these 'mountes *opere topiario*' were probably fairly recent (so attracting Leland's attention), being made for Lady Mary Percy, banished to Wressle after her marriage to Lord Henry Percy in 1527 (Percy had been obliged to marry her, to prevent his attentions to Anne Boleyn, who was then the object of the King's desire.[55]). Topiary work at this time was an innovation – Leland noted two other examples, at Ulleskelf in the West Riding and at Little Haseley in Oxfordshire, both near 'orchards'[56] – and it would be reasonable to imagine that the 'quicksets' round King Henry's mount were carefully clipped into a unified shape, if not into fanciful artificial creations like the lions and dragons which 'stode up wondersly' in the three-dimensional knots at Richmond.

Though Henry VIII's palace and gardens at Nonsuch were rapidly famous (they were created between 1538 and 1547 with the clear aim of rivalling, and outshining, François I's palace and gardens at Fontainebleau), details of the gardens are scant until the end of the century. By the 1540s, Leland could already write 'This which no equal has in art or fame, Britons deservedly do *Nonesuch* name',[57] but, until the 1590s, we know little more than that two parks surrounded the palace and gardens, and that the latter comprised privy gardens, hedged walks and a kitchen garden.

One item however from Henry VIII's time has been accurately identified – the banqueting-house, built between 1538 and 1546, and the subject of excavations in 1960.[58] This garden building, sited some 350 yards away from the palace and its privy gardens, measured 44 by 38 feet, and had two storeys above a cellar. On the roof was a parapet with 'heraldic beasts'. The building was set on a paved and slightly raised platform – an octagonal area, with round 'bastions' at four of the angles, providing a walking space all the way round.

While this banqueting-house at Nonsuch could have been used for a 'complete' entertainment – the chief areas included oven and wine-rack spaces, and there was a separate bakehouse or kitchen nearby – this type of garden feature was at first normally intended to supplement rather than to replace the facilities of the principal building, whether mansion or palace. An early sense of the word 'banquet' implies not a 'feast', the modern meaning, but a *continuation* of the main meal, taken in a separate room, like a 'dessert', when the guests would leave the main dining room while the dishes were removed (French *desservir*, 'to clear away'). Most early banqueting-houses therefore were small, with room for a few *banquets* (benches or seats) and without facilities for cooking. There is a wholly appropriate, and beautiful, example in the garden at Melford Hall in Suffolk. Here the octagonal banqueting-house, built around 1559, stands 150 yards away from the house on a raised platform with a bowling green beside, and with views both into the grounds and out over the wall to the village green.

Comment on royal gardens – and garden pageantry – in this period may end in the summer of 1557 with the visit to Richmond Palace by Princess Elizabeth (second daughter of Henry VIII) to her sister Queen Mary (King Henry's older daughter). 'She went by water . . . in the Queen's barge,' wrote John Nichols,

> . . . which was richly hung with garlands of artificial flowers, and covered with a canopy of green sarcenet wrought with branches of eglantine in embroidery . . . She was received by the Queen [at Richmond] in a sumptuous pavilion . . . in the Labyrinth of the gardens. The walls . . . were checquered into compartments, in each of which were alternately a lily in silver and a pomegranate in gold [indicating Queen Mary's French alliance and Spanish descent].[59]

In November 1557, Queen Mary was dead; Princess Elizabeth succeeded her, and took over much of her sister's, and their father's, pageantry, though without the pomegranates. Nonetheless, it was at Richmond Palace that Elizabeth would die, many years later, in 1603.

Labyrinths

A line from Nichols' description of Princess Elizabeth's visit to her sister at Richmond in the summer of 1557 deserves special attention – 'She was received by the Queen in a sumptuous pavilion . . . in the Labyrinth of the gardens.' If we discount the comments on 'Rosamund's Bower' (see page 26), this appears to be the first reference to an existing garden maze in Britain. Within a few years (1563 or earlier) Thomas Hill was describing how to lay them out (see page 67), but in 1557 Richmond stood alone. By this time Alberti's architectural treatise had stated that the 'Ancients' had labyrinths on the pavements of their porticoes, 'in which the Boys used to exercise themselves',[60] and Sebastiano Serlio in his *Architettura* (IV, xii), first published in Venice in 1537, had included two designs of garden mazes. How the Richmond maze was laid out is difficult to say. From Thomas Hill, and from the illustrations in Du Cerceau,[61] we may conjecture that low, closely clipped evergreens, no more than knee-high, were used – certainly not tall hedges 'well framed a man's height', as William Lawson was to advise in 1618.

Until the close of Queen Mary's reign (1553–58), another type of maze would have been common in many parts of the British Isles – flat, almost two-dimensional mazes cut in the turf, in which the path was no more than the underlying soil, chalk or gravel. That at Breamore in Hampshire has already been mentioned, being possibly of Anglo-Saxon origin (see page 19). Others still survive: for example at Saffron Walden in Essex, Somerton in Oxfordshire, Wing in Leicestershire, Alkborough in Lincolnshire and St Catherine's Hill in Winchester, Hampshire. I say 'still survive' since there were once scores of them, mentioned in documents and noted by topographers and antiquarians from the sixteenth century onwards.[62]

Their purpose is not wholly certain, though the existence of similar labyrinths, laid out in tiles or bricks on the floor of continental churches – in the chapter house of Bayeux Cathedral, for example – has led to the speculation that they were used for acts of penitence, proceeding towards the centre on one's knees. This theory might apply to many of the old turf mazes in the British Isles, since they are often sited close to a church. Others however are not, being on village greens or open downland, and their use seems to have been rather for running races and other jolly games than for the exercise of piety. In many instances their names include references to 'Julian' or to 'Troy' – 'Julian's Bower', 'Troy Farm', 'Troy Castle', and 'Caerdroia' in Wales for example – which link the maze to the *Lusus Troiae*, the 'Troy game', to Aeneas' son Iulus (known earlier as Ascanius) who took part in the game, and to the legend of Daedalus, who built the labyrinth for King Minos of Crete. (An interesting mixture of church and classics occurred at 'Gelyan's [Julian's] Bower' near Louth in Lincolnshire, where in 1544 the mason was paid 3s. 'for making at gelyan bower a new crose'. Where was the cross? Presumably near the entrance, or at the centre of the maze, replacing an earlier stone.[63]) These Virgilian connections were already apparent in the twelfth century, with the comments on the architectural labyrinth of

'Rosamund's Bower', and the equestrian evolutions of young Londoners mentioned by William Fitzstephen (see page 22). Yet this explanation is not all that certain, and the disappearance of most of these mazes after the Reformation has left little fact and a deal of fiction. Even the reason for the neglect of the mazes – that they were a part of the earlier 'super-stition' – is no more than a theory.

The neglect is sure – as Shakespeare wrote in A *Midsummer Night's Dream* (II, i),

> . . . the quaint mazes in the wanton green,
>   For lack of tread, are undistinguishable

– and after the reference of 1544 at Louth, no turf maze is recorded until 1660, when the maze on the green at Hilton in Cambridgeshire was cut by William Sparrow to celebrate the return of Charles II. After Hilton, turf mazes – unlike their hedged counterparts, which thrived until around 1700 – were forgotten until the present age, when they reappeared as a 'new' and intriguing garden feature (see page 324).

Husbandry and Herbals

In this period, there were few books of direct garden interest. Master Fitzherbert's *Book of Husbandry* (1523) is eminently practical, principally to do with farming, and only slightly concerned with gardens.[64] Section 24 tells 'Howe forkes and rakes shoulde be made', but these are more for a farm than a garden. Bees are properly discussed in Section 122, ditching and hedging in Sections 125–127, and grafting, with the proper tools, in Sections 136–139. A few lines (part of Section 146) tell of the wife's garden duties:

> And in the begynnynge of Marche . . . is tyme for a wyfe to make her garden, and to
> gette as many good sedes and herbes as she canne, and specially suche as be good
> for the potte, and to eate; and as ofte as nede shal require, it must be weded, for els
> the wedes wyl overgrowe the herbes.

That's that. Fitzherbert had not read the translation into English verse of Palladius, commissioned by Humphrey, Duke of Gloucester around 1420, nor did, I suspect, many others, so that the ancient Roman's advice went unheeded until Thomas Hill, reading another version of Palladius, referred to him relentlessly in the 1560s (see page 63).

Plant matters, however, were different. Several *herbals* (i.e. lists of plants, generally indicating their uses in medicine, and including a description of each plant, sometimes with a woodcut illustration) were translated into English in this period – Banckes' *Herball* (1525) and *The Grete Herball* (1526), for example – and were followed in 1538 by the first of William Turner's three books on plants, the *Libellus de re herbaria novus*. This was translated, and slightly expanded, in 1548 as *The Names of Herbes*, and in 1551 he produced the first part of *A New Herball*, followed by the first and second parts together in 1562, and the completed three-part work in 1568. The *New Herball* was illustrated with woodcuts, mainly taken from the 1545 edition of Leonhard Fuchs' *De Historia stirpium*.[65] In 1578 Henry Lyte produced *A Niewe Herball*, based on Dodoens' Cruÿdeboeck.

Though Turner (*c.* 1512–68) has been called 'the father of British botany' for his work on the properties of plants, his interest in this history lies in his comments on the presence of various plants in England in his time, his remarks as to where they were grown, and the fact that he himself was a gardener of some enthusiasm. These matters appear particularly in *The Names of Herbes*. He had already travelled widely in England and on the Continent, having contacts with several noted botanists – Ghini, Gesner, Fuchs – and had stayed long enough in Germany to have one garden in Cologne, and possibly a second, maybe in Bonn.[66] Soon after the accession of Edward VI in 1547, he was appointed chaplain and physician to Edward Seymour, Duke of Somerset (the Lord Protector), who had been granted the estate at Syon on the north bank of the Thames, facing the royal park at Richmond. *The Names of Herbes* is dated 'From your graces house at Syon ... 1548', and many of the plants and trees which Turner describes are noted as growing at Syon – so many, and often of sufficient rarity at that time to imply that a collection of plants had been begun there, and indeed that Turner may have been in charge of it. We might note that he includes acanthus, 'one kinde' of cistus, cypress, lily of the valley, pomegranate ('but their fruite cometh never unto perfection'), white narcissus and the Chinese lantern (*Physalis alkekengi*). Though Turner has occasionally been credited with planting the first red mulberries in Britain at Syon Park, he himself states simply that 'it groweth in diverse gardines in England'. Other gardens and parts with interesting plants at the time were Lord Cobham's 'a little from Graves Ende' (see page 71), 'Coome park' (now Coombe, south-east of Richmond Park) and 'my gardine', which was on the south side of the Thames in Sheen.

Turner's interest extended to many wild plants, several of which he notes 'by the Temmes syde about Shene' – like yellow loosestrife

(*Lysimachia*). Some were so common that he need not explain – 'everyman knoweth wel enough where strawberries growe'. He was still happily in the age of *Fragaria vesca*! One garden vegetable was praised for its ornamental value – the 'kidney beane ... or arber beanes, because they serve to cover an arber for the tyme of Summer'.

Not long after *The Names of Herbes*, Turner was appointed Dean of Wells, but was expelled when Queen Mary came to the throne. Reappointed after Queen Elizabeth's succession, he was dismissed in 1564 for nonconformity. In these two periods at Wells his work on *A New Herball* continued, and he is associated with the 3-acre area of the present Deanery gardens.

Turner noted several recent introductions. Half a dozen others should be mentioned, which are now common in our gardens, orchards or hedgerows: the sycamore, brought from the Continent 'in the sixteenth century'; the hop, introduced from Holland in 1524 (previously ale had been made *without* hops); and three fruit trees – the pippin, introduced by Leonard Mascall around 1525, the fig, claimed by some to have been planted first at Lambeth Palace by Reginald (later Cardinal) Pole in 1525, and the apricot, introduced in 1542. A thicket of fig stems and branches still grows beside the east wall of Juxon's Hall at Lambeth Palace, but this is long pre-dated by the fig orchard at West Tarring in Sussex (see page 27). Of the apricot Turner remarked in 1548, 'we have very fewe of these trees as yet'.

In 1576 William Lambarde claimed that the region round Teynham in Kent now counted as the modern *Hesperidum Hortos* or 'Hesperidean gardens'. This was due to the enterprise of Richard Harris, the King's 'Fruiterer', around 1533, when he had planted 105 acres of orchards there with fresh grafts brought in from France and the Low Countries, particularly of sweet cherries and two types of apple – the 'temperate Pipyn' and the 'golden Renate', or 'Reinette'.[67]

4

THE REIGN OF ELIZABETH

I do not think it belittles the interest of medieval gardens to say that garden history in Britain begins as a full, coherent and unified subject in the reign of Queen Elizabeth I. In 1587 the topographer and historian William Harrison produced an enlarged edition of *The Description of England*, with several new sections including the entire chapter 'Of Gardens and Orchards'. In this chapter, he not only states proudly that the country's gardens have improved beyond measure 'within these forty years' so that 'in comparison of this present the ancient gardens were but dunghills and laystows [open drains] to such as did possess them',[1] he also indicates in considerable detail the different aspects of garden activity which shared in this improvement, bringing together many elements which had until then normally been discussed as relatively separate topics.

News from the Continent

This advance in garden interest and activity came about for several reasons, related mainly to eager and extensive contact with new developments on the Continent. The phrase 'the culture of the Renaissance' covers much of this interest, though it is not altogether adequate. England's growing economic and political importance was linked with the drastic realignment of European states, divided since the Reformation into Roman or Protestant groups, and also with the exploration and exploitation of the Americas.

On the Continent, English travellers were impressed by the new and extravagant gardens created in Italy, and also in France, and by the largely classical inspiration of these gardens, related to their design, features, sculpture and architecture. They were impressed by a new type of garden, the *botanic* garden, founded at Pisa in 1543, Padua in 1545 and Leiden in 1587, for the collection and study of all kinds of plants, including newly discovered species from the Americas, the 'new found land'; and they were impressed by the botanists whom they met, either on the Continent or in England, such as Leonhard Fuchs (1501–66), Konrad von Gesner (1516–65), Clusius (Charles de l'Ecluse, 1526–1609), Joachim Camerarius the Younger (1534–98) and Mathias de l'Obel (1538–1616). These scholars, whose work was originally based on Greek or Roman accounts of plants from the Mediterranean region, had gradually come to see that new forms of description and classification were needed to take account of plants from other regions of the world, and the fact that plants were now to be studied for a wider range of purposes than the classical writers (Theophrastus, Dioscorides, Pliny the Elder, Galen) had envisaged.

Above all, English gardens, and the people who designed them and wrote about them, were deeply affected by the flood of newly published texts from the Continent. Many were classical, printed from old manuscripts from the end of the fifteenth century onwards. Many were modern, being by Italian, French or other continental writers, but nearly all influenced by older classical works; and, whether ancient or modern, they were of all kinds – not merely botanic, but historical and biographical (the letters of Pliny the Younger, for example); architectural (*Roman*: Vitruvius; *Italian*: Alberti, Serlio, Palladio; *French*: Du Cerceau); agricultural (*Roman*: Cato, Varro, Palladius; *French*: Estienne; *German*: Heresbach); scientific (*Greek*: Hero of Alexandria); scientific-cum-architectural (*French*: Bernard Palissy); and finally poetic and fictional, including descriptions of imaginary and sometimes fantastic gardens – beginning with Colonna's *Hypnerotomachia Poliphili* (this work has already been mentioned as the first to include illustrations of knots – see page 41).

In virtually every instance the garden elements of these works are slight, parts merely of wider subjects – and properly so, since gardens at any time whatsoever are always a part, not the whole of our lives. Even the imaginative works bring in gardens as a 'change of scene', to allow the reader (and possibly the hero or the heroine) a respite from the strains of battle, shipwreck or courtly intrigue.

Comment on the variety of the imaginative literature is necessary, from the classical *Daphnis and Chloe* of Longus (translated from Greek into French in 1559), a largely pastoral tale, to the French Protestant Saluste Du Bartas' long poem on the Creation, of which *Eden* was published in 1584 (English version in 1598). Other pastoral works, with chivalric elements, are Jacopo Sannazaro's *Arcadia* (Italian, 1504) and

Jorge de Montemayor's *Diana* (Spanish, *c.* 1559), completed in 1567 by Gil Polo (translated into French in 1569, and English in 1598). Almost wholly chivalric was *Amadis of Gaul*, first written in Portuguese, then Spanish, then translated into French and enlarged in 1540–48 (translated into English in 1588), while Ariosto's epic *Orlando furioso* (1532; English version 1591) and Tasso's *Gerusallemme liberata* (1551; English version 1594) combine long tales of knightly combat with episodes in enchanted gardens derived from classical sources.

By the later years of the sixteenth century, these influences from the Continent were therefore extraordinarily varied, and they were at first adopted and adapted in England in ways which may now seen haphazard, inconsistent, and – in real gardens – somewhat timid. In imaginative literature, however, such hesitation was needless, so that the 'magical' gardens in Spenser's *Faerie Queen* (II, xii, the 'Bower of Bliss' and III, vi, the 'Garden of Adonis', published in 1590) are unrestrained in their delight and exuberance, happily combining classical, biblical, medieval and contemporary allusions.

Sir Philip Sidney

Also published in 1590, though written around 1580–1, Sir Philip Sidney's pastoral and courtly novel, *The Countess of Pembroke's Arcadia*, has three garden descriptions, all in the first book. The first and second gardens are not exceptional – though the second does have a sculptured fountain of Venus and the young Aeneas, and a summerhouse containing pictures with classical themes. The third, round a 'lodge' or country residence belonging to King Basilius, is notable both for the complexity of its sources, and for its subsequent influence on several real gardens in England, and it should therefore be examined in detail.

Sidney first describes the situation of the lodge:

> It being set upon such an unsensible rising of the ground as you are come to a pretty height before almost you perceive that you ascend, it gives the eye lordship over a good large circuit, which according to the nature of the country, being diversified between hills and dales, woods and plains, one place more clear, another more darksome, it seems a pleasant picture of nature, with lovely lightsomeness and artificial shadows.

Next comes the lodge's relationship to the garden and to a smaller building:

The lodge is of a yellow stone, built in the form of a star, having round about a garden framed into like points; and beyond the garden ridings cut out, each answering the angles of the lodge: at the end of one of them is the other smaller lodge, but of like fashion, where the gracious Pamela liveth; so that the lodge seemeth not unlike a fair comet, whose tail stretcheth itself to a star of less greatness.

Last, he describes the garden and a banqueting-house:

I was invited and brought down to sup with them in the garden, a place not fairer in natural ornaments than artificial inventions, where, in a banqueting-house, among certain pleasant trees, whose heads seemed curled with the wrappings about of vine branches, the table was set near to an excellent water-works; for, by the casting of the water in most cunning manner, it makes, with the shining of the sun upon it, a perfect rainbow, not more pleasant to the eye than to the mind, so sensibly to see the proof of the heavenly Iris. There were birds also made so finely that they did not only deceive the sight with their figure, but the hearing with their songs, which the watery instruments made their gorge deliver. The table at which we sat was round, which being fast to the floor whereon we sat, and that divided from the rest of the buildings, with turning a vice, which Basilius at first did to make me sport, the table, and we about the table, did all turn round by means of water which ran under and carried it about as a mill.[2]

Let us consider the sources of this description. The first section is virtually a paraphrase from Alberti, *De Re aedificatoria*, IX, ii, on the ideal setting for a country house; a passage taken by Alberti from Pliny the Younger's comments on the setting of his Tuscan villa (*Letters*, V, vi). Sidney also knew his Pliny, as will appear. The star-like lodge, with its smaller lodge at the end of one of the 'ridings' or avenues, could well be an echo of the Palazzo Farnese at Caprarola, north of Rome – converted into a palace between 1547 and 1559 by Vignola from a symmetrical, five-sided fortress – and the related Villa Farnese, the sumptuous yet discreetly hidden garden villa designed by Vignola a quarter of a mile away, under construction from the 1550s and completed in 1587. Though Sidney did not travel so far south in Italy, he was well aware of the cultural and artistic activities of the time, and the marvels at Caprarola could indeed have come to his notice, as did the marvels of the Villa d'Este at Tivoli. Visiting Caprarola in 1581, Montaigne said of the Palazzo that it was 'the most talked about in Italy'.[3]

The banqueting-house, with its table, shady vines and waterworks, comes in the first instance from Pliny, but the 'rainbow' and the artificial birds with water-powered voices come most probably from written reports of the Villa d'Este, which Sidney would have read either in Paris, during his contacts there with the Cardinal d'Este's household in 1572, or in Vienna in 1573, when he met Clusius, then director of the Imperial gardens.[4] The chirping birds in the 'Owl fountain' at the Villa d'Este were directly and exactly inspired by the hydraulic toys described in the *Pneumatica* of Hero of Alexandria (*c.* AD 100); a manuscript of Hero's text was known to Pirro Ligorio, main designer of the gardens at the Villa d'Este, and a Latin version was published in 1575.

Finally, the revolving table, driven by water, close to the chirping birds, is clearly derived from the circular, revolving table-top described in Varro's *De Re rustica* (III, v, 9–17), set in a luxurious private aviary, with songsters close by. Varro's table-top revolves to bring food and drink round to all the guests, while at the same time cold and hot water 'flows for each guest from the table . . . by the turning of cocks'.

Sidney's *Arcadia* became the most widely-read romance of the age, with an immense and lasting influence. Within the ambit of this history it is enough to say that the description of Basilius' garden influenced both real gardens (see pages 77 and 86) and literary gardens, particularly the one in Thomas Nashe's *The Unfortunate Traveller* (1594).[5] Here, Nashe writes of a merchant's 'summer banquetting-house' in Rome, with a paradise-like garden inside, in which the infinity of singing birds are all mechanical. They 'made a spirting sound, such as chirping is', with 'searching sweet water . . . bubling upwards through the rough crannies of their closed bills'. While this comes from Sidney, other details (such as wind-cum-water instruments on the roof, and the pacific, pre-lapsarian nature of everything within the garden – 'no poysonous beast there reposed . . . the rose had no cankers, the leaves no caterpillers . . . Such a golden age . . . was set forth in this banketting house') come most probably from Bernard Palissy's *Recepte véritable* (1563), which includes the detailed 'dessein d'un Jardin . . . déléctable',[6] and from Saluste Du Bartas' vision of *Eden* (1584).[7] Together with Sidney, these two French Protestant writers, separately or on their own, provided the modern literary or technical authority for many future waterworks, grottoes and ornamental streams.

The influences in the later sixteenth and early seventeenth centuries are obviously rich, diverse and indeed confused, bringing together classical, medieval and modern elements. We may add the uncertain but likely reports of travellers, telling what they had seen in Italy and France (like the *Survey of . . . Tuscany . . . in 1596* by Sir Robert Dallington, not published until 1605).

'Within Forty Years Past'

As I wrote at the beginning of this chapter, William Harrison's remarks of 1587 give a wholeness to the subject which has not appeared before. The broad spread of garden activity is clear, stretching out to parks, warrens, woods and water, to the intensive cultivation of saffron, and the importance of bees. He was himself a minor but enthusiastic gardener and plant collector, with some 3 acres at Radwinter in Essex. This garden contained a 'variety of simples' totalling 'very near three hundred of one sort and other . . . no one of them being common or usually to be had'.[8] He admired flowers, herbs, vegetables and fruit, for their beauty, variety, rarity, medicinal virtues and usefulness as food.

Yet if his 'little plot . . . be so well furnished', what should one think of the gardens of the great? He named two great royal gardens, Hampton Court and Nonsuch, and two great private gardens, Lord Burghley's Theobalds, and his patron Lord Cobham's property at Cobham in Kent.

He wrote at length in praise of the new plants brought from abroad, of their beauty and their use – we wonder 'to see how many strange herbs, plants, and annual fruits are daily brought unto us from the Indies, Americans, Taprobane [Sri Lanka], Canary Isles, and all parts of the world'. These discoveries were widely enjoyed – 'there is not almost one nobleman, gentleman, or merchant that hath not great store of these flowers'[9] – and the study, use and breeding of the plants was being advanced by notable botanists, of whom 'the chief workman, . . . the founder . . . is Carolus Clusius, the noble herbarist'.[10]

This progress, Harrison claimed, had come 'within forty years past', and in looking back to the early Elizabethan period, we must examine the several areas of garden interest one by one, to see how they led up to Harrison's and the later Elizabethans' overall enthusiasm.

Good Husbandrie – Thomas Tusser

Like Jon Gardener in the fourteenth century, Thomas Tusser in the sixteenth wrote in a wholly native tradition. In easy, lolloping doggerel, his advice on rural economy was printed first in 1557 as *A Hundredth Good Pointes of Husbandrie* (reprinted 1562, 1570), and much enlarged in 1573 as *Five Hundred Pointes of Good Husbandrie* (often reprinted, in varying forms, until 1744). His theme is the running of a small farm, with its household and with a garden as a minor but valuable part of the whole.

So far as I can judge, Tusser is as wholly 'English' as Jon Gardener, insofar as he makes no allusions at all to classical or modern continental writers on husbandry. Like Jon Gardener again, he does not refer to his own farm or garden, nor to those of other people, even though it is known that he worked farms in Suffolk and Essex, and that his patron for many years, Lord Thomas Paget, had a considerable property, including a garden, at Beaudesert in Staffordshire (see Chapter 14), with which he may indeed have been familiar.

Tusser's text proceeds month by month, beginning in September. In the expanded *Five Hundred Pointes*, he gives a terse 'abstract' for each month, then describes the month's 'husbandrie' more fully. His verse is clear, direct and down-to-earth. Most sections are to do with farming, household matters, ordering of servants, thrifty storage or sale of produce, so that gardens are, simply, a *part* of the many things which the farmer, his wife and servants must care for. In 'Novembers abstract', for example, only one section is to do with gardens:

For herbes good store,
trench garden more.

The other 28 sections range from

Rid chimney of soot,
from top to the foot.

to

No chaffe in bin,
makes horse looke thin.

and

Good horsekeeper will
lay muck upon hill.

His garden advice is as practical as all the rest. 'Wife, into thy garden' he orders, for the garden is her province, distinct from the husband's smallholding or farm. With her servants, her task, in September, is to set out a plot 'with strawberry rootes', the best of which are to be found 'among thornes in the wood' (these are therefore 'wild' strawberries, the European *Fragaria vesca*, not the larger hybrid strawberries from America), and to plant 'Barbery, Respis [raspberries], and Gooseberry'. Her planting is to be orderly, and will be attractive:

The Gooseberry, Respis, and Roses, al three,
with Strawberries under them trimly agree.

Elsewhere (in March), 'good huswives delight' in 'sowing and setting' seeds and roots and cuttings, and giving order to their plot through proper use of tools:

Through cunning with dible,
rake, mattock, and spade,
by line and by leavell,
trim garden is made.

In all this there is no word of statues, or sculptured fountains, no allusion to the classics. Design is no more than implicit, with advice on the right time and materials for your 'trim bower' and your 'arbor' (January), and (in December) on covering over the 'gilleflower' and 'rosemarie gaie' and other plants in 'the knot, and the border'. Instead, 'go looke to thy bees', which will do well near to a garden with flowers.

We should once again remember that native honey was an essential part of the British diet until well into the nineteenth century, while cane sugar was the imported luxury. Hence the beehives which appear in so many pictures of early gardens, and the care which the housewife was advised to take in looking after them – a task pretty well as important as any of her other garden duties. In 1617 William Lawson in *The Country House-Wife's Garden* could write decisively 'And I will not account her any of my good House-wives, that wanteth either Bees, or skilfulness about them'.

The housewife's garden had to be secure, and so quickset hedges must be planted or repaired. Little hedges of box, bay, hawthorn or privet are planted within the garden – not necessarily for ornament, but to dry the washing on (January). All is useful. From trees in the nearby copse, the husband will have brought back long, thin sticks, for use with the peas – 'Stick plentie of bows among runcivall pease to climber thereon, and to branch at their ease' (February); 'runcival' (or rouncival) meant large or sturdy, as with 'marrowfat' peas. As well as peas, beans (broad beans, that is) will have been sown in the winter, along with 'perseneps', while 'cabbegis', 'turneps' and 'carrets' follow in spring. These are named by Tusser among 'Herbes and rootes to boile or butter'. The only nonrhyming parts of Tusser's *Husbandrie* of 1573 are two lists, 'Of trees or fruites to be set or remooved [transplanted]' (January) and 'Seedes and herbes' (March). The first list has some 30 items, mainly orchard trees and soft fruit, while the second contains some 170 different items, divided into seven main sections: 'for the kitchen', 'for sallets and sauce', 'to boile or to butter', 'strowing herbes', 'herbes, branches, and flowers, for windowes and pots', 'herbes to still in Summer' and 'necessarie herbes to growe in the garden for Physick'. While we no longer grow herbs or flowers to strew on the floor, and we might not often distil forms of eyebright, fumitory or plantain to extract their essence, most of Tusser's plants and trees are not particularly obscure, nor would they be desperately inappropriate in an orchard or a garden today. What is to be noted, however, is that Tusser's lists are still firmly of plants from the Old World, little changed from those known in Britain in the late Middle Ages, and that these plants are mostly grown for their *usefulness* – to eat, raw or cooked, to use for scent or flavour, to distil for cordials or medicine, to use as floor covering (to give out fragrance, or to take up dirt) or to provide medical ointments, purges and drugs. Even the 'herbes, branches, and flowers, for windowes and pots' contain many forms of gillyflowers (pinks or carnations), cherished partly for their musky scent, and 'lavender of all sorts' and bay and rosemary, to scent the air within the house, and distract one from less charming domestic odours.

Tusser's precepts would produce a fine, no-nonsense working garden. Trim, ordered, colourful and productive, its management would have left little time for the housewife to 'stand and stare', as W. H. Davies put it. Instead, we might imagine a motto – by Tusser himself, in 'Janueries abstract' set up at the entrance to this tidy, working place:

What greater crime
than losse of time?

Thomas Hill, Londoner

Before his death in or prior to 1576, Thomas Hill or Hyll, who titles himself variously 'Londyner', 'Citizen of London' and 'Gent', produced several books on the interpretation of dreams, on physiognomy, on remedies against the plague, on astronomy (verging on astrology) and on gardening. His garden book appeared in successively enlarged editions and with different titles, of which the earliest to survive, *A Most Briefe and Pleasant Treatyse*, is dated 1563. This is the first book solely about garden matters to be printed in English. There may have been an earlier edition, *c*.1558, but no copy of it has survived. In 1568 it was remodelled as *The Proffitable Arte of Gardening* (reprinted at least six times until 1608) with one extra section on beekeeping and another on grafting, and in 1577, after his death, it was refashioned as *The Gardeners Labyrinth ...* by Dydymus Mountaine (a whimsical variant of his real name), and seen through the press by Henry Dethicke, who dedicated it to William Cecil, Lord Burghley. By 1656 another five editions had followed.

From version to version Hill's text grows longer and more diffuse; and it acquires more illustrations. The 1563 volume has a tiny frontispiece and plans of two mazes; these reappear in *The Proffitable Arte*, with a new frontispiece and plans for several knots. Hill's portrait appears at the beginning of the section on bees. The 1577 *The Gardeners Labyrinth* includes all these woodcuts except the portrait, and adds two new, detailed views.

Though, as I shall show, Tusser and Hill have much in common, nothing separates them so sharply as the opening phrases of each of Hill's three garden texts. The first, in 1563, begins 'it is ryghte necessary (sayth Varro) . . .', and we are instantly given a classical authority for the proper siting of our garden. By 1577, in *The Gardeners Labyrinth*, this is in the second chapter, while the first chapter begins 'The worthie *Plinie* (in his xix. booke) reporteth . . .', going on to trace the invention of 'Garden plots' back to the ancient Romans. Both the 1568 and 1577 books are prefaced by lists of Greek and Roman authors 'from whom this work is selected', and their names are dropped remorselessly throughout Hill's text to give it the full backing of classical authority.

Though many different classical authors are named – 19 in 1568, 28 in 1577 – Hill did in fact draw mostly from three or four, Cato, Varro, Pliny the Elder and Palladius, in whose works the remainder are mentioned, and most of his references go back simply to Palladius, who relied heavily on Cato and Varro. While it is singularly unprofitable to try to work out exactly which texts Hill was using, it remains signally important that, unlike Tusser, Hill did draw so copiously on classical sources. Hill was not alone – in continental Europe at the same time, Estienne and Liébault in 1570, and others, right on to Olivier de Serres (1600) and W.H. von Hohberg (1682) were doing the same, going back indiscriminately to the classical writers or to later borrowers and adaptors such as Crescenzi. Conrad Heresbach produced his *Rei rusticae libri quatuor* in 1570, translated by Barnabe Googe in 1577 as *Foure Bookes of Husbandry*, and much of the garden comment in this work (it is principally to do with farming) runs parallel to Hill. Your garden must be close to the house, away from the barn, close to manure and to running water; the quickset hedge around it may be planted with seeds lodged in a length of old rope, laid in a furrow; even the vegetables and herbs which he describes are much the same.

So we must not think that Thomas Hill was 'original'. Not for a moment. He was profoundly indebted to other writers, mostly classical, and his work is (to a later eye) warped by continual reference to the phases of the moon, governing the times of garden operations. Hill may have believed in this; certainly he acquired the details from his classical sources.

His work is solidly to do with one or another aspect of garden activity. Like Tusser, Hill reckoned that the garden must be a useful part of the household, and so a recurrent theme is the use of each and every plant for physic. By 1577, in the second half of *The Gardeners Labyrinth*, Hill gives a 'necessarie table' listing the medicinal qualities and uses of some 60 plants, from angelica to 'artochoke', 'arage or orage' down to valerian, and, at the letter 'W', a further account of the 'waters' which may be distilled from many of them. So with onions, for example, which we might consider as a vegetable for eating, he proposes nearly 50 uses, most of which would not occur to us today:

> Onions maintaine health, cure ulcers, remove spottes in the bodie, profit the eares running . . . remove the griefe of the stomache, open pilles, clear the eies, remove the pin and web, amend the bloodshotten eies, recover the haires shed away, the biting of a mad dog . . . help ulcers of the privities, paine and noise of the eares, Disenteria, griefe of the loines . . .

> Onions often used, ingender evill humours, procure thirst, swellings, windinesse, head ach, cause to become foolish, they nourish nothing . . . [and much more!]

These products from the useful garden are achieved only through hard work. Drawing on many classical sources, Hill writes copiously on dung; he echoes Palladius in recommending a sloping garden, sited away from the barn (because of dust and chaff which harm the plants), near to the dunghill, and watered by a stream. Weeding is a continuing task, and pests – 'the Garden wormes, the great Moths and Snayles with shelles and without shelles' – are worth several chapters, extended to cover 'Serpents of the Garden', toads, mice, weasels, hail, frost and other perils. I could wish there was advice on the dread but beautiful black, green and yellow caterpillars which devour my verbascum.

All this from 'the skilful *Rutilius*', 'the learned *Democritus*' and a dozen other long-dead experts, writing mainly about farms, gardens and plants in the Mediterranean (hence their advice on the planting of dates, or the elimination of scorpions); but suddenly, Hill brings the modern, English garden into focus: with the recently invented watering pot, a device the Romans did not have:

> The common watering potte ... hath a narrow neck, big belly, somewhat large bottom, and full of little holes, with a proper hole formed on the head to take in the water, which filled full, and the thombe layde on the hole to keepe in the aire ... may be carryed ... [to the proper place].

These thumb pots, as they were called, were made of earthenware, as were the early watering pots fitted with a spout. There were also metal pots, recently available in the London area – 'the body wholly of Copper' – corresponding to our modern watering cans. Hill also describes the 'great squirt' which appears in an illustration in *The Gardeners Labyrinth*, a hand pump little different from the modern stirrup pump, operated from a bucket. This is a 'Squirt made of tinne ... that by force squirted upward, the water breaking may fall as drops of raine on the plants'.

The hard work leads to enjoyment, in a small garden enclosed within alleys and arbours of carpenter's work, made in juniper, ash or willow, grown over with pomegranate, vines, melons or cucumbers (he does not mention the 'arber beans' praised by Turner in 1548), and with lower-growing rosemary, jasmine or roses up the sides. So far, Hill stays close to his Roman texts, and similar structures were made throughout the Middle Ages. The enjoyment likewise is perennial, as the following extract from *The Gardeners Labyrinth* shows:

> The commodities of these Alleis and
> walkes serve to good purposes, the one is that
> the owner may diligently view the prosperities
> of his herbes and flowers, the other for the
> delight and comfort of his wearied mind, which
> he may by himself or fellowship of his friends
> conceyve in the delectable sightes and fragrant
> smelles of the flowers, by walking up and
> downe, and about the Garden in them.[11]

But the *features* within or beside the 'Alleis and walkes' are relatively

A knot pattern of ferocious complexity from Hill's Gardener's Labyrinth. *A version was almost certainly laid out at All Souls College in Oxford in the 1580s.*

A moated garden in London – illustrating a place of assignment with 'Herbers and Bowers fit for the purpose', in Stubbes's Anatomie of Abuses *in 1583.*

This turf maze at Saffron Walden in Essex is one of the finest surviving examples, with four outer 'bastions' or 'bellows' round the central circles.

modern: bowling alleys (1563); mazes (1563), and knots (1568). The 'bowlying allies . . . you shall sift over with the finest sand'; the mazes – one round, one square in plan, and illustrated in all three of Hill's texts – may be set out in low-growing evergreens, 'Isope and Tyme, winter Savery . . . Lavender Cotten, Spike, Marioram and such like . . . for these doe well endure all the Winter thorow greene'. (This is an eloquent, if indirect, comment on the shortness of the Elizabethan flowering season, and the length of their flowerless and leafless winter. Longer-flowering hybrids had not yet been developed, and winter-flowering plants – such as laurustinus – had not yet arrived from abroad.) Both the square and the round maze plans are virtually identical with the low-hedged mazes at Gaillon in France, illustrated in Du Cerceau's *Les Plus excellents bastiments de France* (1576–9), while the round maze, with its four curious 'ears', is essentially the same as the turf maze at Saffron Walden in Essex, thought to be 'of medieval origin'.

For the knots, Hill provides several patterns, one of astonishing complexity, but his text is unhelpful, merely suggesting (among the many 'most delectable flowers', and 'green and sweet herbes' whose cultivation he discusses) plants which will do for 'edges' and 'borders'. The complex pattern does have a strong link with a real garden, since it resembles closely one of the knots shown in the 1580s 'Hovenden' plan of All Souls at Oxford,[12] and it is not at all unlikely that Hill's pattern, available since 1568, served as the basis for the Oxford college knot.

It is intriguing that Hill's text and illustrations say and show nothing to do with garden statuary or garden architecture, apart from modest structures of carpenter's work, nor anything related to fountains, waterworks or pools; his overwhelming deference to classical authors does not once bring out mythological or historical comment. We may explain this partly by suggesting that Hill's learning was wholly from books, and that he was unacquainted with the new highly sculptural and classically-based gardens of Italy and France. Yet just as cogent is the fact that he is 'Thomas Hill, Londoner', and that his books were for those, mainly in London, who had or wanted to make *small* gardens. Another feature which does not appear in his text or his pictures is the 'mount', for looking over one's own garden or out into the countryside, and this may be for the same reason. The several detailed maps of London produced in Hill's time (such as the 'Copperplate' map, c.1553–59; the 'Agas' map, c.1562; and the Braun and Hogenburg map, 1572) show some scores of modest garden plots, extending out behind the houses – for example along Holborn to St Giles, near Bishopsgate and Shoreditch and in Southwark – which are immensely similar in feeling to Hill's pictures. His frontispiece of 1563 could be taken as a representation of any one of many gardens on the (then) outskirts of the city, imagining the house on the near side, and open ground to left, right and beyond. The two main garden views in *The Gardeners Labyrinth* of 1577 have the rectangular shape and four-part subdivisions of beds which appear beside St Mary's Spital at Spitalfields. Hill's pictures are, in fact, much more solidly 'English' than his text, since they are wholly free of classical reference.

'Allies, Gardens, Banquetting Houses'

We should understand that small gardens, like Thomas Hill's and like those in the London maps of the period, were commonplace and largely utilitarian, producing fruit, vegetables and herbs for private use and market sale. John Stow's *Survey of London* (1592, 1603) indicates their frequency – gardens, orchards and tenements or 'holdings' – especially in the spreading areas of 'suburbs without the walls' to the north and north-east of the City and south of the Thames near Southwark, and alternating with cottages, archery butts, tenter yards, taverns, lodging houses and open fields. Characteristic of the *mixture* of land use is the area north of Aldgate:

> . . . called Goswell street, replenished with small tenements, cottages, and Allies, Gardens, banquetting houses and bowling places.[13]

Other garden uses are apparent in the words 'banquetting houses and bowling places'. One of Thomas Hill's woodcuts in *The Gardeners Labyrinth* of 1577 shows a carpenter's work arbour with a cluster of bowls on the ground, which we may match with lines from *Richard II* (1593), III, iv:

> What sport shall we devise here in this Garden?
> . . . Madam, we'll play at Bowles.

Stow's *Survey* indicates – with some disapproval – that places of entertainment, sometimes related to gardens, were frequent in the suburbs, particularly in the neighbourhood of the two playhouses in and near to Holywell, the *Theater* (1576–98) and the *Curtain* (1576–c. 1628), and the comparable establishments in Southwark, the *Bearhouse* (for bear baiting) and the *Playhouse* or *Globe*, built with the materials of the *Theater* in 1598–9. Stow mentions particularly 'Fisher's folly', north of Bishopsgate and not far from Holywell, 'a large and beautifull house, with Gardens of pleasure, bowling Alleys, and such like, builded by *Jasper Fisher*'. In a general way he disapproves of the trend to take open fields 'by means of inclosure for Gardens, wherein are builded many fayre summer houses . . . some of them like Midsommer Pageantes, with Towers, Turrets, and Chimney tops . . . bewraying the vanity of mens mindes.'[14]

Lurid comment on these gardens was made in 1583, in *The Anatomie of Abuses* by Phillip Stubbes:

> In the Feeldes and Suburbes . . . they have Gardens, either paled, or walled round about very high, with their Herbers and Bowers fit for the purpose. And least they might be espied in these open places, they have their Banquetting houses with Galleries, Turrettes, and what not els therein sumpteously erected: wherein they may (and doubtlesse doe) many of them plaie the filthie persons. And for that their Gardens are locked, some of them have three or fower keys a peece . . . one they keepe for themselves, the other their Paramours have to go in before them . . . Then to these Gardens they repaire when they list, with a basket and a boy, where they, meeting their sweet hartes, receive their wished desires.[15]

The accompanying woodcut shows a square, moated garden with several buildings – a house, and small arbours in which 'wished desires' may be accomplished. Stubbes was not alone in his remarks on these uses of the suburban garden. Shakespeare refers to such a place in *Measure for Measure* (c.1604), IV, i, 30–35, 'a garden circummur'd with brick' with a trysting house, and a little-known text of 1598, *Skialethia*, specifically links attendance at one of the London theatres, the *Curtain*, with similar garden visits, as the playgoer 'coming from the Curtaine, sneaketh in To some odde garden noted house of sinne'.[16]

Yet most gardens of this size and in this period were innocent enough, and must have echoed the details of Hill's illustrations fairly closely, whether they were in London, or in a provincial town – like the college gardens at Oxford and Cambridge – or in the enclosed area of a moated manor house deep in the countryside. A garden in the moated forecourt, shown in an embroidery of around 1590, is roughly the same size as that illustrating Stubbes' text of 1583. With water all round (and a handy boat moored to the bank), it is enclosed on three sides by alleys of 'carpenter's work', giving views of the countryside, and on the fourth by the manor house – a building of some size, but rather irregular plan, suggesting a long and varied history. Within the square garden are four rectangular beds, slightly raised, and at the centre, aligned with the rather grand doorway of the house, is a fountain, with a broad circular bowl at the base, a central stem and a second smaller bowl above, bearing an urn

(I think!) from which water is squirting. This feature, and the somewhat elaborate architecture of the building, take us into the sphere of larger gardens, where delight and ornament may vie more strongly with mere usefulness, and where the fascinating enthusiasms of the flower fancier, the plant collector and the botanist may flourish.

While what we would now call 'nursery gardens', providing seed, plants and garden materials, have existed since the early 1500s or before,[17] it is generally true that until the end of the sixteenth century *collections* of plants were either in the gardens of the nobility, or in more modest gardens enjoying noblemen as patrons. Of the smaller kind, we should note those of William Turner and William Harrison, already mentioned (see pages 53 and 59); the garden (in Highgate) of the botanist Mathias de l'Obel or Lobel (1538–1616), whose main residence in England was from 1584 onwards; and the garden of John Gerard (1545–1612) in Holborn (see page 80).

5

GARDENS OF THE GREAT

The main centres which were to encourage the collection of plants and the large development of new ideas were the gardens of the nobility – those of families or individuals such as the Cobhams at Cobham Hall in Kent; the Williams, later Norris, at Rycote and Thame in Oxfordshire; the Hattons at Ely Place in London and Holdenby in Northamptonshire; Lord Lumley at Nonsuch in Surrey; the Earls of Worcester at Raglan Castle in Gwent; Mary, Countess of Pembroke at Wilton in Wiltshire; Lord Edward La Zouche at Hackney in London and later at Bramshill in Hampshire; Sir Walter Cope in London (Cope House, later to become Holland House); Sir Francis Carew at Beddington in Surrey at the end of the century; and, of course, William Cecil, Baron Burghley (1520–98) and his son Robert Cecil, 1st Earl of Salisbury (1563–1612), at Burghley in Northamptonshire, Theobalds in Hertfordshire, Salisbury House in London (beside the Thames, just south of the Strand), and, from 1607, in exchange for Theobalds which was given to King James I, at Hatfield in Hertfordshire. (As this last sentence implies, the story both of Theobalds and Hatfield goes on into the seventeenth century, as is the case with many, if not most, of these gardens.)

At Cobham Hall, several generations were noted for their gardening success. In 1546, the then Lord Cobham was negotiating the purchase of seeds from Antwerp, and in 1548 Turner's *The Names of Herbes* referred both to a plant – French broom (probably what we now call Spanish broom, *Spartium junceum*) – which he had seen 'in my Lord Cobbans garden', and to another – 'Vulvaria ... a stynkyng herbe creapynge by the grounde with leaves of Mergerum or Organe [marjoram or oregano]' – which grew 'in my Lord Cobham's garden at Calice' (i.e. Calais, when Cobham was on service there).[1] In 1577, Barnaby Googe's preface to his translation of Heresbach singled out 'the Lord Cobham, and the Lord Wylliams of Thame' for the excellence of their vineyards.[2] By 1587,

William Harrison chose to name Cobham among the four most notable gardens in the land, along with Hampton Court, Nonsuch and Theobalds. Admittedly, it was Sir William Brooke, 10th Baron Cobham (1527–97) who was his patron, and who had presented him with the living of Radwinter long before, in 1559. Harrison's praise was matched in the same year, 1587, by Francis Thynne, one of the continuators of Holinshed's *Chronicle*, who wrote of 'a rare garden there, in which no varietie of strange flowers and trees do want'[3] – would he had listed them!

In 1576, Sir Christopher Hatton (1540–91), for many years one of the Queen's principal favourites, was granted the lease of Ely Place in London, together with the garden and orchard of the Temple. For rent he paid a red rose, ten loads of hay and £10 a year, while the Bishop of Ely, who had been forced into this agreement by the Queen, kept only the freedom of walking in the gardens and yearly payment of twenty bushels of roses.[4] Ely Place had been noted for its productive gardens and vineyards since the mid-fourteenth century,[5] and Hatton's part in their history is remembered in the nearby 'Hatton Garden'.

Friend and patron of Edmund Spenser, and also of minor writers like James Sanford, a translator from the Italian, the second edition of whose *Garden of Pleasure* was dedicated to Hatton in 1576, Hatton's most important part in the cultural development of the time was the building of his vast new residence at Holdenby in Northamptonshire, begun in the late 1570s and virtually completed by 1583. This huge house, built round two courtyards and with a third or base court in front, was given a symmetry and balance lacking in earlier mansions of its size – attributed to the influence of Italian Renaissance architecture and works on classical architecture (Alberti, Vitruvius, Serlio, Palladio and Du Cerceau) published before 1580. This Italian influence extended to the gardens, which were laid out before the long south front of the house, and for an equal distance out to east and west. In the centre, a great platform some 87 by 110 yards was raised up to be level with the house, and given a complex pattern of knots, while the sloping areas to east and west were laid out in terraces – seven on each side, laid out with 'rosaries', probably rose walks incorporating trellis-work. Below the western terraces was a rectangular pond, and below the eastern terraces was a bowling alley. While most of the house was destroyed in 1651, the outlines of these spacious, ordered gardens remain as a striking early instance of formal gardening on a massive scale, patently designed to match the size and symmetry of the house.[6]

The gardens at Holdenby, planned to fit with the new house, and most probably designed when the house was designed, are the exception. Most often, the 'new' gardens were laid out round older existing houses, as at Raglan Castle in Gwent, where, after the castle had been remodelled in the mid-sixteenth century, the 3rd Earl of Worcester added in 1570–89 a sequence of terraces and ponds, with viewing points and summerhouses, along the valley beside the castle (see page 74). The outlines of these garden features may still be traced in the present fields – the castle itself was damaged and then 'slighted' in 1646, and it, and the gardens, were abandoned.

At Nonsuch, Henry VIII's palace was sold by Queen Mary I to the 12th Earl of Arundel, and later, in 1579, it passed to his son-in-law John, Lord Lumley (d. 1609). Though Nonsuch reverted to the Crown in 1591, and was often visited by Queen Elizabeth, Lumley remained in residence, and his upkeep of and additions to Henry VIII's garden scheme were much admired at the end of the century – by Anthony Watson (who was in Lumley's service) in the 1580s,[7] by William Camden in his *Britannia* (1586), by William Harrison in *The Description of England* (1587) and by the travellers Paul Hentzner, Thomas Platter and Baron Waldstein in 1598–1600.[8]

From Watson and Platter we learn of the varied and lifelike topiary at Nonsuch. Watson listed 'deer, horses, rabbits and dogs', which 'gave chase with unhindered feet and effortlessly passed over the green', while Platter said of these bushy creatures that they were so artfully contrived 'one would think at a distance that they were real animals'. In 1618, looking back over '48 Years (and more) experience', William Lawson wrote about topiary in a similar way:

> Your Gardner can frame your lesser wood to the shape of men armed in the field, ready to give battle; of swift-running Grey-Hounds, or of well-sented and true-running Hounds to chase the Deer, or hunt the Hare. This kind of hunting shall not waste your Corn, nor much your Coyn.[9]

Lawson's illustration shows token figures of a horse and an armed man to represent the topiary, and his text continues with comment on 'mazes well framed a man's height', a curious parallel with both Watson and Platter's remarks about Nonsuch. They both mentioned a maze there, Platter saying that it was 'surrounded by such tall growth, that one cannot get over or through it' – one of the earliest instances of a *tall* hedge maze in England. It might well be that it had simply grown in the years since Henry VIII's reign, and that natural growth allied to a measure of neglect had produced this phenomenon. It remains, however we explain it, a solitary example.

While these features would inevitably have changed with the passing of time, they might indeed have originated in the 1540s. But other features, mentioned particularly by Platter and Waldstein (who go round in different directions!) are evidently later – the monuments and groups of sculpture derived from classical legend. One group (seen by Waldstein) portrayed the labours of Hercules, while the main display, in the 'Grove of Diana', with a summerhouse, grotto, fountain and numerous inscriptions, was to do with the story of Diana and Actaeon – the virgin huntress-goddess surprised while bathing by the hapless hunter Actaeon. This legend had for some time been linked with the image of Queen Elizabeth as the Virgin Queen, in Ben Jonson's words 'Queen and huntress, chaste and fair', and we may reasonably see this section of the Nonsuch gardens as Lumley's extravagant expression of loyalty to the Queen, and also, as recent commentators point out, as further evidence of the arrival in England of an Italian style of gardening.[10]

The fifteenth-century castle at Raglan in Gwent was inherited by William Somerset (3rd Earl of Worcester, c.1527–88) in 1547. Though gardens of a sort were already there, including richly stocked orchards, they were lavishly extended by Somerset and his son Edward (the 4th Earl, 1553–1628) between 1550 and 1628.[11] By 1587, a poem by Thomas Churchyard refers to 'curious knots', 'Pond and Poole' and a 'fountain trim', and the surviving massive terraces to north-west and south-west of the castle date from this time, as did an extensive artificial pool. The 4th Earl added two main features, a formal water garden *above* the main pool, and a long walk beside the castle moat, with 15 alcoves in which were set busts or statues of the Roman emperors. These features, mostly formal in their individual design, were arranged round or near to the castle following its military layout and its position in the sloping terrain.

The castle was seriously damaged in 1646, and then abandoned, so that the outlines and some details of the gardens have been preserved in the meadows which now surround the castle. The geometrical layout of the water garden, with streams running between diamond-shaped islands, was comparable to the artificial island and streams made at Hatfield around 1610 (see page 91). The 4th Earl of Worcester also had a house and garden near London – Worcester Lodge, Nonsuch – which are recorded in a plan of around 1609 by Robert Smythson. Though the garden is square and wholly symmetrical in design, it is only partially aligned with the house, as is the case with many late-Elizabethan and early Jacobean gardens, however grand and however formal the design of the garden itself may be.

From the frontispiece of Gerard's Herball, *1597: a formal garden, with square, raised beds within the formal enclosure. The original drawing was made by John Bol (d. 1583).*

This knot, devised by Sylvia Landsberg for the garden of the Tudor Museum, Southampton, involves 'threads' of box, santolina, savory and germander. The pattern is from Estienne and Liébault, L'Agriculture et Maison rustique, *1570.*
Photo: Hugh Palmer

'An Ancient Gentleman' at Wilton

At Wilton in Wiltshire, in the mid-sixteenth century, the abbey was granted to William Herbert (created Earl of Pembroke in 1551), and the buildings were remodelled for him between 1543 and around 1560. Nothing is known about his or any earlier monastic gardens, but in 1577 the 2nd Earl married Mary Sidney (1561–1621), sister of Sir Philip Sidney, and she, in John Aubrey's words, made Wilton House 'like a college, there were so many learned and ingenious persons'.[12] The first of these in Aubrey's account was 'Dr' Adrian Gilbert, half-brother to Sir Walter Raleigh, who helped her both with 'chemistry' (more properly alchemy) and with garden matters.[13] Concerning the latter there is an isolated, and extraordinary, account by John Taylor, the 'water poet', published in 1623, two years after Mary, Countess of Pembroke's death, and when Adrian Gilbert was indeed 'an ancient gentleman' (he was born in 1550 or before). Taylor had just visited Wilton, now in the hands of William Herbert, 3rd Earl of Pembroke (1580–1630), and he praised Gilbert's 'pains and industry' for making there a most rare garden:

> There hath he . . . used such a deal of intricate setting, grafting, planting, innoculating, railing, hedging, plashing, turning, winding, and returning circular, triangular, quad-rangular, orbicular, oval, and every way curiously and chargeably conceited: there hath he made walks, hedges, and arbours . . . resembling both divine and moral remembrances, as three arbours standing in a triangle, having each a recourse to a greater arbour in the midst, resembleth three in one, and one in three . . . he calls it *Paradise*, in which he plays the part of true *Adamist*, continually toiling and tilling.[14]

While Taylor claimed that this had been achieved 'much to my Lords cost' – i.e. that Gilbert had made the garden for the 3rd Earl – this is unlikely for an 'ancient gentleman' well on in his seventies. This 'Paradise' is much more likely to have been made for Mary, Countess of Pembroke, even in the 1590s, influenced by the garden enthusiasm of Sir Philip Sidney (see pp 56–8), and by the presentation of the garden of Eden in Saluste Du Bartas' *Eden* (1584), translated by Joshuah Sylvester in 1598. We may compare the 'walks, hedges and arbours' of Adrian Gilbert's gardens at Wilton with those enjoyed by Adam before the Fall:

> Musing, anon through crooked Walks he wanders,
> Round-winding rings, and intricate Meanders,

False guiding paths, doubtfull beguiling strays,
And right-wrong errors of an endless Maze.[15]

No other description of this garden survives, nor are there pictures. Mary, Countess of Pembroke herself went on to create another, likewise vanished, garden at Houghton Lodge in Bedfordshire (see page 86). When Taylor next visited Wilton, in 1649, all had changed, giving place to a garden inspired by French examples – a garden which would in turn be modified and changed and changed until the present century (see pp 121–3). Change indeed is the single constant quality of any garden, great or small.

Most subject to change are the gardens of plant collectors, where a season's neglect, or a fiercer than usual winter, or simply *faute d'argent* can reduce to nothing the treasures which have taken years, or a fortune, or both, to amass. One such fancier of rare plants who caught Panurge's 'kind of disease, which at that time they called lack of money' was Edward, 11th Baron La Zouche (*c*.1556–1625). His father dying in 1569, he was during his minority a 'ward of state' in the care of Sir William Cecil, but when he came of age he began to indulge a passion for horticulture so freely that from 1586 or 1587 he had to leave England to live more cheaply abroad. In 1590, he met Sir Henry Wotton at Altdorf, and corresponded with him for some years; he also met and corresponded with the botanist Clusius (Charles de l'Ecluse). Returning to England in 1593, he met the English botanist John Gerard, and the French botanist Mathias de l'Obel (or Lobel), who lived in London from the 1590s until his death in 1616. Though de l'Obel had his own garden at Highgate, he also supervised Zouche's London garden in Hackney, and indeed accompanied Zouche to Denmark in 1598 on a diplomatic-cum-botanical journey. (Much later, between 1615 and 1623, Zouche may even have had contact with John Tradescant (the elder), when Tradescant was working for Lord Wotton (Sir Henry Wotton's half-brother) at St Augustine's in Canterbury, since there is record of discussion with 'Lord Wotton's ... gardener' on Zouche's behalf concerning musk melons.[16])

In 1605, Zouche began to build a grand country residence at Bramshill in Hampshire. There had been a deer park at Bramshill since 1347, and Zouche's new building, finished in 1612, incorporated parts of an earlier mansion. In 1614, the poet William Browne dedicated *The Shepherd's Pipe* to Zouche, celebrating 'the shades Of your delightful Bramshill'. Though the gardens at Highgate and Hackney have vanished entirely, Bramshill still displays a complex and extensive scheme of garden walls, whose erstwhile contents may well have been devised by Zouche and by de l'Obel together.

Within the house, one medium-sized panelled room retains the original painted decorations on all four walls – reproductions of many different plants, such as vines, artichokes, mallows and dianthus, with the occasional snail or butterfly in attendance. There are some 150 different panels, most measuring about 12 by 15 inches, a few 12 by 20 inches, and the paintings seem to have been copied from the woodcuts illustrating de l'Obel's botanic works. These had appeared in various forms from the 1570s onwards, and were re-used in other volumes, notably by Christophe Plantin, and in the 1633 and 1636 editions (by Thomas Johnson) of John Gerard's *Herbal*.[17] The painter could therefore have been working for Zouche, in de l'Obel's lifetime or later, or, possibly, later still for one of Zouche's successors – garden activity at Bramshill continued until the end of the century, with the designing of an additional formal scheme westwards from the house and below the balustraded garden enclosures. While this new garden, for Sir Robert Henley, was later 'landscaped', to become a grassy slope and pool, the plant paintings in the panelled room remain as an astonishing witness of botanic enthusiasm and of de l'Obel's connection with Bramshill. Today the rare plants have gone, but one balustraded area survives as a bowling green, with seats and a loggia and a curiously fashioned pillar for the game of 'troco' (cf. the French word *triquet*), a forerunner of nineteenth-century croquet.

Oranges at Beddington

Another grand house was built by Sir Francis Carew (c.1535–1611) at Beddington in Surrey, which combined in its garden both a passion for plants and an appreciation of design. Several visitors – Baron Waldstein in 1600, Thomas Coryate in the mid-1600s, and Wurmsser von Vendenheym in 1610 – praised the streams, with water so clear you could see figures (presumably in pebbles, or painted on tiles) on the bottom, and the waterworks with classical sculptures ('a Hydra out of whose many heads the water gushes'). Coryate compared these 'many elegant conceits' and the 'rocke . . . framed all by arte' with the shell-ornamented rock and waterworks which he saw in 1610 in the Giusti Gardens in Verona.[18]

Queen Elizabeth visited Carew at Beddington twice – in August 1599 and August 1600.[19] Though she may have wanted to see the house or the waterworks, it is more likely that she was enticed by Carew's fame as a grower of rare and tasty fruit. Already in 1562, Carew was referred to in letters between William Cecil and his agent Thomas Windebank in Paris, concerning Carew's own purchases of orange and lemon trees, and his help in choosing good specimens of lemon, pomegranate and myrtle for Cecil's garden at Burghley.[20] Carew is credited with being the first to grow oranges in England, and the first also to have had an *orangery* – a building specially designed for housing and protecting the trees during the winter. Writing much later – first in 1658, then in 1700 – John Evelyn says the trees 'now over-growne' were 'planted in the ground, and secured in winter with a wooden tabernacle [or cover] and stoves'. In 1700 he says they have been growing for '120 yeares'.[21] A comment by J. Gibson in 1691 gives 'the house wherein they are' to be 'above two hundred feet long', and reports the 'aged' gardener as saying that the orange and lemon trees were (in 1691) 'near one hundred years'.[22]

However, cherries – out of season – were the choice fruit for Queen Elizabeth on her 1599 and 1600 visits to Beddington. The story is told by Sir Hugh Platt in *The Jewel House of Art and Nature* (1608) and in *Floraes Paradise* (1600), that Carew, by

> ... spreading of a Tent over a Cherry tree about fourteen days or three weeks before the Cherries were ripe ... did greatly backward the tree in his bearing, now and then watering the Tent in a sunny day with cold water, whereby the strength of the Sun beams became very weak upon the tree; and when he was disposed to ripen them speedily, he withdrew the Vail, giving a freer passage to the hot and scorching beams of Phoebus.[23]

Sir Hugh Platt (c.1552–1608) wrote several books on the practical aspects of gardening, beginning in 1594 with a work on soils and manures. The practical side comes out in his own use of the 'Carew method' of holding back the ripening process:

> It was my hap to present unto a late Lord Mayor of the City of London 8 green and fresh Artichokes upon Twelfth day [i.e. Twelfth Night], with a score of fresh Orenges, which I had kept from Whitsuntide ... I was also furnished with two hundred Artichokes for my own provision, which continued a service at my table all the Lent ensuing ...

Platt seems to have gardened above all with fruit and vegetables, in several parts of London – at Bethnal Green, where he had a vineyard yielding excellent wine grapes, and at other times at St Martin's Lane, at Bishop's Hall in Middlesex, and at Kirby or Kirkby Hall near Bishopsgate.

The Cecils

In garden matters of this period, person after person and place after place has links with Sir William Cecil, later Lord Burghley (1520–98), or with his second son Sir Robert Cecil, 1st Earl of Salisbury (1550–1612). Some references to Sir William Cecil have already occurred – his friendship with Sir Francis Carew for example. As one of the foremost politicians of his time, he was courted by many, and so received the dedication (among others) of several books related to gardens – for example, in 1577, Thomas Hill's *Gardeners Labyrinth*, and in the same year, Barnaby Googe's translation of Heresbach, *Foure Bookes of Husbandry*. Both Cecils were well acquainted not only with aristocratic garden enthusiasts (we may note as well Robert Cecil's friendship with Sir Walter Cope (d. 1614), and his marriage in 1589 to Lady Elizabeth Brooke, daughter of the 10th Lord Cobham), but also, over two generations, with the two most noted English botanists in the late sixteenth and early seventeenth centuries – John Gerard (1545–1612) and John Tradescant (the elder, c.1570–1638).

Gerard had his own London garden in Holborn, and his first publication, in 1596, was a *Catalogus arborum, fruticum, ac plantarum* listing 1,033 different species growing in his garden. The preface was written by Mathias de l'Obel. The *Catalogus* is the first list in Britain to describe the contents of what we might call a 'botanic garden',[24] and Gerard followed this up before 1598 with a proposal that he should be appointed as a 'Herbarist' to the University of Cambridge, to run a garden in which the 'noble science of physicke' might be furthered through the processes of 'Simpling' – i.e. the study of the medicinal qualities of plants.[25] This proposal was sent to Lord Burghley, whose London garden in the Strand and whose much larger garden at Theobalds in Hertfordshire, Gerard had long been connected with. Burghley seems to have let the matter rest, and our first botanic garden was not founded until 1621 by Henry Danvers, whose intention was similarly the advancement of medicine (see page 144). Meanwhile, in 1607, another botanist, de l'Obel, was appointed *Botanicus regius*, the King's botanist, by James I.

A year after the *Catalogus*, in 1597, Gerard produced *The Herball or Generall Historie of Plantes*, dedicating it to Burghley. His originality, however, is slight. Most of the text is from another Englishman's translation of Dodoens' *Pemptades* of 1583, the woodcuts are mainly from Tabernaemontanus' *Eicones* of 1590, and even the vignette of a garden on his title page, so often cited as a 'typical late-Elizabethan garden scene', is taken from 'April' in a series of months by H. Bol, engraved by A.

Collaert in 1585. Nonetheless, Gerard's *Herball* and its revised and much improved edition of 1633, edited by Thomas Johnson, remained popular and influential for much of the seventeenth century.

We should not ignore the general opinion of the time that plants and their products – leaves, flowers, seeds – were of importance for their *usefulness*, revealed most powerfully in the pages of Richard Hakluyt, where he lists 'things to be indevoured' by merchants travelling to Constantinople and related parts of the Levant. A part of his remarks concerns the earlier and most useful importation of the saffron crocus (see page 34), of value in dyeing, and the largest part of his recommendations is to do with the textile industry and with how the 'Trees, whose Leaves, Seedes, or Barkes, or Wood doe serve to that use' may be 'brought into this realme by Seed or Roote'. He adds immediately 'All little Plants and Bushes serving to that use to be brought in'.[26] Elsewhere he waxes lyrical on the various flowers, vegetables and fruits which have been introduced 'in time of memory', 'as the Damaske rose', which he follows with 'the Turky cocks and hennes', then 'the Artichowe', 'the Muske rose plant', various plums, the apricot, 'and now [1582] within these foure yeeres there have bene brought into England from Vienna in Austria divers kinds of flowers called Tulipas'. He concludes with currants from Zante, tamarisk from Germany, and 'the seed of Tobacco' from the West Indies.[27]

To return to the Cecils. While John Tradescant (the elder) was to be connected with Robert Cecil's new gardens at Hatfield and Cranborne (see page 89), John Gerard had supervised his father's gardens in the Strand and at Theobalds. These were by no means the only houses with gardens which the Cecils possessed. Burghley House in Northamptonshire, built between about 1553 and 1587, was one of Lord Burghley's main residences, and a centre for plant collections from the early 1560s. Little is known of the first gardens at Burghley, though there are remains of avenues, mainly lime trees, which radiated from the house in a landscape now firmly marked by the hand of Capability Brown.

Somewhat later, there was the great house at Wimbledon, begun in 1588 for Burghley's oldest son Thomas Cecil, later Earl of Exeter. The architect is not known, but a plan of the house and garden by Robert Smythson in 1609 shows the detail and extent of a grand formal garden layout. Though begun at a later date than the balanced layouts of Holdenby or Wollaton, Wimbledon's gardens are not aligned symmetrically with the house. All areas, large or small, are square or rectangular, set on the east and south sides of the house, and separated one from another either by thorn hedges or rows of 'lyme trees: both for shade: and swetnes' or cherries. The outer boundaries were mainly walled. The ground slopes up from north to south, so that the several garden areas would have risen up gently in the form of terraces over the house.

Within the walls and hedges, each garden space is self-contained, and given a symmetrical plan – east of the house, four knots of flowers, with thorn hedges 'cutt verie well', round a square pool or fountain. The same plan, but in larger or smaller form, was used for two areas to the south-east and south-west, flanking a square garden due south of the house, with a central banqueting house and a paved surround. To the west lay 'gardens for earbes', an 'orcharde with frute trese' underplanted with roses, and a larger orchard with the trees set widely apart. Further south (and rising upwards) were the lime walk, the cherry walk, a vast orchard with roses to east and west, and finally 'the vyne yarde'. As at Burghley House, these gardens were redesigned, and have now gone entirely, though, as at Burghley, the hand of Capability Brown is still to be seen (see page 220).

Meanwhile, Lord Burghley's great house at Theobalds in Hertfordshire was begun around 1560, and was far enough advanced for Queen Elizabeth to visit him there in 1564. There were to be many more visits – 14 in all by 1596 – some lasting several days.

The garden at Theobalds must have been among the most lavish of its time. By 1587, William Harrison lists it among the four best in England, and from 1591 the comments on royal visits and the remarks by individuals enable us to see the garden both in its normal state of excellence and as a setting for royal entertainment. The overall plan is not clear, but abundant details are recorded. Its size was such that 'one might walk two myle in the walkes, before he came to their ends',[28] and the moat or canal round it was, according to Paul Hentzner in 1598 'large enough for one to have the pleasure of going in a boat, and rowing between the shrubs'.[29] Hentzner saw also 'labyrinths', a marble fountain, 'and columns and pyramids of wood and other materials' – these might have been related to 'heraldic beasts' – and a two-storey banqueting-house, with leaden fish-cum-bathing tanks above, and a dining chamber and a room below with busts of the first 12 Roman emperors. In 1600, Baron Waldstein's account adds to Hentzner's that the central fountain was fitted with 'concealed pipes', to spray 'unwary passers-by'. There was a sundial and armorial displays. Another fountain had, floating in the water, 'a little ship of the type they use in the Netherlands . . . complete with Cannons, flags, and sails'. The banqueting-house, with its upper ornamental tank, had 'in two of the corners of this pool . . . two wooden water-mills built on a rock, just as if they were on the shore of a river'.[30] Jacob Rathgeb, in 1592, and Waldstein both describe the rockwork grotto, fountain, sculptured people, animals and trees within the hall of the palace[31].

It is curious, considering John Gerard's claim in the *Herball* to have been connected with Theobalds for 20 years, that contemporary comments on the floral element for the gardens are sparse: hedges, bushes, woodland, but little more. Baron Waldstein states simply 'in the garden you see lilies and other flowers growing among the shrubs'. It was not until 1618 that an Italian visitor remarked that one saw the King's arms 'designed to perfection in mixed borders of mignonette and pinks'.[32] By 1618, however, Theobalds had been the King's property for 11 years, acquired from Sir Robert Cecil in exchange for the old episcopal palace at Hatfield in 1607. King James had paused for four days at Theobalds in 1603 on his long progress south from Scotland, and had so much liked the place that he soon resolved to acquire it for himself. The hunting was good, the house palatial, and the gardens fine – it seems that he much appreciated the labyrinthine hedge-lined alleys, where he 'recreated himself in the meanders compact of bays, rosemary and the like overshadowing his walk'.[33]

Beyond the bedding with the royal arms, it is not known whether James did much to develop the gardens at Theobalds, apart from the planting of mulberries (see page 90). His successor, Charles I, certainly made extensive pools with islands in 1625–8, though these are not mentioned in the 1650 survey, which concentrates on the variety and number of fruit trees and bushes, and the several summerhouses. The gardens – and palace – then decayed, being lost in the mid-eighteenth century.[34]

'Entertainments'

The references to the gardens of the 1580s and 90s are largely to do with layouts and features which were meant to last – in garden terms at any rate – and some, like the gigantic terraces at Holdenby, can still be seen. Their plans were largely enclosed, walled, like the gardens of cloisters and palaces; we may think, for example, of Penshurst Place and of Knole, both in Kent. At each of these an earlier building was given an enclosing yet adorning wall, which left the house in one corner of an extensive walled rectangle, an area which could hardly be 'gardened' except in a geometrical way. Begun at Penshurst in the 1570s and at Knole in the last years of the sixteenth century, these walls have survived to the present day, and have ensured the continuing foursquare division of the gardens, however varied the treatment of smaller parts has been from age to age. From the beginning, and up to the present, the walls have also served both as a protection for the house and as a physical and visual barrier between the gardens and adjacent parkland. For Penshurst, there is a passage by Ben Jonson – in *To Penshurst*, first published in 1616 – praising both park and garden. Among the delights of the park are 'thy walkes for health, as well as sport', and 'Thy Mount, to which the Dryads do resort', while the garden excels for its fruit, a quality maintained today:

Then hath thy orchard fruit, thy garden flowers,
Fresh as the ayre, and new as are the houres.
The early cherry, with the later plum,
Fig, grape, and quince, each in his time doth come:
The blushing apricot and woolly peach
Hang on thy wals, that every child may reach.[35]

While Jonson makes it entirely clear that Penshurst is a seat with noble owners, the usefulness of the garden's products links it with Jon Gardener and Thomas Hill.

In these and other gardens of the period there were also short-lived shows, entertainments and festivities which used the gardens as an essential background or setting, and which survive today only insofar as written descriptions have been preserved, or, in one instance, a drawing was engraved and duplicated.[36] The extravagance of these entertainments may be compared with that of the 'pageants' mounted by Henry VII and Henry VIII (see pages 42 and 44). But there is one striking difference: whereas the earlier events were put on by the monarch in or outside a royal palace, these entertainments for Queen Elizabeth were put on by her courtiers in or beside their private mansions. As a result, the mansions, and their gardens, were often refurbished, extended or altered for these occasions, while the gardens (if not the palaces) of the Queen were not notably developed. It is true that John Norden praises the fountain set up in a courtyard at Hampton Court in 1590 (Jacob Rathgeb in 1592 explains that it has an 'ingenious water-work' for wetting the ladies), Paul Hentzner adds that rosemary was trained up the walls 'to cover them entirely', and in 1599 and 1600 respectively Thomas Platter and Baron Waldstein praise the variety of plants in the arbours, the life-like and original topiary, and the maze – with varied flowers and fruit trees, two fountains and the added delight of bird-song.[37] But beside the praise lavished on private aristocratic gardens of the time, this is not remarkable. As for the Queen's palace at Nonsuch, its much admired garden features – topiary, a maze and much sculpture – seem to have been largely the work of Lord Lumley, who was the owner from 1579 to 1591 (see page 73).

The 'entertainments' provided for the Queen by her courtiers have been much discussed. Those at Kenilworth in Warwickshire in 1575 are among the most famous, and are recorded in a long description by Robert Laneham, together with a set of the verses composed for the occasion by George Gascoigne and others.[38]

Robert Dudley, Earl of Leicester, who provided these entertainments, had owned Kenilworth Castle since 1563, and the Queen had visited him there once before, briefly, in 1565, when she was given a relatively modest reception. On this second occasion the festivities lasted for 19 days, 9–27 July 1575. Laneham's account tells of an exhausting programme, with ceremonious meetings and greetings, addresses, dialogues, plays, masques and dances by a crowd of characters, mostly classical, but some vehemently not. All this alternated with many long sessions of hunting in the park, with bear baiting, mummers, morris dancers, fireworks, an Italian contortionist, a comic wedding, a pageant by actors from Coventry, an aged comedian called Captain Cox and much, much more.

While praising the park at Kenilworth in his introductory paragraphs – it is 'beautified with many delectabel, fresh, and umbragious bowerz, arberz, seatz, and walks'[39] – Laneham does not mention the *garden* until he is near the end of his account. While it was probably completed so as to be ready for the Queen's visit, it may have been used only as a place of elegant retirement for the Queen and her favoured attendants, away from the much larger and boisterous crowds present at the principal amusements. Certainly it was not designed as the splendid centre for the occasion, as was the case at Elvetham in Hampshire in 1591 (see page 87). Laneham himself, who chronicled the events, did not see the garden until the gardener – 'my good freend *Adrian*' – let him in, 'as the garden door was open, and her Highness [the Queen] a hunting'.

It was not extensive – Laneham says 'an aker or more of quantitee' – and its site may still be seen on the north side of the castle, beside the enclosing outer wall, and, since 1973, adorned with a formal scheme of low box hedges and fragrant herbs. The 1575 garden was virtually rectangular, with a terrace along its northern side (made most probably by widening the sentinels' walkway). The terrace was adorned with 'obelisks, sphearz, and white bearz' (the bear, with a 'ragged staff' was Leicester's heraldic emblem), with an arbour at each end. It overlooked a garden scheme divided into 'Four eeven quarterz', each with a slim, fifteen-foot obelisk at the centre. The quarters (probably designed as knots, though Laneham does not say as much) were set with 'redolent plants and fragrant earbs and flowers ... deliciously variant', and with apple, pear and cherry trees. Against the mid-point of the terrace was a large and elaborate aviary. In the middle of the four quarters was a sumptuous marble fountain, topped by the 'ragged staff', which included in its complex sculpture bas-reliefs of marine divinities, overlooking the waters of the pool, stocked with 'carp, tench, bream, and for varietee, perch and eel'. Round the basin were water jets for the spectators – 'water spurting upward with such vehemency, as they should by and by be moystned from top to toe; the hee's to sum laughing, but the shee's to more sport'.

Fountains, fruit, flowers, scent, birdsong – and from one point or another the view of the people in the outer court, on the surrounding lake or in the park with its deer – all 'woorthy to be calld Paradys'. It was not a new or original scheme, however delightful Laneham may have thought it. The features were not notably different from those at Richmond or Hampton Court in the first half of the century, with fruit trees and regular flower beds overlooked by alleys leading to arbours, and with sculptured fountains and 'heraldic beasts'. Its site, vaguely but not exactly aligned with an unsymmetrical castle and adjacent buildings, is immediately comparable with the situation of the gardens and their châteaux in Du Cerceau's contemporary plans and bird's-eye views of, for example, Montargis, Gaillon and Valori in France.

Among the Earl of Leicester's guests were several of the Sidneys, including Sir Philip Sidney, only a month back from three years of travel on the Continent, and his sister Mary, then aged 13. There is no record of what either of them thought of Leicester's garden, but to Sir Philip at least it may have seemed less subtle, less allusive than it might have been. By 1580, his idea of 'Basilius' garden', in the *Countess of Pembroke's Arcadia* (see page 76) was far removed from the 'four even quarters' of Kenilworth, as would be his sister's gardens, first at Wilton and later at Houghton in Bedfordshire.

When Sidney himself wrote texts for later entertainments for the Queen – at Woodstock in September 1575 and at Wanstead in 1578[40] – he kept to modest pastoral themes, prefiguring the rural aspects of the *Arcadia*. The use of garden settings for these entertainments came later (after Sidney's death in 1586), in the 1590s. In these years, the Queen made several visits to Lord Burghley's estate at Theobalds, where there were festivities of a grand kind; another equally if not more grand event was at Elvetham in Hampshire, and less costly entertainments were offered at Cowdray in Sussex and at Bisham in Berkshire.

At Theobalds in 1591 an elaborate poetic performance took place, with a summons addressed from the Queen via Sir Christopher Hatton (of Holdenby) to the 'Heremite of Tybole' – i.e. to the elderly, and now widowed Lord Burghley – and with three speeches (composed by George Peele) addressed to the Queen, from a hermit (who has been disturbed in his ten years' contemplations by the widowed Burghley), a gardener and a mole-catcher. The gardener was laying out a maze, with a centre of eglantine, the Queen's most special rose – 'so green that the sun of Spain at the hottest cannot parch it'. While hermit and gardener were serious, the mole-catcher brought in a comic tone, an equal part of these occasions, as it was in much stage drama of the period. This part-serious, part-humorous theme was taken up again in early 1594.[41]

Later in 1591 the Earl of Hertford welcomed the Queen and her entourage as his guests for four days – Monday evening to Thursday forenoon, 20–23 September – at Elvetham in Hampshire.[42] His residence was not palatial, his gardens were slight, and so 'on the sodaine' he raised several temporary buildings and created a temporary, but vast, garden setting for the entertainment. While the buildings were made to look like garden walks – 'the outsides ... were all covered with boughs, and clusters of ripe hasell nuttes, the insides with arras [tapestry with figures and designs], the roofe ... with works of ivy leaves' – a far greater matter was achieved 'by handy labour'. This was 'a goodly Pond, cut to the perfect figure of a half moon'. Dug out within sight of the Queen's rooms, 'under the prospect of her gallerie windowe', the pond was large enough to hold three islands ('notable grounds'), one a ship, one a fort and one an island like a 'Snayl Mount rising to four circles of green privie [privet] hedges, the whole in height twentie foot, and fortie foote broad'. And then there were a dozen or so little boats, and, necessarily, a 'presence seate' or 'canopie of estate' for the Queen to sit in and watch what went on, on those wet September days in 1591. What was presented was no doubt intended to be like the *naumachies*, the artificial 'naval' battles staged in Roman times, and later in Renaissance Italy, when, for example, a part of the Piazza Navona in Rome or an area in front of the Palazzo Pitti in Florence was flooded to create a temporary lake and marine battlefield. At Elvetham, the *naumachia* was between the spirits of the water and the land (not immensely different from the jollities at Kenilworth in 1575), with the sea god Nereus and attendant tritons, the sea goddess Neæra and her attendants, and the woodland god Sylvanus and his train. Much poetry and much rain – on Thursday, for example, 'it was a most extreame rain'; and all gone. We may argue now, where the 'goodly Pond' ever was.[43]

Not all these entertainments were so lavish. At Cowdray in Sussex in 1591 and at Bisham in Berkshire in 1592, the Queen was given entertainment of a gentle rural kind, where, at Cowdray, she was greeted by a 'pilgrime' and then by a 'wilde man' in 'my Lorde's walkes', and at Bisham a 'wilde man' appeared and spoke approvingly of the two daughters of the house who were 'on stage' as shepherdesses. Neither was expensive, compared with the 'half moon' pond at Elvetham but both were wholly in the fashion of the chivalric-pastoral scenes of Sir Philip Sidney's *Arcadia*, or Thomas Lodge's *Rosalynde*.

6

OF GARDENS AND GROTTOES

Sir Robert Cecil

While Sir William Cecil, Lord Burghley, is one of the main links in the garden activity of the late sixteenth century, his son Sir Robert Cecil, later 1st Earl of Salisbury, is a notable figure to introduce the reign of King James I. Receiving the Hatfield estate in exchange for Theobalds in 1607, Cecil quickly began to build, taking down most of the old palace, and raising an entirely new building some 100 yards away. Garden work involved several experts, including Mountain Jenings (or Jennings) around 1609 (he had worked at Theobalds, and returned there later in connection with the King's mulberry plantations), John Tradescant (the elder) from 1610 until 1614 or 1615, and in 1611–12 Salomon de Caus, the French hydraulic engineer. Sir Francis Bacon, Cecil's cousin, also corresponded on garden matters, both giving and receiving advice. At roughly the same time, the Cecil property at Cranborne in Dorset was remodelled, the house being rebuilt and enlarged between 1608 and 1612, and the gardens developed from 1610 – Tradescant and Jenings were sent there once or twice at the end of the year.[1]

Since then the gardens at both properties have been much altered, particularly in the later nineteenth and later twentieth centuries. At Cranborne, remains of a mount attributed to Tradescant may be seen, and some of the present terraces to the east of Hatfield House may correspond to those of Jenings' and Tradescant's period.

In Tradescant's time at Hatfield, the lavish and varied plantings included 30,000 vines, given by the wife of the French ambassador, 500 fruit trees, the gift of the French queen, and hundreds of cherry trees and mulberries (probably white mulberries, *Morus alba*, though this is uncertain).[2] The latter had been recommended by King James, for the raising of silkworms (which will feed on the leaves, though they do not like the leaves of the red mulberry, *Morus nigra*), and in 1608 Cecil ordered 500 mulberry trees for himself. In the next year, 1609, an order was issued to the Lords-Lieutenant in all counties in England that they should encourage mulberry planting, and a book, *Instructions for the Increasing of Mulberie Trees* by William Stallenge, was published. There seems to have been confusion in the importation of cuttings – red rather than white – and the scheme did not prosper. King James, however, had properly ordered mulberries for himself, and payment for their care at Theobalds was made in 1608.[3] Another area of 4 acres was planted for King James westward from St James's Park, becoming known as the Mulberry Garden or Gardens. Though it was not a commercial success, a part of the area survived in the 1650s and became a fashionable, if disreputable, pleasure garden until 1673, praised both by Evelyn and Pepys. By 1703, the site had been absorbed into the grounds of Buckingham House, a building which remained until the early nineteenth century, when it was replaced by Nash's Buckingham Palace.[4]

One other instance of the royal mulberry experiment should be mentioned – at Oatlands in Surrey. By 1616, the plantations of mulberries there must have been both mature, extensive, and of the right kind of tree, as a silkworm house was built in that year, designed by Inigo Jones.[5] How the manufacture of silk prospered we do not know, but some years later, in 1630 (long after he had left Hatfield) John Tradescant was appointed keeper of the 'gardens, Vines and Silke-Wormes at Oatlands', a post which he kept until his death in 1638, and which was then held by his son, John Tradescant (the younger), until around 1648.[6] The buildings at Oatlands were destroyed in the 1650s and the gardens neglected, to such an extent that the eighteenth-century developments there have virtually no relationship to the gardens made a century before.

Returning to the older Tradescant in 1610, at Hatfield he was concerned above all with the acquisition of plants, for which he travelled extensively in 1611 and later years (see page 127). The design of the gardens was at first the work of Jenings and Thomas Chaundler, while Salomon de Caus followed an earlier engineer, Simon Sturtevant, in designing waterworks. At Theobalds in 1602, Jenings had already begun waterworks for Cecil involving a stream, and it is possible that a part of the Hatfield scheme was related to this earlier project. At Hatfield the upper ground eastwards from the house was given a series of terraces, with fountains set symmetrically within a formal layout. This was the 1611 design of Salomon de Caus.

De Caus had come to England in 1607 or 1608, and had worked at Somerset House in London for the Queen, Anne of Denmark, and at

Richmond for Henry, Prince of Wales. He left in the middle of 1613 in the train of Princess Elizabeth, who went to Heidelberg as the bride of Frederick, Elector Palatine, and who later became known as Elizabeth of Bohemia, the 'Winter Queen'.

At Somerset House he was engaged in 1611–12, and possibly as early as 1609, to make waterworks involving an elaborate rock-cum-grotto which was eloquently admired in 1613 by J. W. Neumayr.[7] This feature resembled, and apparently surpassed, the marvellous artificial mountain-grotto at Pratolino in Italy. At Richmond, for the Prince of Wales (who died in 1612 aged 19) de Caus was involved in similar projects from the end of 1610, but in 1611 he became subordinate to Constantino dei Servi, an Italian, and it is hard to give de Caus all that much credit for these uncompleted works.[8] His later publication, *Les Raisons des forces mouvantes* (1615), and his superlative achievement at Heidelberg in the 'Hortus Palatinus', created between 1615 and 1619 and commemorated in his *Hortus Palatinus* of 1620, are notable in their transmission *back* to England by his brother (or nephew) Isaac de Caus in the 1630s (see page 121), when they are set in a new and different framework.

To return to Hatfield: below the terraced formal area and further to the east, was the 'dell', with a stream, pool and 'island'. The 'island' was diamond-shaped, bisected by a lesser stream, with a central building which may have been a banqueting-house. Lesser buildings nearby include one which may have been a grotto. In 1611, for the stream and grotto (if that is what it was) Tradescant bought 'on Chest of Shells with eyght boxes of Shells' from the Low Countries, and de Caus likewise arranged for a consignment of 'coquilles' to be sent.[9] These shells were intended both for the walls and sides of these features, and also to be set in the bed of the stream to glisten and sparkle in the running water. They were sometimes arranged in lifelike patterns, and sometimes accompanied by ceramics of snakes or fish.

Similar shell decoration was to be found at Beddington in the early 1600s (see page 78), and it should be noted that this was a central feature of the decoration of grottoes recommended by the French Protestant ceramic artist Bernard Palissy in 1563 in his *Recepte véritable*, and in the grottoes which he executed at Chenonceaux, Écouen and the Tuileries.[10] I have already mentioned the descriptions of grottoes and waterworks in Palissy, Sidney, Du Bartas and Nashe, and the additional influence of real and spectacular garden features of this kind seen by travellers in Italy and France. By the early seventeenth century the possibilities and complexities of these influences are astonishingly diverse, notably in one grotto – at Greenwich – and in a more general way in the varied gardens, garden writings and gardening contacts of one man – Sir Francis Bacon.

✠ *A Grotto at Greenwich*

In 1613, J. W. Neumayr described a grotto he saw in the grounds at Greenwich. Having referred briefly to a sculptured fountain in the middle of the garden, he continues:

> Further on you reach a Grotto, like a little house, mostly open at the front and at the two sides, with strong iron bars. Round the walls are three separate arches, decorated like all the adjoining wall with shells, mussels, mother of pearl and all sorts of rare stones and sea-growths. Out of this at some points grew flowers, grass and various beautiful plants. In the central arch was a life-sized sculpture, half woman, half horse, likewise made with sea-shells and mussels, and pouring out water onto the ground. In the two other arches were other sculptures, also gushing out water. On the ground were rocks from the shore, piled up like cliffs. At some places, there were also flowers and twiggy bushes growing out, and there was also a little turf. On the wall, sitting on a branch, was a cuckoo, which the gardener made to sing by means of the water. As well as this the roof of the house was open at some points, protected by sliding frames so that the birds, which flew round and about in great numbers, could not escape. [The aviary is then described.][11]

We do not know for sure when this feature was built, though it has been suggested that it was designed by Salomon de Caus, who may have worked at Greenwich around 1611 for Queen Anne. Whether de Caus was or was not the designer, however, the inspiration for this combination of sculptured waterworks, artificial chirping bird and aviary comes clearly enough from King Basilius' banqueting-house in Sidney's *Arcadia*, with an addition of shellwork *à la* Palissy. The pastoral-chivalric source is even more certain when one notes that Neumayr commented also on a viewing tower in the highest part of the park, named 'Le chasteau de Millefleur'. The name is inaccurate – in 1598 the same tower was seen by Paul Hentzner, who stated that it was 'called Mirefleur, supposed to be that mentioned in the romance of Amadis of Gaul'.[12] In *Amadis* it is in fact one of the English strongholds of Queen Oriana, and therefore absolutely suitable as a name for a tower in the English Queen Elizabeth's park at Greenwich.[13]

Sir Francis Bacon

Sir Francis Bacon's part in this history is far greater than his essay 'On Gardens', published in 1625, a year before his death. Born in 1561, his long legal, political, philosophical and literary career included garden matters only as a small yet brilliant part. Bacon, like many of those who have had penetrating and decisive thoughts about gardens – looking forward to Sir William Temple, Horace Walpole or Gertrude Jekyll, or back to Pliny the Younger – saw them only as a *part* of man's affairs; and yet his view was singularly rich and stimulating.

Long before the essay 'On Gardens', he had designed gardens for himself or for others. In 1594, he took on lease the property at Twickenham Park, which remained his until 1606. In this time (in fact by 1601) the poet John Donne wrote 'Twicknam Garden' (in *Songs and Sonnets*), pleading to the lady of the moment:

> Love let mee
> Some senslesse peece of this place bee;
> Make me a mandrake, so I may groane here,
> Or a stone fountaine weeping out my yeare.[14]

Bacon himself was not, I understand, subject to such ecstasy, but still, as he wrote, 'found the situation of that place much convenient for the trial of [his] philosophical conclusions'.

The design of 'that place', Twickenham Park, is happily recorded by Robert Smythson in 1609, three years after Bacon left and one year after the arrival of Lucy Harington, Countess of Bedford. While the design may well have been altered in its details in 1608–9, the overall layout must still have been Bacon's invention. It was wholly geometrical – a series of circles within a framework of squares, and with lesser circles in the 'corners', instantly reminiscent of the maze designs at Saffron Walden in Thomas Hill's *The Gardener's Labyrinth* (1577), and in Du Cerceau's plans of Gaillon in *Les plus excellents bastiments de France* (1576–9). The scale however is far larger, comparable with the equally geometrical scheme in the botanic garden at Padua (a quartered square within a circle, with forms of circle within each of the quarters of the square). There was, it seems, no element of water in this garden of Bacon's. The outer *squares* were hedged, one hedge of 'thorn and quick sett', the next of 'trees cut into Beastes', the next of rosemary, and the fourth and innermost hedge of fruit trees. The central *circles* were of lime or birch. In the 'corners' steps led to circular areas (blank on Smythson's plan), which may reasonably have held pavilions for viewing the centre of the garden.

Bacon's second garden design (or one in which he was influential), at Gray's Inn in London, dates from around 1597 to 1609. There he is credited with a principal part of the design (now an extensive L-shape) of the 'walks', terraces running north and then east, overlooking the main buildings of Gray's Inn. The garden area was walled in 1597–8, and the terraced walks running north-south were then planted with many elms, as well as beech, sycamore and cherry, and lavish additional planting of smaller shrubs and flowers – privet, quickset (probably hawthorn), roses, woodbine, pinks and violets. The quantity of privet and quickset ordered (20,000 of each) indicates an extensive hedging scheme, which may have involved one or even two mazes.[15] In 1608–9, Bacon had a mount, with a summerhouse, built mid-way along the main north-south terrace. This was demolished in the later eighteenth century, but the 'walks' survive, and might still be found conducive to 'philosophical conclusions'.

Bacon's third garden was at Gorhambury in Hertfordshire. He inherited the estate in 1601, and soon decided that the waterless site of the main house was unsatisfactory for garden making. 'If the Water could not be brought to the House, he would bring the House to the Water' – and so, over several years, he developed gardens round the medieval fishponds a mile or so to the north-east, and eventually built a mansion, Verulam House, beside these new gardens. 'Here', Aubrey writes, 'his Lordship much meditated, his servant Mr Bushell attending him with his pen and ink horne to sett downe his present notions'.[16] We shall hear of Bushell again (see pages 98 to 99). But Bacon's work at Gorhambury was not merely meditative. He set out long and broad avenues of mixed planting – elm, chestnut, beech and others – between the old house and his new garden residence. When Aubrey saw them in 1656, their leafy tops had come to resemble 'workes in Irish-stitch', 'a most pleasant variegated verdure'.

Under the 'great and shadie' oaks of the woodland, Bacon planted 'some fine flower, or flowers, some whereof are there still [1656], viz. paeonies, tulips, . . .', and at the eastern end of the walks, beside Verulam House, he had a fruit garden, 'some thicketts of plumme-trees with delicate walkes; some of rasberies. Here was all manner of fruit-trees . . . and . . . choice forest-trees'. Here the walks were adorned with 'elegant sommer-howses well built of Roman architecture' – adornment, presumably, being classical columns and pediments.

At another angle to Verulam House were the 4-acre water gardens, which Bacon laid out in ways which paralleled the 'islands' at Hatfield and Raglan (see page 91 and 74), and the streams and grotto-work at Beddington and Greenwich (see pages 78 and 92). Aubrey gives a plan of the central island, with a 'curious banqueting-house of Roman architecture', surrounded with regular walks and hedges. Far earlier, in 1608 (around the time the gardens at Hatfield were laid out) Bacon himself wrote about this garden, that he wanted it to include round the elaborate central house-and-island a further group of islands, each with plants or statues of a distinctive kind – a matter which he may have discussed with his cousin, Sir Robert Cecil.[17] Most important is Aubrey's comment, to do with Bacon's actual achievement, that his ponds

> ... were pitched at the bottomes with pebbles of severall colours, which were work'd in to severall figures, as of fishes, etc. which in his lordship's time were plainly to be seen through the cleare water, now over-grown ...

Aubrey adds that 'if a poor bodie had brought his lordship halfe a dozen pebbles of a curious colour, he would give them a shilling, so curious was he in perfecting his fish-ponds'.[18]

All gone. In Aubrey's time the several 'sommer-houses' were 'yet standing, but defaced, so that one would have thought the Barbarians had made a conquest here', and much later, 'in the remarkable hot Summer of 1802', Charlotte Grimston was able to examine the bed of the fishponds for traces of the shell and pebble ornament, but 'could not find the smallest remains of them', and 'only slight traces' of the banqueting-house.[19]

We do not hear much of underwater decoration in later years, though grottoes with fantastic shell ornaments will flourish. Bacon was disgraced in 1621, at the height of his influence in garden matters. In 1625 his essay 'Of Gardens' was published, together with others, such as 'Of Building' and 'Of Masques and Triumphs' which had not appeared before. He died in 1626, and his other work related to gardens, 'centuries' or sections V and VI of *Sylva sylvarum*, was published posthumously in 1626.[20] It is proper to note these dates, since his gardens, designed or supervised by himself, come long before his writings on the subject, and since these writings are also at remarkably different levels – so much so that they might almost have been composed by different people. While 'Of Gardens' deals with a 'prince-like' scheme of not less than 30 acres, discussing the design, the aesthetic quality, the flowers, ornamentation and pleasurable aspects of the garden, Bacon's much longer remarks in *Sylva sylvarum* are severely practical, seeing these factors from the viewpoint of the intelligent gardener, as matters of experiment and continuing work, which could mostly have been followed in a garden of half an acre or less by an enthusiast such as Walter Stonehouse in the 1630s, or John Rea in the 1650s.

'Of Gardens' must be among the best known of all writings on the subject. I note only the principal points:

- Bacon outlined a scheme of planting which would yield enjoyment – flowers, foliage, fruit or fragrance – throughout the year, giving a *Ver perpetuum* or perpetual spring. Today, with the development of longer-flowering varieties, and the introduction of winter-flowering plants, this is not by any means impossible, but in 1625 it was ambitious and unusual. We need only think back to Thomas Hill in 1563, urging that mazes should be set with evergreens, 'Isope and Tyme ... and such like ... for these doe well endure all the Winter thorow greene'. There was no question of *flowers* – the green leaves would be an ample comfort.

- Bacon insisted on a layout which was firmly geometrical, framed with hedges and walks, several of them built up and over as green architecture, with pillars and arches of carpenter's work, and some with 'a little *Turret*' big enough 'to receive a *Cage* of *Birds*'. These hedged walks are similar to the grand fantasies proposed in Vredeman de Vries' *Hortorum viridarumque formae* of 1583, and to those admired later by Thomas Coryate in 1608 in the Tuileries Garden in Paris – '700 paces long ... artificially roofed over with timber worke, that the boughes of the maple trees ... doe ... cover it cleane over. This roofed walke hath six faire arbours advanced to a great heigth like turrets'.[21]

- Bacon disliked knots, and topiary 'images', though he approved of topiary in architectural forms – pyramids and columns. (It is curious, therefore, that the 1609 Smythson plan of his Twickenham Park garden (see page 93) indicates one hedge with 'trees cut into Beastes'. It could be that Bacon changed his mind between the early 1600s and his essay in 1625, or that the topiary 'Beastes' were added by Lucy Harington when she acquired Twickenham Park in 1608. We do not know.)

- At the centre he required a mount with a banqueting-house – as on the island at Gorhambury – and with a symmetrical setting comparable (or so I imagine) to the circles and squares of Twickenham Park.

- With fountains, he urged that they should not stagnate – the one practical point in 'Of Gardens' – and that they should be adorned with gilded or marble statues. In ornamental pools, like those at Hatfield and Gorhambury, 'the Bottome' should 'be finely Paved, And with Images'. His essay 'Of Building' provides for a 'grotto' or 'place of shade' as a part of the house in the 'under story towards the garden', which is an interesting link between the two essays, since Bacon clearly conceived the house (a princely one) to have a *public* and a *private* side, the garden being mainly on the private side.

- Beyond the main garden, with its mount and alleys and fountains, Bacon wanted a 'Heath', which we might describe as a fairly formal area of grass and ornamental shrubs, underplanted with flowers. He wanted it 'to be framed as much as may be, to a *Natural wilderness*', but this term means no more than 'without a formal layout'. The ground should be scattered with 'little *Heaps*, in the Nature of *Mole-hills*', planted with flowers and herbs – thyme, pinks, periwinkle, violets, wild strawberries, cowslips, lily of the valley and similar 'Low Flowers', which should be accompanied by carefully trained and pruned standard shrubs – roses, juniper, holly, barberries, redcurrants, gooseberries, rosemary 'and such like' – not what the twentieth century understands by a 'natural wilderness'!

The garden sections of Bacon's *Sylva sylvarum* are, as I have said, vastly different in their concern. They deal with experiments, some which Bacon himself performed, some which he has heard of, and others which he proposes should be made. He examines, empirically or theoretically, an astonishing range of botanical and horticultural questions: the germination of seeds; the relative merits of different dungs and fertilisers; the importance of different situations for different plants; the usefulness of digging; the importance of water; how to retard flowering or fruiting (Had he read Sir Hugh Platt on cherries (see page 79)? With roses he says that delaying them 'is an experiment of pleasure'); the usefulness of shade – as with growing wild strawberries beneath borage; plant associations, known or hypothetical; layering and grafting; pipless or stoneless fruit; the nature of thorns and prickles; and much more. These are practical matters which any gardener, however small the garden, could appreciate. They are topics that do not need a 'prince-like scheme' for their study – Jon Gardener, Thomas Tusser or Thomas Hill could have tried them out in their gardens, with a garden shed and an area of no more than half an acre. But – and this difference is crucial – they did not. They did not have Bacon's questioning curiosity, relying rather on 'common sense', on received knowledge derived from other gardeners or from writers in the past.

A 'Delicate Grotto'

Bacon's influence extended far into the seventeenth century. His favourite secretary, Thomas Bushell (1594–1674) left him around 1620, and by 1626 was established at Enstone, near Charlbury, 12 miles north-west of Oxford. Here by chance he discovered a cave in the 'hanging of a hill', with 'pendants like icecles as at Wookey hole'. With a stream nearby, Bushell was able to convert this cave into a 'delicate grotto', with a house above. Its two main rooms were his study – 'hung with blacke Cloth, representing a melancholly retyr'd life like a Hermits' – and his bedroom, with a bed 'hung by 4 cordes . . . instead of bed postes'.[22]

Beneath, the grotto was a complex marvel, incorporating pneumatic and optical devices derived from Hero of Alexandria, from the Villa d'Este, Pratolino, Sidney's *Arcadia*, Bacon's Gorhambury, and other texts and other gardens – de Caus' *Raisons des forces mouvantes* and the watery marvels of Schloss Hellbrunn, outside Salzburg, are the most likely. Bushell himself ascribed the inspiration to Bacon, writing that when the cave – that 'desolate Cell of Natures rarities' – was discovered,

> I (in imitation of that excellent Lords sublime fancy) beautyfied the same with Ornaments of contemplative Groves and Walks, as well as artificial Thunder and Lightning, Rain, Hail-showers, Drums beating, Organs playing, Birds singing, Water murmuring, the Dead arising, Lights moving, Rainbows reflecting with the beams of the Sun, and watry showers springing from the same Fountain.[23]

Other visitors paid attention to the many joke fountains which ingeniously spat, dripped, squirted and streamed on the unwary.

Bushell's garden round about was small, but likewise modelled on Bacon's Gorhambury. In its 'neat, curious, long Walkes' and 'contemplative Groves', Bushell and his two musical servants, Jack Sydenham and Mr Batty, could in fine weather 'walke all night', very much as Bushell had attended on the meditative Bacon.

Two royal visits to Enstone in the 1630s brought fame briefly. Then came the Civil War, and Bushell left, never to return. In 1674, the Earl of Lichfield made more joke-fountains, and later the house, grotto and gardens declined into a place of entertainment. Again, by the 1840s, it had all gone, like Bacon's water gardens at Gorhambury.

These gardens both seem to have embodied something of the qualities which Robert Burton praised as 'the most pleasant of all outward pastimes' in *The Anatomy of Melancholy* (1621):

... to walk amongst orchards, gardens, bowers, mounts and arbours, artificial wildernesses [cf. Bacon's 'heath', or 'natural wilderness'], green thickets, arches, groves, lawns, rivulets, fountains, and such-like pleasant places, like that Antiochian Daphne.[24] [The rural beauty of Daphne was loved by the Emperor Julian, and William Kent's landscape garden at Rousham was later to be seen as its English parallel.]

Much of Burton's praise goes well with the earlier gardens at Theobalds, Hatfield, Beddington and the like, and extends onwards to the Fanshawe, Danvers and Harington gardens to be discussed shortly (see pages 102–9). However, many other gardens developed in the first decades of the seventeenth century show less experiment, though much enthusiasm.

Gardens for Castles and Mansions

Again and again in this history the siting and layout of a garden was affected, decided even, by 'outside' factors – social, economic or political – leading to results which may now seem intriguing or even incongruous. Thus, as in previous periods, gardens created in the reign of James I were often laid out in spaces related to an existing castle or mansion – spaces which may have been larger or smaller, more or less regular, according to the military importance or the degree of security of the site.

At Lulworth Castle in Dorset, begun around 1608, the relatively regular shape of the castle allowed correspondingly regular gardens to be developed on each of its four sides; these were further enlarged later in the century into an impressive formal scheme. In contrast, at Bolsover Castle in Derbyshire the Fountain Garden is sited within the walls of the thirteenth-century inner bailey, beside the pseudo-medieval Little Keep, designed by Robert Smythson and begun around 1610. The garden, laid out around 1612, is set in an irregular circle of walls, and some – myself, that is – would dearly wish to know how the space was filled with knots, beds and statues. By 1628, the Venus Fountain, also designed by Smythson, had been erected in an octagonal pool at the centre of this garden, and in 1634 the garden was the setting for Ben Jonson's *Love's Welcome to Bolsover*, a poetic entertainment for Charles I and Queen Henrietta Maria.

There is a comparable constraint in the site of the garden at Haddon

Hall in Derbyshire. Here the ground slopes down steeply on the south-eastern side of the medieval hall, which was much enlarged around 1600. The garden which was created soon afterwards was therefore formed by a sequence of terraces of varying height and width, following the outline of the hall and the slope of the ground. After prolonged neglect (thereby avoiding direct destruction), the terraces and the garden were thoroughly restored in the first half of the present century.

At Audley End in Essex the great house, the largest of all Jacobean 'prodigy houses', was built between about 1605 and 1614 for Thomas Howard, Earl of Sussex, and matching formal gardens were laid out as well. But no illustrations survive, and the earliest view and plan, by Henry Winstanley, of around 1676, have scant indications only, with names linked to empty spaces, to hint of what glories *might* have existed before 40-odd years of neglect: two bowling greens in the western court-yard, another to the east, bare grass quarters in the 'mount garden' to the south, and two squares of 'cherry garden', a 'wilderness' and 'great pond' to the north-east. At Audley End therefore (as at Holdenby in the 1580s) a grand garden was made to suit with the house; but it has disappeared – indeed, it went early on – and we now value Audley End for its landscape gardening, created in the eighteenth century.

From Melford Hall in Suffolk (where the octagonal banqueting-house was built around 1559) there are details, in a letter of 20 May 1619 by James Howell, which go far to fill in the gaps for these gardens. Howell (staying as guest of Sir Thomas Savage, who was owner of Melford Hall and its 340 acres of gardens, park and warren from 1609 to his death in 1635) wrote happily of the varied delights of the place:

> ... the Park, which for a chearful rising Ground, for Groves and Browsings for the Deer, for rivulets of Water, may compare with any ... the great House, whence from the Gallery one may see much of the Game when they are a-hunting. Now for the Gardening and costly choice Flowers, for Ponds, for stately large Walks, green and gravelly, for Orchards and choice Fruits of all sorts, there are few the like in England: here you have your *Bon Christian Pear* and *Bergamot* in perfection, your *Muscadell* Grapes in such plenty, that there are some bottles of Wine sent every year to the King.'[25]

Sir Thomas's wife Elizabeth was also the owner of St Osyth Priory in Essex, which possessed a comparable deer park and gardens, and it is reasonable to imagine similar activity on that estate (much changed in the eighteenth and nineteenth centuries).

Ventures in Scotland and Ireland

In Scotland and Ireland, apart from occasional references to monastic gardens, this history does not really start until the early seventeenth century. Even then it is a scantily documented subject, related above all to the few garden areas within the protection of castle walls. Thus at Edzell Castle in Kincardinshire a garden was made within a rectangular walled area in 1604 by Sir David Lindsay. What was the layout of this space – 173 by 144 feet? We do not know, but the elaborate pattern of niches or recesses on three of the four walls, designed presumably for plants and with related bas-reliefs, implies a corresponding sophistication in the planning of the garden itself. The present layout and planting, dating from the 1930s, are excellently matched with the surrounding walls, though they are probably more elaborate, and more carefully tended than any original scheme may have been.

The modern reconstruction of the Edzell garden may have been encouraged by the evidence of the 'King's Knot', a pattern of rectilinear knots set just outside the walls of Stirling Castle, and laid out for James VI of Scotland, James I of England, in the 1620s. Today the outlines, strongly three-dimensional, of two large square knots may still be seen, as we look down from the castle. In the early eighteenth century Daniel Defoe saw the gardens on this site, already in decline:

> ... but how fine they were I cannot say, though the Figure of the Walks and Grass-plots are plainly to be seen. They seem to have been very old fashioned, but might be thought fine for those Times ...'[26]

Though we may peer downwards at the marked relief of these knots, the details of design and planting remain a secret.

In Ireland, statements in the earliest years of the seventeenth century are glum. Around 1600, Fynes Moryson wrote that he had seen only two parks in Ireland, one belonging to the Earl of Ormond, the other to the Earl of Kildare, though he had written elsewhere of *England*, that no other country of comparable size 'alloweth such great proportions of lands for parks to impale [enclose] fallow or red deer'. The reason for Ireland's dearth of parks, he explained, was that it was 'often troubled with rebellions', which ran counter to the fertility of the soil and the mildness of the climate.[27] With this comment Sir John Davies, in 1612, would have agreed – 'at this day there is but one park stored with deer in all this kingdom ... the earl of Ormond's near Kilkenny'.[28] The grounds and gardens of Kilkenny Castle will reappear in this history in the 1680s (see page 146).

One 'garden' had, however, been reported in this time – in 1599, the Earl of Essex's unhappy expedition to Ireland had involved the capture of the castle at Caher, on an island in the River Suir. Beside the castle was a garden, and to it, or into it, '300 menne' were sent to occupy and defend the place.[29] But their stay was brief, and was hardly related to fruit or flowers. . . .

I would dare to suggest that modern gardening 'begins' in Ireland in the 1630s, with a topiary work outside the Primate's palace at Drogheda. From 1624 until 1655, the post was held by Archbishop Usher, and he, or possibly his predecessor, laid this out in the 'pretty neat garden' close to the palace:

> Upon a bank, these words, in fair great letters, are written: 'O man, remember the last great day.' The bank is bare, the proportion of the letters is framed and cut in grass.[30]

How the text was displayed is not too clear – 'cut in grass' implies a lawn, of sorts, which would have been improbable at that time. Might it therefore have been in letters cut out in grass or turf, with 'bare' ground surrounding? The contemporary use of topiary is so common, that we may wonder whether the letters were not in box – or other shrubs – set in a grassy background. The stern message, 'in fair great letters', can be matched with one laid out far later, in the 1890s, in letters of box on a half-circular gravel terrace overlooking the gardens at Monreith in Wigtownshire; it read 'Homo quasi flos egreditur et conteritur'.[31]

'Busied About New Workes'

The letters of John Chamberlain (1554–1628) are mainly political or personal, but they touch on a few gardens with illuminating effect, particularly on Ware Park in Hertfordshire, the property of Sir Henry Fanshawe (father of the poet Sir Richard Fanshawe). On 22 April 1606 Chamberlain wrote from Ware Park to tell of the illustrious company, including Sir Christopher Hatton, from Kirby Hall in Northamptonshire (of the Hatton family from Holdenby (see page 72), which had been acquired by King James), and on 15 October he wrote again, mentioning Sir Christopher Hatton once more and 'such a quoil about gardening, that a man cannot be ydle though he do but look on'.[32]

This 'quoil' ('agitation' or 'bother') concerned a new garden, 'wholly translated, new levelled, and in a manner transplanted' (a matter some of us have experienced in our own gardens), where at the centre, instead of a knot, Sir Henry Fanshawe had installed a small version of 'a fort, in perfect proportion, with his rampars, bulwarkes, counterscarpes and all other appurtenances ... an invincible peice of worke'. Without a sketch of some sort we cannot be sure, but this 'fort' was probably a form of mount. With its angular star-like plan it might conceivably have been paralleled by the house and gardens made by Mary, Countess of Pembroke in this period or shortly after (she died in 1621) at Houghton Lodge in Bedfordshire. There, according to John Aubrey, she laid out a scheme recreating the house and gardens in Sir Philip Sidney's *Arcadia*, already mentioned several times in this history. Aubrey's comment is brief, and tantalising – 'The architects were sent for from Italy. It [Houghton Lodge] is built according to the description of Basilius' house in the first book of the *Arcadia* ... It is most pleasantly situated and has four vistas, each prospect twenty-five or thirty miles'.[33] Did the architects from Italy build the banqueting-house, with grotto, waterworks and aviary from the *Arcadia*, as well? Once more, we do not know. These examples – Fanshawe's fort, and Houghton Lodge – end the direct influence of Sir Philip Sidney.

At this time another observer, Sir Henry Wotton, remarked on Fanshawe's garden enthusiam – to do with flowers:

> He did so precisely examine the *tinctures* and *Seasons* of the *flowers*, that in their *settings*, the *inwardest* of which that were to come up at the same time, should always be a little *darker* than the *utmost*, and so serve them for a kind of gentle *shadow*, like a piece, not of Nature, but of *Art*.[34]

Here we have something new and exciting. It is an invention, a novelty, comparable with Bacon's wish for a 'Ver perpetuum', a perpetual spring – with the hope of flowers, or the colour of flowers, through much of the year. Similar techniques were employed by Sir Thomas Hanmer in Wales in the 1650s, and much later, though they did not think of Fanshawe, nor of Hanmer, by the herbaceous ladies and gentlemen of the nineteenth century. We do our best today.

Fanshawe's garden, according to Chamberlain, was in 1609 enriched with flowers from Sir Ralph Winwood, of Ditton Park in Buckinghamshire,[35] and a few years later, in 1613, the general layout was drastically altered, being witnessed and to some extent directed by Sir Henry Wotton. The changes were again noted by Chamberlain, who adds that they were being urged on with excessive attention from Wotton, another of Fanshawe's guests. This time, the fort has been moved, and replaced by a water garden:

> We are busied about new workes, and bringing of waters into the gardens, which have succeeded so well that we have a fine fountaine in the lower garden where the fort was, (yf you remember the place) and a running streame (from the river) between the knotts and the rancks of trees in the brode walke or alley ...'[36]

If Wotton succeeded in influencing the design of this garden, as Chamberlain claimed he was trying to do, he may have wished it to show variety and surprise in its different levels. He recommended this quality in 1624 in *The Elements of Architecture*, saying that gardens 'should be *irregular*, or at least cast into a very wild *Regularity*'. He praises one garden (without identifying it), 'for the manner perchance incomparable', which began from 'a high walk like a Tarrace',

> ... from whence might be taken a general view of the whole *Plot* below, but rather in a delightful confusion, than with any plain distinction of the pieces. From this the *Beholder* descending many steps, was afterwards conveyed again by several *mountings* and *valings*, to various entertainments of his *sent* and *sight* ... everyone of these diversities, was as if he had been *magically* transported into a new *Garden*.[37]

While Wotton may well have been thinking of gardens on sloping terraced sites which he had seen in Italy, he could also have known a garden site developed in England, at (West) Lavington in Wiltshire, in this period. It was the property of the Dauntsey family, which came to Sir John Danvers (c.1588–1655) on his marriage to Elizabeth Dauntsey in 1628. The Danvers and Dauntsey families had been connected for some time, and Sir John Danvers may indeed have been influential in the creation of the garden there before the marriage. John Aubrey wrote of Danvers that he 'first taught us the way of Italian gardens. He had well travelled France and Italy, and made good observations'. Aubrey's lines on the Lavington garden might almost have been written with Wotton's recommendations at his elbow – or lodged somewhere in his most capacious memory:

> The garden at Lavington is full of irregularities, both naturall and artificiall, [i.e.] elevations and depressions. Through the length of it there runneth a fine cleare trowt stream; walled with brick on each side ... In this stream are placed severall statues ... Among severall others, there is a very pleasant elevation on the south side of the garden, which steales, arising almost insensibly, that is, before one is aware, and gives you a view over the spatious corn-fields there [a quality which Wotton praised

as 'a *Lordship* ... of the *Eye*',[38] anticipating somewhat Addison's praise of rural landscape in 1710–12 – see page 166] ... It is almost impossible to describe this garden, it is so full of variety and unevenesse.[39]

Though altered by later lawns, paths and plantings, the Lavington garden is still there, on an undulating site, with traces of Danvers' terraces, and crossed at its lower levels by the stream.

Sir John Danvers was praised by Aubrey for two gardens – Lavington, just mentioned, and his garden (and house) in Chelsea. If the Lavington garden was 'full of variety and unevenesse', the garden of the London house, which was begun around 1622, was far less so, at least in its general plan – a large, tree-lined oval or circle of grass (a bowling green), surrounded by a path, set in a square.[40] To the south, on the river side, was the house, with views both ways – out to the river, and back to the garden. One had to descend steps, leading to left or right, to arrive at the general level of the garden, with a plantation of shrubs and low trees in between oneself and the central oval of lawn. Statues, several commissioned from Nicholas Stone, stood in or beside this area, and more – as in an Italian garden of the late-sixteenth or seventeenth century – were set beside the paths leading to the central lawn. At the far northern end, a walk with flanking pavilions and central banqueting-house had been slightly raised with the earth dug out from a trench running the width of the garden. At the centre, and lowest point, of the trench, was a little grotto, over which a bridge joined the banqueting-house to the garden.

Some commentators have tried to show that this plan revealed the irregularity praised by Wotton,[41] but this lacks conviction, set beside the 'variety' of Lavington. Aubrey's text of 1691 stresses the difference between the two sites, Lavington originally 'uneven, and irregular', while Chelsea 'lay plain (flatt)', so that there 'the business was to make elevations and depressions'.[42] More to be regarded are the statues, chosen for their mythological or pastoral interest, and it may well have been these, linked with the garden's geometrical similarity to his own garden at Twickenham Park, that made Sir Francis Bacon enjoy the place – Aubrey writes that Danvers 'was a great acquaintance of the Lord Chancellor Bacon, who took much delight in that elegant garden'. The pleasure might also have come from the fragrant herbs, praised by Bacon in his essay. At Chelsea, Danvers 'was wont in fair mornings in the summer to brush his beaver-hat on the hyssop and thyme, which did perfume it ... and last a morning or longer'.[43]

Danvers is mentioned by Aubrey for one other gardening venture, at Cirencester in Gloucestershire. Again, the phrases are brief – 'The mount in the garden of the great house there (built by old Sir John Danvers) is called Grismund's Tower'.[44] We may correct Aubrey in one respect – Grismund's Tower was far older than Danvers' time. It was probably a small medieval fortification, and was noted by John Leland in the 1540s as 'a steepe round biry [bury or mound] like a wind myl hill ... called Grismundes Tower, for Gusmundes Tower, as theie say. The place is now a waren for conys'.[45]

What Danvers did is uncertain, though most likely, he made the medieval mound into a viewing platform, perhaps like the 'fort' at Ware Park, or like the top of the banqueting-house he was to build at the end of his Chelsea garden. By the early eighteenth century, the mound had resumed its antique reputation – the antiquarian Stukeley in 1721 wrote 'behind my Lord Bathurst's garden is another mount, called Grismunds or Girmonds, of which several fables are told: probably raised by the Danes when they laid siege to this place'.[46] There is no mention of Grismund's Tower in the 'landscaping' elaborated by Lord Bathurst and Alexander Pope (see page 179).

Sir John Danvers had two older brothers, of whom the second, Henry Danvers (1573–1644, created Earl of Danby 1626), engaged in two important garden projects, one large-scale, the other of only 4 acres. By 1617 he had assumed the Rangership of Cornbury Park in Gloucestershire, where in the early 1630s the sculptor and architect Nicholas Stone (who had executed statues for his brother at Chelsea) was engaged to remodel the old house. Cornbury Park dates from the early Middle Ages, with a medieval hunting lodge, the core of the present house. Danvers' garden activity consisted principally in the establishment of long intersecting avenues, out into Wychwood Forest, work which was remodelled or consolidated with the advice of John Evelyn in 1664.[47]

In 1621 Henry Danvers founded the Oxford Botanic Garden, where, in 1631–3, Nicholas Stone was engaged 'for to mak 3 ston gates'[48] (the main gate – the Danby Gate – and the two smaller ones still stand). The decade and more needed for the building of the gates to commence was a part of the garden's slow beginning. It was the first university botanic garden in Britain (John Gerard's proposal of c.1597 – see page 80 – having failed). An attempt was made at the end of 1636 to engage John Tradescant (the elder), who had worked at Hatfield, as keeper, but he died in 1638. Four years later, in 1642, the first keeper to be appointed was Jacob Bobart (1599–1679).[49]

The plan of the Oxford Botanic Garden, as reproduced by David Loggan in 1675, and apparently based on the original layout, is comparable in its strict geometry to the contemporary gardens at Twickenham Park, by Sir Francis Bacon, and at Chelsea, by Sir John Danvers, and like them it looks backward to the formal designs of the sixteenth century and before – indeed to the cloister gardens of the Middle Ages. It is, I would maintain, one of the last important designs to survive from the period of the Renaissance, before the arrival of a 'new' and different garden aesthetic from France in the 1630s. It is governed – as were the initial designs for the botanic gardens at Padua (1545) and Leiden (1587) – by a special belief, not possible before 1492, and indeed not conceivable in earlier Christian times. This is the belief that a botanic garden, for the reception, study and diffusion of plants, should be divided into four equal parts, to accommodate the leafy floral treasures brought back from the four quarters of the world – the four continents of Asia, Africa, Europe and America, the 'new-found land'. Oxford's quartered garden, laid out in the 1620s or early 1630s, is therefore an intriguing compound of ancient – the extreme of formality – and adventurously modern, with the wish to receive new plants from the as yet unknown 'new world'. In its design, set beside the gardens at Gorhambury, Ware Park and Lavington, it is no less than antique.

Gardens of the Harington Family

One other group of gardens dating from the early part of the seventeenth century must be mentioned, connected with the Harington family. Sir John Harington came into possession of Combe Abbey in Warwickshire through his wife in 1581, and had been building and gardening there with enthusiasm for several years when, in 1603, he was entrusted with the care of Princess Elizabeth, daughter of King James. Created Lord Harington in that year, he kept the Princess at Combe until 1608, when she was allowed her own household at Kew, in which Harington continued as her senior advisor. A painting of her, aged 6 (c.1603), by Robert Peake the Elder shows her with a background of the Combe Abbey grounds – a wooded river scene, with an elaborate wooden temple-cum-arbour of several storeys to one side, a bridge and palisaded hunting ground to the other.[50] The *Memoirs Relating to the Queen of Bohemia* by 'one of her Ladies', and edited by Lady Frances Erskine around 1770, refer to these gardens in enticing but possibly inaccurate terms, which do however seem in accord with the background of Peake's painting. There was at Combe 'a little wilderness at the end of the Park, on the banks of a large brook ... [with] a small lake, in which there was an island covered with underwood and flowering trees and plants ... for nine months in the year they formed a continual spring'. Such phrases bring Sir Francis Bacon's 'Of Gardens' to mind, as well as the 'dell' at Hatfield and Bacon's Gorhambury. On the island there was also 'an aviary, the back and roof of which were formed of natural rock', and in the adjacent wilderness Lord Harington had built 'little wooden buildings in all the different orders of architecture'.[51]

Princess Elizabeth went on to marry Frederick, Elector Palatine, in 1613, becoming known as the 'Winter Queen', and was involved in the creation of the great terraced gardens at Heidelberg, designed by Salomon de Caus. Lord Harington had accompanied her on her journey out to Heidelberg, but died at Worms in 1613.

On his death, the Combe Abbey property was inherited by his daughter, Lucy Harington (c.1580–1627), and remained hers until 1622. We do not know if she continued with the gardens there, as all trace of them from that period has gone, obliterated by formal gardens in the 1680s, Capability Brown's landscaping in the 1770s, and further formal work in the 1860s. Lucy Harington's interest in gardens does seem, however, to have been considerable. In 1594 she married Edward Russell, 3rd Earl of Bedford, and in 1608 acquired the house and garden of Twickenham Park, which had been Sir Francis Bacon's until 1606. In 1609 Robert Smythson produced a plan of this property showing the firm geometrical design of the main garden – presumably Bacon's work – and also an empty rectangle above the house and to the right of the large formal garden, inscribed 'kichin gardin'. This, we may safely assume, was the centre for the Countess of Bedford's vegetable enthusiasm – in 1614, Giacomo Castelvetro dedicated his *Brief Account of the Fruit, Herbs and Vegetables of Italy* to the countess. We may imagine, charitably, that some of the vegetable ingredients for his and the Countess's recipes were sown, planted and harvested in this plot.[52]

At a grander level the Countess of Bedford may have influenced two other sites – Woburn Abbey in Bedfordshire and Moor Park in Hertfordshire. At Woburn, the grotto-room, which still survives, was built before the death of the 3rd Earl in 1627, and may indeed have been urged more by the Countess of Bedford than by her husband. The designer is not known, though it has been attributed on stylistic grounds to Isaac de Caus (1590–1648), who was to work for the 4th Earl of Bedford in London in the 1630s.[53] It is a large vaulted room, encrusted with shell and rockwork designs on walls and ceiling, and with several arched recesses which would have had water dripping down over the rough protuberances, though there do not seem to have been any water-jokes of the sort which Thomas Bushell installed at Enstone, or which we may still see at Schloss Hellbrunn near Salzburg. Hydraulic toys excepted, the Woburn Abbey grotto is probably as large and as sumptuous as the *influence Italian style* ←

Italian grottoes which English travellers had admired and wished to recreate, with an abundance of sea-gods and goddesses, shell-chariots, putti and dolphins. It is possible even to compare it with the Italianate grotto which Louis XIV had constructed at Versailles in 1666–7, holding Girardon's sculptured groups of Apollo, his horses, and the sea-goddess Thetis and her nymphs.[54] This comparison has a further validity, since the grottoes at Woburn and Versailles each mark a high point in the imitation of Italian practice, after which the developments in Britain and France were to take a somewhat different course. No other grotto of the size and character of the one at Woburn was made in Britain (though there were many smaller ones), and Louis XIV had his Versailles grotto destroyed, moving Girardon's sculptures to another part of the gardens.

The other property that the Countess of Bedford was involved with, Moor Park in Hertfordshire, came into the Bedford family in 1617, and according to Sir William Temple (1628–98), writing in 1685, the garden there was created by the Countess of Bedford, presumably not long before her death in 1627. However, in the next few years – until 1630 – the property belonged to the 3rd Earl of Pembroke (1580–1630), son of Mary, Countess of Pembroke, the sister of Sir Philip Sidney. The Earl (like his brother the 4th Earl) was interested in garden matters, and Temple's comments of 1685 on Moor Park, which look back to 'when [he] knew it about thirty years ago' and therefore to well after the Countess of Bedford's death, may therefore apply in truth to the garden of the 3rd Earl.

In the end, I think, the owners are less important than what happened. The Moor Park garden was laid out in the late 1620s or early 1630s, and from Temple's description, its plan ('the perfectest Figure of a Garden I ever saw') had a unity and overall harmony which was distinctly new. It brings us to a particular type of small or middle-sized garden which became common in Britain in the middle decades of the century, and which is discussed in the next chapter.

7

'THE BEST FIGURE OF A GARDEN'

Throughout the seventeenth century, many gardens were made, or extended, following the general lines of later Elizabethan and Jacobean garden practice, and varying according to the means and interests of the owners, the size of the ground available, and the disposition of the house and its related buildings. The garden areas were generally square or rectangular in plan and separated from each other by hedges or walls, allowing the different parts to be used in their different ways, for ornament, for amusement, and for the varied purposes of a 'working' garden-cum-farm – for herbs, vegetables, fruit, vines, bees and fish.

This general observation on the most common plan can be given precise reference, since sufficient examples survive or are documented to indicate its widespread acceptance through much of the seventeenth century as an 'average' or 'standard' design, and it was even praised as a kind of ideal garden model. The total garden area was usually modest, between half an acre and 2 acres, though occasionally rising to 4 or 5.

The pattern appears pictorially in William Lawson's *A New Orchard and Garden* of 1618. This is one of the best known of garden plans, enjoyed for the tiny figures in the six 'squares' or 'compartments', and for the comments at the side and in the main text. Lawson set out his advice in *A New Orchard* as the fruit of '48 years (and more) experience', which *might* suggest that the plan had been in his experience, known as a working model since the 1570s; his references to topiary and mazes have already been mentioned in comment on these features at Nonsuch in the 1580s (see page 73). But I am not aware of any garden scheme from that period which was closely comparable with Lawson's. More significant are the figures and comments, which imply again and again that the constituent parts are merely *suggested* as desirable, useful, pleasant elements, which must depend as always on the site, one's means and one's interests, though Lawson does suggest most persuasively that use and delight can be combined, with a mount at each corner of his site. Each mount bears a tiny building, two with stills to produce essences, medicines and liquors; and each mount overlooks a river – so that 'you might sit in your Mount, and angle a peckled Trout, sleighty Eel, or some other dainty Fish' – while the mounts themselves will be 'covered with Fruit-trees, Kentish Cherries, Damsons, Plums, etc', with 'stairs of precious workmanship; and in some corner (or more) a true Dial or Clock, and some Antick works' (i.e. a sundial and sculpture). To this Lawson adds the need – in one's mount – for 'silver-sounding Musick, mixt Instruments, and Voices, gracing all the rest'. To end, he asks – and we need not reply – 'How will you be wrapt with Delight?'[1]

Noticeable in the schematic nature of Lawson's plan are the *narrow* spaces to left and right, for large areas of 'walkes', 'Orchard' and 'stone-fruit', and the twice-repeated 'ifs', against the letters 'O' and 'P'. Apart from saying at letter 'B', 'Trees twenty yards asunder', there is no suggestion of size – length, breadth or acreage – at any point. We are left with the basic pattern – the house facing a rectangular garden area, divided lengthwise by a central walk or path and crosswise by two other walks, giving a pattern of six equal-sized squares, *possibly* on sloping ground, with some sort of terracing, and *possibly* with a river (or pond) at one end or the other, and symmetrically placed mounts at two or four of the corners.

Lawson was a country clergyman, and by no means wealthy. Most probably, therefore, his own garden, if it had this shape and most of the suggested features, came at the very largest to 3 or 4 acres, *including* the walks and orchard areas. The principal oblong of six squares was therefore likely to have covered no more than 2 acres, possibly less. Sir Francis Bacon's proposal in 1625 for a 'prince-like' scheme required 30 or more acres, and is of quite another nature – as is indeed the scheme laid out at Wilton from 1632 onwards, with a general plan not too dissimilar from Lawson's, but measuring 400 by 1,000 feet (over 9 acres) for the main rectangular area, without counting any outer parts (see Chapter 8).

More to the point is the Reverend Walter Stonehouse's orchard and flower garden in the 1630s, which contained a listed total of 866 different plants in an area little more than 2,000 square yards, or a trifle below half an acre.[2] Again, writing in the 1650s, Sir Thomas Hanmer allows that 'large grounds' with labyrinths and 'variety of alleys' may have to be between 5 and 12 acres, 'but it suffices most gentlemen to have only a square or oblong piece of ground of between three-quarters and one and a half acres'.[3] Not many years later, John Rea's *Flora, Ceres and*

Pomona of 1665 recommended a small, rather than a large, 'ill-furnished and ill-kept' garden, and suggested around half an acre for a gentleman and $1\frac{1}{2}$ acres for a nobleman, these areas to be divided into two parts, roughly one third for flowers, two-thirds for fruit. John Evelyn's garden at Sayes Court, near Deptford in Kent, came to occupy about 10 acres, no more, within a larger property of 100 acres or so, which remained as field and farmland.[4]

To finish this set of comments on the area of these seventeenth-century gardens, Sir William Temple's words in 1685 should be quoted, which bring us both to the size, the disposition and the details of the plan. Writing that English (and Dutch) gardens were generally smaller than those in Italy, while those in France and Brabant were of an intermediate size, Temple stated that 'our Gardens' were 'seldom exceeding four, six, or eight Acres, inclosed with Walls'.[5] A few pages later, design is discussed – the qualities needed for 'the best Figure of a Garden'. It has to be either 'a Square or an Oblong', and on flat or falling ground, sloping down from the house; and Temple thought the best of these to be 'an Oblong upon a Descent'. Because this entails terracing, steps and stairs, and levelling of the several areas, it is more costly than a flat garden, but it is preferable for 'the Beauty, the Air, the View'.[6]

Temple wrote from experience of the many variants on this type of garden which he must have seen, and particularly of two: his own, in Staplestown, Co. Carlow, where he lived from around 1655 until the early 1660s, and that of the Countess of Bedford at Moor Park in Hertfordshire, which he visited in the mid-1650s. The Irish garden, at Staplestown House, is not mentioned in Temple's writings, but it appears in a sketch made by Thomas Dineley in 1680, which shows it to have had the essential plan and size I have described.[7] Its rectangular outline, on falling ground, with the house set symmetrically at the upper end, corresponds with that of the garden at Moor Park in Hertfordshire. This was, Temple wrote in his essay of 1685, 'the perfectest Figure of a Garden I ever saw, either at home or abroad', and, according to him (we have no other witness of this now vanished garden), it had been made 'with very great care, excellent Contrivance, and much Cost' by the Countess of Bedford. This lady – born Lucy Harington, and married to Edward Russell, 3rd Earl of Bedford – died, like her husband, in 1627, which would mean that the garden was made before then, and I have suggested in the previous chapter that this garden might in fact have been laid out, or at least perfected, by the next owner, the 3rd Earl of Pembroke, in the years 1627–30.

For the detail, Temple explains that the Moor Park garden – 'an Oblong upon a Descent' – was exactly aligned with the house, which stood at the higher end of the site. The garden extended downwards in a sequence of three rectangular areas. The first was a gravelled terrace with bay trees (probably in tubs) and three sets of steps down to 'a very large Parterre'. The second area was quartered by paths, and adorned with eight statues and two fountains. Both the first and the second areas were flanked by colonnades (with balustraded walks above), and were therefore limited in their outlook to the upward (towards the house) and downward view. The third and lowest area – 'the lower Garden' – was again reached 'by many steps flying on each side of a Grotto that lies between them'. This was 'embellish'd with Figures of Shell-Rockwork, Fountains and Water-works', while the garden was 'all Fruit-trees ranged about the several Quarters of a Wilderness which is very shady' – an area divided by regular paths and given a 'wild' character (in comparison with the open gravelled terrace and parterre above) by the upward and sideways growth of the trees.

This 'sweetest place ... may serve for a Pattern to the best Gardens of our manner', Temple concludes; and then he speculates, whether 'other Forms wholly irregular' may not exist, which may 'be very agreeable', and relates that the Chinese (so he has heard from travellers) love gardens which are 'without any order or disposition of parts' – a quality they call 'the *Sharawadgi*'. Swiftly, Temple rejects the thought of imitating this irregularity, and turns to praising a foursquare garden he has heard of at the Cape of Good Hope, quartered (like the Botanic Garden at Oxford) to receive 'the Trees, Fruits, Flowers, and Plants that are native and proper to each of the four parts of the World ... There could not be in my mind ... a nobler Idea of a Garden'.[8] (Temple's reference to the *Sharawadgi* was then forgotten for many years, until first Joseph Addison in *The Spectator* (no.414) in 1712, and then others – Alexander Pope in 1724 and Robert Castell in 1728 – took it up as one of the excuses for the new 'landscape' gardening.)

Between Lawson's plan of 1618 and Temple's 1685 recollection of what he had seen around 1655 – that is, between the sketched *suggestion* of an ideal and the *description* of its achievement – there are many examples, differing according to the house, the site, the means and the interests of the owner. Having indicated their general shape, and the range of size, a further selection, in rough chronological order, may be added to show their geographical spread, and the wide differences in their detail.

In England there were Wakerley in Northamptonshire and Snitterton Hall in Derbyshire. Wakerley is now an archaeological site, as the house – built soon after 1613 for Sir Richard Cecil – was demolished in 1633, and the property was abandoned. The outlines of house and gardens, closely adhering to the type I have defined, remain visible in aerial

The sunken knot garden with maze beside the Old Palace at Hatfield. Created by Lady Salisbury in 1980–1, the patterns are strictly faithful to those appearing in Elizabethan sources.

Dineley's sketch of Sir William Temple's house and garden, in Staplestown, Co. Carlow. It has the essential layout of what Temple later called 'the best Figure of a garden'.

Thomas Dineley's 1684 sketch of 'Trouscoad' or Trawscoed (anglice Crosswood) in Dyfed shows again the standard layout of many seventeenth-century gardens, an enclosed, geometrical scheme aligned on the house.

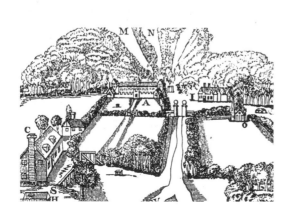

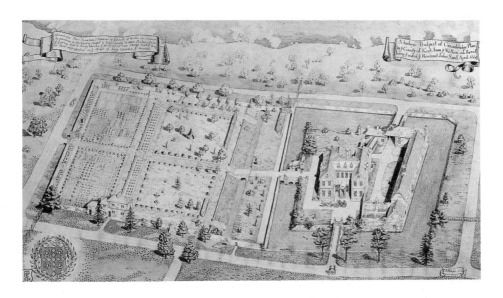

C. E. Kempe's drawing of the house and garden at Groombridge Place in 1884. The layout dates from the 1670s, and has been accurately maintained ever since.
© Country Life

A garden in the French manner was laid out at Longford Castle in the 1660s, largely obliterated by Capability Brown, and then restored. The present herbaceous scheme outlines earlier formality.

photographs, having been altered little or not at all in the 20 years of their active use.[9] At Snitterton Hall, however, a similar garden was created from 1631 onwards, but was progressively extended, or altered, in later periods, so that additional areas of garden extend to the side of the original plan.[10]

In 1635 Sir William Brereton travelled through Scotland and Ireland. Upon landing in Ireland, at Carrickfergus in Co. Antrim, he noted especially Joymount, the property of Sir Edward Chichester (d. 1648). Here the rectangular layout I have outlined was apparent: matching the balanced proportions of the main rooms of the house were a 'fine garden and mighty spacious orchards', with a pair of dove houses (pigeon cotes) 'placed one opposite to the other in the corner of the garden, and 'twixt the garden and orchards'.[11]

At Hillesden in Buckinghamshire, a new house, on a new site, was built in the late 1640s by Sir Alexander Denton, after the first house there had been destroyed in 1644. On falling ground before the house, a new garden was made, with the components of parterre and terrace, a second terrace overlooking a rectangular pool or 'canal', and a further, firmly embanked terrace with a curved, nearly semi-circular 'bastion' at the centre, aligned – as all the rest of the scheme – with the centre of the house and with fine views further downhill. This new house was destroyed early in the nineteenth century, but the garden outline is shown on the 1833 1-inch O.S. map (sheet 45), and the lowest terrace with its curved centre section can still be seen.

At Hillesden, the erection of a new house allowed a fully axial garden scheme to be laid out, while the fall of the land governed the number of terraces. At Groombridge in Kent, another new house was built (approximately between 1652 and 1674) within the site of an older, moated building. While the new building was given a regular form, with which the garden outside the moat could be aligned, the garden itself, an enclosed rectangle of $3\frac{1}{2}$ acres, was laid out on ground which rises *up* northwards from the house, so that each of the crosswise divisions of the garden constitutes an embankment or small terrace-walk, lifting the level of the ground higher and higher as it gets further from the house. The central north-south path, aligned on the house, is broken by short flights of steps at these crossings, and also rises steadily through the main rectangular areas as they slope upwards. It achieves an interest which few such long straight paths can share, through the slight changes in level and the varied forms of hedge which flank it, with occasional gate-piers or steps to suggest 'here is something new' – anticipating by many years the 'enticement principle' of Hidcote and Sissinghurst. As in the Lawson plan and in a few other examples of this garden type, there is a long

[handwritten margin note: old sites → being re-used].

walk – at Groombridge, named 'Paradise Walk' – running the length of the garden, *outside* the garden wall, and itself enclosed on the outer, eastern side by a privet hedge.

It has been suggested that John Evelyn advised the owner, Philip Packer, on the design of the garden, while the new house was being constructed. His comment (*Diary*, 6 August 1674) that there was 'a far better' site for the house nearby, 'on a graceful ascent', might however imply that Evelyn was not satisfied with what had been done, and would have preferred the house to be *above* the garden, with views downwards toward the old moated site. Without more details, one may merely reflect that at his own garden at Sayes Court he aimed for a considerable variety of features, and seemed not to be interested in the quality of overall balance. At Groombridge the gardens have received devoted attention since the 1880s, and their present pre-eminence may not have been so striking in 1674.

Beginning in 1654, another garden of this type and size was made at Coltness near Altertoun in Clydesdale, for the newly-married Thomas (later Sir Thomas) Stewart.[12] He enlarged the existing house, set the farm in order, and refashioned the garden – an area of 3–4 acres Scots, or some 5 acres English measure. Here his work was largely from scratch – the gardens were 'much improven and inlarged'. The main area, south of the house, was in the general pattern I have been describing, but affected by the lie of the land, which sloped sideways, falling from east to west; and the *use* of the garden was much more practical than in many other examples.

The slope of the ground meant that the first garden area in front of the house had to 'fall into three cross taresses'. 'The tarras fronting the south of the house was a square parterre, or flour-garden', while the areas to east and west, 'the higher and lower plots of ground', 'were for cherry and nut gardens'. On the eastern side, above the cherry and nut plantations, were walnuts and chestnuts (presumably *Castanea sativa*, the Spanish or edible chestnut), and on 'the slope bank' east of the parterre was a 'strawberry border'.

The rectangular area then extended south (and probably with a continuing east-west slope) with 'a high stone wall, for ripening and improving finer fruits', and with 'a good orchard and kitchen garden, with broad grass walks, all inclosed with a good thorn hedge; and without this a ditch and dry fence, inclosing several rows of timber trees for shelter'. The latter are a variant on Lawson's walks outside the principal garden, this time designed as wind-break and plantation combined.

The modest yet practical scheme of the Coltness garden must be compared with another garden, far larger (some 14 acres including the house), laid out in Ireland, at Listowel in Co. Kerry, between 1661 and 1668.[13] This scheme was executed by William Fitzmaurice, 20th Baron of Kerry (1633–97), who succeeded his father in 1660. In the early 1660s, he had the house remodelled to a design by Inigo Jones, and laid out an aligned area of gardens and orchards which corresponded closely in its outline with the framework of the Lawson plan, and indeed with Temple's 'perfectest Figure of a Garden'. With a central axis dividing the ground, three equal areas extended away from the house, flanked by two 'walks' on one side and a strip of woodland on the other. The three garden areas, extending from the house, were 'the Lawn', the kitchen gardens and the apple orchards. While much of this area has reverted to agricultural use, ditches remain to indicate most of the boundaries and divisions, and may be compared with the 'ditch and dry fence' extensively used at Coltness in the same period, often in combination with 'a good thorn hedge'. There were apparently no water features at either Coltness or Listowel, and at Listowel, being a level site, there was no element of terracing either.

In Wales, between the 1660s and 1684, a further group of these gardens appeared. In 1684 Thomas Dineley accompanied the Duke of Beaufort on a 'progress' through the Principality, and his manuscript account is copiously illustrated, including sketches of houses, some with courtyards and gardens. Particularly striking is his view of 'Trouscoad' (Trawscoed or Crosswood) in Montgomeryshire, built in the early seventeenth century. Tredegar in Monmouthshire and Ruperra Castle in Mid-Glamorgan (completed 1626) also fit into this garden pattern.[14] Dineley's sketches can be paralleled by a painting of 1662 – the anonymous view of *Massey's Court, Llanerch*.[15] This garden, in Denbighshire, was laid out apparently after the owner, Mutton Davies, had returned from his Grand Tour in Italy, and because the scheme included statuary, a step-cascade to one side and fountains, it has been suggested that it was 'Italian' in character.[16] This is, however, a misreading of the details for the whole. The Llanerch garden had once again the standard seventeenth-century plan I have been describing, with a main, enclosed rectangle of garden areas split into three smaller rectangles, divided from each other by terraces. In this instance, the house (obviously older than the garden) stood to one side of the first and highest garden area, and lesser plots, with fruit trees or vegetables, extended to the sides, as the site allowed. As in Lawson's plan, summerhouses stood at several corners of the enclosures, and at the foot of the Llanerch garden, parallel plantations of trees sloped down to a circular pool with a Neptune figure in the centre – aligned on the central axis – another variant on the 'river' which may run 'under your Mount' in Lawson.

The 1660s gardens at Llanerch were firmly swept away by 'landscaping' in the eighteenth century, but in the late 1920s a formal garden framework was restored near the house, designed by Percy Cane (see page 316). As at Llanerch in the 1660s, a large 'river', or at least a linked set of pools, was the last or lowest feature of the garden at Sudbury Hall in Derbyshire, begun around 1660 and finished by 1670. This is shown in another painting, by J. Griffer or Griffier,[17] displaying the layout as seen from the bottom of the garden, looking up towards the house. Like the Llanerch garden, this one has an enclosed main rectangle (aligned here with the new house), with a first terrace adorned with urns and statues, then a large quartered lawn with four statues and a central fountain, then a lawn – it might have been termed a 'wilderness' – planted with evergreens and with another central fountain. From this last enclosed area, iron gates, and steps, led out to a broad transverse walk and to the set of pools, which – like the Llanerch pool – had a central statue of Neptune with a trident. To left and right of the main scheme were long plantations with 'walks'.

These examples may be continued with another 'wished-for' or 'ideal' (though modest) scheme, that of John Aubrey for his property at Easton Piercy in Wiltshire. In 1669, he considered modifying his house and refashioning his garden, but did not carry out the scheme – 'I sold it in 1669', he wrote in his *Natural History of Wiltshire* but his sketches and a few notes survive to demonstrate what he would have liked to do. As at Llanerch and at Sudbury, there would be have been classical and Italian features, more indeed than in any of the other examples I have discussed. Aubrey was, after all, an antiquarian. He would have included several sculptures, in and out of grottoes, and fountains, and the outside of the house would have been reshaped to resemble an Italian villa. Yet his garden would have been both small – barely over an acre in area, compared with 2–3 acres for Sudbury and 2 acres for Llanerch – and firmly based on the type of plan I have described. It was to have been an enclosed rectangle, aligned with the house, and divided into three roughly equal areas by terraces. This 'oblong upon a descent', as Temple called it, would have had in this instance a stream crossing the lowest area, rather than passing outside the enclosure. The 'lie of the land', a neighbouring house, and the boundaries of the property would have dictated a slight irregularity in the 'walk' to one side and in the enclosure of the lowest area. Both Lawson and Temple, and Stewart at Coltness, would have seen Aubrey's design as yet another variation upon a shared and much copied scheme.

Towards the end of the seventeenth century this 'type' of garden plan became less common, while the greater garden schemes become ever more diffuse and extensive. The last, and one of the fullest proposals to incorporate the rectangular plan divided into three sections, aligned with the house at one end, is set out in 'An Essay of a Country House', printed at the end of Timothy Nourse's *Campania Foelix* of 1700. Much of this book is to do with husbandry, rather than gardening, and Nourse's enthusiasm for trees may be traced back to John Evelyn. Yet, from the start, he is emphatic that man, and man-directed order, must correct the 'Original Curse of Thorns and Bryers' which permeates the vegetable world. This order is especially apparent in the garden scheme he outlines at the end of the book.

Each of the three areas measures 120 by 60 yards, giving an overall length to the garden of 180 yards, and an area of just over $4\frac{1}{2}$ acres. In contrast to most of the examples of this type, Nourse's garden has the house set at the *bottom* end of the plot, with the three areas rising up, and divided by terraces 9 feet high. A central axis, aligned with the house, runs the length of the garden, as do walks or paths along the sides, with steps up at each terrace. As with earlier examples, the part by the house is laid out with borders, flowers and evergreens, and a central sculptured fountain; the second area contains dwarf fruit 'as Cherries, Apples, some choice Pears, &c. cut and shap'd into little round hollow Bushes'; and the third area – like Temple's wilderness in 1685 – is wholly 'design'd for Boscage', with a great variety of trees, evergreen or deciduous, and with a wealth of flowers growing beneath. It is indeed a conscious imitation of a part of Sir Francis Bacon's 'princely garden', aiming to 'represent a perpetual Spring'.

Yet Nourse's scheme ends with another matter – the view outwards from the highest point of the garden:

> ... and thus at length the Prospect may terminate on Mountains, Woods, or such Views as the Scituation will admit of.

Bacon had said nothing of this, nor Lawson nor Temple in describing the arrangement of the 'best Figure of a Garden'. Nourse looks forward – to gardens which look outward, to the landscape beyond.

8

'THE NOBLEST IN ALL ENGLAND'

In 1632 Isaac de Caus began to lay out the new garden at Wilton in Wiltshire for the 4th Earl of Pembroke, and his work continued for some years, being to some extent complete by 1635. He followed this, in 1636, with extensive remodelling of the south front of Wilton House, working with advice from Inigo Jones, with whom he had already collaborated on the Banqueting House at Whitehall.[1]

Isaac de Caus was either the brother or nephew of Salomon de Caus, and must have had considerable experience of Salomon de Caus' work, both through his actual garden creation at Heidelberg, and through his two garden-related books, the *Raisons des forces mouvantes* of 1615 and the *Hortus Palatinus* of 1620. Features from the garden and the books, such as details of the fountains and the grotto, and of the elaborate 'carpenter's work' designs for the hedges, were more or less duplicated at Wilton. Though de Caus' work at Wilton has practically all disappeared (only his grotto façade survives, having been moved to another part of the grounds), we know a great deal about it from the book *Wilton Garden*, published around 1645 and generally attributed to de Caus, and from later drawings, particularly those of William Stukeley.[2] De Caus obliterated the earlier garden made by Adrian Gilbert (see page 76), and laid out an oblong scheme, 400 by 1,000 feet, conceived from the outset as being exactly related to a new south front for Wilton House, virtually twice the width of the existing building. By 1635 the garden had been laid out, and its main lines were to survive until the early eighteenth century, imposing, symmetrical, and no doubt, as John Evelyn wrote on 20 July 1654, for many years 'the noblest in all *England*'. Yet even in its infancy, this garden was robbed of a part of its intended majesty. In 1635, the Earl of Pembroke experienced severe financial difficulties, aggravated

in the next few years,[3] and the proposed design for the new south front
to Wilton House was reduced, so that it extended only half-way across
the garden – from its eastern side to the central north-south axis. Stukeley's view of 1723 shows this with poignant clarity. The 'new' south
front is grand enough, in all conscience, and we admire it unreservedly
today. Yet it is only a part of what the initial garden design envisaged.[4]

This explanation of the early stages of Isaac de Caus' garden and house
scheme at Wilton helps, I hope, to make clear the importance, and the
novelty, of his work. The garden was deeply different from the earlier
creation of Salomon de Caus at Heidelberg, in that it was exactly calculated in relation to the house. The main view in the book *Wilton Garden*
shows it from a somewhat raised viewpoint, as if from a terrace, balcony,
or *piano nobile* in the house itself. This view may be compared at once
with similar views of the Luxembourg Gardens in Paris, laid out in the
1620s, where in 1644 (he had not been in France before) John Evelyn
wrote with interest and astonishment that

> ... the Parterr is indeede of box; but so rarely designd, and accurately kept cut; that
> the mbrodery makes a stupendious effect to the Lodgings which front it.[5]

Evelyn's comment shows how new was the idea, for an Englishman, of
patterns executed principally in box (the Elizabethans, as we have seen,
used edgings of much more variety) and of a layout which was deliberately
planned to go with the 'Lodgings', the garden front, of the house. The
French themselves were aware of the novelty of their garden designs
from the early 1600s, noting their difference from traditional Italian
schemes, and by about 1608 a visitor from England, Thomas Coryate,
had remarked on this at the Tuileries in Paris and at Fontainebleau.[6] The
French term *parterre* implies a design which is *on* or *along the ground*,
and which is therefore meant to be seen from a higher, slightly raised
viewpoint, as from a terrace or the upper windows of a house. The
parterre, whether a single design or one composed of several elements
divided by walks, tends therefore to have an overall unity, related to that
viewpoint – unlike a group of 'knots', which may be of widely different
patterns even if their normally square outlines are of equal size.

This appears instantly from the main view of the Wilton garden. Here
the parterre is in the area closest to the house, extending in equal and
exactly identical sections to the right and left of the main axis. Next
comes an area of clipped trees, again divided exactly to left and right,
and crossed by the irregular but carefully concealed course of the River
Nadder, and lastly, furthest from the house, is the relatively open and

simply laid out area of lawn and paths leading to the grotto at the end of the central axis. The grotto, fitted with hydraulic jokes and toys, and adorned with sculpture, was comparable with that at Greenwich, built by 1613, and the contemporary 'desolate Cell of Natures rarities' elaborated by Thomas Bushell at Enstone. The 4th Earl of Pembroke was, like the 3rd Earl, a son of Mary, Countess of Pembroke, sister of Sir Philip Sidney. In the Wilton grotto, there was a final echo of Basilius' summerhouse and aviary, from Sidney's *The Countess of Pembroke's Arcadia*. Beyond the grotto, to the south, the ground rose up, and by 1700 the axis was extended towards a statue of Marcus Aurelius on the skyline.

The controlled gradation of detail, from the elaborate uniformity of the parterre to the open grass and sparsely planted trees before the grotto, is confirmed in the detailed pictures from de Caus' *Wilton Garden*. All is related to the house, so that the best, the master view, is obtained from the house itself, from the slightly raised position of the *piano nobile*. The accompanying text refers to a 'little Terrass raised for the more advantage of beholding' the details of the embroidery and flanking beds of flowers – a further indication that these features were meant to be viewed from above. De Caus' garden at Wilton was in its essential lines attempting, and achieving, what designers in France had been striving to create since around 1600: a unified design, in which all parts are related, and have their individual interest in relation to the one controlling viewpoint – the principal rooms of the house.

Grandeur – Restrained

If we enquire, why Wilton's example encouraged so few followers, we find two simple and related answers. First, Wilton was a project for house and garden combined, and on the grandest scale, whose emulation might not have seemed appropriate in smaller properties; and second, the worsening political situation, leading to the outbreak of the Civil War in 1642, discouraged grand building and grand gardening. It is no coincidence that from 1642 until the Restoration in 1660 garden history in Britain is notably concerned, not with 'gardening grandly', but with the quieter, more modest and practical activities of botany, plant collection, the growing of fruit and vegetables, and with writing about these things while living in rural retirement (see Chapter 8).

One garden in the French style did in fact come quickly after Wilton – or a least a part of one, at Wimbledon. Charles I had bought the property in 1639, and in the refurbishment of the earlier garden scheme he had the area southwards from the house redesigned by the French gardener André Mollet in 1642, and an area to the east altered to become an 'orange garden', with a large orangery built to one side. From a later view of Wimbledon from the south, dated 1678,[7] which offers a glimpse of scrollwork parterres aligned with the south front of the mansion, we may venture to assume that Mollet laid these out in 1642 – he had had considerable experience, and published *Le Jardin de plaisir* in 1651 with numerous parterre designs. In 1649, however, this garden area – the 'lower level' of the 'upper or great garden' – was said by the Parliamentary Surveyors to contain in the 'middlemost' area 'eight several squares, and well ordered knotts' – knots, rather than parterres.[8] It may well be that the Surveyors' concern with garden terminology was slight, set beside the need for urgent and competent valuation – they reckoned that the plants in the knots, the box borders and the 'Flanders bricks' used as pavers were 'worth £60', with £20 more for the central alley of paved stone, and a further £29.8s. for the 'rails, spired posts, and statues' in this area. The rails and posts went round the 'knotts', much as they had done in Henry VIII's gardens at Hampton Court, and we may question therefore whether Mollet's work was really all that different from the earlier pattern laid out in the 1590s, and recorded by Robert Smythson in 1609.

The 'Oringe Garden', however, as described by the Surveyors, was both the same in area and general layout as the space in Smythson's plan, and yet suddenly different. While before it was, no more, no less, an enclosed garden with four knots and a central fountain, it had now become a place for special plants – citrus trees – with a special building, 'one large Garden House ... fitted for the keeping of Oringe trees ... worth £66.13s.4d.'. Here (the survey is dated 'November 1649') were 'now standing in square boxes, fitted for that purpose, forty-two Oringe trees bearing fair and large oringes ...'. A lemon tree and 'one Pomecitrus tree' was also kept in this building, and '6 Pomegranet trees' and other young orange trees were overwintered elsewhere.[9]

This new building for the royal garden at Wimbledon may be linked with a similar building in the garden of the palace at Oatlands in Surrey. Here in 1633 'an orrenge Garden' was enclosed 'for the keeping of orange trees in winter', and given an 'adjoyning ... shedd' and 'Colehouse'. John Tradescant (the elder) was in charge, and made a bowling green nearby at the same time.[10] The 'shedd' with the 'Colehouse' may count, until further candidates are proposed, as the first orangery in England. The word 'orangerie' – meaning a place to keep orange trees – appeared for the first time in France in 1603, and plant fanciers in France and in

England had already tried to grow them. Much later, John Evelyn, and then J. Gibson, claimed that Sir Francis Carew at Beddington in Surrey (see page 79) was the first to grow and to shelter orange trees in England, but Carew's building was in fact a permanent *cover*, built over the trees, rather than a special building to which they were taken in the winter, like the 'Shedd' at Oatlands or the 'large Garden House' at Wimbledon.

In this period – between 1630 and 1660 – there was no doubt much garden development, but there is little evidence of anything of a grand, foreign or adventurous nature. In the 1620s King Charles' favourite, George Villiers, 1st Duke of Buckingham did set off garden works at New Hall in Essex and at Burley-on-the Hill in Leicestershire, and Buckingham, one might think, would have been in touch with the new French style – John Evelyn, at least, could record in his *Diary* for 14 August 1654 that Burley was *à la moderne*. Both at New Hall and at Burley, Buckingham planted trees with enthusiasm – a task which was probably supervised by John Tradescant (the elder) – and the various avenues at New Hall were admired in their early maturity by Evelyn (*Diary*, 10 July 1656), especially the mile-long quadruple avenue of limes leading to the south front of the mansion. These limes were felled in 1798, and the approach drive has since been shortened and replanted as a single but still impressive avenue. Something similar was achieved for the eastern approach to Burley-on-the-Hill, to judge from a plan copied from a mid-seventeenth-century original.[12] Lesser avenues are also indicated on this plan, aligned on the house from south-east, south-west and west-south-west, and there are three descending terraces to the south, which would have given not only a commanding view to those who were there, but also revealed the house in its place of authority on the crest of the slope. This house was destroyed in the Civil War, but the *grandes lignes* of the terraces and some of the avenues were taken up again in the late 1690s to make one of the most impressive formal layouts in the country.

The partial destruction of the garden layout at Burley-on-the-Hill in the Civil War, and its re-establishment later in the century is typical of the fate of several gardens set out in the pre-war period, and the lack of clear detail to do with their first form sometimes makes it hard to say whether what was begun in the 1630s and 40s did or did not respond to the new ideas on garden design which were then active in France. This is, I think, the case at Longford Castle in Wiltshire, where a formal garden to the south of the castle is shown in a view of about 1680 by Robert Thacker.[13] Probably, this layout was the one restored around 1654, after a pre-war garden on this site had been damaged in the conflict, but this is not a certainty. Similarly, Jan Sieberechts' paintings of the garden at Longleat in Wiltshire, executed between 1675 and 1678, show

The steeply sloping terraces at Powis Castle were probably begun by William Winde in 1697.
Italianate in feeling, they survived the threat of 'landscaping' by William Emes in the 1780s.

This walk at Barncluith in Lanarkshire is part of a 1690s scheme of five terraces overlooking
the steep, wooded valley of the river Avon – 'a very Romantick Garden'.

a small, but regular scheme aligned with the front of the house.[14] While this in its simplicity (two square lawns, each with a circular fountain, flanking the central path) and its symmetrical alignment is essentially post-Restoration in spirit, it is known that a garden existed on this site in the later sixteenth century. At what point, or points, did the stages of its century-long transformation occur? Even the stage marked by Sieberechts' paintings did not last. As at Burley-on-the-Hill, the formal scheme at Longleat of the 1670s was to be enlarged immensely by the end of the century.

Survivals – Knots and Mounts

Though a regular 'type' of garden developed in the middle decades of the seventeenth century, and though the new French formality had briefly made an appearance at Wilton in the 1630s, the design of most gardens did not alter noticeably until the 1670s or later. Indeed, the development of garden design and the laying out of big new gardens might both be said to have slumbered throughout the 1640s and 1650s, during the troubles leading to the Civil War (which began in 1642) and the execution of Charles I in 1649, and during the ensuing Commonwealth, which ended with the restoration of Charles II in 1660. Instead we may discern a more modest form of garden activity, sometimes linked with a prudent retirement from public life, and coupled again and again with a deep interest either in garden flowers, often including botanic enquiry, or in useful gardening (allied with husbandry in general), or in both. Obviously these interests did not begin to develop only when England moved towards the Civil War. That merely provided further reasons for modest rather than innovative, for studious and practical rather than ostentatious gardening.

We must first consider a few remarkable survivals of Jacobean (or even Elizabethan) garden features, which led towards the plant enthusiasms of the mid-seventeenth century. The garden of St Augustine's at Canterbury is of interest here, since it began as a monastic garden, became royal property at the Dissolution, and later, in 1612, was acquired by Edward, Lord Wotton (1548–1625; he was half-brother to Sir Henry Wotton, whose garden enthusiasm has already been noted – see page 104). The buildings which remained from the monastery were still considerable, and the grounds covered more than 20 acres. Here in 1615 came John Tradescant (the elder), who was in charge of the gardens intermittently until around 1623, and to whom may be attributed both the cultivation of several choice or uncommon plants, and the design and elaboration of the garden plan.[15]

The garden at St Augustine's had numerous features, and in 1635 these were outlined by a visitor with an eye for gardens, Lieutenant Hammond (he commented shrewdly on the new garden at Wilton, and on Bushell's grotto at Enstone in the same year). Hammond tells of 'the faire gardens and Orchards, sweet walkes, Labirinthlike wildernesses and Groves; rare Mounts and Fountaines', which, with the buildings, made up 'neere 20. or 30. Acres'. The 'honest Head Gardiner' led him along the 'long walkes', into the 'pretty contriv'd wooddy Mazes' and up the 'high Mounts'. Most of all in 'this delicate Garden and Paradise', with its orchard and fruit, its long lime-tree walk and 'fragrant, and delicious Flowers', he admired a fountain:

> ... a neet and curiously contriv'd Fountaine, of pure cleere water, knee deep and 4. square, and in the midst a little greene Island and Charon in his Boat; upon the Banke lyes Snakes, Scorpions and strange Fishes, which spout forth water about the Ferrimans eares and his Dog's, which is convey'd away by the turning of a Cocke.[16]

Once again the type of ornamental water feature described has already been remarked on at Beddington, Hatfield, Greenwich and Gorhambury. Hammond's visit was in 1635, some 12 years after Tradescant's work at St Augustine's had stopped. That the features from Tradescant's time were still maintained, however, is indirectly confirmed by a plan of the garden and surrounding area dating from about 1642,[17] showing the grounds divided into two areas of trees (probably orchards) and three large separate square areas of knots, each divided by walks. By the 1640s, such knots – geometrical, and one definitely 'labyrinthine', and remarkably similar to the circles (with 'ears' or 'bastions') set within squares at Sir Francis Bacon's Twickenham garden – were distinctly old-fashioned, being in essence the same as those illustrated in the *Maison rustique* of 1600, or William Lawson's *Country House-wife's Garden* of 1617. The property was still occupied by Lord Wotton's widow, Lady Margaret (1581–1659), who experienced difficulties to do with recusancy for many years, which may well have restrained her from changing her garden.

Knots may have been old-fashioned in the 1640s, but they survived in many British gardens until the end of the century as simple geometrical patterns (often no more than *strips* of box hedging, with gravel of one or more colours in the spaces). Two further instances from the 1640s may be cited. The first was at Bishopscourt in the Isle of Man, where in the late 1640s Daniel King sketched two views of the gardens. While one shows a bowling green edged with low clipped hedges to the east of the medieval buildings, the western view shows a layout of four different knots, divided by walks, and enclosed by low hedges.[18] While the different geometrical plans of these knots are clear enough, one cannot tell what plants were involved.

The other example is at Darfield in Yorkshire, where Walter Stonehouse (1597–1655) laid out a pattern of four knots in a virtually square plot, with a fifth knot to one side. Stonehouse was rector at Darfield from 1631, and in 1640 he drew up plans of his knots, and an alphabetical list of the plants in his garden. The list was revised in 1644, with a total of 866 different plants. On the plans, the 'best garden', which contains the five knots, has letters and numbers along the borders and beside each part of each knot to indicate which plants are set at each and every point – in the five main knots, there are 158 different kinds.[19] A devoted plant collector as well as gardener, Stonehouse had links with several of the most noted plant enthusiasts of his time. His garden had another feature of a traditional kind – running north-south beside his orchard there was a narrow 'mount or high walke', 80 feet long and lined with seven cherry trees to the west and eight 'olde plum-trees' to the east.

The mount, like the knot, was a feature of some antiquity by the 1640s. Most often a single raised hillock, to give a view (whether over the garden or further afield), it could also be a raised walk – we might think not much different from a terrace – and if of reasonable length, then good enough for a bowling alley. In one form or the other, with or without an accompanying building, it lived on until well into the eighteenth century. Before returning to Walter Stonehouse and his love of plants, other mounts of this period should be recorded.

Two notable fortress-mounts survive at Dunham Massey in Greater Manchester and at Marlborough in Wiltshire. The former appears in several views of the 1690s, showing rings of low hedges and a small tower at the top, though it is now no more than a hillock with trees. The latter was visited by John Evelyn on 9 June 1654 – 'the Mount; to which we ascend winding for neere halfe a mile: It seemes to have been cast up by hand'.[20] 'Cast up by hand' it was, being a Norman motte-and-bailey. The winding path upwards (as at Wressle in the East Riding, described by John Leland in the 1540s) remains at Marlborough today, while an eighteenth-century grotto in the side of the mount was readorned by Simon Verity in the 1980s. Another possible fortress-mount is glimpsed briefly in a painting of about 1640–50 of Aylesford Friary in Kent,[21] where a steep, possibly conical mount stands to one side of the mansion. Steps lead upwards, but the top – platform or summerhouse or even a chapel? – is hidden by trees. Right at the edge of the painting, a turf or low-hedged maze is dimly seen.

For pleasure, there were mounts at St Augustine's in Canterbury and another at Burley-on-the-Hill in Leicestershire by the 1620s (when John Tradescant (the elder) was working first for Lord Wotton at St Augustines and later for the Duke of Buckingham at Burley). The mount at Burley, well to the west of the house, overlooked a bowling green. Several such mounts were tiny, little more than a 'pimple', like the 'promontory' overlooking the water at Beckett Park, near Shrivenham in Oxfordshire, on which a summerhouse (or fishing or Chinese pavilion) was built around 1635, designed possibly by Inigo Jones.[22] Another 'pimple'-like mount was in the garden at Boscobel in Shropshire. Surmounted by a small summerhouse, it was there in 1651, when it was used for part of one Sunday by King Charles, who 'commended the place for its retiredness'.[23] Equally small was the mount in the garden at Wadham College, Oxford – part of a scheme laid out in 1651. This mount has now gone, but is clearly shown in an engraving by David Loggan in *Oxonia illustrata* (1675). Standing at the centre of a set of four square beds, each quartered by low hedges, the mount has a single flight of steps up to the platform at the top, where a statue of Atlas holds a globe on his head. Nearby, at New College, a mound or mount had existed close to the city wall since 1529–30, when 500 wagon-loads of rubbish were tipped there. Why there, and for what purpose is not made plain, but a substantial mount was created and remained there, receiving occasional attention from the college gardener in the 1590s and in the following decades.[24] In 1647 the mount was used for the celebration of Prince Charles' birthday, and then, early in 1649, 'perfected with steps of stone' and hedges round the walks. Engravings by Loggan in 1675 and by William Williams in 1732 show the mount with a four-sided pyramidal shape and two separate walks, linked by steps, below a final square platform at the top. Between the college buildings and the mount there were four square knots, aligned on the central steps. One was laid out with the royal arms, one with the arms of the college founder, William of Wykeham, one with a strap-work pattern, and one set out as a sundial. Both mount and knots survived in this form until well on into the eighteenth century, around 1760, when the knots were removed in favour of open lawn, and the mount – or mound, as it is now called – was 'landscaped' as a grassy tumulus, with plantings of trees which have since risen dense and irregular over the old symmetrical structure.

Not all mounts were square or circular in plan; sometimes they were a kind of terrace, and notable examples were made. Sir Edwin Sandys (1561–1629) took possession of Northbourne in Kent in 1613 or 1614, and shortly afterwards built Northbourne Court, with an impressive and, I think, unique garden enclosure facing the mansion. Bar a few ruins, the house has gone – almost completely demolished in 1750 – but the great brick-walled terraced enclosure, 75 yards wide and 200 yards long, still stands as it did in the 1620s, a wholly 'artificial' construction, involving a double terrace to left and right and a triple terrace at the far end of the U-shaped structure. The view outwards, over fairly level fields, is not exciting, and I would think that the mount-terraces at Northbourne Court were intended mainly to provide *inward* views, down to the enclosed lawn, over to the mansion, up from the mansion, and from one part of the raised terraces to another – as they do today, with superb plantings along each level, and along each side.

Northbourne lacks contemporary comment, as does the decoy-garden at Tackley Manor in Oxfordshire, though there is an excellent illustration of its plan. Here a highly formal group of ponds – so formal as to be 'ornamental', but serving as valuable fishponds and decoys – was laid out around 1620 (a gateway bears this date), possibly for John Harborne, owner of Tackley Manor between 1612 and 1651. In 1623, the 3rd edition of Gervase Markham's *Cheape and Good Husbandry* was embellished with the plan 'for the better satisfaction and delight' of those who want to lay out good fishponds.[25] The plan shows a scheme of four ponds, two square and two triangular, each containing an island or rather a peninsula, since the appropriate square and triangular islands are each connected to the mainland by a narrow isthmus (or causeway). Each island rises up in turn to a mount, while at the upper end of the layout, beyond the two square ponds, the ground is dug out and raised to provide a long terrace-walk (or mount – it is called such in the plan). This has a fine view over the ponds and their separate mounts, and is both long and broad enough to serve as a promenade and bowling green – just like the raised walks at the end of the formal gardens at Hamstead Marshall in Berkshire, begun in the 1660s, and at Kirby Hall in Northamptonshire, begun in 1685.

Mounts and John Evelyn

John Evelyn (1620–1706), the diarist, traveller, founder-member of the Royal Society, writer of 30-odd books and pamphlets on a multitude of topics, was also – and with emphasis – an enthusiast for gardens, gardeners and plants, and their history in all its ramifications.

We may begin with his concern with several mounts, as they bring together the different types and uses I have outlined, and indicate also the variety of his interests, which were only slightly affected by the nascent French garden style. In May 1643, following his father's death in December 1640 and the outbreak of civil war in 1642, he decided to withdraw from society and live quietly in the country. How many British gardens have been born, following their owner's decision to leave the town? This Evelyn did, first, in 1643, making a garden 'study' and 'some other solitudes and retirements' at his brother's property at Wotton in Surrey, and then going abroad for most of a decade, observing many a garden in France, Germany and Italy on the way. His first garden works at Wotton included 'a triangular Pond or little stew [fishpond], with an artificial rock'.[26] His brother George continued with alterations, and architectural advice came also from another relation, Captain George Evelyn.

Nine years later, in February 1652, John Evelyn returned to Wotton, advising his brother to remove a 'mountaine [a mount] ... with a moate within 10 yards of the very house'. This was done, the spoil from the mount filling up the moat, and a far more imposing terraced slope was given to the hillside further south,[27] so that a temple front and grotto (designed by Captain George Evelyn) could be recessed into the slope, with a viewing platform at the highest point, having a prospect northwards, back over the garden to the house and beyond. It was, and is, an impressive scheme, from the terrace of the house to the temple and mount, and from the viewing platform back to the house.

While the scheme of garden and mount had considerable symmetry, the house itself remained a 'complicated multi-gabled Tudor jumble',[28] larger but not dissimilar in character to Sayes Court, near Deptford in Kent, which John Evelyn bought in 1652. Sayes Court was essentially a farmhouse, surrounded by areas of meadow and orchard on fairly level ground, bounded by a stream to the east. The garden area was about 10 acres, in an estate of 100 acres or a little more. On 14 January 1653, Evelyn wrote in his *Diary* 'I began to set out the *Ovall Garden* at Says Court ... and this was the beginning of all the succeeding *Gardens*, *Walkes*, *Groves*, *Enclosures* and *Plantations* there', and he drew up a detailed plan, with 125-odd numbered references at the side, in this period. The plan contains a long raised rectangular terrace walk or mount giving views over several areas, like the one at Tackley Manor in Oxfordshire (see page 131). Though this mount looks large enough for a bowling green, Evelyn laid out two separate bowling greens, one to each side of the straight path leading up to the front of the house.[29]

Evelyn later proposed one other mount, with a far different purpose from those with which he was involved at Wotton or Sayes Court. This is described and sketched, in his unfinished garden opus the 'Elysium

Britannicum', which he began in the 1650s and enlarged and amended until 1699. It is a pyramidal mount with a flat top, looking rather like the one at New College, and with a vaguely similar layout of geometrical beds in front.[30] But its aim was not entertainment; it was intended for a 'philosophical garden', a garden for the study of the world's plants – a botanic garden. The idea of such a mount, with its four sides facing the north, south, east and west, and therefore shady, sunny and so forth, comes from Olivier de Serres' *Théâtre d'Agriculture* of 1600. Though Evelyn never in fact built such a mount, the garden at Sayes Court contained several areas for the cultivation of rare plants, as well as an aviary, a nursery, an 'elaboratorie' or laboratory and a score of other features – groves, orchards, a milking area, a pond for carp and another pond with an island, on which grew fruit, asparagus and a mulberry tree.

Sayes Court has gone, though we remember Peter of Russia's stay there in early 1698, devastating the hedges (and more), for which Evelyn was awarded £150.[31] More important in the history of gardens in the 1650s is the fact that the gardens of Sayes Court contained many different elements grouped loosely together by hedges, walls and paths, but not given any overall regularity. We might reasonably compare Evelyn's plan, adapting a host of different features to the requirements of a real situation, with William Lawson's plan (and his *comments* on this plan in his text) back in 1618 (see page 110). Lawson and Evelyn share a practical approach to design which was characteristic of most gardens in Britain in the first half of the seventeenth century.

Decades later, in the 4th edition of *Sylva* (1706) and in his eighty-sixth year, Evelyn produced a proposition for a vast symmetrical scheme to be planted with forest trees. (It is in fact much less of a garden scheme, and more one for a wooded park.) The main area is a square of many acres, quartered and subdivided into 'sixteen blunt triangles … consider'd as pretty large fields', and in its alignment with the house and in the balanced arrangement of lesser spaces – for fruit, vegetables, gardens and fountains – it is patently derived from the great 'regular' gardens which had recently been laid out in Britain, following the examples in France and the Netherlands. On the previous page of *Sylva*, Evelyn had praised some of these British achievements, and the 'most laudable undertaking' of Leonard Knyff in drawing them. But he does not insist on the regularity of the design,

... intending this as an idea only of something which I conceive might be both convenient and graceful, or to be varied into other figures, according to the pleasure of the owner'.[32]

Reality, he implies, may impose a somewhat different order.

Apart from Wotton and Sayes Court, designed for his brother and for himself, Evelyn gave 'advice' on several other gardens – for example at Cornbury House in Oxfordshire in 1664, at Euston Hall in Suffolk in 1671 and 1677, and at Cassiobury Park in Hertfordshire in 1680 – the advice often being to do with the planting of trees. Details are scarce, and, so far as I know, Evelyn himself designed only one large garden of a firmly regular kind – the 400-yard long terrace and semi-circular central bay, with 'crypta' resembling a Roman bath and tunnel, at Albury Park in Surrey. This scheme, with related 'canals' and a secondary terrace, was elaborated for his friend Henry Howard (1628–84), later Duke of Norfolk, whom he had seen during his travels in Italy in 1645–6, and who began, at Albury in 1655, 'to build, and alter the gardens much'. Gardens at Albury had already been developed in the 1630s by Henry Howard's grandfather, the collector Thomas Howard, 2nd Earl of Arundel, and had received something of an 'Italian' character, to judge from one of Wenceslaus Hollar's views, showing an arcaded terrace, possibly the front of a grotto, set into the hillside.[33]

Evelyn stayed with Henry Howard for a fortnight in 1662, and by 21 September 1667 could write 'I accompanied Mr *Howard* to his Villa at *Alburie*, where I designed for him the plat for his Canale and Garden, with a *Crypta* thro the hill &c'. The day before he had been with Howard in London, and had persuaded him to give his grandfather's collection of antique fragments (we know them since as the 'Arundel Marbles') to the University of Oxford. This conjunction gives a special sense to Evelyn's advice at Albury; he was proposing garden features there of a *classical* kind, commemorating poetic and architectural triumphs of the Roman past. Three years later, according to his *Diary* entry for 10 October 1670, Evelyn went again to Albury 'to see how that Garden proceeded'. It was 'exactly don according to the Designe and plot I had made'. The details given recall the direction of Evelyn's interest: 'The *Crypta* through the mountaine in the parke, which is 30 pearches [165 yards] in length, such a *Pausilippe* is nowhere in England besides'. Evelyn added briefly 'The Canals wer now digging, and Vineyards planted'. What Evelyn had helped to produce was a memorial, in England, of two monuments from classical Italy – the grotto and tunnel at Posilippo, near Naples. There a long tunnel pierces the mountain, and above it, at one end, are ruins said to be the 'tomb of Virgil'. Evelyn's commemoration at Albury is indeed formal, and the semi-circular arcaded bay is reminiscent of several such features he had seen in Italy – at the Villa Mondragone or the Villa Aldobrandini in Frascati, for example.

Later designers and painters focused on the idea of 'ruins' at Posilippo, rather than Evelyn's terrace and central bay (we may think of Joseph Wright of Derby's paintings of 'Virgil's tomb' in the 1770s), but such an interest would not have been shared by Evelyn in the 1660s.

Evelyn's interest in gardens was linked to a host of other subjects. We need only look at his assorted contributions to the Royal Society to see that his *Fumifugium: or, the Inconvenience of the Aer, and Smoake of London Dissipated* (published 'by His Majesties Command' in 1661) is both an exercise in what we might call 'town planning', and a proposal for a great series of flowery fields round the east and south-west of London which must even then have seemed fantastical. He suggested that vast fields, of 20, 30 or 40 acres 'or more', should be separated by broad plantations (150 feet wide 'or more') of flowering and odoriferous shrubs, edged with 'Beds and Bordures' of scented flowers, while the central fields should be planted with wild thyme, beans or peas – not, however, with cabbage, 'whose rotten and perishing stalks have a very noisom and unhealthy smell'.[34] No one has followed this advice, though we might, indeed, think it worthwhile, and J. C. Loudon proposed something similar and equally utopian in 1829 (see page 249).

Evelyn's *Sylva*, first published in 1664, has likewise a double thesis. Originally an argument that more trees should be planted, for ships for the navy, it was printed together with *Pomona*, to do with fruit trees, and the *Kalendarium Hortense*, which tells us, the gardeners, what to do throughout the year.

Much of Evelyn's writing on gardens is derived from his massive and unpublished text 'Elysium Britannicum', a work begun in the 1650s, never completed, but intended as a comprehensive survey of every aspect of gardens – their history, cultivation, uses, planting and so forth. Much of *Sylva*, both in 1664 and in its enlarged editions (the 4th in 1706), comes from the 'Elysium' as does *Acetaria, or a Discourse of Sallets* in 1699. He was also an energetic translator of foreign works, including *The French Gardiner*, in 1658, from Nicolas de Bonnefons' text of 1651, and *The Compleat Gard'ner*, in 1693, from Jean de la Quintinie's text of 1690. We should note that Evelyn's son, John, also translated René Rapin's Latin poem (first published in 1666) *Of Gardens* in 1673.

Though Evelyn was profoundly interested in gardens, his interest in plants and plant collections seems to have been less thorough. Certainly, he ordered a collection of dried plants and flowers, 'an *hortus hyemalis*' or 'garden for the winter', when he was at the botanic garden in Padua in 1645 (*Diary*, 1 August 1645), and his *Diary* records visits to the Oxford Botanic Garden in 1654 and 1675, to the Chelsea Physic Garden in 1685, to the garden at Wadham College in Oxford in 1654, and several visits to the gardens of Fulham Palace in the 1680s. At each of these, he noted 'curious' plants, that is those which were rare, or had extraordinary qualities, like the 'Sensitive plant' (*Mimosa pudica*), which he was shown at the Oxford Botanic Garden. But his contacts with plant enthusiasts, such as Sir Thomas Hanmer, were fewer than with those interested in garden design.

The plant enthusiasts continued right through the seventeenth century, following on from John Gerard, John Tradescant and John Parkinson. Often, they had gardens of their own, like Sir Thomas Hanmer at Bettis-field, and frequently wrote about their interests, producing books (several being catalogues of plants in a particular collection or of plants in a certain region), and corresponding with like-minded experts, travellers, collectors, botanists, nurserymen and gardeners. When Thomas Johnson (c.1600–44) re-edited Gerard's *Herball* (1633, 1636), he had already made botanic forays with a group of friends to Hampstead Heath and Kent, described in the *Iter Plantarum Investigationis* of 1629, and in 1634 he published the first part of his *Mercurius Britannicus*, considered as an initial stage of a botanic survey covering the whole of Britain.[35] In 1650, William How published his *Phytologia Britannica*, and John Ray's *Catalogus Plantarum* appeared in 1660, describing the flora of the Cambridge region. Ray's *Catalogus ... Plantarum Angliae* was then published in 1670.

Some of these volumes were, of course, connected with the work of botanic gardens, and the seventeenth century saw the foundation of four of these – Oxford (already mentioned) in 1621, the Chelsea Physic Garden in 1673 (founded by the Society of Apothecaries), the physic garden at Edinburgh in 1670, and, around 1687, the physic garden at Trinity College, Dublin. In 1680, Robert Morison, Professor of Botany at Oxford, published Part 2 of his *Historia Plantarum Oxoniensium* (Part 1 never appeared), and Part 3 was published in 1699 (after Morison's death) by Jacob Bobart (the younger), keeper of the Oxford Botanic Garden. From the Edinburgh garden, in 1683, came James Sutherland's *Hortus Medicus Edinburgensis*, with the subtitle *A Catalogue of the Plants in the Physical Garden at Edinburgh*.

In addition to these books and the botanic gardens, there were the private collections, notably at Fulham Palace, where from 1675 to 1713 Henry Compton was Bishop of London, and where he established a small but famous arboretum, mainly of trees from North America. One other private collection that should be recorded was at Moira in Co. Down, where Sir Arthur Rawdon collected exotics from several countries, including the West Indies and the Levant, in the 1690s. From Moira, he sent specimens to Henry Compton at Fulham, to the Chelsea Physic Garden, and to other correspondents on the Continent. For these plants, he built the first 'stove' or hothouse in Ireland. He had also 'a great number of samples of them, very well preserved, in paper'.[36]

SIXTEENTH-AND SEVENTEENTH-CENTURY INTRODUCTIONS

c.1500	Holm oak (*Quercus ilex*)	Italy
c.1500	Norway spruce (*Picea abies (excelsa)*)	Scandinavia, W. Russia
c.1500	Red mulberry (*Morus nigra*)	Persia
c.1542	Apricot (*Prunus armeniaca*)	China
1547–8	Bear's breeches (*Acanthus mollis*)	Italy
before 1548	Strawberry tree (*Arbutus unedo*)	Mediterranean and Italy
1548	Stone pine (*Pinus pinea*)	Italy
c.1550	African marigold (*Tagetes erecta*)	Mexico
1569	Clematis (*Clematis viticella*)	Spain
1570s	Tomato (*Lycopersicon esculentum*)	South America
1578	Tulip (*Tulipa gesneriana*)	Turkey via Holland
1580	Crown Imperial (*Fritillaria imperialis*)	Turkey via Vienna (1576)
c.1580	Hyacinth (*Hyacinthus orientalis*)	Turkey via Padua
c.1582	Oriental plane *Platanus orientalis*	Persia via S.E. Europe
1585	Potato (*Solanum tuberosum*)	South America
1593	Yucca (*Yucca gloriosa*)	Central America
1596	Judas tree (*Cercis siliquastrum*)	Eastern Mediterranean
1596	White mulberry (*Morus alba*)	China
before 1597	Sunflower (*Helianthus annuus*)	Western N. America via Spain
before 1597	Laurustinus (*Viburnum tinus*)	Southern Europe
before 1597	Marvel of Peru (*Mirabilis jalapa*)	Southern C. America
before 1597	Nasturtium (*Tropaeolum minus*)	South America
before 1597	Common lilac (*Syringa vulgaris*)	Eastern Europe
1597	Phillyrea (*Phillyrea latifolia*)	N. Africa, S. Europe
by 1616	Horse chestnut (*Aesculus hippocastanum*)	Balkans
c.1620	Common larch (*Larix decidua*)	Central Europe
by 1621	Evening primrose (*Oenothera biennis*)	North America
before 1627	Lobelia (*Lobelia cardinalis*)	North America
before 1629	Passion flower (*Passiflora caerulea*)	Central America
before 1629	Strawberry (*Fragaria virginiana*)*	North America
by 1629	Red runner beans (*Phaseolus coccineus*)	Central America
c.1629	Stag's-horn sumach (*Rhus typhina*)	Eastern N. America
c.1629	False acacia (*Robinia pseudoacacia*)	Eastern N. America
1632	Canadian columbine (*Aquilegia canadensis*)	North America
1637	Virginia creeper (*Parthenocissus quinquefolia*)	North America
c.1640	Swamp cypress (*Taxodium distichum*)	Southern N. America
before 1648	Golden rod (*Solidago canadensis*)	North America
c.1656	Virginian maple (*Acer rubrum*)	Eastern N. America
1659	Cedar of Lebanon (*Cedrus libani*)	Lebanon
c.1663	London plane (*Platanus* × *hispanicus*)	
by 1688	Tulip tree (*Liriodendron tulipifera*)	North America
c.1688	Box elder (*Acer negundo*)	North America
1699	Sweet pea (*Lathyrus odorata*)	Sicily

* In 1821, this was crossed with *Fragaria chiloensis*, introduced from Chile in 1721, creating the forerunner of today's large varieties.

9

'So Mightily Improved'

The entry in Samuel Pepys' *Diary* for 16 September 1660 reads:

> From thence to the Park, where I saw how far they had proceeded in the Pell-mell,
> and in making a river through the Park, which I had never seen before since it was
> begun.

King Charles II had returned to England at the end of May 1660, and the
transformation of the irregular ground at St James's Park had started not
many weeks later. The long straight avenue of the Mall, with double lines
of trees, was laid out along the north-west boundary, and a straight canal,
half a mile in length, was formed from a scattering of ponds in the old
hunting park. The new canal ran roughly east-west, from the buildings
of Whitehall towards Buckingham House. By 1661 the poet Edmund
Waller had published 'On St. James's Park, as lately improved by His
Majesty', in which he exclaimed:

> For future shade, young trees upon the banks
> Of the new stream appear in even ranks:
> The voice of Orpheus, or Amphion's hand
> In better order could not make them stand.[1]

The gardens of Hampton Court were redesigned in the same period,
notably by the addition of a semi-circular garden area in front (to the
east) of the palace, with a semi-circular canal along its outer boundary.
From the centre point of the palace, three vistas radiated outwards into
the park, the central vista being a canal and those to left and right being
tree-lined avenues. John Evelyn saw them in 1662, and remarked 'The
Park formerly a flat, naked piece of Ground, now planted with sweete
rows of *lime-trees*, and the Canale for water now neere perfected'.[2] Related

avenues were also planted in Bushy Park, northwards from the palace. With different replantings these avenues all survive today, as does the canal, though what the details of the large semi-circular garden (now known as the Fountain Garden) were is not clear. The Fountain Garden was thoroughly developed (or completed) by William III in 1689.)

The park at Hampton Court was, and remains, 'a flat ... piece of Ground', with only a slight fall to the east, an accident which has produced the one defect in an otherwise masterly plan. The straight canal, aligned on the centre of the palace, is about five feet lower than the level of the semi-circular garden, and is not clearly visible from the garden except from the outer edge of the semi-circle. From the royal apartments it shows fairly well, but is only seen at its absolute best from the roof of the palace, an experience enjoyed around 1701–3 by Celia Fiennes, who wrote after her visit 'The leads give a vast sight all about of the parke and gardens'.[3]

At the Restoration in 1660, the 'French formal garden' was already accepted as the fashionable garden style – as Evelyn would say, it was '*à la moderne*'. Yet Louis XIV, its supreme exponent, via André Le Nôtre (1613–1700), France's greatest garden designer, had hardly begun to show the world how superbly splendid – impressive or oppressive, depending on the viewpoint – such creations could be. Though Louis' rule began in 1643, his elaboration of Versailles did not really begin until after Nicolas Fouquet's disgrace at Vaux-le-Vicomte in September 1661, and Louis' secondary marvels at Trianon and Marly were neither of them undertaken until the late 1670s, when Versailles had become too overwhelmingly public even for that most public of monarchs.[4] Meanwhile his family, his ministers and his courtiers were to make similar, and sometimes only slightly less grand gardens – Chantilly, Meudon, Sceaux, Maintenon, Rambouillet and a score of others – which, most of them, left the earlier glories of Fontainebleau, Saint-Germain, the Tuileries and the Luxembourg somewhat in the shade.

It was a continuing and astonishing development, at least until Louis' death in 1715 (going on indeed well after the reaction in Britain had engendered a new and constrasting style). Until the end of Louis' reign, observers from other countries repeatedly expressed their amazement at his gardens. In response, they too continued to make more and more extensive and authoritative garden schemes in their own countries. The imitations appeared not only in England but all over Europe, from Madrid to Stockholm, from St Petersburg to Naples. Remaining in England, we may note the words of an English writer, Dr Martin Lister, who wrote in 1698 of the vastness of St Cloud and Versailles, 'these Gardens are a Country ... we cannot afford to lose so much Country as these Gardens take up'.[5] By and large, Lister's assessment was correct – the vast extravagance of Versailles could not be matched in Britain. But by 1698 there were many gardens there which bid fair to rival all but the most magnificent in France, and many more were to follow.

Charles II returned from long years of exile as a willing and grateful admirer of the French king. It was no coincidence that as Louis turned to the creation of vast formal gardens as an expression of cultural supremacy, Charles should emulate his benefactor's enthusiasm, and indeed endeavour to employ French garden designers. André Mollet, who had already worked for Charles I at Wimbledon in 1642, probably advised on the work at St James's Park in 1660, and may also have been at Hampton Court and Greenwich in the early 1660s. His brother Gabriel was certainly closely connected with the care of St James's Park in 1661, as was his other brother, Charles Mollet, from 1663. Gabriel died in 1662, André in 1665 or 1666, and an Englishman, John Rose took over in 1666 as 'keeper of St. James's Garden'.[6] Somewhat later, Rose was sent to Versailles to meet Le Nôtre, and to study the gardens there.

The King evidently hoped that Le Nôtre himself might be persuaded – or allowed – to come over to England, but there is no contemporary proof that he did. There is, however, one garden plan partly in his handwriting for a section of the grounds at Greenwich – a design which was never executed, and which could have been supplied by Le Nôtre from France.[7] The Greenwich plan was probably for Queen Henrietta Maria, who died in 1666, and it is of interest that the exact area of Le Nôtre's design has remained an open grassy space within a larger geometrical scheme, as if waiting to be laid out. This larger formal layout, executed in the mid-1660s, was aligned on the Queen's House, and stretched uphill into the park (i.e. to the south-east) with a series of 'Giant Steps' rising up to the terrace, beside which the Observatory was built in 1675–6. The 'Giant Steps' can now be perceived only with the eye of faith, but the terrace and the course of several of the great avenues crossing the park remain.

Le Nôtre, therefore, did not come to England. But one fanciful yet charming anecdote about him has value, however, in showing the extent to which rigid geometrical forms were taken for granted in garden and landscape design, and how any irregularities stood out in contrast. In 1693–4 the Swiss traveller Béat de Muralt was in London, and later related a story of how Le Nôtre had been invited over by Charles II to redesign St James's Park, after the initial creation of the straight canal and the tree-lined Mall in 1660–1. According to de Muralt, the Frenchman arrived, and observed that, apart from these two large geometrical features, 'the rest was a meadow, grazed by deer and cows', which seemed to 'bring the country into the town'. His conclusion was that 'this natural simplicity, this rural – at points even solitary – air was somehow nobler than anything he could devise, and he persuaded the king not to change it'.[8] Looking at bird's-eye views of the park, drawn in the 1690s – the time of de Muralt's anecdote – it is hard to see it as a scene of 'natural simplicity . . . rural . . . even solitary'.

Nature, we may suppose, is in the eye of the beholder as much as beauty. Within a few years, Lord Shaftesbury was to write that 'things of a natural kind' are 'more engaging' and have a 'magnificence . . . beyond the formal mockery of princely gardens'.[9] But between 1660, when King Charles had the canal in St James's Park laid out, and around 1710, geometry in garden design – that is, French-style geometry – became an ideal. If not Le Nôtre himself, then other French gardeners worked in Britain, as did gardeners from the Netherlands who had had French experience, and gardeners from Britain who had been across to the Continent and seen French gardens with their own eyes.

Le Nôtre's nephew, Claude Desgots (d. 1732), was consulted with regard to Cliveden in Buckinghamshire in 1713, and at Bulstrode in the same county in the early 1700s. Another Frenchman, M. Grillet, designed the cascade at Chatsworth in Derbyshire in its initial form around 1694, and another, Nicolas Huet, helped design the terraces on this steeply sloping site. The Huguenot Daniel Marot designed the 'embroidery' parterre for the great semi-circular garden at Hampton Court in 1689, thereby completing the project begun by Charles II in 1662. Marot's design for the 'Great Parterre' survives in a signed watercolour drawing, dated August 1689, and in a panoramic painting by Leonard Knyff of around 1702.[10] Marot had probably been told to prepare the great design some while before August 1689, as an entry in John Evelyn's *Diary* for 16 July of that year states 'I went to Hampton Court, about businesse, the Council being there; A greate appartment, and spacious Garden with fountaines, was beginning in the Parke, at the head of the Canale'. The fountains – 13 in all – were set in a complex and splendidly unified semi-circular pattern of *broderie*, low hedges of clipped box scrollwork enclosed by gravel paths lined with small pyramidal yews, and given vivid contrast by coloured gravels and areas of grass.

Marot had already worked for Louis XIV at Marly, and then, after the Revocation of the Edict of Nantes in 1685, he had emigrated to the Netherlands, where he designed the gardens at Het Loo for William of Orange. At Hampton Court there were in fact several gardeners who had come over from the Netherlands after the accession of King William – Hendrick Quellenburg, Samuel van Staden and Caspar Gamperle, for example, while another French Huguenot, Jean Tijou, was responsible for 12 superb wrought-iron gates and screens there.

Another Frenchman, Guillaume Beaumont, is known to have been at Hampton Court in 1689, before moving north to Levens Hall in Westmoreland, where he laid out the formal garden for Colonel Grahme.[11]

Grillet's cascade at Chatsworth survives amended and enlarged, as do Tijou's screens at Hampton Court, and we may still admire Beaumont's ground plan at Levens, adorned with topiary marvels, certain of whose saplings he planted in the 1690s. Then, around 1705, the amiable and distinguished French diplomat (but less distinguished soldier) Maréchal Tallard was held prisoner at Nottingham after his capture at Blenheim in 1704, and had his own little garden laid out beside his residence, Newdigate House. He may have designed it himself, or had a French gardener do the work, or had it designed 'to suit with Versailles' by George London and Henry Wise, who first reproduced the plan in the second edition of their *Retir'd Gard'ner* of 1706.

George London (d. 1714) and Henry Wise (1653–1738) are both supposed to have served as apprentices under John Rose (who had been to Versailles) at St James's Park, and London twice visited Versailles. His second visit, in 1698, was in the suite of William Bentinck, 1st Earl of Portland (1649–1709). Bentinck was himself a garden enthusiast – his main estate in Holland, Soesdyke, was renowned for its plant collection, which supplied choice items for the greenhouses of Hampton Court – and William III gave him the sinecure of Superintendent of the Royal Gardens. In 1700 he acquired Bulstrode in Buckinghamshire, where the highly geometrical layout was determined by George London, involving consultation with Claude Desgots, Le Nôtre's nephew.

'Instruction' came also to Britain in the form of books on gardening by French writers, many of them in English translation. André Mollet's *Le Jardin de plaisir* (1651), with a sheaf of garden designs and parterre plans, was translated as *The Garden of Pleasure* in 1671; also first published in 1651 was Nicolas de Bonnefons' *Le Jardinier françois*, which John Evelyn translated as *The French Gardener* in 1658. The Jesuit poet René Rapin's *Hortorum libri IV* (1666) was published in English verse in 1673 as *Of Gardens*, translated by Evelyn's son John; another version, by John Gardiner, appeared in 1706.

Jean de la Quintinie, the director of Louis XIV's splendid fruit and vegetable garden at Versailles, produced his *Instructions pour les jardins fruitiers et potagers* in 1690, and this was translated into English by John Evelyn (senior) in 1693 as *The Compleat Gard'ner*. In 1699 this was reissued, abridged and amended by George London and Henry Wise.

London and Wise also translated François Gentil's *Le Jardinier solitaire* of 1704 and Louis Liger's *Le Jardinier fleuriste et historiographe* of 1706, which was published as a two-volume work under three different titles in the same year, 1706 – firstly, as *The Retir'd Gard'ner*, then as *Le Jardinier solitaire* and finally, as *The Solitary or Carthusian Gardener*. Last in this selection of French garden books is A. J. Dézallier d'Argenville's *La Théorie et la pratique du jardinage* (1709), a work which is a virtual codification of French formal gardening practice. This appeared in English in 1712, translated by John James as *The Theory and Practice of Gardening*.

Beside these, several of which ran into further editions, there were other less important works from France, accompanied of course by numerous volumes by British writers on aspects of husbandry and horticulture, especially to do with trees, fruit and vegetables, and botanic cataloguing and classification. Though British observers commented briefly and instructively on garden design, in theory or practice, it is hard to claim that any British book was published in this period which really extended the ideas provided in the French texts mentioned above, unless John Reid's *The Scots Gard'ner* of 1683 is included – a work which is for the most part firmly to do with the utilitarian side of gardening (see p. 152). John Evelyn's massive 'Elysium Britannicum' certainly discusses all kinds of gardens, their composition, contents and design – but it was never published.

In contrast, however, are the many and detailed views of houses and their gardens published in Britain from the 1680s onwards, showing in bird's-eye perspective the achievements in formal style of the later seventeenth and early eighteenth centuries. Some of these views are by British artists – Robert Thacker, Henry Winstanley and David Loggan have already been mentioned, and later there were Thomas Badeslade, John Harris (the elder) and John Harris (the younger). Others are by French, German and mainly Dutch artists – for example, John Slezer, John Drapentier, Leonard Knyff and John Kip. Some of these artists are also known for their paintings and sketches, but their work is mainly found in topographical and architectural collections, published from the 1680s onwards. The best-known are probably Knyff and Kip's *Britannia illustrata* (1707), James Beeverell's *Les Délices de la Grande Bretagne* (1707), and the four volumes of *Vitruvius Britannicus* (I, II and III by Colen Campbell, 1715–1725; IV by T. Badeslade and J. Rocque, 1737).[12]

I have, I hope, set the scene for the development of gardens in the French style in Britain between the Restoration and the early eighteenth century. In this style, the gardens and avenues are related to the house, and best seen from the house – probably best appreciated both in their intricacy and their extent from a raised viewpoint, such as the central apartments on the first floor or *piano nobile* of the house, or from a balustraded viewing platform on the roof or 'leads', or from a little tower or cupola built on top of the roof.

The degree of symmetry in the alignment of garden with house and the success of this alignment, both in France and in other countries like Britain where the style was followed, depended on several factors, notably the symmetry of the house itself (an old house might not possess a 'regular' façade, and might suffer also from 'irregular' wings or adjoining buildings) and the suitability of the terrain. It is in fact rare to find a house-with-garden of an extensive kind which is as fully balanced in its axial alignments as the designs proposed by the writers of garden books.

Hugh May and Others

Up and down the country, gardens and parks, with avenues and 'vistos', were laid out beside existing houses, laid out to match remodelled houses, or laid out round new houses as parts of a single and integrated scheme. Most often – as at Hampton Court – the building (whether palace, mansion or house) was already in place, and so the gardens and wider developments had to be designed round an unsymmetrical centre. This was the case at Cornbury in Oxfordshire. Earlier, in the 1630s, the house had been altered by Nicholas Stone for Lord Danby, founder of the Oxford Botanic Garden. In 1663 the architect Hugh May (1622–86) was there, designing new stables and setting out 'the walkes in the *Park*, and Gardens' for Henry Hyde, styled Viscount Cornbury (1638–1709). May had studied for a while in the Netherlands before the Restoration, and his work, mainly architectural, extended occasionally into garden design. A year later, in 1664, John Evelyn went out to Cornbury in company with May 'to assist the Planting of the *Park*'. May's stables were admired, and together they 'design'd an handsome Chapell'. Evelyn noted that the park was walled round (it had indeed been emparked in the early Middle Ages), that the 'lodge' there was 'a pretty solitude, and the Ponds very convenient'.[13]

Only a few days earlier, Evelyn had been consulted by Viscount Cornbury's father, Edward Hyde, 1st Earl of Clarendon, 'to project the Garden' of his new London house in St James's Street. While the latter was small, the park at Cornbury was of great size, encompassing some 800 acres of Wychwood Forest, with areas of open ground and a long chain of stream and pools leading to the River Evenlode. In this wooded parkland there are still several long intersecting avenues, some radiating from the house, first designed by Lord Danby, and then extended by May and Evelyn. Later, in 1689, a further straight approach was developed, when William Talman and George London collaborated to design a bridge over the Evenlode to the north-east, for an entrance drive between the house and the village of Charlbury.

Similar magnitude appears at Cassiobury Park in Hertfordshire, where a sixteenth-century building was first remodelled and then virtually demolished in the construction of a new house for Arthur Capel, Earl of Essex (1631–83). The architect was again Hugh May, his work extending from 1674 until 1680. As at Cornbury, he was also involved in laying out a grand scheme of walks through the 700 acres of park and woodland. At Cassiobury, however, another garden expert is named, Moses Cook or Cooke, who was engaged on both park and gardens from around 1669 until the mid- or late 1670s. In 1676 he published *The Manner of Raising, Ordering and Improving Forest Trees*, a work commended by Evelyn in the 1679 and 1706 editions of *Sylva*, and of influence with John Reid, whose *Scots Gard'ner* appeared in 1683. Moses Cook dated the preface to his book from Cassiobury in 1675, and claimed that he had worked on the gardens there as early as 1669. In 18–21 April 1680, the ubiquitous Evelyn was at Cassiobury, staying for three or four days with the Earl of Essex, admiring Hugh May's architectural work and the 'Walkes, Ponds, and other rural Elegancies', which were due both to May and Cook, and to the Earl himself – 'no man has been more industrious than this noble Lord in Planting about his seate'. Evelyn noted that the site was too cold for some trees, though '*Black-Cherry* trees prosper' (i.e. the wild or gean cherry, *Prunus avium*). In a separate phrase, he added 'The Gardens are likewise very rare, and cannot be otherwise, having so skillfull an Artist to governe them as *Mr Cooke* . . . Here is an incomparable Collection of the choicest fruits'.

A year later, in 1681, Cook went into partnership with Roger Looker, John Field and George London to found the nursery at Brompton Park.[14] It was almost certainly his competence with fruit trees which brought him into this concern, soon to become the principal source of trees and shrubs for Britain's expanding park and garden activity. Field died in 1687, Looker by 1689, and Cook sold his share in the partnership in 1689. Henry Wise had joined the concern 1687, and from 1689, therefore, London and Wise were in charge, both expert in raising and shipping plants and in designing gardens. London was himself engaged at Cassiobury around 1697 in further work – the whole displayed in Kip's engraving of around 1700.[15] These gardens have now gone, effaced by the Grand Union Canal in 1796, by Humphry Repton's landscaping in 1801–2, and above all by the sideways growth of Watford, bringing housing, a public park and a golf course.

Hugh May was probably the architect who designed Holme Lacy House in Herefordshire around 1673, and he may also have been responsible for the garden areas to the south and south-west. From the late seventeenth century, the great yew hedge, and the terrace leading to the orangery still remain, but most other features were much remodelled in the nineteenth century.

In the 1660s, the Duke of Ormonde had his garden at Kilkenny Castle, Co. Kilkenny, remodelled – a 'French gardener' is recorded there in 1664 – and it is possible that Hugh May designed a fountain within a garden banqueting-house there at that time.[16] The gardens – 'Bowling green, Gardens, Walks, Orchards, and a delightful Waterhouse adjoining to the B. green' (containing May's fountain) – were admired by Thomas Dineley in 1680.[17] Later they declined, but Kilkenny Castle deserves a further note in the history of gardens, since it was the home of Lady Eleanor Butler, who ran away in 1778 with her friend Sarah Ponsonby, and settled in 1780 in Llangollen, to create there a *ferme ornée* of international fame.

By 1670 May was given a post, worth £200 p.a., as 'inspector of French and English gardeners at Whitehall, St. James's, Greenwich and Hampton Court'.[18] Little is known of this post beyond its title, and May's part in Restoration gardening remains shadowy. Nonetheless, one item about him, recorded by Pepys in 1666, shows him to have been absolutely 'up to date' in garden development. On 22 July 1666, he and Pepys talked together, walking 'up and down' at Whitehall (could it have been in St James's Park?), 'discoursing of the present fashion of gardens to make them plain, that we have the best walks of gravell in the world, France having none, nor Italy; and our green of our bowling allies is better than any they have'.[19] 'To make them plain' – what clearer sign is needed, to show the move towards *expansive* garden plans, with a conscious wish to have gardens that are open, extensive and – one might hope – showing the extent of the owner's control over the surrounding land?

Pepys reported further that May preferred these walks and open spaces adorned 'only with a little mixture of statues, or pots, which may be handsome', the latter containing 'such or such a flower or greene as the season of the year will bear'. He had no use for flowers in the main parts of the scheme – 'for flowers, they are best seen in a little plat by themselves; besides, their borders spoil the walks of another garden' (i.e. of any much used part of the design).

May's assertion to Pepys in 1666 that British gardens had qualities which made them – in some respects – superior to those in other countries was matched by a common consciousness that, at the least, the making of gardens had become an important part of British life, and that there was a certain character to British gardens which made them different from those existing before the Restoration. While this is a perennial claim (only a few decades later Daniel Defoe was to state that the love of gardening came to Britain with William of Orange, and William Harrison had seen it as one of the benefits of Queen Elizabeth's reign), it was made with more strength and coupled with a greater exuberance in garden making in the later seventeenth century than in most other periods. Sir William Temple, in 1685, saw this progress 'in the Elegance of our Gardens, in the Number of our Plants; and . . . in the Variety of fruits', all 'in three or four and twenty years of His Majesty's Reign'.[20] Shortly after, John Aubrey wrote that 'in the time of King Charles the Second gardening was much improved . . . there is now, 1691, ten times as much gardening about London as there was Anno 1660'.[21]

It was not, however, a one-sided matter. Aubrey added that 'especially since 1683, there have been exotick plants brought into England no lesse than seven thousand' – in other words, Pepys' and May's interest in 'plain' gardens with gravel walks and lawns was not the only aspect of gardens to be admired. In 1665, John Rea, in *Flora, Ceres and Pomona*, lamented that 'many gardens of the new model' might have 'good walls, walks, and grass plots', but lacked the 'most essential adornments' of flowers; and in 1677 John Worlidge (or Woolridge) complained in his *Systema Horti-Culturae* that 'the new mode of Gravel Walks and Grass-plots' had 'banish'd out of their Gardens Flowers, the Miracles of Nature'.[22] He added, '. . . it's hoped that this new, useless, and unpleasant mode, will like many other vanities grow out of Fashion', but he must have been disappointed. For many years flowers were to be the affair of specialists, of collectors, to be grown in particular parts of the garden where they did not impinge on the grand views of walks, avenues and canals. For their part, 'collectors' did not stop – not for a moment. Some were enthusiasts of modest means, while some were resolute in their extravagance and internationally famed for their collections. J. Gibson's 'Short Account of Several Gardens near London . . . in December 1691' has a fascinating selection of grand and less grand gardens with a special interest in exotics, from royal establishments to the Chelsea Physic Garden, from commercial nurseries to small private gardens. Wholly typical is the reference by another writer, Thomas Dineley, in 1684, to the *separate* garden for exotic plants established by Richard Myddleton of Chirk in Clwyd – on their return to Chirk Castle, the party

> . . . made an halt at an Admirable Walled GARDEN of Trees Plants Flowers and Herbs of the greatest rarity as well foreign as of Great Britain, Orrenge and Lemon

Trees the sensitive Plant &c., where in a Banqueting house a Collation of choice
fruit and wines was lodged ... [it] would gratify not only the nicest Florist ... but
the most skilfull Arborists ...[23]

Parts of the garden walls still survive, as does the banqueting-house (now
named Whitehurst House) and an archway dated 1651, but the rare
botanic contents have gone, vanished long ago.

For the most part, however, the main areas of fashionable gardens
from the 1660s onwards were not noted for flowers, a situation which
was to continue (with rare, notable exceptions, like the Duchess of
Marlborough's flower garden at Blenheim in 1708–9[24]) for much of the
next century, throughout the epoch of the landscape garden. Only in the
relatively minor form of the *ferme ornée* or 'ornamented farm', in the
hands of Philip Southcote at Wooburn in Surrey (from 1735 onwards –
see page 190) was there an attempt to plant flowers as a principal part of
the scheme.

One collector who created a fine formal garden at the same time as he
'collected' was Sir Christopher Hatton (1632–1706), the fourth of that
name, who began to redevelop and extend the grounds beside Kirby Hall
in Northamptonshire in 1685. The house, begun in 1570, had been
variously altered in the seventeenth century, and the gardens, seen by
John Evelyn in August 1654, were then given only moderate praise. But
the 1685 developments were both extensive, coherent and, by chance,
enduring, since the gardens were neglected (not destroyed) after Sir
Christopher's death, and restoration has only been undertaken in our
own time, facilitated by the undisturbed stone edging of the four main
beds in the area beside the house. Hatton's full scheme extended 100
yards westwards from the house and 600 yards to the south – a long
rectangle, divided into several sections, the most formal in the area
immediately beside the west front of the house. South of this was a
'wilderness' and orchard beyond, the whole scheme enclosed to north
and west by sizeable artificial terraces. The northern terrace is still wide
enough to accomodate a bowling green – like the one at Hamstead
Marshall in Berkshire – while the western terrace stretches south for 250
yards, with a lesser terrace extending beyond. A 'privy garden' to the
south-east of Kirby Hall, which is understood to have held the collection
of rare plants, has gone, though traces remain of four rows of trees which
converged on the house from the north.[25] Sir Christopher's brother was
the 'incomparable Charles' (1635–*c.*1705), whose correspondence either
back to Kirby Hall or with botanists such as John Ray (who dedicated
his *Historia plantarum* of 1686 to Charles Hatton), tells us much of the

continuing enthusiasm for plants and the complicated international and inter-professional links of the collectors.

Grander than either Cornbury, Cassiobury or Kirby was – and is – the garden and park at Boughton in Northamptonshire. Here the gardens came by 1700 to some 150 acres, with many hundreds of acres of park and woodland round about. The gardens and park are principally the creation of Ralph Montagu (?1638–1709), from 1705 1st Duke of Montagu, who was three times ambassador to France between 1669 and 1679, and who expressed his admiration for the French manner of garden design as early as 1669. The house was rebuilt in distinctively French style soon after 1683, and the gardens were developed from 1685 onwards, their execution being in the hands of a Dutch gardener, Van den Meulen, employed at Boughton until 1717. Though the gardens and surrounding parkland were indeed further developed by the 2nd Duke of Montagu after 1715 (by his death in 1749 the avenues round the house totalled some 22 miles), the first and principal achievement was complete by 1709. Indeed, a great deal had already been achieved by 1700, when the French exile, Saint-Evremond, lamented being unable to visit them again and not seeing 'the fine House, the fine Water-Works, the fine Ducks ... the Cascade, the Octogon, the Water-Sheafs, and the Water-Spouts'.[26] By 1712, the topographer John Morton produced a long description of the many and elaborate parterres and waterworks, for example,

... below the Western Front of the House are Three more remarkable Parterres: the Parterre of *Statues*, the Parterre of *Basins*, and the *Water* Parterre; wherein is an Octagon Basin whose Circumference is 216 yards, which in the middle of it has a *Jet d'Eau* whose height is above 50 feet, surrounded with other smaller Jets d'Eau.[27]

To give a Versailles-like extent to the regularity of the scheme, the River Ise had been 'canalised' into long straight sections totalling most of a mile, to which the several waterworks were linked. Later, the '*Water* Parterre' described by Morton became a rectangular pool 200 by 170 yards in extent, whose shallow outline remains, crossed by the straight canal of the River Ise at the lowest point of the main garden axis. On the far side, and somewhat to the south, there is still a large 'mount' formed from the soil excavated to make this 'Broad Water', as it was called. These later developments, between 1726 and 1731, involved the advice of Charles Bridgeman (see page 163). The change from the complexity of the '*Water* Parterre' to the still formal but simple rectangular pool is characteristic of the evolution of the formal garden in its later stages.

'No-body Hath Adventured'

In Wales, in Ireland and in Scotland, the creation of grand formal gardens in the French style came later, and generally in a less extensive (and expensive) form, for political, religious and economic reasons. Sir Thomas Hanmer (writing to John Evelyn) commented in 1668 that, in his part of Wales, not a few of the gentry had started 'to plant both flowers and trees, and have pretty handsome little grounds, but no-body hath adventured upon large spacious ones'.[28] I have already mentioned the gardens at Llanerch, made in the 1660s, and those at Tredegar, made from around 1690 onwards, both of them relatively modest in their size (Tredegar boasted an orangery, beside which was a parterre laid out in inert materials – coal dust, crushed shells and fragments of brick[29].) Not until the mid-1690s and early 1700s did 'grand' formal gardens appear in Wales – at Powis Castle in Powys and at Chirk Castle in Clwyd.

At Powis, changes to the medieval fabric had begun by 1684, when Thomas Dineley made his visit, but it is likely that the three long terraces below the castle were given their full ornate form by William Winde from 1697 onwards. The terraces, with elaborate balustrades, steps, a central viewing platform, aviary and orangery, overlook an enclosed 'valley', laid out initially with lawns and formal pools. This scheme lingered on, in neglect, until the end of the eighteenth century. In 1784, the journeying John Byng was shocked by the state both of the castle – 'hourly falling into decay' – and the gardens,

> ... which were laid out in the wretched taste of steps, statues, and pavillions, not even the fruit attended to; the balustrades and terraces are falling down, and the horses graze on the parterres!!![30]

Happily, a plan to 'landscape' (in other words, to destroy) the terraces was not adopted, though the formal pools were removed, and so the terraces survive, topped with gigantic clipped yews and planted at the lower levels, early in the present century, with flowering trees and shrubs.

Such survival was less complete at Chirk, where an even more extensive scheme with parterres and lengthy avenues was laid out between about 1705 and the late 1720s, only to be swept away by William Emes (or Eames) in the 1760s. Slightly later than the formal garden at Chirk, came that at Erddig in Clwyd, made for John Meller in 1718–33. Here, a resolutely formal and symmetrical garden was laid out, aligned on the house with central axis of path and pond, and flanking lawns and groves enclosed in a rectangular wall. This scheme has most happily survived, being restored and replanted in the 1970s.

In Ireland, these formal gardens were somewhat later to arrive, because of the profoundly unsettled political situation in the 1680s. One or two were, however, laid out at that very time. The ardent collector Sir Arthur Rawdon had a formal garden at Moira in the 1690s, which was extended by his successors, and at Kilruddery, Co. Wicklow, a scheme of singular beauty was laid out from the 1680s by the Earls of Meath. The long parallel canals in front of the house, leading to a lime avenue beyond, would have impressed Louis XIV himself. At Carton, Co. Kildare, in the 1690s, a squared-out scheme was made to one side of the house, and long radiating avenues formed a grassed semi-circle on the other. This was much changed later in the century.[31]

Three more formal gardens in Ireland, made in the 1730s, reflect the lateness of Chirk and Erddig in Wales. At Mount Ievers, Co. Clare, between 1731 and 1737, the new house was given a canal along its front, and a large square of garden with symmetrical pond and avenues on the other side; at Powerscourt, Co. Wicklow, the first stage of the terraces, with a parterre design, was begun in 1731–41, a scheme which was to be magnified by Daniel Robertson in 1843, and splendidly completed 'by several hands' by the 1890s; and at Pakenham Hall, Co. Westmeath, linked basins and a canal, 1,200 feet long, followed by another 'near a mile in length' were laid out from the house in the early 1730s. These canals and the linked basins have gone, but were described and sketched in 1736.[32] It is not without interest that this elongated water-scheme is close in date to that at Shotover in Oxfordshire, laid out from 1718 to around 1730, one of the last formal water schemes to be devised, and similar also to the canals and cascades illustrated in the frontispiece to Philip Miller's *Gardener's Dictionary* of 1732. Within a decade or so, such schemes were to be considered old-fashioned.

'When Full Grown'

While a few formal gardens were laid out in Scotland soon after the restoration of Charles II, as at Hamilton Palace in Lanarkshire, their general development was slow, held up by the political uncertainties which continued until the uprisings of 1715 and 1745. In 1689, the English traveller Thomas Morer commented that 'their avenues are very indifferent, and they want their gardens, which are the beauty and pride of our English seats'.[33] This may be contrasted with remarks by James Macky in *A Journey through Scotland* of 1723, and by Daniel Defoe in the third volume of his *Tour through the Whole Island of Great Britain*, published in 1726. These writers both commented with admiration on the many new gardens, particularly their avenues and surrounding plantations, which would soon grow to an impressive size. For Macky, for example, Floors Castle in Roxburghshire 'will soon be very noble', and at Tyninghame in East Lothian the plantations were praised for the grandeur they would have 'when full grown'.

A book on formal gardening had, however, been written by a Scotsman and published some years before Morer's dismissive 'very indifferent'. It was John Reid's *The Scots Gard'ner*, a thoroughly practical volume which appeared in 1683. It concentrates on the raising of vegetables, fruit and herbs, with respectful reference to John Evelyn's *Kalendarium Hortense*, and Moses Cook's *Manner of Raising ... Forrest-Trees* of 1676, and has little on the gentler or more elegant sides of the subject. Early on it states that 'the Kitchen-Garden is the best of all Gardens', and in a later section, on the raising of kitchen vegetables and herbs, it adds 'Weeding ... may be accompted the most material part of Gard'nery', a realistic parallel to George Wither's earlier and terse 'The *Spade*, for *Labour* stands'.

Nonetheless, *The Scots Gard'ner* does briefly consider both beauty – with an engaging 'However I will here take a little turne among the Flowers' plus a three-page list – and design.[34] Most of the first part discusses planning, levelling, preparing and laying out the ground, beginning with a plan 'first on Paper', since here 'we see faults plainly'. Reid's taste is rigidly geometrical, and culminates in a plan of squared gardens within a larger octagonal enclosure crossed by diagonal avenues, which is so fiercely symmetrical we may doubt if it was ever laid out in practice.

The nearest example I can suggest of a garden laid out to Reid's plan was at Drumlanrig Castle in Dumfriesshire, where a terraced scheme begun in the mid-seventeenth century was elaborated in the 1720s, and admired by Defoe. It contained eight garden areas set round the house at the centre, and still survives in grand outline, though much has been reduced to lawn.

While quite a few properties might have earlier terraces and formal gardens near the house – like Hamilton Palace, which had three formal terraced parterres in 1677 and a vast park – planting round about (with the related possibility of grand avenues through the plantations) was generally more recent. At Yester in East Lothian, an astonishing complex of garden features was recorded in about 1690 by the painter Emanuel de Witt, with statues in the quartered parterre, a central fountain, a summerhouse on a mount, a labyrinth, a canal, a cascade and a grotto. For Macky, in his 1723 *Journey*, this was still 'very spacious and fine', but beyond, there was 'the best planted Park I ever saw'.[35] By the mid-1730s, the house had been rebuilt by William Adam, but the plantations were yet larger and the gardens still survived, to be described in a part of Samuel Boyse's 'Retirement':

> Full, in the front, an ample circle lies,
> Where trees on trees in soft succession rise . . .
> Beyond, the fair-dispos'd parterre is seen,
> With flow'rs adorn'd, and slopes of lively green;
> A crystal fountain in the centre plays . . .
> Four statues, equal, rise on every hand . . .[36]

At Hopetoun House in West Lothian, another formal garden was laid out, probably by Sir William Bruce, in 1696 or a little later. Here, Macky again praised the parterre, comparing it favourably with Canons Park in London. 'But,' he added, 'the Views here are prodigiously more expansive.' He listed several of them, ending with 'several Visto's from each of the many Walks that run from this Parterre . . . and through the great Avenue fronting the Palace, your View terminates on *North Berwick Law* . . . at thirty Miles Distance . . .'[37]

Dalkeith Palace (or House) in Midlothian had been drastically remodelled around 1701, and was praised by Defoe as the 'finest new House in Scotland', but Macky was more careful when praising the gardens and park. Much was still to come: 'And from the Gate of this Court is to be an Avenue through the Park . . . a Mile long . . . On the East Side there's a natural Amphitheatre; in the Bottom of which are to be Water-works, and a Flower-Garden . . .'[38] A plan of the gardens at Dalkeith of about 1700 shows, in fact, a constricted and only partially regular layout, including two knots with geometrical patterns.[39]

The most intriguing of these late seventeenth-century Scottish sites is, I feel, the terraced garden at Barncluith in Lanarkshire. The house (at least the tower) and gardens were possibly begun as early as the late 1630s, though the architectural development of the five steep terraces overlooking the River Avon took place probably in the 1690s. When Macky was there in the 1720s, he described a place in marked contrast with the open and extensive gardens and parks which were in the course of creation. Barncluith, he wrote,

> . . . is a very Romantick Garden . . . which consists of seven [probably 'five'] hanging
> Terras-Walks, down to a River Side, with a wild Wood full of Birds on the opposite
> Side of the River: in some of those Walks, are Banquetting-Houses, with Walks and

Grotto's, and all of them fill'd with large Evergreens, in the Shapes of Beasts and Birds.[40]

Macky's choice of the adjective 'Romantick' here is an early but accurate use of the word to suggest something related to 'romance', a story of an old-world kind. Happily these terraces above the narrow gorge of the Avon have largely survived, after providing impetus in the early nineteenth century for praise of ancient gardens. They were restored in the 1890s, when several views, together with their plan and elevation, were reproduced in articles on old Scottish gardens by J. J. Joass and R. S. Lorimer (see page 286).

'Our Heroick Poets'

Not long before George London's death in 1714, Joseph Addison had praised London and Henry Wise for their 'fine Genius for Gardening'.[41] Though his own preference was for 'the beautiful Wildness of Nature', he had singled them out as 'our heroick Poets' for their achievements in the formal style, and lauded their success in the grounds of Kensington Palace, where they had cleverly converted an old gravel pit from 'such an unsightly Hollow with so beautiful an *Area*', balancing it with an adjacent mount. This happy transformation also provided the background for Thomas Tickell's poem 'Kensington Garden' (1722), which had a frontispiece showing the central area, a design of immense formality.

By 1712, London and Wise had been involved in designing or redesigning many gardens. Soon after London's death, Wise withdrew from the Brompton Park nursery, but continued as a designer and as supervisor of several of the royal parks until 1727. In his last years, he collaborated several times with Charles Bridgeman (c.1680–1738), who may have worked for a while in the Brompton Park nursery from around 1709 onwards.[42] By 1727, the 'heroick' style was falling from favour, in England at least, and by Wise's death in 1738 a new fashion was definitely in the ascendant (see Chapter 10).

The table on page 155 lists the main sites where either London, Wise or both of them were engaged, showing where possible when their work occurred. Some commissions may have been settled within a year – for example, Maréchal Tallard's little garden at Nottingham, if indeed they were the designers. Others, like the gardens and park at Blenheim, extended well over a decade, and included collaboration with other people – designers, gardeners, architects and, of course, the owners themselves. Often enough – as at Longleat – an earlier layout already existed, and might well have been altered again, sometimes more than once.

GARDENS AND PARKS WHERE GEORGE LONDON (D.1714), OR HENRY WISE (1653–1738), OR BOTH WERE ENGAGED

1681	Brompton Park nursery founded by London, Looker, Field and Cook	
By 1689	London and Wise sole partners at Brompton Park	
1688–	Chatsworth, Derbyshire	G.L. and H.W.
1688–95	Chelsea Hospital, London	G.L. and H.W.
1689–1712	Kensington Park, London	G.L. and H.W.
c.1690	Grimsthorpe Castle, Lincolnshire	G.L
c.1692	Dyrham, Gloucestershire	G.L.
c.1693	Hampton Court, Herefordshire	G.L.
1692/3	Hodsock Priory, Nottinghamshire	G.L.
1696	Stonyhurst, Lancashire	G.L. and H.W.
1696	Melbourne, Derbyshire	G.L. and H.W.
'late 1690s	Badminton, Gloucestershire	G.L. and H.W.
1697	Cassiobury Park, Hertfordshire	G.L.
1698–9	Castle Howard, Yorkshire	G.L.
1699–c.1715	Windsor Castle, Berkshire	H.W.
1699–	Chicheley, Buckinghamshire	G.L.
1699–	Hampton Court, Middlesex	G.L. and H.W.
c.1700	Staunton Harold, Leicestershire	G.L. and H.W.
1700 (or later)	Bulstrode, Buckinghamshire	H.W. (or Claude Desgots)
1701	Lumley, Co.Durham	G.L.
1701	Rokeby, Co.Durham	G.L.
1701	Burley-on-the-Hill, Leicestershire	G.L.
1701	Newby, Yorkshire	G.L.
c.1702	St James's Park, London	G.L. and H.W.
1704/5–1716	Blenheim Palace, Oxfordshire	H.W.
c.1705	For Maréchal Tallard, Nottingham	G.L. and H.W.
post 1706	Canons, Middlesex	G.L.
1706–	Wanstead, Essex	G.L.

In their earlier work – as at Chatsworth, Kensington Park or Badminton – their designs must have seemed fully abreast of current fashion, and were, like Melbourne in Derbyshire, aimed 'to suit with Versailles'. At Chatsworth, as I have said already, a Frenchman, Grillet, was called in to design the great cascade, modelled on those of St Cloud and Marly, and the vast geometrical gardens as a whole were, as nature *redesigned*, in striking contrast with the surrounding hills – in Defoe's words, in 1727, the latter formed 'a waste and houling Wilderness' which, wholly unexpectedly, led the stranger to 'the most pleasant Garden, and most beautiful Palace in the World'.[43] Defoe's praise here may be seen in a slightly different light, when compared with his description of the situation and the gardens of Drumlanrig Castle, in the second edition of his *Tour*. Again, there is 'so glorious a Palace', and 'such fine Gardens', 'standing in a wild and mountainous country'. But his opening comparison shows an assessment of the situation which rejects altogether any liking for nature in the raw: '*Drumlanrig*, as *Chatsworth* in *Derbyshire*, is like a fine Picture in a dirty Grotto, or an Equestrian Statue set up in a Barn.'

At Badminton, with a large and not dissimilar enclosed geometrical layout round the house, the countryside was also brought under the visual and aesthetic control of the house and its owner – exactly *à la* Versailles. In 1698, Celia Fiennes wrote that 'the Gardens are very fine and Water works', with no other detail, but she said, much more generously, that the house and park stood

> ... on an advanc'd ground with rows of trees on all sides ... and you may stand on the leads and look 12 wayes down to the parishes and grounds beyond all thro' glades or visto of trees.[44]

This comment – we may remember her standing on the 'leads' at Hampton Court around 1701–3 (see page 139) – might, I imagine, have been matched had she visited Blenheim and seen the two-mile Grand Avenue extending northwards from the palace, over Vanbrugh's bridge and on to the Ditchley Gate. She would also have seen, south of the palace, Wise's bastioned formal gardens – their military outline making them indeed the design of 'heroick Poets' – and nearby the 8-acre kitchen garden, likewise bastioned to resemble a fortress. Wise's design took until around 1716 to complete, by which time the fashion for such grandeur was coming under attack. Vanbrugh's great bridge, crossing the tiny River Glyme, was seen in that year by Sarah, Duchess of Marlborough, as 'that ridiculous bridge', such was its disproportion in the crossing of a little stream, and in the late 1760s Wise's formal gardens would be swept away, and Vanbrugh's bridge would be redeemed in the genial landscaping of Capability Brown, producing one of the supreme man-made landscapes in our experience. While Vanbrugh's palace remains, Wise's gardens are now visible only in the immense, indeed stupendous, walls of the kitchen garden.

At Castle Howard, in Yorkshire, London was consulted in 1678, and the architect Talman at about the same time. London proposed grandiose avenues, a parterre, a big kitchen garden and a symmetrical network of paths ('a Star') laid out in Ray (or Wray) Wood to the north-east of the house. Apart from the last item (the 'Star' of paths in Ray Wood), these features were largely executed in the next 20 years, though in several ways more superbly, and with unexpected developments, since the owner, Charles Howard, 3rd Earl of Carlisle, took a large part in the designing of both house and gardens, and since Vanbrugh, who replaced Talman as architect by about 1700, designed many of the singularly prominent architectural features in the gardens and wider landscape.[45]

The rejection of London's formal layout in Ray Wood is referred to in 1718 in Stephen Switzer's *Ichnographia Rustica*, as being halted by 'his Lordship's superlative Genius', and replaced by a diverting 'Labyrinth' of winding paths. Garden and landscape work at Castle Howard was to continue until the 1740s, to be acclaimed by later commentators as one of the supreme examples of the landscape garden (see page 194).

10
ALL CHANGE

'Is There Anything More Shocking?'

According to Daniel Defoe, writing in the mid-1720s, King William III (1689–1702) introduced to this country

> ... the love of gardening ... his majesty was particularly delighted with the decoration of ever greens, as the greatest addition to the beauty of a garden, preserving the figure of the place, even in the roughest part of an inclement and tempestuous winter.[1]

These 'ever greens' were, of course, evergreen bushes set out in symmetrical patterns and trimmed into artificial shapes, as was appropriate in the formal gardens of the time. Shortly after – in 1727 – the garden designer Charles Bridgeman (d. 1738) worked with Henry Wise on a report to the new king, George II, entitled 'A State of the Royal Gardens, from the Revolution, to the Year 1727'.[2] In this report the high cost of maintaining the gardens was ascribed to

> ... their Minute Forms and Compositions, which were the Fashion at the time they were made; And to the great Collections of Orange and other Exotick Trees ... And to the many kinds of Evergreen Trees, and Espaliers of all sorts, which are also very numerous, and grown to extraordinary size, and loftiness, and which yearly increases the labour and expence in keeping.

The solution, Bridgeman suggested, was 'to put the Oranges ... and other Exotick Trees ... and also the several kinds of clip'd Evergreens out of the Gardens' – in other words, to get rid of them. With the 'Oranges' and 'Exotick Trees', this did not happen – the royal collections continued. But the other advice – to scrap the evergreen topiary, now over-large and correspondingly difficult and costly to trim – was generally accepted. (This was not always the case. In the Fountain Garden at Hampton Court, the radiating obelisks of yew were kept, and later much neglected, so that Thomas Jefferson wrote of them in March 1786 'Clipt yews grown wild'.[3] Today, those very yews heave up like constipated mushrooms, a much loved familiar sight, yet grotesquely out of scale, and making the palace look like a doll's house.)

In 1727, by and large, topiary was becoming old-fashioned. J. Gibson's enthusiastic report of 1691 was nearly 40 years old, and for several decades 'greens' had been grown with diligence. In the sketches of Edmund Prideaux, taken in the West Country and in East Anglia around 1725, many of the houses have delightful patterns of 'greens' set in the main formal garden areas – for example, at Prideaux Place, near Padstow in Cornwall, at Heanton Satchville, Mothecombe House and Netherton Hall in Devon, and at Forde Abbey in Dorset. These were to go, sooner or later, as fashion or finance dictated. In 1739, the fourth volume of *Vitruvius Britannicus* (pl. 73–4) shows a bowling green at Heanton Satchville, bare as a button, where Prideaux's view had offered globes, cones and cakestands of topiary, set round statues and low patterns of box.[4] Bridgeman's advice is clear: if there are other possibilities, get rid of your topiary.

Defoe himself, having praised King William for encouraging the use of clipped evergreens, commented revealingly on 'the gardens of Count Tallard' at Nottingham. Here after his capture at the Battle of Blenheim (1704), the French commander, Maréchal Tallard, Duc d'Hostun (1652–1728), was allowed to reside as a privileged prisoner of war, and made his own garden, 'a small, but beautiful parterre, after the French fashion'. His garden plan was illustrated, with notes, in the second edition of George London and Henry Wise's *The Retir'd Gard'ner* (1706), and again, without notes, in Beeverell's *Délices de la Grande Bretagne* (1707 and 1727). It was a small (half acre) but delicious example of a French formal garden. Or so it was in 1706. By 1727 Defoe added 'But it does not gain by English keeping'. It was by then (in spite of Defoe's praise of King William's garden enthusiasm) out of date, and, like the clipped evergreens condemned by Bridgeman, it was doomed to go.

By the late 1720s, a new fashion was 'coming in'. Ideas which had been put forward a fair while before were beginning to have their effect. The theory went back at least 20 years, to the remarks of Lord Shaftesbury (Anthony Ashley Cooper, 3rd Earl of Shaftesbury, 1671–1713), possibly to those of Sir William Temple in 1685, and to those of Joseph Addison

(1672–1719) and Alexander Pope (1688–1744). The development was slow, partial and hesitant, and it was not until the mid-1730s that a genuinely 'new' kind of garden, the landscape garden, began to be created in its entirety. When Addison wrote against topiary in the *Spectator* (no. 414) of 25 June 1712, complaining that 'we see the Marks of the Scissars upon every Plant and Bush', we should be also be aware that shortly afterwards, also in the *Spectator* (no. 477), of 6 September 1712, he wrote in praise of George London and Henry Wise as 'our heroick Poets' for creating the 'several little Plantations' and the 'seeming Mount' from an existing gravel pit near to Kensington Palace.

In this later essay Addison pointed out that 'there are as many kinds of Gardening as of Poetry', equating the 'Makers of Parterres and Flower Gardens' with 'Epigrammatists and Sonneteers', while the work of 'heroick Poets', like London and Wise's scheme at Kensington, was considered altogether more grand and formal. His own taste could be accommodated as the '*Pindaric* Manner', which is 'irregular', and imitates 'the beautiful Wildness of Nature, without affecting the nicer Elegancies of Art'. In other words, he was admitting that several approaches to garden design were possible, and that he did not in fact reject any of them. Again, we should appreciate that his phrase 'the beautiful Wildness of Nature' was applied to his own garden, 'a Confusion of Kitchin and Parterre, Orchard and Flower Garden'. He claimed indeed that it was like 'a natural Wilderness', but neither 'Wildness' nor 'Wilderness' had the strength that we might attribute to these words today. His pride was in the *flowers* of his garden, growing 'in the greatest Luxuriancy and Profusion'.

In the first decades of the eighteenth century, therefore, no wholesale departure from formal gardening took place. As with Addison's phrases, we should beware of putting too much trust in James Thomson's lines, in 1730, referring to Bubb Dodington's garden at Eastbury in Dorset, designed by Charles Bridgeman in the early 1720s. This layout – vast, geometrical and formal – has now reverted to mounds and hillocks in mainly agricultural land, but in its heyday it was one of the last great formal gardens in the British Isles. Yet to Thomson (in the 1730 version of *Autumn*), it contained

> ... the green majestic walks
> Of, Dodington, thy seat, serene and plain;
> Where simple Nature reigns.[5]

Again, we should note that several of these commentators were not, or may not have been the keenest of gardeners themselves. Addison's own garden at Bilton in Warwickshire has disappeared without contemporary comment, and remarks around 1800 suggest that what then remained was firmly formal, while Lord Shaftesbury doesn't seem to have gardened at all.[6] Shaftesbury in fact referred to gardens – in *The Moralists*, 1709 – as a matter which should urge us to thoughts beyond man-made formal schemes, but with a wholly moral, rather than an aesthetic, aim. Like John Evelyn in 1657, writing to Sir Thomas Browne in the last years of the Commonwealth of his idea of a 'society ... of Paradisean and Hortulan saints', for whom 'caves, grotts' and other 'irregular ornaments of gardens do contribute to contemplative and philosophicall enthusiasme',[7] Shaftesbury saw these 'irregular ornaments' as guides to the truth of the natural world, and thence to God, its creator. His much-quoted phrases, preferring 'the rude rocks, the mossy caverns, the irregular unwrought grottos and broken falls of waters, with all the horrid graces of the wilderness itself' to 'the formal mockery of princely gardens',[8] were not meant so much as propaganda for 'new' gardening (in contrast to the 'princely gardens' of Louis XIV), but as guidance of a moral kind. Elsewhere in his writings he urges 'remember ever the gardens and groves within', the 'inward walks and avenues' – if these are neglected, then all our efforts are in vain. Then, 'what are gardens ... what are dirt-pies?' – they are all foolish diversions, just so many 'rattles'.[9]

Other writers, like John Dyer, in his poem *Grongar Hill* (1726), or James Thomson in *The Seasons* (1726–30) were not really concerned with gardens, but with the countryside, a larger and freer prospect of the English scene. In contrast Addison and Alexander Pope were concerned, far more than they were with gardens, with the activities of people in the town. Both were profoundly city-centred, involved in the carefully contrived artificialities of social and cultural life. Pope is the author of *The Rape of the Lock* (1712 and 1714), the *Dunciad* (1728) and the *Essay on Man* (1733), while Addison in 1713 produced his verse tragedy *Cato*, a deliberate attempt to create a work for the British stage which would respond to the demands of French classical tragedy.[10]

Above all, in this movement from the formal to the natural in gardening, we should note that it took time, that it proceeded gently, bit by bit. In 1728, the writer and garden designer Batty Langley asked 'Is there anything more shocking than a stiff regular garden?' – a question which is, for us, quaintly at odds with the stiffness and regularity of parts of his designs, and with the views which he drew of ancient ruins, designed to be the termination of vistas or avenues, and painted on movable canvas screens.[11] All the while, great formal layouts were still wholly in favour on the Continent – Louis XIV was active in developing the great gardens at Marly until a few months before his death in 1715, and British visitors on the Continent remarked, often quite viciously, on the formality of French or Dutch parterres until the Revolution in 1789.[12] At the same time, however, in Britain great formal planting schemes with avenues and vistas were still under way, enthusiastically admired by James Macky and Daniel Defoe in the 1720s in the Scottish parts of their different tours, while in Hertfordshire, at St Paul's Walden Bury – no more than 28 miles from London – one of the most lovely of all formal schemes was not laid out until the early 1730s.

'Virtuoso Grand Jardinier'

The most important garden designer in this transitional period – after George London and Henry Wise, and before William Kent – was Charles Bridgeman (c.1680–1738). He appears to have worked for London and Wise in the Brompton Park nursery in the early 1700s, and under Wise at Blenheim in 1709. He was, or became, well-acquainted with architects such as Sir John Vanbrugh and James Gibbs, working with them on several projects, particularly at Blenheim, Stowe, Eastbury and Claremont. His patrons and friends included Edward Harley, 2nd Earl of Oxford, and the poets Matthew Prior and Alexander Pope. It was Prior who referred to Bridgeman as the 'virtuoso grand jardinier' for his work at Down Hall in Essex (see page 172). He went into partnership with Henry Wise in 1726, and in 1728 he replaced him as Royal Gardener, a post which he held until his death in 1738.[13]

The following table lists the main sites where he is thought to have worked (designing a part or the whole), in rough chronological order.

CHARLES BRIDGEMAN'S MAIN GARDEN WORK

1709 onwards (mainly 1716–1730s)	Blenheim Palace, Oxfordshire; contract for maintenance, 1726
1713/14–c.1730	Stowe, Buckinghamshire
c.1715	Chiswick House, Middlesex
c.1718–1730s	Eastbury, Dorset
1719–21	Purley Hall, Berkshire
c.1720	Claremont, Surrey
1720–5	Wimpole Hall, Cambridgeshire
1720–6	Down Hall, Essex
early 1720s	Rousham House, Oxfordshire
1722–6	Kedleston Hall, Derbyshire

mid-1720s	Dawley, Middlesex
1724	Marble Hill House, Middlesex
1725–7	Houghton Hall, Norfolk
1726	Chicheley Hall, Buckinghamshire
1726–31	Boughton, Northamptonshire
1726–33	Kensington Gardens, London
c.1726	The 'theatre' in Alexander Pope's garden, Twickenham, Middlesex
late 1720s	Shardeloes, Buckinghamshire; design (unexecuted) possibly by George London, not Bridgeman
late 1720s – mid-1730s	Richmond (gardens and park), Surrey
1730–8	Amesbury Abbey, Wiltshire
c.1730	Farley Hall, Berkshire
1730s	Gubbins, Hertfordshire

Bridgeman wrote no books on garden design, and so, to learn of his style, we must look at his plans, at contemporary views of his work, and at contemporary comment. With precaution, we may also see the books and plans by Stephen Switzer (1682–1745), who worked with Bridgeman at the Brompton Park nursery in the early 1700s, as offering parallel and comparable advice. Switzer published *The Nobleman's, Gentleman's and Gardener's Recreation* in 1715, enlarged to two volumes as *Ichnographia Rustica* in 1718. In 1742, the latter was reissued, enlarged to three volumes.

The most instructive comment on Bridgeman came in 1724, when Lord Perceval wrote to Daniel Dering describing recent work at Stowe in Buckinghamshire. A small terraced formal garden had been laid out on the south side of a relatively modest mansion in the 1680s (mentioned by Celia Fiennes around 1694, and reproduced in a sketch of about 1690[14]). Bridgeman's work at Stowe began in 1713, and in 1719, if not before, Vanbrugh was engaged to remodel the house and design garden buildings. Other architects who worked there in Bridgeman's time included James Gibbs and William Kent.

Perceval, in 1724, admired the views of 'the bewtiful wooded country', visible beyond the gardens thanks to the use of a ha-ha (see page 167). This device, a ditch or sunken fence, allowed the gardens to appear 'three times as large as they are. They contain but 28 acres'. The long slope leading up to the house now involved the Octagon Lake, flanked by twin pavilions, and a symmetrical vista up to the parterre and the house, 'which, standing high commands a fine prospect'. In 1734, the French artist Jacques Rigaud recorded several views of Stowe, published in engraved form by Bridgeman's widow, Sarah, in 1739. His views show this main axis clearly and in detail, and show also Bridgeman's skill in linking several such vistas into a complex and impressive scheme. The house and other buildings or monuments terminated the views, which, though straight, were varied – a path, a hedge-lined avenue, a long canal, a stretch of lawn. As Perceval wrote, 'Nothing is more irregular in the whole, nothing more regular in the parts, which totally differ one from the other'.[15]

Looking back from near the year 2000, the 'irregular' of Perceval's description is trivial, no more than the accommodation of an asymmetrical site, soon to be extended to ten times the area. But we may agree that the *regularity* of the parts lay in their geometrical arrangement round one or another architectural feature – at Stowe, the canal and amphitheatre linking Queen Caroline's monument and the Rotunda. The same regularity can be found in the arrangement of the lake and amphitheatre at Claremont, and, on a smaller scale, in the different sections of the layout at Down Hall.

In short, Bridgeman's manner was a much simplified formal style, with one or more axes, usually from the house, directed to a notable garden feature – a geometrical pond, a monument, a temple, an obelisk – flanked or connected by curving (if not wriggling) paths, leading from one area to another. This can seem a poor thing on paper, but, between the house and the Octagon Lake at Stowe, or from the lake to the amphitheatre at Claremont, or from the house down to the temple at Purley, these vistas still survive as splendid achievements, however changed since Bridgeman's time.

His contemporaries, such as Switzer, knew also that the detailed formality of topiary and parterre would no longer please their patrons. With or without Bridgeman's advice, other less formal yet still geometrical layouts were made. At Shotover in Oxfordshire, around 1718 or in the early 1720s, the great canal was laid out *à la* Switzer or *à la* Bridgeman, stretching away from the mansion for over half a mile, like the Long Water at Hampton Court, but with lawn between the house and the canal, rather than the intricacy of Hampton Court's Fountain Garden. By the mid-1720s, the vista had been completed with a Gothic pavilion, designed probably by William Townesend, who had worked on a stylistically similar remodelling at All Souls' in Oxford.[16] This Gothic styling at All Souls, with its pointed arches and battlements, was another move away from continental models, being the first attempt at a return to a native British architecture, followed (or paralleled) by the mock-Gothic castle, Alfred's Hall, at Cirencester, begun in 1721 (see page 180). The great canal at Shotover stretches eastwards from the house. To the west, another straight axis, an avenue, is flanked by the curving, twisted paths common in Bridgeman's and Switzer's designs. Here, in the late 1720s, William Kent may have contributed to the layout, and certainly designed an obelisk and an octagonal temple.

Switzer himself is noted for his design work at Grimsthorpe Castle in Lincolnshire, where in the 1720s he modified a 1690s layout by George London by simplifying the parterres and enclosing a large part of the scheme – both parterres and adjacent woodland – with a bastioned terrace walk, allowing extensive views out over the countryside (as the ha-ha wall was soon to do all over the country). At Castle Kennedy in Wigtownshire, a large garden was created in Bridgeman's or Switzer's style in the early 1730s, extending from the ruins of the castle (burnt out in 1717) along a narrow isthmus bounded by the Black Loch to the north-east and by the White Loch (Loch of Inch) to the west. Garden plans were drawn up by William Boutcher in 1722, and William Adam may have supplied others by 1730, but it is possible that the owner, Lord Stair, may, like many other proprietors at this time, have decided much of the plan for himself. Though in parts overlaid with impressive nine-teenth-century plantings – an avenue of monkey puzzles and rho-dodendrons round part of the Round Pond – the main lines of the 1730s layout survive in remarkable completeness, with a broad gently terraced slope, down from the castle, the two-acre Round Pond and the Belvedere or terraced mound, strongly reminiscent of the amphitheatres at Eastbury and Claremont. Other viewing terraces, notably Mount Marlborough, are comparable with Switzer's bastioned terrace walks at Grimsthorpe, both for their 'military' connection, and for their purpose in allowing views into the gardens and out to the landscape.

One other garden in a comparable style must be mentioned – Thorndon Hall in Essex, the property of the 8th Lord Petre (1713–42), a passionate botanist and plant collector. In 1732, aged only 18, he married and moved to Thorndon Hall, and set about extending and landscaping the grounds with exceptional energy. By 1733, a French surveyor named Bourginion had drawn up a plan, crossed by long axial avenues, between which other regular features were set – an 'octagon' for systematic plant-ing of new seeds and plants from abroad and various formal pools – as well as a multitude of wriggling paths, serpentine pools (one involving a menagerie) and broader areas of woodland. South of the house was a vast lawn, rolled with a 'great Rowler for Rowling the Park', pulled by two horses, or by four if used all day.[17] The site was later landscaped by Capability Brown, and then amended as a golf course and country park, but Petre's fame as a collector survives. By his death, over 60,000 trees had been planted, his 'stoves' or greenhouses were the largest in the country, and Peter Collinson wrote to Linnaeus in 1744 that Petre's death was 'the greatest loss that botany or gardening ever felt in this island'. He provided plants for his relative Philip Southcote at Wooburn (see page 190).

The New Theory

The *objections* to gardens in a formal style were of a practical, aesthetic and political nature. On a practical level, they were costly to maintain; aesthetically, they were artificial (as with topiary – see Joseph Addison, *The Spectator*, no. 414, 25 June 1712; Alexander Pope, *The Guardian*, no. 173, 29 September 1713), and, since they were enclosed, they ignored the wider countryside (see Addison, *The Spectator*, no. 414, 25 June 1712); and from a political viewpoint, they were the expression, in garden form, of a generally tyrannical attitude – centred in Louis XIV's Versailles – and thus at odds with the spirit of liberty which was supposed to be a part of British life (see Addison, *The Tatler*, no. 161, 20 April 1710).

The *aims* of the new commentators were accordingly to make gardens that were 'natural' rather than 'artificial'. This general and by no means original plea had a particular sense in the early eighteenth century – that the area of the garden should, if possible, look out to the encircling countryside, and to some extent be laid out in harmony with it. Addison put this most cogently in *The Spectator* (no. 414) of 25 June 1712 when he suggested that country and garden could be joined into a pleasing whole:

> Why may not a whole Estate be thrown into a kind of Garden by frequent Plantations? ... Fields of Corn make a pleasant Prospect ... [and with] the natural Embroidery of the Meadows ... some small Additions of Art ... Trees and Flowers ... a Man might make a pretty Landskip of his own Possessions.

Addison's word 'Landskip' has a special *painterly* sense, implying a 'Landscape painting', which is discussed below, but which does not hinder the general idea that the garden should come to resemble and to be united with the countryside. In 1731, Pope's *Epistle to Lord Burlington* stated that the true garden (true to 'nature' and the 'Genius of the Place') 'calls in the Country', to be an essential part of the garden.

The *characteristics* of the new gardens responded to the objections and aims I have outlined:

- They tended to be more 'open', directed outwards to the countryside, and in consequence less and less house-centred. This was, of course, fundamentally opposed to the idea of the French formal garden, in which the house – or mansion or palace – was essentially the focal point of the garden scheme; it was, in British terms, a marked and increasing divergence from the seventeenth-century rectangular gardens described in Chapter 7, with the house set firmly at one end of a set of linked geometrical areas.

- They tended to be larger – an almost inevitable result of their outward-looking nature. There was here an understandable progression, from Chiswick in Middlesex (14–15 acres according to John Rocque's plan of 1736) to Rousham in Oxfordshire (25 acres) to the vastness of Stowe (Buckinghamshire) or Castle Howard (Yorkshire). By 1755, gardening was defined as 'the modern art of *laying out ground*',[18] a process which stretched outwards to the countryside, rather than coping with an enclosed and therefore *limited* space.

- Being more open, and often larger as well (frequently making use of the deer parks which still survived round many mansions), they included a larger amount of grass, whether it was called a bowling green, a lawn or a meadow, and contained correspondingly less of a floral kind, whether in formal layouts or arrays of pots. Gardens with flowers most certainly continued, often in urban regions, in collector's gardens, or in separate and tidily segregated areas within the larger schemes. It was not until the later 1730s, at Wooburn Farm in Surrey, that the 'new' gardens were deliberately given floral displays, even though Addison had praised his own garden in 1712 as being 'a Confusion of Kitchin and Parterre, Orchard and Flower Garden', where his flowers 'grow up in several Parts of the Garden in the greatest Luxuriancy and Pro-fusion'.[19]

The specific *features* of the new gardens were at first no more than two, but both vastly important – the ha-ha wall and the serpentine path.

The Ha-ha

This feature, invented early in the eighteenth century, was crucial, no less, in the development of the new gardens, since it enabled the owner to 'look out' into the countryside without the need for a wall, or some other barrier, to keep cattle away from the garden and grounds immediately beside the house. It was, to exaggerate a little, an 'invisible wall', in the form of a ditch, dug out carefully along the outer boundary of the garden, deep enough to prevent cattle from entering the garden and to allow the owner and visitors to look outwards – to the countryside and encircling 'nature', without the visual impediment of a wall, hedge or railings.

Horace Walpole's familiar comment and definition must, I think, be repeated. Looking back from the late 1760s, he saw the ha-ha as 'the capital stroke, the leading step to all that has followed' in the creation of the landscape garden; he added 'I believe the first thought was Bridgeman's'. This 'capital stroke' was 'the destruction of walls for Boundaries, and the invention of fossés [ditches] – an attempt then deemed so astonishing that the common people called them Ha! Ha's! to express their surprise at finding a sudden and unperceived check to their walk'.[20]

The ha-ha is a vivid illustration of the essential artificiality of all gardens – and no harm in that – since it demonstrates how the amiable wish to 'embrace nature' is tactfully but firmly stopped by the sunken wall, however great the visual enchantment beyond may be.

The ha-ha was first named, in French, as 'le ah-ah', by A. J. Dézallier d'Argenville in his *La Théorie et la pratique du jardinage* of 1709. This work was translated into English as *The Theory and Practice of Gardening* in 1712 by John James, who wrote of an 'Opening, which the French call a *Claire-voie*, or an Ah, Ah, with a dry Ditch at the Foot of it ... At present we frequently make Thorough-Views, call'd *Ah, Ah* ... This Sort of Opening is, on some Occasions, to be preferred, for that it does not shut up the Prospect'.[21]

The thing itself, the ha-ha, seems first to have appeared at Blenheim in Oxfordshire by about 1712. At this time the great formal gardens of George London and Henry Wise had already been established, and Charles Bridgeman was taking over their care. In 1712, William Stukeley visited Blenheim and wrote 'The garden is ... taken out of the park, and may still be said to be part of it, well contriv'd by sinking the outer-wall into a foss, to give one a view quite round and take off the odious appearance of confinement and limitation to the eye'.[22]

Today we may see excellent – and by this I mean convincing – examples of the ha-ha all over the country. At Blenheim, to the south of the palace, the present ha-ha wall may even be a part of the one described by Stukeley in 1712. At Stowe, in Buckinghamshire, there are long stretches of ha-ha wall which were a part of Bridgeman's scheme in the 1720s, the extent beside the Lake Temples being immediately apparent and convincing. In 1724, Lord Perceval commented on the excellence of Bridgeman's work at Stowe, and added 'what adds to the bewty of this garden is, that it is not bounded by walls, but by a ha-hah, which leaves you the sight of the bewtiful country ...'[23] Perceval may, however, have been referring to an earlier and less extensive ha-ha, replaced in the 1730s. At Rousham in Oxfordshire, we may see a stretch of ha-ha which responds to Horace Walpole's later claim that William Kent 'leaped the fence, and saw that all nature was a garden'. For my money, the ha-ha at Rousham is the best, but there are scores of others – as at Bowood in Wiltshire (the work of Capability Brown much later in the eighteenth century), or, even in the present age, at Villiers Park in Oxfordshire or at Phoenix Park (the Dublin Zoo) in Ireland.

To conclude, in the 1960s, it is proper to record that my mother was at the Dublin Zoo – in my company – and was alarmed by the apparent freedom of a hippopotamus. She ordered me to get to the manager, and was barely comforted when I explained that the hippopotamus was a vegetarian, and was effectively confined by a ditch which was really there but which she had not noticed, so skilfully had it been designed. The ha-ha is indeed an extraordinary invention, and though it may first have come from the French, its essentially negative and invisible quality makes it an intriguingly British part of the history of gardens.

'I Invented the Serpentine'

The wavy, serpentine or snake-like line, as used for the outline of a path, a stream, a hedge or border, was adopted in the early eighteenth century as a gentle alternative to the straight lines and sharp angular corners then dominating the perspectives of the formal garden. The 'S'-shape, composed of sections of a circle, was still geometrical, rather than haphazard or irregular. Its use, therefore, often involved a kind of compromise, with its wavy lines used for minor paths set within larger rectilinear outlines. As the serpentine line became more familiar, or less daring, less regular curves could be adopted, becoming commonplace by the mid-century and replacing the 'S'-shape I have described.

Though it was used above all in the 1720s and 30s, the serpentine line was known earlier, and its invention as a water feature in a garden was claimed in the 1660s by Matthew Wren, Bishop of Ely (1585–1667), who wrote (apparently in the margin of his copy of Wotton's *Elements of Architecture*),

> For disposing the current of a river to a mightie length in a little space, I invented the serpentine, a form admirably conveighing the current in circular and yet contrary motions ... with walks and retirements betweene, to the advantage of all purposes, either of gardening, [or] planting ... In brief, it is to reduce the current of a mile's length into the compass of an orchard.[24]

Wren's phrases presumably refer to an orchard-garden and stream of his own. We do not know. The use of streams that 'wind in a serpentine way without order, and turn in the open spaces around the trees' was described, surprisingly, by Le Nôtre in 1694, writing a note about his 'Bosquet des Sources' at Trianon[25] – a single instance of informality in the gardens of Louis XIV.

In British gardens clear evidence appeared in the 1720s, when Lord Bathurst developed his Buckinghamshire estate at Richings (or Riskins), and claimed 'that he was the first person who ventured to deviate from straight lines, in a brook which he had widened at Ryskins'. He added that a visitor, taken to see the 'new improvement', 'asked him to own fairly, how little more it would have cost, to have made the course of the brook in a strait direction'.[26] Not long after, in the late 1720s or early 1730s, the straight canal at Chiswick, Lord Burlington's property, was given 'serpentine' shape, which it retains today. This is considered to have been the work of William Kent, by about 1733 (see page 178), though the pictorial evidence of one painting, dated round 1727, may mean that the canal had already been made to meander – slightly – before Kent's time,[27] and that Kent's work was to make the canal even more 'natural', and to add the web of meandering paths, particularly to the south-east, which are shown on John Rocque's map of 1736.

Within a year or two of the changes at Chiswick, in 1730–31, the actual Serpentine between Hyde Park and Kensington Gardens was formed at the request of Queen Caroline. Long thought to be the work of William Kent, it is now attributed to Charles Withers (the Surveyor-General of Woods and Forests).[28] The Serpentine, linked with the Long Water, was formed from a string of ponds crossing the park, which in turn received their water from the River Westbourne. These ponds were the earlier work of George London and Henry Wise, and their transformation into the Serpentine was completed in May 1731 (as recorded in the *London Journal* of 1 May that year). The Serpentine remains today much as it was then, with the addition of fountains and sculpture in the 1860s at the north end of the Long Water.

Kent did, however, achieve one named serpentine feature, the 'serpentine rill' at Rousham, when he worked there in the late 1730s. This feature, a thin, sinuous stream flowing some 200 yards, past the Cold Bath and down to the Great or Octagon Pond, is the most striking survivor of the serpentine enthusiasm – its construction is patently artificial, being a simple masonry trough some 9 inches wide, as is its continuing and accurate 'S'-shaped course.

One could cite many more examples in the 1740s. By 1753 the fame of the serpentine line reached its peak in William Hogarth's *Analysis of*

Beauty, where the 'S'-curve is hailed as the 'line of beauty', and his frontispiece shows the many points where this line may be seen and appreciated – the curves of a fiddle, a lady's leg and so forth. Hogarth's illustration does not however touch the garden scene. It was left to an anonymous poet, visiting William Shenstone's garden of The Leasowes (near Halesowen, not far from Birmingham) in 1756, to sing the praises of the 'waving line' in the landscape:

> Yon stream that wanders down the dale,
> The spiral wood, the winding vale,
> The path which wrought with hidden skill,
> Slow twining scales yon distant hill
> With fir invested – all combine
> To recommend the WAVING LINE.[29]

The Leasowes, the most famous of the eighteenth-century *fermes ornées*, covered a good 150 acres, and had room enough for these serpentine delights. But other gardens were far smaller, and more open to ridicule. In 1753, the year of Hogarth's *Analysis*, Francis Coventry mocked 'Squire Mushroom' for his crowded garden – 'less than two acres' – in which the first sight is 'a yellow serpentine river, stagnating through a beautiful valley, which extends near twenty yards in length'.[30] This was only one of Squire Mushroom's errors – we shall return to them soon.

'On Classic Ground'

In 1701, Joseph Addison addressed a poetical 'Letter from Italy' to Lord Halifax, describing his delight in the countless reminders of the ancient world:

> For wheresoe'er I turn my ravished eyes ...
> Poetic fields encompass me around,
> And still I seem to tread on classic ground.[31]

Addison's phrase 'to tread on classic ground' echoed through British gardens in the first half of the eighteenth century, and it was the principal among several 'excuses' for change in garden styles in that period.

Though the owners and designers may not have thought of Addison, they did think that their gardens and parks were echoing important aspects of the classical concern with agriculture and with gardens. It is a dual concern, in which the two parts can overlap – the interest in rural retirement in Roman times, and the interest in the Roman garden.

Beatus Ille . . .

'Happy the man' began Horace, in the second Epode, 'who, far from mercenary things . . .', and then continued by describing the peaceful, productive farmer who delves, plants and grafts – and supervises – far from the troubles of the town. Virgil had said the same, more whole-heartedly, in the *Georgics* (II, 490ff. and IV, 125ff.),[32] and a variety of British farmer-gardeners took up the theme, particularly in the 1720s and 1730s.

'Withdrawal to the country' when times are difficult is a common enough occurrence, and has often been linked with garden enthusiasm, notably in ancient China. But in Britain, in relation to the early eighteenth century, it is of especial interest, since it played a central part in the change in garden style. John Evelyn in 1652–3, and Abraham Cowley in the early 1660s may have chosen to garden as an alternative to less attractive political and social activities, but they did not set out to garden in a new or different way.

The same might still be said of the gardening of the poet diplomat Matthew Prior (1664–1721), who retired to Down Hall in Essex in 1720. He wrote a happy 'Ballad of Down Hall' describing his first visit to the place, probably in late 1719:

> There are Gardens so stately, and Arbours so thick,
> A Portal of Stone, and a Fabric of Brick

He was also warned by his companion that although it was modest, it was probably costly:

> I show'd you DOWN-HALL, did you look for VERSAILLES?
> If you have these Whims of Apartments and Gardens,
> From twice Fifty Acres you'l n'er see Five Farthings.[33]

Quickly, Prior saw his retirement as a felicitous echo of ancient Roman practice – 'Down in itself considered I love more than Tully his Tus-culum, or Horace his Sabine field'. He had already engaged Charles Bridgeman (whom he terms his 'virtuoso grand jardinier' and 'operator hortorum et sylvarum') to redesign the grounds. What was proposed, and agreed between them was, however, far from resembling a Roman farm. 'We have laid out squares, rounds and diagonals, and planted quincunxes at Down',[34] he wrote on 29 December 1720, and Bridgeman prepared two plans which are, apart from the serpentine stream and the wriggling lesser paths, wholly orthodox and formal.

Prior died in 1721, and the estate reverted to his friend and benefactor, Lord Harley, for whom Bridgeman completed the garden scheme in 1726. From this period a hornbeam approach drive still survives, and a small temple attributed to James Gibbs, though the other features have gone, largely superseded when the present Down Hall was built in 1871–3, with extensive formal gardens.

Matthew Prior may well have been the last in this period whose 'retirement' was given so formal a setting. Others chose to emulate the ancient Romans in their farms, their gardens and their architecture more directly, since this could be seen as a deliberate move away from the formality and artificiality of the previous age.

Lord Bolingbroke (Henry St John, Viscount Bolingbroke, 1678–1751) was probably the first to put this into practice. He had been in exile abroad since 1715, and between 1720 and 1724 he had developed the garden and grounds at La Source near Orleans. In 1721 he wrote to Jonathan Swift, telling him:

> You must know, that I am as busy about my hermitage, which is between the Chateau and the Maison Bourgeoise, as if I was to pass my life in it ... Send me some mottos for groves, and streams, and fine prospects, and retreats, and contempt for grandeur, &c.[35]

Bolingbroke's interest in 'country life', albeit as an amused and superior spectator, may be assumed from the bucolic verses of John Gay's *Shepherd's Week*, which had been dedicated to him as early as 1714. The 1721 letter to Swift, with the ideas of the 'hermitage', 'retreats', and 'contempt for grandeur', must be read with a certain caution. In the 1680s, Louis XIV's most extravagant garden project, at Marly, had at first been qualified by Louis himself as a 'hermitage', and Bolingbroke's layout at La Source (rather like Prior's at Down Hall) seems to have been both resolutely formal and relatively grand.[36] By 1725, he had returned to England and acquired an estate at Dawley in Middlesex – some 400 acres. Dawley House was soon renamed 'Dawley Farm', and by 1728 Alexander Pope wrote to Swift that he had overheard Bolingbroke 'agree with a painter for £200 to paint his country-hall with trophies of rakes, spades, prongs, &c., and other ornaments, merely to countenance calling this place a farm',[37] a description corroborated in 1748 by Lady Luxborough, Bolingbroke's sister, in a letter to William Shenstone:

> When my brother Bolingbroke built Dawley, which he chose to call a Farm, he had his hall painted in stone-colours, with all the implements of husbandry.[38]

Lord Bathurst likewise developed his Buckinghamshire estate at Richings (or Riskins) along the lines of a farm (including the 'serpentine' stream already referred to on page 170). Looking back in 1742 at Bolingbroke's and Bathurst's garden interests, Stephen Switzer applied the term '*La Ferme Ornée*' (an ornamented or ornamental farm) both to Dawley and to Richings, linking it with 'the Method used by the *Romans* of old'.[39] Looking back from slightly later, Joseph Spence would claim around 1752 that Philip Southcote (c. 1699–1758) was the 'first that brought in the garden farm, or *ferme ornée*', adding that 'Mr Southcote began his garden in 1734'.[40]

These attributions of the term are clearly a matter of degree. The idea of retirement to a 'farm' partly modelled on the antique was taken up more fully and more thoughfully both by Southcote at Wooburn in Surrey, and by William Shenstone (1714–63) at The Leasowes near Halesowen in the Midlands from the mid-1730s (see page 197). Meanwhile, others had developed the idea of imitating Roman *gardens*, again, we may think, as an excuse for gardening in a new and different way. Features from Roman gardens had of course been imitated before, notably in Renaissance Italy,[41] and the sculpture, fountains and hydraulic amusements of Elizabethan and Jacobean gardens were largely derived from the same classical sources. But from the 1720s onwards there was a fresh interest in Roman gardens, and indeed in the 'antique', particularly the architecture of the ancient world and its reincarnation in the designs and buildings of the Renaissance architect Andrea Palladio. One ancient Roman writer, Pliny the Younger, had left detailed descriptions of his country villas and their gardens, particularly in *Letters* II, 13 and V, 6, which were easily available in current editions of his complete letters, and given particular emphasis in individual works: first, briefly, by Vincenzo Scamozzi in 1615, and then by J. F. Félibien in 1699 (the latter work reprinted many times).[42] In addition, Pliny's importance in the theory of the Roman villa had already been acknowledged by Alberti, whose architectural work *De Re aedificatoria* was translated into English as *Ten Books of Architecture* by Giacomo Leoni in 1726.

Two years later Robert Castell produced *The Villas of the Ancients Illustrated*, with texts and translations of the appropriate letters by Pliny, and passages from Varro, Virgil and Columella, with commentary and lavish illustrations. Castell's book was dedicated to Lord Burlington, who had been active since 1715 in building and gardening at Chiswick, in ways which clearly referred to Roman and Palladian examples (see page 176). Castell is a shadowy figure, and his importance in garden history is probably slight – his book was produced privately for only 116 subscribers, with a small number of extra but less lavish copies, and has never been reissued. Though dedicated to Burlington, it is not at all clear whether he sponsored the work – Castell was imprisoned for debt in the same year, 1728, and died of smallpox, still in prison, in 1729.[43] Apart from one reference in the 1742 edition of Stephen Switzer's *Ichnographia Rustica*, Castell's book (his only work) appears to have been ignored until the 1760s and later.[44]

Nonetheless, Castell must be given attention here, since he echoes a part of Burlington's work at Chiswick, and, very slightly, hints at a change in the development of the Chiswick gardens in the 1730s. Pliny states that his Laurentian and Tuscan villas – are within agricultural estates, but his descriptions are above all to do with the villas, and then with their gardens, which are mainly in a highly formal style. The villas and formal gardens therefore take up most of Castell's commentary, and most of his illustrations. However, unlike other commentators on Pliny, Castell shows in his reconstructed *plan* of the Tuscan villa large areas of countryside round about. In his *commentary* this part of the plan is barely mentioned, but another passage in Pliny receives particular attention. Pliny's text (*Letters* V, 6) states that in the middle of one ornamental part of the garden there is, unexpectedly, an area which looks like the open countryside (*ruris imitatio*). In Castell's plan this part is tiny, but his commentary is expansive. He suggests that this is one of three ways of garden design – simple fields, the formal layout, and, in the third, a 'Manner, where . . . *Hills, Rocks, Cascades, Rivulets, Woods, Buildings*, etc. were possibly thrown into such an agreeable *Disorder* . . . like so many beautiful *Landskips*'.[45] By 'Landskips' he means 'landscape paintings', a direct echo of Joseph Addison, writing in 1712 that 'a Man might make a pretty Landskip of his own Possessions', and he continues with a reference to the 'present Manner of Designing in China' – 'a close Imitation of Nature' – which is similarly derived from Addison (*Spectator*, no. 414, 25 June 1712), harking back to Sir William Temple's earlier '*Sharawadgi*' (see page 113). It certainly has nothing to do with Pliny.

11

BURLINGTON, KENT, POPE – AND PARADISE

Chiswick

Richard Boyle, 3rd Earl of Burlington (1695–1753) returned from his Grand Tour in 1715. He had been abroad for a year, spending most of the time in Italy, admiring the sculpture and architecture of the ancients, and the architecture and painting of Renaissance Italy. On his return he began not only extensive alterations to his London residence, Burlington House, but also designing small buildings for the garden of his 'country' house at Chiswick, and developing the layout of the garden itself. While the ideas and designs for both buildings and gardens were Burlington's (influenced by his experience in Italy, and his parallel study of the work of Inigo Jones), the execution of architectural matters was largely by Colen Campbell, and the gardens may have been laid out by Charles Bridgeman.

Burlington went again to Italy in 1719, for a short visit in which he made a particular study of the buildings, architectural drawings and writings of Andrea Palladio and Vincenzo Scamozzi. On his return, in December 1719, he was accompanied by the young painter William Kent (1685–1748), who had been studying and working in Italy for several years (Burlington had met him in Italy as early as 1714). Kent was to remain attached to Burlington, as employee, friend, adviser and resident in Burlington House, until his death in 1748.

Burlington had, however, begun his garden activities at Chiswick without Kent, and indeed many years before Kent was involved with garden matters at all. Burlington was his own designer, aided and advised by cultured friends. In July 1716, John Gay addressed an 'Epistle' to

Lord Burlington – subtitled 'A Journey to Exeter' – which began

> While you, my Lord, bid stately Piles ascend,
> Or in your *Chiswick* Bowers enjoy your Friend;
> Where *Pope* unloads the Bough within his reach,
> Of purple Grape, blue Plumb or blushing Peach;
> I journey far.[1]

These 'Chiswick Bowers' were set out in an area of ground related not to the Chiswick Villa which we know today – Burlington did not begin that until 1725, a decade after the gardens were begun – but to Chiswick House, a large Jacobean mansion to the north-east of the present villa. Chiswick House had been bought by Burlington's grandfather in 1682, and stood on the site until 1788, long after Burlington's death. The gardens in their early form, until the 1730s, were predominantly formal, with a straight avenue extending away to the north-west, and dividing at a *patte d'oie* or 'goose-foot' into three separate avenues, each with a building or monument at the end.

In 1736, John Rocque produced a plan of the gardens, with views of the garden buildings in the surrounding margins. While certain aspects of the layout reflect the work of William Kent in the 1730s, the buildings are mainly Burlington's, imitated or derived from ancient Roman or Palladian models, and given garden settings of considerable formality. It has been suggested that, both in his first garden buildings (the Orangery, the Casina, the Ionic Temple) and in the villa itself, Burlington was creating a kind of garden museum or showplace in honour of Palladian architecture. Inigo Jones, Britain's first admirer of Palladio, is commemorated by his Gateway, brought from Beaufort House in Chelsea to Chiswick by Burlington in 1736, and re-erected to the north-east of the mansion, near to the now vanished Orangery. The villa itself (built 1725–29), with statues of Palladio and Jones to left and right at the entrance, was designed purely as a place for intellectual and aesthetic activity, whether as study or amusement. It had no kitchens, no dining room, no bedrooms – these were kept firmly in the large older mansion, Chiswick House. The internal decoration of the villa, influenced again by the designs of Inigo Jones and his pupil John Webb, was largely executed by William Kent, and it is probable that Kent did not have any part in the development of the gardens until this was finished, around 1730 or 1731.

Rocque's plan of 1736 shows a lengthy 'river' or canal on the south-western side of the villa, much as it is today. This was dug out by 1719, the spoil providing a sizeable terrace on the southern side, giving views out to the Thames. At first the canal was more or less straight, and flanked on its northern side by two geometrical pools, set to left and right of the Ionic Temple – shown in paintings by around 1729–30.[2] When Kent joined in the garden work at Chiswick, the area round the canal and the canal itself were most to be affected. Between the main straight avenue and the canal, he laid out a long regular area of lawn overlooked by the new villa, with a hedged semi-circular apse-like enclosure at the further end. This was adorned with ancient statues, said to have come from Hadrian's Villa near Tivoli, alternating with stone seats and term statues. This feature, called the *exedra*, is reminiscent of the semi-circular ending to Pliny's riding ground in his Tuscan villa, and may be linked with Robert Castell's *Villas of the Ancients Illustrated*, published in 1728. Kent first designed a stone semi-circular ending for this area, which was not used, and which reappeared as the Temple of British Worthies at Stowe (see page 186).

Kent also lessened the formality of the two pools beside the canal (these have now gone altogether), though leaving the exactly circular pool, with its central obelisk, in front of the Ionic Temple – to my mind, one of the most lovely *small* formal garden areas in the world. His main and great garden work at Chiswick was to do with the canal. This he deliberately made more serpentine, exaggerating its already slightly sinuous outline, so that it came to look like a wholly natural lake, an original part of the country landscape. Though the serpentine line had been introduced some years before at Richings, Lord Bathurst's estate in Buckinghamshire, Kent's treatment of the canal at Chiswick makes it the first large lake in the western world to be presented as a *natural* rather than an *artificial* feature, as something which had existed in the area of the garden long, long before the garden itself was designed.

At the southern end of the canal, Kent produced another novel feature, a cascade set in a ruin – an *artificial* ruin. As with the *exedra*, more than one design was considered – a formal squarish affair, with water pouring out from a central arch, was built by about 1730, to be replaced by the 'ruined' cascade, probably in 1738. This design – three arches of roughly constructed stones, clearly dilapidated, with crumbling or collapsing boulders at the sides – appears among the views surrounding Rocque's plan, and we may view it today, the first *deliberately* ruined garden structure in Britain. It has been suggested[3] that Kent was inspired by the 'rustic' cascade at the Villa Aldobrandini at Frascati, which he would have seen in Italy, and which G. B. Falda illustrated in 1675.[4] While this is indeed likely, we should be aware that Kent sensibly increased the air of antiquity, of ruin, to make his cascade look, like the lake into which it flows, as if it is immensely old – in deliberate contrast with the newly constructed temples, obelisks and villa nearby.

Kent's garden activity began around 1730, after he had been occupied for over a decade with painting, book illustration and architectural work – designing buildings, large and small, and features within buildings, including furniture. Quite a number of his garden buildings survive, in gardens which he did not design, or where his landscaping has been overlaid or obliterated, but his surviving gardens are few indeed. His work was not widespread: Carlton House (gone), Chiswick, Claremont and Esher Place (gone) in London and north Surrey; Holkham, and possibly Raynham in Norfolk; Euston in Suffolk; and near to Oxford, Rousham, Shotover, Stowe in Buckinghamshire, and Badminton in Gloucestershire. Beyond a drawing for a wild yet Italianate scene at Chatsworth (a proposed replacement for Grillet's cascade), there is little else. It is not a lot, and his reputation has owed much to Horace Walpole's superlative comments, in the essay 'On Modern Gardening', written long after Kent's death.[5] Alas, the garden Walpole qualified as 'Kentissime' – Esher Place – has gone. Two plates by John Rocque in *Vitruvius Britannicus* (1739, pl. 110–11) tell of multiple vistas, riverside walks, temples and monuments, and there is a surviving design by Kent for a Chinese building at Esher, possibly the earliest example of garden chinoiserie in the British Isles.[6]

'Extensive or Forest Gardening'

We do not know what part Alexander Pope played in the forming of Chiswick, though his praise came early, and continued. He took friends to view the villa and the gardens, and in 1731 he published his *Epistle to Lord Burlington*, in which his advice on garden design stretches out to larger and more varied scenes than Chiswick – notably to Stowe, and, I think, to Cirencester, with a glance of some satisfaction towards his own small garden at Twickenham.

Long before 1731 and the *Epistle*, Pope had been advising Lord Bathurst, at Richings (see page 174) and then at Cirencester. His first visit to Bathurst's property at Cirencester was in 1718, some three years after Bathurst had begun to rebuild Oakley House there and to plant and develop the parkland to the west. Work on Oakley House (now Cirencester House) began in 1714, and in 1716 Bathurst added to the adjacent land by purchasing Oakley Wood and Sapperton Manor further to the west. This gave him control over a five-mile stretch of ground westward from the house (which stands on the west side of Cirencester, close to the church), which he proceeded to plant with a rich variety of trees, the areas of woodland and parkland being defined by majestic grassy rides. The longest of these, the Broad Avenue, was aligned on Cirencester church, and stretches five miles out to Sapperton; the Elm Avenue extends for a mile west from the house to Queen Anne's Monument (1741), and other rides cross or connect these in several directions, linked by large intersections – the Hexagon, Seven Rides and Ten Rides.

This was gardening on a vastly greater scale than at Richings – it was indeed what Stephen Switzer had called 'extensive or forest gardening' in his *Ichnographia Rustica* in 1714. It has been suggested that the dimensions of this 'forest gardening' may be best compared with those of the French creations, made in the seventeenth century, of Fontainebleau and Compiègne,[7] though these were both linked to royal palaces, and were not given the thoughtful planning which Bathurst achieved. Later, after many a visit to Bathurst at Cirencester (and after many others to Richard Boyle, Lord Burlington, at Chiswick) Pope wrote admiringly, 'Who plants like Bathurst, or who builds like Boyle?'[8]

Bathurst's scheme at Cirencester was not executed all at once – it took many years to reach maturity. In 1721 Pope wrote of the 'future and as yet visionary Beauties that are to rise in these Scenes',[9] and a good while later, in 1735 or 1736, George (later Lord) Lyttleton wrote from Stowe (where he was composing inscriptions for the temples in the Elysian Fields) that 'lord Bathurst's seat is a vast design; and when it has time to grow and form itself, there will be nothing in England equal to it, in the great French manner [an echo of Stephen Switzer's 'grand manier'] ... But at present it is only a fine sketch, and most of its beauties are in idea'.[10] We should note this evidence of slowness in garden growth, and contrast it with the commoner signs of decay and dereliction recorded in this history.

The rides or avenues at Cirencester survive to this day. They were brilliantly planned, not simply from a single great house in the French fashion, but crossing the country from viewpoint to viewpoint, with fine features at the intersections, probably designed by Bathurst himself – the Hexagon (1736), the Horse Guards, Pope's Seat and others. Of these vistas, those from the tower of Cirencester church must be among the noblest in Britain – a double view, first to the house, and beyond it to Queen Anne's Monument; and then, to the right, the second view out to the horizon along the Broad Avenue.

One building, deep in the woodland, a third of a mile away from Ten Rides, was begun (or elaborated from something much simpler) in 1721, with Pope's advice, and finished in 1732 or soon afterwards. This is Alfred's or King Alfred's Hall. Contemporary therefore with Burlington's temples and monuments at Chiswick, it is not in the least

Palladian, but deliberately Gothic, with battlements and pointed windows, some of the latter from a much older manor house at Sapperton. It is generally accepted as the first mock-Gothic castle in Britain, the ancestor therefore of the many would-be medieval buildings in British eighteenth-century gardens, from Hagley, Mount Edgecumbe and Stowe, all the way to Fonthill Abbey. Jonathan Swift slept in it, or its immediate ancestor, when Bathurst was beginning its Gothic transformation, and Mrs Mary Pendarves (later to become Mrs Delany) wrote to Swift in October 1733 reminding him of this, and adding that it 'is now a venerable castle and has been taken by an antiquarian for one of King Arthur's, "With thicket overgrown, grotesque and wild" '.[11]

Another early work, possibly a 'first', at Cirencester is the Lake, begun around 1736. Far later therefore than the canal or 'river' at Chiswick, it is also far larger – some 12 acres in area – and deliberately irregular and 'natural' in outline. Sited within the Home Park, and relatively close to the house, it was not aligned with any of the avenues, and is therefore free of any trace of geometrical planning.

'His House, Embosom'd in the Grove'

Alexander Pope moved into his Twickenham house in 1719 after several months' negotiation. He lived there until his death in 1744. Though he had already had much garden contact and had given much advice, this was the one garden he designed for himself – yet with advice and help from others. In the mid-1720s, Charles Bridgeman came with a team of workers and rapidly laid out a tiny 'theatre' in one corner, and William Kent may also have helped at different times – he certainly designed vases and urns as ornaments.

It was, beside Richings, Chiswick and the vastness of Cirencester, a small property – under 5 acres. Looking back to the 3 5 acre type of formal garden in the previous century, Pope's garden was, however, both in its layout and its details, profoundly different. To begin with, the house, with a small river frontage, was separated from the garden by the Hampton road (in 1992, the A310); it did not in any way 'overlook' the garden. By 1722 Pope had a tunnel dug under the road to connect his house and the garden area. This tunnel, which became known as the Grotto, was enlarged and elaborated in the early 1740s. It is now the only part of his property to survive – the house was demolished in 1807, and the gardens were radically altered and much built over then and in the present century.

A throng of friends, fellow writers and artists joined with Pope in the elaboration of his garden. By 1720 John Gay could write to Pope, congratulating him on the progress he had made in house and garden, and by early 1723 could write to Jonathan Swift that 'Pope has just now embark'd himself in another great undertaking as an Author, for of late he has talk'd only as a Gardiner'.[12] The 'great undertaking' was the translation of the *Odyssey*, to follow his earlier and remarkably well-paid translation of the *Iliad*. It is proper to repeat that Pope's urbane versions, in ten-syllable rhyming couplets, are a vital part of his cultured and social career, and that his house and garden were equally the setting for meetings of sophisticated town-dwellers, far more than they were the abode of a solitary lover of nature. His own lines, written in the 1720s, make this clear enough:

> His House, embosom'd in the Grove,
> Sacred to social Life and social Love,
> Shall glitter o'er the pendent green,
> Where Thames reflects the visionary Scene.[13]

The theme of 'social Life' continues even in his grotto – in the 1740s, his elaboration of this area into a miniature representation of the mineral subterranean world led him to identify the different rock or fossil specimens with their donors.[14]

If we look at the inventory of his furniture and effects at Twickenham, made after his death, the garden offers a modest list of 20 urns, three statues and four 'Busstos' with varied pedestals and supports, and '10 Wood Chaires & two Arm Windsor Chaires'. But in the house, there are scores, no less, of pictures, some paintings, some prints. Many are not identified – 'upon the Best Staire Case. 29 Prints in Black Frames' – but many are, as portraits. Only nine are designated as 'Land Skips', whether of country scenes or of gardens.[15]

To the garden itself: for such a famous site there was scant illustration in Pope's lifetime. His gardener, J. Serle, who had worked for him from the mid-1720s, published plans of both garden and grotto a year after his death (Serle was later employed at Prior Park, Bath, by Ralph Allen), and there is one sketch by William Kent. Otherwise, we depend on letters, particularly by Pope to his friends – notably the letter to Edward Blount of 2 June 1725, with details of the grotto. The garden, though small, was filled with different features – a vineyard, stoves (where he grew pineapples), an orangery, a kitchen garden with vegetables (broccoli and fennel come to mind) and a selection of fruit trees, some obtained from Philip Miller at the Chelsea Physic Garden, and a 'garden house'. Roughly at the centre of the garden was an open lawn – the bowling green – approached through a formal 'grove' of lime trees, laid out in quincunx. To vary the viewing angles one large and two small mounts were constructed, and the relatively small dimensions of the garden were disguised by belts of trees or bushes along the boundaries, avoiding the cramping effect of walls. Urns and statues were carefully placed, and, at the far end of the garden, lines of cypresses led towards an obelisk erected in 1735, in memory of Pope's mother, who had died two years before.

Looking back from the 1990s, this may seem formal. But Pope's plan has no house as a central point, and its many features are most thoughtfully spaced, concealed and divided. Kent's one sketch, of the 'Shell Temple', shows a distinctly unclassical building backed by an irregular grove, with one small archway (the garden entrance to the grotto) offering a glimpse of the Thames. This sketch may be dated to the mid-1730s, as the writer Aaron Hill had written to Pope in late 1733 about 'a little obelisk of Jersey shells [i.e. oyster shells]' which Hill had constructed in his own garden, and enclosing a gift of a parcel of shells 'to embellish your *marine temple*, by inserting them, among the *Hollows*, between those large shells, which compose it'.[16]

At this time Aaron Hill had further thoughts on grottoes, described in two letters in 1734, outlining a proposal for a complex yet regular structure, with linked areas of grottoes to designate power, riches, honour and learning, a central 'temple of happiness' and a liberal addition of statues and urns. The design (never executed) is old-fashioned for the 1730s, harking back I suspect to Bernard Palissy's *Recepte véritable* of 1563, but the decoration with shells was certainly fashionable, and would have appealed to Mrs Delany, whose shellwork enthusiasm is discussed below (see page 202).[17]

Pope's Twickenham grotto first involved fancy – here he could contemplate. A sketch by Kent captures him in this state; another, by Kent or Lady Burlington, shows him beneath the rock and fossil arches, hand poised to write. Then came geology, as he tried to make the walls of the grotto resemble aspects of a mine in the West Country. In the 1740s, Pope made sketches for his alterations, and wrote in 1741 his 'Verses on the Grotto', where he instructs visitors

Approach. Great NATURE studiously behold!
And eye the Mine without a Wish for Gold.[18]

Pope's grotto ended therefore with a thoughtful attempt to show some part of the marvels of the mineral world, moving away both from indiscriminate collections of 'curiosities', and from the classically inspired watery caves of the seventeenth century.

'All Gardening is Landscape-Painting'

Earlier sections of this history have discussed the developments which led towards the 'landscape garden', from the 1700s until the 1730s. In this progression Alexander Pope and William Kent emerge as important figures, with particular connections with Lord Burlington at Chiswick and with Pope's own garden at Twickenham. By the mid-1730s, two salient attitudes had become generally accepted – that gardens should be related to the vision of landscape painters, and that they should be 'free', 'natural' and unconnected with the formalities of Louis XIV's Versailles. A lesser but related expectation was that they should also eschew the smaller-scale topiary figures common in gardens in the 'Dutch' style.

In 1734 these matters came together. Sir Thomas Robinson, writing to Lord Carlisle, remarked that:

> There is a new taste in gardening just arisen ... a general alteration of some of the most considerable gardens in the kingdom is begun, after Mr Kent's notion, viz to lay them out and work without level or line ... This method of gardening is the more agreeable as, when finished, it has the appearance of beautiful nature.[19]

In the same year Pope is reported as saying that 'All gardening is landscape-painting',[20] a phrase and a date which fit in with Philip Southcote's words, reported by Joseph Spence around 1752 but referring back to his gardening at Wooburn, begun in 1734 – ''tis all painting'.[21]

'Without level or line' and ''tis all painting' – what a change from Thomas Tusser's words in 1573 – 'by line and by leavell / trim garden is made'! Of course, 'trim gardens' were still made in the restricted areas of urban properties. Joseph Spence himself designed many such between 1731 and his death in 1768,[22] and, with diminishing frequency, gardens with formal layouts utterly dependent on 'line' and 'leavell' were occasionally made, such as the scrollwork parterre set out at Chatelherault, near to Hamilton Palace in Lanarkshire, in the mid-1730s, or the simpler but immensely more extensive diamond-shaped plan at St Paul's Walden Bury of around 1730. But the idea that landscape painting was the model for the garden designer to imitate was for some decades virtually a belief: the garden should resemble a *picture* rather than the projection of a *plan*, and the picture should be of a *landscape* rather than of a garden, of nature and the countryside rather than something contrived and clipped into topiary or parterre.

As Joseph Addison wrote in the *Spectator* of 25 June 1712 (no. 414), 'if the natural Embroidery of the Meadows were helpt and improvd by some small Additions of Art . . . a Man might make a pretty Landskip of his own Possessions'. Addison did not say, what kind of 'landscape painting' he had in mind, though by the 1760s those commenting on garden landscapes had no doubt, referring again and again to the works of Claude Lorrain (1600–82) and of Gaspard Dughet (1615–75, known also as Gaspard Poussin), and of their followers and imitators, including Salvator Rosa (1615–73). By 1712, the year of Addison's essay, the Earl of Shaftesbury was eagerly collecting paintings by Claude and 'Poussin' (possibly Nicolas Poussin, rather than Gaspard), and in 1713 William Kent, studying architecture and painting in Italy, was instructed by his patron Burrell Massingberd to acquire copies 'after Poussin and Clodio Lorenzo'. In later years Kent himself owned several Claudes and Gaspards, either originals or copies.[23] For the most part such paintings were of Italian scenes, whose atmosphere was heightened by the inclusion of figures and buildings related to the myths or history of ancient Greece or Rome. The vision, therefore, in these English landscape gardens was for a long time most strongly Italian.

From 1731 to 1764, ''tis all painting' was virtually unquestioned. From the former year, Alexander Pope's *Epistle to Lord Burlington* gives the instruction

> In all, let *Nature* never be forgot.
> Consult the *Genius* of the *Place* in all.

This is apparently an order to study and respect the natural characteristics of the site when creating a garden; yet his '*Genius* of the *Place*' is seen to operate as a painter rather than a gardener – the Genius '*Paints* as you plant, and as you work, *Designs*'. In his *Anecdotes*, Joseph Spence looks back at Pope and Kent as 'the first that practiced painting in gardening', and at another point specifies, a trifle obliquely, when he comments on Lord Cobham's long-elaborated work at Stowe 'Lord Cobham began in the Bridgeman taste: 'tis the Elysian Fields that is the painting part of his gardens'.[24] Here he is referring first to Charles Bridgeman (d. 1738), who was principally responsible for the grandiose and largely formal layout at Stowe from 1713 onwards, and to William Kent, whose span at Stowe extended from the early 1730s to his death in 1748. While Kent's first work at Stowe seems to have been to design garden buildings – the

Temple of Venus (by 1732) and the Hermitage – he later took part (with his employer Lord Cobham) in the complex creation named the 'Elysian Fields', the valley lying to the east of the main north-south axis, hidden from that axis by trees and immediately different in its character.

The 'Elysian Fields' at Stowe involve a small valley with a stream, groups of trees on the gentle upper slopes on either side, and a scattering of buildings. At the top end, there is a grotto, its design related to Kent's cascades at Chiswick and Rousham, and near the centre, there is a modest cascade, falling through a low three-arched bridge, which leads the stream (here called the Styx, the name of the river in the underworld dividing the living from the dead) into the most open part of the valley. On one side, there is Kent's Temple of British Worthies (c.1735), a semi-circular arcade with spaces for the busts of 16 great and good Britons of the past, from Alfred to the Black Prince, Queen Elizabeth, Milton and Pope. Many of these were chosen for having lived at one point or another in their existence in conflict with the ruler, party or government in power – like Lord Cobham himself. This temple, or arcade, looks across the stream to another temple higher up on the opposite slope – the circular Temple of Ancient Virtue (c.1735). It once held four statues, of Homer, Socrates, Lycurgus and Epaminondas (the poet, philosopher, law-giver and general of antiquity) to match the 'British Worthies' of more recent times. The inscriptions in both temples were probably by George Lyttelton, Lord Cobham's cousin, who would soon 'improve' his property at Hagley in Worcestershire with buildings and monuments of a similarly poetic and historical kind (see page 200). Kent's Temple of Ancient Virtue was modelled on the Temple of the Sibyl at Tivoli, a building which he saw on his travels in Italy, and which he would also have seen in various settings in the paintings of Claude Lorrain and Gaspard Dughet. The temple at Stowe was the first version of the Temple of the Sibyl to be built in a British garden, and was to be followed by many more – for example, at Wentworth Castle, on the terrace at Rievaulx and at Bramham Park, all in Yorkshire, and at Highclere in Hampshire. The poetic culmination was at Ermenonville in France, where in 1776–7, as the 'temple of Philosophy', it was built at last in a *ruined* form, echoing the ruined original at Tivoli, and conveying the poetic message that the 'edifice' of philosophy still awaited the great philosopher of the future to bring about its completion.[25] At Stowe, Kent's Temple of Ancient Virtue needs indeed to be in a 'complete' form, since its poetic message is of an already achieved moral perfection which we should endeavour to imitate. As if to mock our present inadequacy, Kent did in fact design a little *ruined* temple nearby (it has long since disappeared) named the 'Temple of Modern Virtue' (c.1737).

If the 'Elysian Fields' at Stowe are 'the painting part' of the gardens – a three-dimensional evocation of a Claudian landscape – they are still only a part of a far larger whole. At Rousham in Oxfordshire, however, Kent's work (between about 1736 and 1741) effectively remodelled the whole of a much smaller existing scheme, to make the gardens, some 25 acres, into a sequence of different pictorial compositions. Nearly all were given a 'classical' feeling by the use of sculptures or architectural features, and also given a wider feeling of landscape from the varied views of the Oxfordshire countryside, seen beyond the meandering course of the River Cherwell, which forms the eastern boundary of the gardens. Within the gardens, therefore (the house overlooks the bowling green and the ground further out along one axis, but is not in evidence elsewhere), there is a continuing and compelling sense of natural yet poetical scenery, with little geometry, but carefully placed sculpture, terms, seats and balustrades, a freely flowing river and winding paths, a pool and rustic cascade of apparent age (like that at Chiswick), an arcaded viewing shelter ('Praeneste') and a temple ('Townesend's Building'), which offer a score of different 'landscapes' of a classical kind. In his essay 'On Modern Gardening' of 1770, Horace Walpole looked back at Rousham (which he had praised in 1760 as 'the best thing I have seen of Kent') and wrote: 'The whole is as elegant and antique as if the Emperor Julian had selected the most pleasing solitude ... to enjoy a philosophic retirement.'[26] When we look out from Venus' Vale over the course of the Cherwell, or from the sculpture of the Dying Gladiator, or from Townesend's Building, we are indeed enjoying an elegant, antique and pleasing solitude. But Walpole forgot, or decided not to mention, the thirteenth-century Heyford Bridge which closes the northern end of the gardens, and the two distinctly un-classical objects which Kent engineered in the further part of the eastern axis from the house – the Gothic flying buttresses and cross, which he added to Cuttle Mill to make it look like a small medieval chapel or hermitage, and the gaunt three-arched 'Eyecatcher', which he set on the distant skyline (both c.1735–38). These objects – the genuinely medieval bridge and Kent's mock-medieval structures – have nothing to do with the ancient classics or with paintings of the Italian landscape; but they have a great deal to do with Britain's native landscape and its ancient history, both matters of growing interest to garden makers in this period.

Kent had in fact already designed two other buildings related to Britain's national past, for the royal grounds at Richmond (again the setting was a scheme laid out by Charles Bridgeman) and commissioned by Queen Caroline. Kent's Hermitage (c.1731–2) and Merlin's Cave (1735) housed, respectively, busts of five notable British scientists, philosophers and theologians – Boyle, Newton, Locke, Wollaston and Clarke – and six figures including the magician Merlin, Merlin's 'secretary', Queen Elizabeth and Minerva, goddess of war, wisdom and the arts.

While these people, real or mythical, are not impossibly different from those commemorated at Stowe – and lead on likewise to the philosophers celebrated at Ermenonville – their settings, the Hermitage and Merlin's Cave, were strongly tinged with the new ideas of garden fashion. The Hermitage, though classical in design, was roughly constructed, and had apparently sunk in parts into the ground, and Merlin's Cave included a thatched roof, Gothic buttresses and an ogive central door. Added to these native qualities was the custodian, the 'thresher poet' Stephen Duck (1705–56), who had been 'discovered' in 1725, writing verse in rural obscurity. Raised to public notice, and envy, as 'Cave and Library Keeper', he was unavoidably subject to a part of the mockery provoked by Queen Caroline's garden enthusiasm (already in 1727 she was seen by the poet Edward Young as 'very fine at Richmond, with Canals, Plantations, Terraces and Popularity'[27]).

Apart from these buildings, Kent's share in this move towards a more native style is uncertain, though in 1753, five years after his death, he was said to have 'imitated nature even in her blemishes, and planted dead trees and mole-hills, in opposition to parterres and quincunxes'.[28]

Such antique and native wildness was to continue and to prosper for much of the century; but the parallels between garden making and landscape painting of an Italianate kind were for some time even more important. In 1762, considering the completion of his central vistas at Stourhead in Wiltshire, between the Pantheon and the grotto on one side of the lake, and the Temple of Flora, the Roman bridge and the parish church on the other, Henry Hoare wrote with satisfaction '[it] will be a Charmg Gaspd [Gaspard] picture'.[29] Two years later, William Shenstone's 'Unconnected Thoughts on Gardening' were published, summing up his garden experience, and stating that his subject was not kitchen or parterre gardening, but 'landskip, or picturesque-gardening'; this was to cover the 'home scenes' of a property (the 'distant images' and 'blue distant hills' were classed as 'prospects') and 'should contain variety enough to form a picture upon canvas; and this is no bad test, as I think the landskip painter is the gardener's best designer'.[30]

While this view undoubtedly encouraged the general idea that certain elements of a landscape painting à la Claude were desirable, if not essential, in a landscape garden, it remains a curious inconsequentiality that in this period few landscape painters of merit ever designed gardens. They may sometimes have painted them as part of their subject matter (often as a background, with the owner and his family in front), and it is easy to think of examples by George Lambert, Arthur Devis, Richard Wilson, Thomas Gainsborough or Joseph Wright of Derby. We may turn the professions round, and note as truly that in this same period those who designed gardens were not renowned for landscape painting. Alexander Pope, we are told, studied painting in his youth, but his teacher, Charles Jervas, was a portraitist. William Kent trained as a painter, it is true, but his finished works are both mediocre to poor and unrelated to gardens, and his garden sketches, engaging and instructive though they may be, have only the rarest connection with 'landscape' as an art. His view of Venus' Vale at Rousham is a happy exception.

Indeed, the landscape painters I have named, and most of those who followed for the rest of the century – Philip James de Loutherbourg, Thomas Jones, John 'Warwick' Smith, John Robert Cozens and the great Turner – were interested more and more in landscape of a native, rather than an Italian kind; and the later ones moved also towards scenes of a 'sublime' – rough, savage, violent – rather than a gentle or idyllic character, thus, in general, moving beyond the kinds of landscape which most gardens could offer. This change was slow, and not perceived for many years, when eventual awareness of it heralded the beginnings of a return to formal gardening, which triumphed again for most of the nineteenth century. In 1782, the topographical writer and artist William Gilpin differentiated his admiration for the 'picturesque' scenery of the Lake District from the poet William Mason's love of landscaped gardens – 'You are the patron of *improved nature*: my delight is in its *wilder scenes*'.[31]

Nine years later Sir Joshuah Reynolds, who had been reflecting upon Gilpin's writings on the picturesque, made an absolute separation between the art of painting and the art of gardening. He objected to Gilpin's wish to enliven gardens by making them picturesque:

> I cannot approve . . . of your idea of reforming the art of gardening by the picturesque of landscape painting. It appears to me undervaluing the art of gardening, which I hold to be an art that stands on its own bottom, and is governed by different principles.

These 'principles' are that the garden 'ought to have . . . the marks of art upon it: . . . it should appear at first sight a cultivated spot – that it is inhabited, that everything is in order, convenient, and comfortable; which a state of nature will not produce'.[32]

But all this is a long way on from the 1730s and 1740s, when Philip Southcote had stated ''tis all painting', and William Shenstone agreed.

Their 'painting' involved a variety of buildings – at Southcote's Wooburn, from 1734 onwards, an 'octagon' (possibly designed by Lord Burlington), a ruined chapel, another Gothic building, one or two bridges, a 'menagerie' with Gothic trimmings for hens and ornamental birds, and further seats and alcoves – and essential *variety* in the spacing of these buildings and the planting of trees, shrubs and flowers. Again and again, Southcote used terms from painting to explain his ideas – 'perspective, prospect, distancing and attracting' – 'perspective' meaning 'looking *under* trees to some further object', 'prospect' meaning 'looking *by* trees', and 'by distancing you may make an object *look three times as far off* as it is. This is done by narrowing the plantation gradually on each side, almost to a point at last . . .'[33]

Wooburn Farm covered some 130 acres, of which about 35 were 'ornamented', and the remainder used as pasture or arable land. A stream was extended through part of the farm, with a long serpentine 'U' section near the house. The ornamentation with the buildings and the stream was co-ordinated by a walk through and round the property:

> All my design at first was to have a garden on the middle high ground and a walk all round my farm . . . from the garden I could see what was doing in the grounds, and by the walk could have a pleasing access to either of them.[34]

This walk was therefore essentially different from the paths of earlier formal gardens, radiating from the house or the mansion. Its aim was to reveal the garden, the grounds and the countryside, all from continually changing viewpoints and from varying distances; and it was itself ornamented – 'these walks are adorned not only with plantations of wood but with spots and beds of flowering shrubs and other flowers to fill up angles, and other shrubs to diversifie the scene'. So wrote Dr Pococke after a visit in 1757,[35] and Joseph Spence drew an 'Order of Planting after Mr Southcote's Manner' which fills in the detail of a section of a walk. On the outer side, the boundary of the property, there were different large trees, then lesser trees, then shrubs; next came a border with three rows of flowering plants – tall ones, such as sunflowers, hollyhocks, crown imperials and golden rod, at the back; then middle-sized flowers – stocks, Canterbury bells, wallflowers, lavender and half a dozen more; and crocus, snowdrops and primroses at the front, edged with a line of pinks. The walk itself, sanded over, came next, and was bounded on the inner side with a fence to enclose the sheep or cattle in the fields.[36]

'The Enchanting Paths of Paradise'

Among the amateur garden creators of this period, two of the most important were Charles Hamilton (1704–86) and Henry Hoare (1705–85). They had been at Westminster School together for two or three years, and remained in contact. Hamilton borrowed money for his garden endeavours from Hoare's Bank in London (directed by Henry Hoare), and Henry Hoare consulted Hamilton on garden matters.

Hamilton acquired land at Painshill in Surrey from 1738 onwards, and sold the property – some 200 acres – in 1773, while Hoare inherited the Stourton estate in Wiltshire – some 3,000 acres – from his father in 1725, and began to develop the gardens at Stourhead, within the Stourton estate, in 1741. He retired to London in 1783, leaving his grandson, Sir Richard Colt Hoare in charge of the property.

Both these gardens, begun in the 1740s and developed with knowledge of each other over the next three decades, reflect the ideas and interests of the new enthusiasm for 'nature', for the 'landscape' and for 'painting', which had been elaborated as an alternative to the formality of the previous age. Both gardens were begun from scratch, and had therefore no earlier elements of a formal or geometrical kind to be accommodated or concealed. But even more important than the effect of this 'clear field', is the exceptional fact that in neither garden can the house be seen.

For Hamilton at Painshill this was partly to do with money. He never had enough to pay for a new house which he wanted to build in a part of his landscape, and had to make do with an old, modest and unassuming farmhouse in a corner of the property (in fact, like William Shenstone at The Leasowes, whose farmhouse, however, lay at the centre of the estate). Not far away, and equally hidden from the gardens he created, is a walled kitchen garden, which he used both for vegetables and for special flowers. For Hoare, it was far more clearly a matter of choice. His Palladian mansion at Stourhead has its own views, prospects and park, but from it, no glimpse whatever of the gardens is allowed.

In both gardens, therefore, there is no direct, straight or visible link between them and the house. No formal avenue connects them, merely a choice of winding paths. Once within either of these gardens – and this is immensely rare at any point in the thousands of years of garden history, go back as far as you will – you are in a region gardened for the sake of the garden, not the house; gardened for pleasure, delight and poetry. Both represent an attempt to create an earthly paradise, within the limits, of course, of the creator's purse (Hoare was far more wealthy than Hamilton) and his understanding, in the 1740s, of what such a paradise might comprise.

Both gardens have large, artificial yet natural-looking lakes. At Pains-hill, Hamilton pumped water up from the adjacent River Mole to make a long, sinuous and convincing sheet of water along his southern bound-ary. At Stourhead, Hoare dammed the water from hillside streams to enlarge and unite a group of earlier fishponds, his lake being as 'natural' as Hamilton's, if the stretch of dam is ignored. Beside and around these lakes are buildings of a wholly poetic and allusive kind; in none of them can one sleep, work or live, except in an occasional 'picnic' manner. Hamilton's buildings are far slighter than Hoare's, since he lacked money to build them solidly, like the great Pantheon or the Temple of Apollo at Stourhead. But Hamilton's buildings are equally as poetic, as related to the inspiration of ancient architecture or poetry, or the paintings of Claude, Gaspard or Salvator Rosa, or thoughts of medieval England, as anything Hoare devised. At Painshill, there is rather more of the med-ieval, the ruined, the Gothic and the wild, so that Hamilton's pinewoods were thought to recall scenes from Rosa. His Mausoleum probably inspired Sir William Chambers' 'ruined arch' at Kew; his Gothic Temple and the distant Gothic Tower, built around 1760, are complete buildings, while his Ruined Abbey of around 1770 tells of the inexorable march of time. For his Hermitage, built in 1750, he tried unsuccessfully to engage a live, solitary, chaste and abstemious hermit, and his elaborate Grotto, laid out to his design by Josiah Lane by 1765, was for years a triumphant recreation of the caves around the Gulf of Naples, celebrated by Virgil.

At Stourhead, independently, or occasionally with influence from Painshill, Henry Hoare created a gentler but equally poetic paradise. A Virgilian theme is apparent in the Grotto (made before Hamilton's), with sculptures of the nymph and river god, the nymph accompanied by Alexander Pope's elegant verses translated from the Latin.[37] A classical sense is obvious from the view westwards over the lake towards the Pantheon. Seen from such a point, close to St Peter's, the parish church of Stourton village, or from a few yards northwards beside the Temple of Flora (where one might have arrived after walking through the woodland paths from the mansion), the lake and woodland view is comprised of mainly classical buildings – nearby, the Temple of Flora (1744–5) and the Roman Bridge (1762); opposite, across the lake, the Pantheon (1754–6) and the Grotto (c.1748), and, high up on the southern slope, the Temple of Apollo (c.1765). This last building was also in the nature of an archi-tectural novelty when it was erected, since its original, among the ruins at Baalbec, had only recently been discovered and delineated in Robert Wood's *Ruins of Balbec and Palmyra* of 1757.

The main pool in Venus' Vale at Rousham – 'a philosophic retirement' unseen from the winding river Cherwell beyond.

The spacious scheme at Castle Kennedy was laid out in the 1730s. The Round Pool is surrounded by later plantings, and an avenue of monkey puzzles leads away to Lochinch Castle.

If you stand over by the Pantheon, however, and look to the east, there is a different 'poem' to appreciate. Beside the Temple of Flora and the Roman Bridge, the view now includes the Gothic monuments of earlier English history – the parish church and, nearby, the Bristol High Cross, re-erected at Stourhead in 1765. As Henry Hoare wrote to his daughter in 1762, when the Roman Bridge was being built near, but not too near, to the church, 'the View of the Bridge, Village and Church altogether will be a Charmg Gaspd [Gaspard] picture,'[38] – in other words, the view was to look like one of Gaspard Poussin's paintings. The Gothic and the medieval did in fact appear at Stourhead a little later, in the form of a hermitage (now gone), imitated from Hamilton's at Painshill (Hoare proposed himself as resident hermit in 1771),[39] and the tall three-sided tower, Alfred's Tower, built around 1769–72 on the far north-western edge of the Stourton estate.[40]

Few gardens, of this or any other period, have such a full independence from the house, from service buildings, from the world of work and business. Comparisons, partial but worthwhile, may yet be drawn with the long walk eastwards from the house at Castle Howard in North Yorkshire, where the gently winding terrace, flanked with statues, leads away to Vanbrugh's Temple of the Four Winds (1726–8). Here, from a bastion overlooking an immense area of field, wood and moorland, the visitor faces the distant Mausoleum, designed by Nicholas Hawksmoor in 1728, and the Roman or New River Bridge of around 1740. No houses, no vegetable garden can be seen, only, as Horace Walpole wrote in 1772, 'the grandest scenes of rural magnificence'.

We may think also of Studley Royal and of the Rievaulx Terraces, both in North Yorkshire. At each of these sites, at Studley in 1768 and at Rievaulx around 1758, the respective owners were able to fulfil earlier ambitions of acquiring land related to adjacent ruins. At Studley, these were the ruins of Fountains Abbey, which could now conclude the long, winding path beside the River Skell from John Aislabie's perfect crescent pools and temple, while at Rievaulx the half mile or so of terrace walk, set between a Tuscan temple at one end and an Ionic temple at the other, could now overlook the ruins of Rievaulx Abbey far below. At Rievaulx, as at Painshill and at Stourhead, the owner's house, Duncombe Park, is far away and out of sight. The visitor to the terraces is in a world of poetry, gazing at the ever changing and unreachable spectacle of the abbey ruins while advancing along the high curving terrace, and aware meanwhile of the classical temples, one round, one rectangular, which stand entire and unruined at either end of the grassy walk.

A last comparison from this period is with the vast, yet intensely private landscape at West Wycombe House in Buckinghamshire. This landscape, with lake, plantations and buildings, is the creation of Sir Francis Dashwood (1708–81), the lake being formed in the late 1730s and various temples and other buildings being added from around 1740–80.

While West Wycombe House was remodelled between about 1739 and 1771 by several architects, and forms a conspicuous feature from many viewpoints, the details of the landscape are again and again of a personal, rather than a public, kind and such that the 'affairs of the world', of politics and the city, are not involved. Temples, as at Stour-head, are unrelated to humdrum concerns – the Temple of the Winds, in rough flints, and the Temple of Music being situated on the main island in the lake. The little Temple of Venus beside the lake has a suggestive lower entrance, while the lake itself was at one time 'laid out by a curious arrangement of streams, bushes and plantations to represent the female form'. Later, more discreetly, it was made to resemble a swan. High up on the neighbouring hillside, stands St Laurence's Church, on the tower of which Dashwood erected a gilded sphere, large enough to admit a group of enthusiasts, while vertically below, in 1748–52, deep in the chalk of the hill, Dashwood's workers scooped out the labyrinthine 'Hell-Fire Caves'. Near to the church and, like the church, visible from the park below, the roofless hexagonal Mausoleum was built in 1764–5. In Dashwood's day, it bore no Christian tokens at all, and Dashwood's own monument has no reference to Christianity. Yet the Mausoleum was built, to Dashwood's order, partly within and partly outside the consecrated ground of the churchyard. Hedging his bets.

In the Elysian Fields at Stowe, the Temple of Ancient Virtue rises beyond the river Styx. Glimpsed to one side, the parish church, where Capability Brown was married in 1744.

From the Grotto at Stourhead: the Temple of Flora, the Bristol High Cross, St Peter's Church, the Roman Bridge – in all, 'a charming Gaspard picture'.

12

'DIVINI GLORIA RURIS'

William Shenstone

At this point in the eighteenth century, it is difficult to know how much contact there was between garden enthusiasts in different parts of Britain. Many were amateurs, owners of property which might be 'improved', and the property itself could be large or small, from spacious estates like Stowe, West Wycombe, Stourhead or Hagley to Alexander Pope's or Horace Walpole's five or more acres. If they lived near London, or had a London residence, their links with other enthusiasts might be greater; if their estate was far from London, their contacts depended on their wealth (allowing extensive travel to London or elsewhere), on their circle of friends and visitors, on their political, religious and social connections, and, of course, on the degree and quality of their enthusiasm. To draw the web of connections produces a patchy scheme at best.

To come to William Shenstone (1714–63), he owned a small grazing farm of about 150 acres near Halesowen, not far from Birmingham, and had a relatively small income. Leaving Oxford in 1737 without a degree, he returned to The Leasowes (a local term meaning 'the meadows'), and, apart from rare visits to London, he remained mostly at or near The Leasowes for the rest of his life, visiting friends at Hagley (the Lyttletons), at Barrells (Lady Luxborough), Radway near Edge Hill (Sanderson Miller) and Enville (Lord Stamford), corresponding copiously with them and with other friends such as Richard Graves, Richard Jago and Thomas Percy, and receiving innumerable visits from friends and strangers, as his *ferme ornée* became more and more renowned, being as much visited and as praised (in its way) as Alexander Pope's Twickenham, Lord Burlington's Chiswick or even Lord Cobham's Stowe.

For all his eventual fame, Shenstone's own garden circle was essentially local, and astonishingly unconnected with the gardens and gardeners in other parts of Britain. The lack of contact between Shenstone and Philip Southcote is puzzling – there is no evidence that Shenstone ever visited Southcote's property at Wooburn, and his letters have only one oblique reference to Southcote. (We might add, that Southcote does not seem to have designed gardens for other people.) Nor does Shenstone say anything directly about William Kent.

With, or probably without, Southcote's influence, Shenstone's *ferme ornée* was clearly in the same mould as Wooburn, but with advantages of contour – slopes, valleys and cascading streams – which Wooburn lacked, and with views out, towards the western hills, which few could equal. These natural advantages were so great that one tactless visitor remarked, that at The Leasowes 'Nature must claim the chief merit', thus rousing Shenstone's gentle reply, 'that he hoped he had done something for Nature too'.[1] He began shaping his sloping pastures round a less than elegant farmhouse in the early 1740s, and his walk and its ornamentation occupied him just as it had Southcote at Wooburn. In comparison, Shenstone's was longer, and – though his lack of money stopped him from building grand structures – it was studded with dozens of different viewing (or *reflecting*) points, in the form of seats, benches, urns, statues, bowers, alcoves, an obelisk, a Gothic screen, a root-house and a ruin. From Robert Dodsley's description and plan of The Leasowes, published a year after Shenstone's death, we may trace over 40 of these points, mostly with seats and mostly with inscriptions, in Latin or English, which suggested to the visitor what thoughts or feelings were appropriate. One of the first in the itinerary was characteristic. Passing down a narrow, tree-shaded valley – 'at once cool, gloomy, solemn, and sequestered', you reached a small 'root-house, where on a tablet were these lines:

> Here in cool grot, and mossy cell,
> We rural fays and faeries dwell;
> Tho' rarely seen by mortal eye,
> When the pale moon, ascending high,
> Darts thro' yon limes her quivering beams,
> We frisk it near these crystal streams.[2]

A 'root-house' was a building made from the large and irregularly shaped roots of trees (the gaps were filled with lesser twigs, clay or plaster), and it was both primitive and antique in character, and less costly than a building in brick or stone. For Shenstone, on £300 a year, this was important. The long catalogue of his garden ornaments has some 30 or more seats and benches, 'rustic', 'gothic', with a 'screen' or 'bower', but few items of a costly kind – the 'Priory ruin' which was made partly from materials from the remains of Halesowen Abbey nearby, the 'Temple of Pan', an 'obelisk' and a couple of statues.

But for the visitor (unless in a grumpy mood, like Dr Johnson, whose comments are condescending, and to whom all this was at best no more than 'an innocent amusement', though Shenstone had laboured 'to point his prospects, to diversify his surface, to entangle his walks, and to wind his waters', which 'he did with such judgement and such fancy as made his little domain the envy of the great'[3]), what mattered was the variety of sentiment, grave or gay, learned or personal: 'Virgil's Grove', the 'lover's walk', a memorial to the late Miss Dolman, inscriptions to friends and poets, alive or dead, a cheery toast 'To all friends round the Wrekin!', and, at the highest point in the property, overlooking The Leasowes and the distant hills, 'DIVINI GLORIA RURIS' – 'the glory of the divine countryside'.

Today, a fragmentary yet still lovely walk survives, past stream and groves and open grass, as does the expansive view, of 'the noble concave in the front, and the rich valley'. Robert Dodsley compared it with a 'punch-bowl, ornamented with all the romantic scenery the Chinese ever yet devised' – 'the highest idea one's boon companion could possibly conceive of human happiness. He would certainly wish to swim in it'.[4]

Shenstone's influence spread out from The Leasowes to reach many nearby garden enthusiasts and many others who visited him on their travels, the degree of influence varying, of course, with the visitor's ability, means or freedom to implement the ideas Shenstone's creation provided. In the immediate circle of admirers was Henrietta, Lady Luxborough (c.1699–1756), living at Barrells in Warwickshire, a small estate to which her husband had banished her in the 1730s. This property is now firmly restored to agriculture, but for a few years, from the early 1740s until her death, she gardened actively, and wrote copiously about and around it to Shenstone. The idea of the *ferme ornée* was known to her already – Lord Bolingbroke (of Dawley in Middlesex – see page 173) was her half-brother – and she wrote happily of an intended visit to Shenstone's *ferme ornée*, to be followed by his visit to her *ferme negligée*. Though the exact layout of her garden is hard to reconstruct, the details and the activities are numerous and beguiling – the stocking of roots 'for future root-houses'; the design and composition of a memorial urn with inscriptions for the poet William Somervile; the Virgilian delights of a beehive in her library; making – and changing – a ha-ha ('The Ha-Ha is digging', and then, three months later 'to consider the Ha! Ha! to be lowered two bricks'); and above all, the various walks and areas of 'shrubbery', where, as Philip Southcote had done, she had many flowers.

One letter alone tells of 'great variety of cowslips, primroses, ragged-robbins, wild hyacinths both white and blue, violets . . . large bushes of Whitsun-roses . . . lilac . . . syringa . . . sweetbriar . . . roses'.[5]

Her own concerns are mingled with comment on Shenstone's progress, in 'Virgil's Grove', or in experiments with an Aeolian harp (this, in 1748–9, just after their joint friend James Thomson had produced his 'Ode on Aeolus's Harp', printed by another friend, Robert Dodsley). This 'instrument' – a sounding-box with taut, tuned strings made to vibrate by the wind – was favoured at this time, and later, as the source of 'natural' music.[6] And Lady Luxborough discusses other gardens, briefly or at length – Mr Cambridge's 'seat on the Severn' (Whitminster in Gloucestershire), and Hagley in Worcestershire, where in 1748, she was looking forward to seeing 'Mr Lyttleton's castle', which Shenstone had described in an earlier letter.[7]

'Mr Lyttleton's castle' was built in 1747–8. Designed by Sanderson Miller (1717–80), it was for George Lyttleton and his acquaintances an excursion into an untried region – the Gothic. This castle, built as a ruin, with one bigger and several lesser towers, is the earliest mock-Gothic ruin in Britain, to be compared only with the ruined arches on the skyline at Mount Edgcumbe in Cornwall (c.1747). Though an oddity, a curiosity, fully deserving the appellation 'folly', which had been applied to William Kent's earlier 'Eyecatcher' at Rousham and to a host of other garden buildings in the eighteenth century, it is also an architectural *experiment*, a daring venture into an outmoded style – the Gothic – and into an untried form – the ruined – which had previously been approached only in paintings or in slight and tentative reality, at Alfred's Hall at Cirencester, and at Kent's Cuttle Mill and 'Eyecatcher' at Rousham. Such experiment was to be continued at Hagley in 1758–9, when James Stuart ('Athenian' Stuart) designed and built the Temple of Theseus, the first building in the eighteenth century to display the primitive Doric style. Within a year, Stuart was to design another temple in the primitive Doric style at Shugborough in Staffordshire. Shugborough had been extensively developed from the 1740s onwards for Thomas Anson and his brother Commodore (later Lord) Anson, and they too were well-known to Lyttleton and to Shenstone. By 1747, there was a 'Chinese' house in the grounds there, recalling Anson's visit to Canton during his circumnavigation; artificial ruins followed, many classical reconstructions, and even, around 1770, a pagoda.[8]

To return to the Gothic at Hagley, Shenstone and Lady Luxborough were eager witnesses to the developments there. In June 1748, Shenstone wrote to her that 'Mr Lyttleton has near finish'd one side of his Castle. It consists of one entire Tow'r, and three Stumps of Towers, with a ruin'd

Wall betwixt them'. He added a sketch.[9] These comments go well with Horace Walpole's, who saw the castle in September 1753, and wrote approvingly to Richard Bentley that it 'has the true rust of the Barons' wars'.

In June 1751, between Shenstone and Walpole, Dr Pococke visited Hagley and wrote a long description. In this he relates that one of the walks leads to a hill 'on which is built a ruined castle . . . a beautiful effect. This castle is seen in different views from many parts of the lawns and wood'.[10] Pococke's remark is helpful – the castle was not there as a place to live in or to use, but to be *seen* from 'many parts of the lawns and wood'. Lyttleton's enthusiasm had also produced an 'Ionic rotunda', a seat dedicated to James Thomson, and a column dedicated to the Prince of Wales. These, like the Gothic castle and the Temple of Theseus, all remain.

Between 1754 and 1760, Sanderson Miller also designed the new house at Hagley in a partly Gothic mode, and earlier had added substantial Gothic items to his own property at Radway in Warwickshire – first the Cottage (1744), then his house, Radway Grange (enlarged *c.* 1745), and in 1746–50 the octagonal Edge Hill Tower, reminiscent of Guy's Tower at Warwick. Miller also designed garden features for Lord Stamford at Enville in Staffordshire at about the same period, notably a 'Gothic greenhouse', a hermit's house, a castellated wall and a Chinese temple, while Shenstone advised on the laying out of walks through the grounds.

Faced with the grandeur of the mansion at Hagley, and the impressive architectural qualities of many of the garden buildings, it is easy to forget that Hagley too was given walks like those at The Leasowes, Barrells or Enville, where the varied prospects, near and far, were meant to inspire the visitor with a kind of religious delight in the wonders of nature. In 1777, a stirring claim to this effect was made by Joseph Heely, writing of the 'beauties' of the park at Hagley:

> Here, methinks, if any where, among such tranquil bowers, where peace and pleasure seem to dwell, the villain would be disarmed from executing his dark and bloody purposes; and every passion that corrodes the human breast, be lulled into a perfect calm.[11]

'The Rurality of It'

The *ferme ornée*, or something pretty similar, reached Ireland in the 1740s with Mrs Delany (1700–88), together with her passion for shell ornament, whether in the house or in the garden. Born Mary Granville, she was married to Alexander Pendarves in 1717 or 1718, and was widowed in 1724. In 1731 she travelled to Ireland to visit friends. Waiting near Chester for the boat to Dublin, she had time to call at Eaton Hall, the Grosvenor property, where she noted 'the gardens are laid out in the old-fashioned taste with cut work parterres and wilderness enclosed in hedges'.[12] Though she expressed admiration for the gardens, and she was to see many more in the formal style in Ireland, her own preference was for a more natural approach – as we shall see.

Having arrived in Dublin, she quickly became acquainted or re-acquainted with Jonathan Swift, with Dr Patrick Delany (whom she married in 1743) and others, and her travels in Ireland were soon under way. In 1732 she wrote from Killalla in Co. Mayo 'we were hard at work, gathering a fresh recruit of shells to finish the grotto'.[13] This may have been her first venture into shell grottoes, and they, and gardens – if we may unite them – remained a passion with her. In 1732 she wrote to Dr Delany at Delville, outside Dublin:

> I already delight in your garden; pray have plenty of roses, honeysuckles, jasmine and sweet briar, not forgetting the lily of the valley . . .[14]

Back in England in 1733, she wrote to Swift of her visit to Cirencester and Alfred's Hall, and then, in 1736, she told him that she has been busy making a shell grotto – it gave her 'full employment' – for her uncle Sir John Stanley at 'North-End' in Fulham.[15] Much later, in 1750, she sent consignments of shells to her brother, for a grotto she had designed for him at Calwich Abbey, near Ashbourne in Derbyshire, and later still she helped the Duchess of Portland with the design and ornamentation of a grotto at Bulstrode in Buckinghamshire.

Mrs Delany's interest in grottoes and gardens is one of the links in this history between England and Ireland in the early to mid-eighteenth century. During her first visit to Ireland in 1731–3 she had observed and advised on other people's gardens. When in 1744 she moved to Ireland after marrying Dr Delany, the 11-acre property at Delville became her home. Dr Delany had begun to develop the grounds some years before, around 1724, and he had stayed briefly with Alexander Pope in Twick-enham in 1728, by which time Pope was well on with the elaboration of *his* five acres. Though we do not know exactly how each part of the Delville property had been set out, a long letter by Mrs Delany describing the garden soon after her arrival in 1744 shows that it was far nearer in spirit to Bolingbroke's Dawley, or to Philip Southcote's Wooburn

Farm (begun in 1734–5 – see page 190) than to Pope's garden at Twickenham:

> The back part of the house is towards a bowling green that slopes gently off down to a little brook that runs through the garden; on the other side of the brook is a high bank with a hanging wood of ever-greens, at the top of which is a circular terrace that surrounds the greatest part of the garden, the wall of which is covered with fruit-trees, and on the other side of the walk a border for flowers, and the greatest quantity of roses and sweet briar that I ever saw; on the right hand of the bowling green towards the bottom is placed our hay-rick, which is at present making . . .

Other parts of the garden were obviously due to be developed further:

> On the left hand of the bowling green is a terrace walk that takes in a sort of parterre, that will make the prettiest orangery in the world, for it is an oval of green, planted round in double rows of elm-trees and flowering shrubs with little grass walks between them, which will give a good shelter to exotics.

Elsewhere,

> . . . the ground rises very considerably . . . there is a path that goes up that bank to the remains of an old castle (as it were) from whence there is an unbounded prospect . . . under it is a cave that opens with an arch to the terrace-walk, that will make a very pretty grotto; and the plan I had laid for my brother at Calwich . . . I shall execute here . . .

The sense of the *ferme ornée* then becomes particularly clear:

> In the middle, sloping from the terrace, every way, are the fields, or rather paddocks, where our deer and our cows are kept, and the rurality of it is wonderfully pretty. These fields are planted in a *wild way* with *forest trees and with bushes* that look so naturally you would not imagine it to be the work of art.

Even then, she had not finished. There was 'a very good kitchen garden and two fruit gardens' which were to be 'set in order', and 'several prettinesses' which she was unable to explain – 'little wild walks, private seats, and lovely prospects'. She ended with 'the beggar's hut',

> . . . which is a seat in a rock; on the top are bushes of all kinds that bend over; it is placed at the end of a cunning wild path thick set with trees and it overlooks the brook which entertains you with a purling rill.[16]

Mrs Delany's own sketches of the Delville garden date from 1744 onwards, and these and her continuing correspondence show that the 11 acres were cared for and developed unceasingly. Shellwork, for a grotto and for interior decorations, was a continuing passion, and there were additions also of a nine-pin alley, an auricula stand, a further greenhouse, a house and enclosure for exotic birds, and a bridge. All this kept her, and Dr Delany, most happily occupied until his death in 1768. It was costly too – a wag wrote that Dr Delany was

Quite ruin'd and bankrupt, reduc'd to a farthing
By making too much of a very small garden

– an echo of the impecunious but equally happy Matthew Prior at Down Hall (see page 172).

While her own *ferme ornée* progressed, Mrs Delany found time to see – often several times – other gardens in Ireland, which were as frequently 'new' as they were old-fashioned. At Dangan in Co. Meath, for example, the grounds were being 'improved' in 1732–3 in the formal manner, with three straight canals, and temples and classical statuary.[17] By 1748, the canals had been 'softened', and joined into a single, 26-acre lake with islands – and varied small ships, 'one a complete man-of-war' – round which were two dozen or so obelisks and other monuments and a sizeable fort.[18]

Another larger garden and park began slightly later, in 1739 or 1740, when John, 5th Earl of Orrery, came to manage the estate of Caledon, Co. Tyrone, after his marriage to Margaret Hamilton in 1738. He had already gardened in a relatively formal way at Marston House in Somerset – Stephen Switzer had designed a long terrace with cascades for him there in the late 1720s, and in Badeslade and Rocque's *Vitruvius Britannicus*, IV, of 1739 there is a bird's-eye view of the house and gardens. Switzer had come to Ireland to work at Breckdenstown, Co. Dublin, around 1719, and he may well have come again for the first stages of the work at Caledon. By the later 1740s, Lord Orrery's enthusiasm was turning towards wilder schemes, notably a bone-house and a hermitage. The former is the sole remaining relic of the garden structures at Caledon,[19] and was inspired to some extent by an earlier 'ossified edifice' at Kedleston in Derbyshire. The hermitage (or root-house) was, according to Mrs Delany in 1748, the first of Lord Orrery's projects to be completed. It was on an island, of about an acre, with appropriate plantings,

The scrollwork parterre at Chatelherault in Lanarkshire. One of the last formal layouts in Britain, it was made in the 1730s, and accurately restored in the 1980s.

The 'Swift and Swans Island' in the garden of Delville, Dublin. A sketch of part of her *ferme ornée, recorded by* Mrs Delany in 1743. Courtesy of National Gallery of Ireland.

... and in the midst is placed an hermit's cell, made of the roots of trees, the floor is paved with pebbles, there is a couch made of matting, and little wooden stools, a table with a manuscript on it, a pair of spectacles, a leathern bottle; and hung up in different parts, an hourglass, a weatherglass and several mathematical instruments, a shelf of books, another of wooden platters and bowls, in short everything that you might imagine necessary for a recluse.

To this (extraordinary in 1748, long before the 'hermitages' of Painshill and Stourhead), she adds that

Four little gardens surround his house – an orchard, a flower-garden, a physick-garden, and a kitchen-garden, with a kitchen to boil a teakettle or so: I never saw so pretty *a whim so thoroughly well* executed.[20]

True, the *idea* of the hermit was by now well under way – William Shenstone and Lady Luxborough referred to each other as hermits, and to their respective residences as hermitages in this time – but the *construction* of a hermitage at Caledon in 1748 was a novelty. Mrs Delany might also have witnessed extensive and extraordinary Gothic developments at Belvedere, Co. Westmeath, a property of Robert Rochfort, Lord Bellfield (later Lord Belvedere). In 1742, Lord Bellfield began the building of a villa to the north-east of Lough Ennell. His architect was Richard Castle, who worked also in Ireland at Carton and Powerscourt, both properties with earlier formal, and later landscape, layouts. At Belvedere, the demesne included several Gothic structures, some influenced by Thomas Wright, who travelled in Ireland in 1746–7, published his *Louthiana* in 1748 on the antiquities of Co. Louth, and in 1755 and 1758 published his two volumes of *Universal Architecture*, with designs for arbours and grottoes.[21]

Wright's *Louthiana*, a work of eminent obscurity, refers several times to Henry Rowlands' *Mona Antiqua Restaurata* of 1723, to do with sacred groves, the wooded and Elysian circles of Britain's ancient inhabitants. His views show embanked circles, grown over with trees, and a tree-shaded hermit's cell. From Wright's designs for Belvedere came the Gothic arch, the gazebo or summerhouse, octagonal like Philip Southcote's at Wooburn, and the huge – no less – 'jealous wall', built around 1760, to blot out the view of Lord Bellfield's brother's house nearby.[22]

Corby Castle and Sir John Clerk

While Southcote, Shenstone, Mrs Delany and not a few others were – and continued to be – fascinated with the *ferme ornée* (it went on easily into the 1820s with the 'Ladies of Llangollen' – see page 236), others turned to the attractions of wilder scenery. The earliest, and among the most striking, example of this was at Corby Castle, near Carlisle in Cumberland. Here, in the period 1720–40, Thomas Howard introduced sculpture, inscriptions, a complex summerhouse and cascade, a classical temple, and other memorials along the wooded and steeply sloping southern side of the River Eden. These were connected by paths, particularly the Green Walk, stretching half a mile along the bank. Cascade, temple and Green Walk are recorded in a plan of 1729, and by 1734 a visitor, Sir John Clerk, could report on the 'very agreable winding walk ... some artificial grotos ... a large walk ... beautified all along with grotoes and Statues of the Rural deities, at the end of this walk next the house is a Cascade 140 feet high'.[23]

Among these 'Rural deities' was probably the one-eyed giant Polyphemus, often called the 'Corby Giant'. Other sculptures were soon added – Clerk noted that the estate was 'vastly improven' in 1739, and in 1750 Dr Pococke saw and admired the 'cascade and water works adorned with grotesque works and statues'.[24] In the nineteenth century, the Green Walk was extended downstream to terminate with a statue of St Constantine, a statue of Nelson was set near the foot of the cascade, and other figures were added, but the essential quality and profound beauty of the site remains. It was, I suspect, the first example in the eighteenth century of a site where the landscape dictated how the garden and its features should be arranged. The 'genius of the place' was indeed respected at Corby.

Sir John Clerk visited Corby Castle at least four times, and his admiration for Thomas Howard's achievement led him both to model parts of his Scottish estate, at Penicuik in Midlothian, on Corby, and to acquire carp and tench for a pool, and trees for his plantations from Thomas Howard.

Already in 1726 Clerk had written most of a long poem, 'The Country Seat', in which he had outlined his views on the links between house and landscape. With repeated glances at classical precept, his comments are mostly practical, the most valued part of an estate being the orchard. On the choice of plants, his view is indeed conservative. While 'Philosophic Gardiners' and the 'curious Botanist' may experiment with citrus fruit or grapes, or other 'exotick Plants', his advice is to live from what Nature has provided in one's own region:

She with a Mother's tender Care bestows
On ev'ry Region all such Fruits and Herbs
As most are fitted for th' Inhabitants

and again, in puritan tones,

... those who are on true Improvements bent
Must with our Nat'ral Products be content.[25]

Such an attitude runs parallel with that of other Scottish 'improvers' at this time. While James Macky in the early 1720s noted again and again the establishment of new and promising plantations on the great estates, the Society of Improvers in the Knowledge of Agriculture in Scotland was founded in Edinburgh in 1723, and a number of landowners in the Lothians were active in the planting of woodland and orchard trees, and the amelioration and extension of their vegetable and garden stock. Notable were Sir James Justice (1663/4–1736) and his son James (1698–1763) at Crichton, Sir John Foulis at Ravelston (from the 1680s) and at Woodhall, Andrew Fletcher, Lord Milton (1692–1766) and his family at Saltoun, and Sir Francis Kinloch (1676–1747) and his family at Gilmerton.

Much of their concern was with 'estate management' rather than gardens or parks – in the practical tradition of John Reid's *The Scots Gard'ner* of 1683 – but they were variously interested in garden plants as well. They had links with their compatriot Philip Miller in the Chelsea Physic Garden, and James Justice the younger was particularly active in horticultural and botanic matters, growing many exotics at Crichton, including the first pineapples in Scotland in a famous 'Pine Apple Stove', illustrated in 1732, and publishing *The Scots Gardiners Director* in 1754.[26]

But it is a feature of most of the wilder garden landscapes, from Corby onwards, that their planting – often copious – was rarely other than with native trees and shrubs. While Clerk's plantations at Penicuik were largely governed by prudence, parts of his landscaping were profoundly influenced by the natural beauties of Corby, particularly those views near the River Esk and the cave or tunnel leading to Hurley Park, with a pond and cascade nearby. As at Corby, these natural elements were enriched with classical allusions. In 1742, Clerk wrote proudly, he 'made the antique Cave at Hurley ... it resembles the Grotto of Pausilipo at Naples'.[27] This cave still exists, rough and gloomy like parts of the valley

The steep cascade at Corby Castle, admired from the 1740s by travellers in search of the picturesque, the wild and the sublime ... Nelson's statue was added around 1810.

at Corby, and profoundly different in character from 'the design and plot ... with the crypta through the mountains' which John Evelyn had supervised at Albury in Surrey, some 70 years earlier – regular and Italianate, 'such a Pausilippe is nowhere in England' (see page 134).

Piercefield and Wilder Scenes

From around 1750 and in the next decade or so, several other wild or partly wild landscapes were developed, as Corby had been, by the addition of memorials, sculpture, seats and inscriptions. Their degree of wildness was to a great extent linked to the physical qualities of the property and its surroundings, so that Ilam in Staffordshire appeared 'a very pleasant seat' to Dr Pococke in 1751, with a hill he could compare with the second and third pyramids in Egypt (he had indeed seen them), and with the 'curiosity' of the two streams which emerged from underground passages. By 1774, Dr Johnson could remark that 'Ilam has grandeur tempered by softness ... As [the walker] looks up to the rocks his thoughts are elevated; as he turns his eyes on the vallies, he is composed and soothed' – in comparison with the 'horrors' of Hawkstone (see page 213); and by 1789 John Byng (later Viscount Torrington) could admire 'the most picturesque and beautiful scenery' at Ilam – 'here nature has done wonders' – but regret that the copious stream had not been made to produce 'a wonderful cascade over the rocks'. He preferred the wilder (and wholly unlandscaped) scenery of Dovedale nearby.[28]

Other more savage scenes were landscaped at this time, the most important being Piercefield in Monmouthshire (c. 1750), Hackfall in Yorkshire (c. 1750), Plompton Rocks in Yorkshire (c. 1755) and Hawkstone in Shropshire (from the late 1750s). It is significant that Edmund Burke published his *Philosophical Enquiry into our Ideas of the Sublime and the Beautiful* in 1756 (revised edition, 1757), in which he distinguished the soft and pleasing qualities of the beautiful from the wild or violent or even terrifying qualities of the sublime. In this division, it is easy to understand that many a garden, like many a gentle agricultural scene, may be beautiful, while a landscape, including perhaps a ruin or a hermitage, may be sublime; and it is possible to see how the liking for ever sublimer forms of landscape could at last take the eighteenth-century enthusiast right out of the realm of gardens into scenes of a wholly natural kind. In such a situation, the design of gardens returns to what is beautiful, eschewing the wildness which was admired at places such as Piercefield.

Piercefield was, and remains, a site of striking natural beauty. In the 1750s, the owner, Valentine Morris, elaborated a walk running mainly along the high winding eastern edge of his property, bounded on that side by the River Wye, which curves and bends between level fields on the Gloucestershire shore, and steep, even precipitous, wooded slopes on the Welsh side. In this task, Morris was helped and advised by another amateur, the poet Richard Owen Cambridge, who had recently laid out his own grounds beside the Severn at Whitminster. Morris's river walk was adorned with a series of viewing places, alcoves or seats, rather like William Shenstone's walk at the Leasowes. These viewpoints – the Alcove, the Platform, the Double View, the Lover's Leap and others – offered mostly a series of remarkable contrasts, between the high clifftop seat and the distant placid farmland, or (at the Double View) between the high woodland overlooking the Gloucestershire fields far below to the east, and the wide Welsh countryside to the west. The 'Giant's Cave' carried the path through a tunnel in the cliff, like Sir John Clerk's cave at Hurley in the Penicuik estate, and – as still at Corby – had a stone giant over the entrance. There was also a 'Druid's Circle', one of the first, if not the very first, miniature Stonehenges constructed in Britain. Another was proposed by the eccentric Philip Thicknesse (a builder of several hermitages) in 1768–9 near his Monmouthshire farm outside Pont-y-moel, and in 1787 General Conway erected the 'Druid's Temple' near his residence at Park Place in Berkshire, using 45 stones from a prehistoric circle discovered in Jersey in 1785. Horace Walpole cheerily named it 'Little Master Stonehenge'.[29] This passion continues; a fine version of the stone circle at Avebury was created by Ian Pollard at Hazelbury in Wiltshire around 1988 (see page 328).

Arthur Young visited Piercefield in 1768, William Gilpin in 1770, John Byng in 1781, and a host of others. All agreed that the views outwards were the chief merit – 'singularly grand, and romantic; affording every charm of rock, wood and water'.[30] Gilpin indeed (whom we have already noted for preferring 'wilder scenes' to gardens) objected gently to Valentine Morris's shrubberies:

> As the embellishments of a house; or as the ornament of little scenes, which have nothing better to recommend them, a few flowering shrubs may have their elegance and beauty: but in scenes, like this, they are only splendid patches, which injure the grandeur, and simplicity of the whole.

Gilpin continued with lines which might have been penned by William Robinson in The Wild Garden a century later, objecting to formal shrubberies:

It is not the shrub, which offends: it is the *formal introduction* of it. Wild underwood
may be an appendage of the grandest scene. It is a beautiful appendage. A bed of
violets, or lillies may enamel the ground, with propriety, at the root of an oak: but
if you introduce them artificially in a border, you introduce a trifling formality; and
disgrace the noble object, you wish to adorn'.[31]

Robinson could not have put his point – in 1870 – more clearly (see page
279).

At Hackfall, a rocky, wooded slope with extensive views and cascading
streams, William Aislabie attempted another variation on Corby – and
something vastly different from his father's tranquil formality at Studley
Royal. From around 1750, he added several buildings overlooking the
gorge of the River Ure – a banqueting-hall, Mowbray Castle (an
eyecatcher) and, lower down, Fishers Hall, a rustic temple and a grotto.
Already in 1751, Dr Pococke could admire 'an octagon Gothick building'
(probably Fishers Hall); and by 1800 – such was the development in
taste – Sir Richard Colt Hoare, grandson of Henry Hoare, creator of
Stourhead, could deride Studley's pools – 'the water in all its parts is
detestable; narrow, round, oval canals ...' – and the next day, after
visiting Hackfall, write rapturously that 'it is impossible to convey by
words a proper idea of the beautiful disposition of wood, rock and water,
which nature has here so happily displayed'. Admiring the prospects,
the 'rapid and rocky River Ure' and the woods, he said little about the
buildings, and concluded 'I seldom have seen so delightful and pleasing
a scene, never, I think in a garden and seldom in nature'.[32]

A similar treatment of wild but promising terrain was undertaken in
the mid-1750s at Plompton (or Plumpton) Rocks near Harrogate in
Yorkshire, not so far from Hackfall. At Plompton, Daniel Lascelles made
a dam, in order to build up the water from a series of small ponds into a
sizeable lake. This, in turn, transformed a group of rocky outcrops into
a spectacular sequence of cliffs, among and over which seeds, saplings
and shrubs were set in profusion (the suppliers being Telford or Perfect,
both based in York). Apart from massive ball finials on the dam, the
architectural part of the scheme was merely a boathouse, and Lascelles'
planned mansion was not built.[33] 'Much visited by parties from Harrogate', Plompton was inspected by Sir Richard Colt Hoare in 1800, and
given modest praise.

Hoare wrote far more fully about Hawkstone in Shropshire the following year. He noted properly that the 'principal beauty' of the hilly
grounds lay in their being 'placed in flat country without any other
similar features in the neighbourhood'. West of Hawkstone Hall the
ground forms a group of steep hilly outcrops, abruptly overlooking the

level landscape towards Wales. From the late 1750s, these hills and cliffs had been treated as a 'sublime' landscape, first by Sir Rowland Hill (d. 1783), then by his son Sir Richard Hill (1733–1809).

There was already a medieval ruin on Red Castle Hill. In and along the crest of the facing cliff – Grotto Hill – Sir Rowland dug out a sequence of cave or grotto chambers, adding a ruined arch at one end, and several apertures in the sandstone wall to display the vast and vertiginous prospects below and beyond. This Dr Johnson saw in 1774:

> ... striking scenes and terrific grandeur. We were always on the brink of a precipice, or at the foot of a lofty rock ... The whole circuit is somewhat laborious, it is terminated by a grotto cut in the rock ... with many windings and supported by pillars, not hewn into regularity, but such as imitate the sports of nature ...
>
> The Ideas which it forces upon the mind, are the sublime, the dreadful, and the vast. Above, is inaccessible altitude, below, is horrible profoundity ...
>
> He that mounts the precipice at Hawkstone, wonders how he came hither, and doubts how he shall return. His walk is an adventure and his departure an escape.[34]

Johnson was then aged 64, overweight, and not a lover of mountains. His phrases hardly describe a garden, but are nonetheless instructive, telling of his reluctant admiration of the sublime, and of his awareness that this kind of scenery, and its manipulation by human beings, was one of the interests of the age. Looking back (once again) we may see that Hawkstone, as perceived by Johnson in 1774, was far, far different from Twickenham, or Wooburn, or Stowe, so different, in fact, that many people then, later, or even today might think it was not a garden at all. By 1801, other features had appeared: Sir Richard Colt Hoare saw the Obelisk (1795), the 'Tahitian Hut' (now gone, but a significant reminder of Cook's Pacific discoveries, like the surviving monument to Cook at Stowe), and the $1\frac{1}{2}$-mile stretch of Hawk Lake, added to the north by William Emes (or Eames) in the mid-1780s. He also saw the hermitage, and its hermit.[35]

The sinuous extent of Hawk Lake is a significant addition at Hawkstone, inspired by the work of Capability Brown, whose gentler schemes – *beautiful* rather than *sublime* – were to resolve and direct the questions of garden design until the end of the eighteenth century.

13

'ONE BROWN'

In the summer of 1751, Horace Walpole visited Warwick Castle. Two years before, work had begun to remove a set of four parterres near the castle, and to replace them with an expanse of lawn stretching down to the river. Walpole was delighted, and wrote to his friend George Montague, 'The castle is enchanting; the view pleased me more than I can express, the river Avon tumbles down a cascade at the foot of it. It is well laid out by one Brown who has set up on a few ideas of Kent and Mr Southcote.'[1]

By this time Lancelot Brown was 35 years old. Born in 1716, he worked from around 1732 until 1739 for Sir William Loraine of Kirkharle Tower in Northumberland, engaged on the estate, and eventually laying out a part of the grounds. Moving south in 1739, he was employed by Lord Cobham at Stowe from 1741, becoming head gardener, and probably being responsible for the execution of some of William Kent's designs in his final work at Stowe, particularly the laying out of the Grecian Valley, though even this is not certain. While working at Stowe, Brown was recommended by Lord Cobham for other landscaping projects – at Warwick Castle, as we have seen, in 1749, a connection which continued until at least 1761, with extensive landscaping in the park south of the Avon; at Packington Hall, also in Warwickshire; and at Croome Court in Worcestershire. Lord Cobham died in 1749, and Brown left Stowe for London in 1751, with further work under way – at Petworth in Sussex, for example. He rapidly became established as the most successful garden (or rather, landscape) designer of the time. In 1764, he was appointed Master Gardener at Hampton Court, a post which he held until his death in 1783, with Wilderness House as his official residence. His responsibilities extended to the royal properties at Richmond and Kew. At the same time he was appointed Gardener at St James's.[2]

From the mid-1760s, he employed the draughtsmen Samuel Lapidge and John Spyers to help with the surveying necessary in his commissions, and in 1770 he made the architect Henry Holland (1745–1806) his partner. Their best-known collaboration was at Claremont in Surrey. In 1773, Holland married Brown's daughter Bridget.

Brown was involved in over 200 commissions in England, probably none in Scotland, a handful in Wales, and possibly one in Ireland – undated, at Slane Castle, Co. Meath. Not long before his death, Brown was asked (for the second time) by the Duke of Leinster to go over to Ireland, but, according to Walpole, 'excused himself saying *he had not yet finished England*'. The table on pages 216–17 lists, in chronological order, the most important of these commissions. Often, they extended over several years, sometimes with intervals. His work frequently continued that of earlier designers, for example, Charles Bridgeman or William Kent, or obliterated even earlier designs of a formal kind. Time has operated with equal indifference on Brown, so that his work has, again and again, been overlaid or overwhelmed by following fashions or suburban sprawl.

Brown was given the nickname 'Capability' because of his habit of referring to the 'capabilities' which he perceived in grounds he was asked to improve. The nickname came early, and was widely known, so that when Brown's son, Lancelot, began at Eton in 1761, he was rapidly called 'Capey'.[3]

Brown's landscaping is characterised by its simplicity – broad sweetly contoured expanses of grass, stretching between the uncluttered garden front of the house and an adjacent lake or stream; the lake or stream, winding in the valley, made to appear of some size, often majestic; and gently curving plantations or belts of trees enclosing the boundaries, providing a continually changing setting for a walk or drive round the grounds. A bridge, a temple or a monument might give a focus to the scene but, unlike the gardens of Charles Bridgeman or William Kent, Brown's landscapes, as he designed them, had few of the objects, and far fewer of the classical 'hints' which were so common in gardens until the mid-eighteenth century.

Though many of his plans survive, Brown wrote no textbook, and only one letter which outlines his general principles. This letter, written in June 1775, was to an Englishman, the Revd Thomas Dyer of Marylebone, who had asked Brown's advice for a friend in France, who wanted instruction on how to lay out his garden in Brown's manner. Brown replied to Dyer with a plan, adding:

> In France they do not exactly comprehend our ideas on Gardening and Place-making which when rightly understood will . . . be exactly fit for the owner, the Poet and the Painter.

IMPORTANT GARDENS AND PARKS WITH DESIGNS
BY CAPABILITY BROWN

1740s	c.1740 (possibly)	Kiddington, Oxfordshire
	c.1739–40, 1742–6, 1752–60	Wotton House, Underwood, Buckinghamshire
	1741–51	Stowe, Buckinghamshire
	1749–50	Warwick Castle, Warwickshire
1750s	1750–1	Packington Hall, Warwickshire
	1751 onwards	Croome Court, Worcestershire
	1751 onwards	Petworth House, Sussex
	1751–6	Kirtlington Park, Oxfordshire
	1754	Belhus, Essex
	1754–6	Burghley House, Northamptonshire
	c.1756	Garrick's villa, Middlesex
	1756	Madingley Hall, Cambridgeshire
	1756, 1775–9	Sherborne Castle, Dorset
	1757	Longleat, Wiltshire
	1757, 1762–6	Bowood, Wiltshire
	1758	Wrest Park, Bedfordshire
	1758, 1772	Harewood House, Yorkshire
	c.1759, 1770	Burton Constable, Yorkshire
	c. 1759	Trentham Park, Staffordshire
1760s	c.1760–73	Syon House, Middlesex
	c.1760	Alnwick Castle, Northumberland
	1760	Chatsworth, Derbyshire
	1760	Corsham Court, Wiltshire
	1761	Castle Ashby, Northamptonshire
	1762	Holkham Hall, Norfolk
	1763	Tottenham Park, Wiltshire
	1763–6	Audley End, Essex
	1763–82	Milton Abbey, Dorset
	1763–74	Blenheim Palace, Oxfordshire
	1764	Dodington House, Gloucestershire
	1764	Wimbledon Park, London
	c.1764	Caversham Park, Berkshire
	c.1764	Prior Park, Somerset
	1764–74	Luton Hoo, Bedfordshire
	1764–83	Responsibilities at Richmond and Kew, Surrey
	c.1765–8	Weston Park, Staffordshire
	1766–72	Thorndon Hall, Essex
	1767	Wimpole Hall, Cambridgeshire
	1767	Ashburnham Place, Sussex
	1767–9	Euston Hall, Suffolk
	1768–74	Compton Verney, Warwickshire
	1769–82	Wynnstay, Clwyd
	1769 onwards	Claremont, Surrey
1770s	1770	Highclere Castle, Hampshire
	early 1770s–76	Coombe Abbey, Warwickshire
	1771	Brocklesby Park, Lincolnshire
	1771	Grimsthorpe Castle, Lincolnshire
	1772	St John's College, Cambridge
	1773–5	Benham Park, Berkshire
	1775–6	Newton Castle (Dynevor), Caernarvon
	1775	Cadland, Hampshire
	1776 onwards	Sheffield Park, Sussex
	1776, 1781	Berrington Hall, Herefordshire

	before 1777–8	Longford Castle, Wiltshire
	1777	Southill Park, Bedfordshire
	1777	Chilham Castle, Kent
	1777	Sledmere House, Yorkshire
	1778	Moccas Court, Herefordshire
	1778–9	Nuneham Courtenay, Oxfordshire
1780s	1781	Llewaney, Flintshire
	1781	Heveningham Hall, Suffolk
	1781	Sandleford Priory, Berkshire
	1782 and later	Woodchester Park, Gloucestershire
Notable unexecuted plans		
	1776–8	The Backs, Cambridge
	Uncertain date	St James's Park, London (adapted by John Nash in 1828–9)

This elevated yet general aim demanded:

> . . . a good plan, good execution, a perfect knowledge of the country and the objects in it, whether natural or artificial, and infinite delicacy in the planting etc.

This last point, the planting, is the only one which Brown amplifies:

> . . . since so much Beauty [depends] on the size of the trees and the colour of their leaves to produce the effect of light and shade . . . as also the hideing what is disagreeable and showing what is beautifull, getting shade from the large trees and sweets [fragrance from the flowers] from the smaller sorts of shrubs etc.[4]

Brown's plan for this does not survive, nor, alas, do we know the identity of the French owner or his garden, so that Capability's advice can only be seen in a most general way. For detail, we must look at some of his remaining schemes, which show his treatment of trees, grass and, above all, of water. With trees, Brown, like Bridgeman and Kent before him, was not an enthusiast for new species. Though he is known to have planted copious quantities of trees in his encircling 'belts' and adjacent 'clumps', his choice fell mainly on oak, elm, beech, ash and lime, adding Scots firs and an occasional cedar to give contrast. As with John Evelyn in the century before, this planting was both aesthetic – it 'conceals the bounds', in Alexander Pope's phrase – and firmly practical, to produce saleable timber. At Chatsworth, Brown transformed the setting for the house and its immediate gardens by ringing the high moorland horizon with trees. Previously, this had 'neither hedge, house or tree', but presented the stranger with 'a waste and houling wilderness', as Daniel Defoe had termed it, in alarming contrast to the 'most pleasant garden' below. Brown's plantings hid this 'endless moor' with a wooded circle, emphasising even more strongly the paradise within.

Brown's schemes rarely approached the sublime (of Hawkstone, for example – see page 213), but stayed within the gentler sphere of beauty and what is beautiful, in the words of his letter to Thomas Dyer. One of Edmund Burke's definitions of beauty, in his *Philosophical Enquiry into our Ideas of the Sublime and the Beautiful* (1756, revised 1757) comes astonishingly close to a part of Brown's achievement:

> Most people must have observed the sort of sense they have had, on being swiftly drawn in an easy coach on a smooth turf with gradual ascents and declivities. This will give a better idea of the beautiful ... than almost any thing else.

Burke's 'smooth turf with gradual ascents and declivities' could hardly have served as an exacter reference to Brown's perfection of the long, grassy slopes at Audley End, Longleat, Petworth or Bowood.

Brown's lakes and his treatment of water are his supreme achievement. Before his time, artificial lakes had often been made in gardens, and often made to look 'natural' – at Chiswick, Painshill, Stourhead and Stowe, for example. During Brown's time, others were to be made, imitating his work, from the modest three-stage lake at Whiteknights Park in Berkshire (mid-1770s), and the lake at Welbeck in Nottinghamshire, designed by Francis Richardson and observed at its birth by Mrs Delany – they are 'floating a valley', she wrote on 7 September 1756[5] – to Robert Adam's fine expanse at Kedleston in Derbyshire (from 1758 onwards), and to the largest of them all, Virginia Water in Surrey, in the southern part of Windsor Park, made by Thomas Sandby in 1749–54, and enlarged in 1782.

By the 1770s, such lakes were a frequent yet relatively novel and decidedly fashionable part of a landscape garden. In 1779, William Mason published the third book of his long poem *The English Garden*, celebrating the appearance of gardens which merited national pride, and citing the artificial landscape lake as one of their most impressive features. He questioned, and answered himself as follows:

> Is there within the circle of thy view
> Some sedgy flat, where the late ripen'd sheaves
> Stand brown with unblest mildew? 'tis the bed
> On which an ample lake in crystal peace
> Might sleep majestic.[6]

What Brown did – generally better than the others – was to block the lower end of a valley with a dam, a weir or a sluice, to hold up the waters from whatever stream or streams were there. At Kiddington, he used the little River Glyme, which he employed again at Blenheim, so that he could exclaim, after creating his most famous lake there to give a purpose to Vanbrugh's bridge, 'Thames will you ever forgive me' – for keeping the waters of the Glyme away from their destination, the Thames (or so we are told – there is no clear authority for the phrase). At Audley End, he used the River Cam, barely more than a streamlet at this point. Later in its course, at Cambridge, Brown was to propose the widening of the River Cam along the Backs, but his plan was never executed, stifled by the committees of academe.

At Syon Park, Brown used both the little stream which had been dignified as the 'Duke of Northumberland's river', to make two connected lakes, and the great sweep of the Thames itself, which was opened up to view from the house by means of a ha-ha wall. At Syon, it is instructive to examine the upper end of the first lake, to discover how its source – a trickling stream – is concealed by a curling change in direction in the bank. In this way, the disparity between the insignificant source and the noble winding lake goes unperceived. When Brown was engaged at Syon in 1760, the Duke of Northumberland also employed him to improve his northern seat at Alnwick Castle. Here again, Brown widened a river, the Aln, with weirs, and characteristically 'beautified' the slopes between the castle and the river, by removing the rough and irregular rocks which lay scattered here and there, and turfing the ground smoothly. Had an enthusiast for the sublime landscaped this part, overlooked by the castle's 'Gothic pile', how different might the treatment have been!

Sometimes the streams Brown dammed to form his lakes were small indeed. At Sandleford Priory in Berkshire (now St Gabriel's School), 'Brown's Pond' and other small lakes were formed in 1781 for Mrs Elizabeth Montagu from a sequence of medieval fishponds, fed by several nameless streamlets. As much applies at Prior Park in Bath, where the gardens, laid out by Ralph Allen between 1734 and 1743 (with some advice from Alexander Pope), had been embellished in 1756 with a Palladian bridge, itself splendid, designed probably by Richard Jones and inspired by the two earlier examples at Wilton and at Stowe. When erected, its appearance in the garden scheme must have been similar in kind, if not immensity, to that of Vanbrugh's bridge at Blenheim – a large bridge, crossing a stream little wider than a ditch. Around 1764 (in fact while he was working on Blenheim), Brown was called in. He simplified the slope down from the house, and gave the bridge its aesthetic justification, exactly as he was doing at Blenheim, by creating an expanse of water which the bridge could cross. Only the most grotchy of visitors would carp at the dam, concealed beneath the very span of the bridge.

We should note other excellent lakes by Brown at Longleat, at Petworth, at Wimbledon, at Harewood, and at Bowood – the last to my mind being Brown's finest surviving landscape scheme. Here he penned in the waters of two streams, the Whetham brook and the Washway, to make a branched and winding lake $1\frac{1}{2}$ miles long. A hamlet was removed when the lake was made (as also happened at Milton Abbey in Dorset and at Nuneham Courtenay in Oxfordshire, long before Brown was employed there, just as the small village of Henderskelf was moved at Castle Howard much earlier in the century), so that round the several miles of the lake shore there were simply the house and its related buildings, a mausoleum, sweeping lawns (with a ha-ha) and belts of trees.

Nowadays, the big house has gone (in 1955–6), leaving the elegant stable courts, chapel and related buildings, the mausoleum and a small Doric temple, set up on the opposite side of the lake in 1864. In the panorama, therefore, both in the 1760s and today, we do not look at, reflect on or even read a series of monuments; rather we walk, and pause, and walk round the lake, enjoying the sight of nature improved, a landscape with a lake in perfected form. In these scenes, the house, the mausoleum and the Doric temple are points we may simply view from a distance – though we may enjoy the nearer approach. For the most part, we enjoy these scenes in a *changing* perspective, as at the Rievaulx terrace in Yorkshire, created around 1758 not by Brown but by Thomas Duncombe, to enjoy the evolving views below of Rievaulx Abbey.

If, like Brown, you create a lake by damming a stream, the dam itself presents an opportunity. It allows the additional pleasure of a cascade. At Blenheim, Brown's cascade is a masterpiece, away round the corner of the lake, so that the sense of the lake's permanence should not be impaired. At Bowood, his work was improved around 1785 by Charles Hamilton, of Painshill, who was inspired by one of Gaspard Poussin's paintings of the falls at Tivoli. Help came also from Hamilton's grotto-builder, Josiah Lane, who added a grotto and cave called the 'Crooked Mustard' and the 'Hermit's Cave'.[7]

Not all Brown's work required a lake. At Warwick Castle, for example, there was already the Avon, and at Nuneham Courtenay, the Thames. Here, Brown genially exposed or concealed the stream, as he did at Syon, to 'make the most' of this essential element. Mention of Nuneham Courtenay invites a mildly malicious note on Brown's grassy sweeps, brought there up to the very doors of the house. At the very doors, in 1786, Fanny Burney stepped out of her conveyance into wet grass, up to the fetlocks:

The Palladian Bridge was built at the foot of the gardens at Prior Park in 1756. Brown 'landscaped' the scene in the 1760s, creating the sequence of pools around the bridge.

From the clifftop, looking through the 'ruined arch' towards the Red Castle at Hawkstone – the arch a 1770s creation of Gothic fantasy, the Red Castle a genuine medieval ruin.

We stopped at the portico, – but not even a porter was there; we were obliged to get out of the carriage by the help of one of the postilions, and to enter the house by the help of wet grass, which would not suffer me to stay out of it.[8]

I should add that not all Brown's attentions to earlier gardens involved wholesale change. At Hampton Court, where he was Master Gardener for nearly 20 years, he changed little, and added little beyond planting the now famous Black Hamburg vine; and at Wrest Park, his serpentine river-and-woodland-walks stretch in an accommodating U-shape round the great formal canal, left untouched, unchanged since Thomas Archer's pavilion was built there around 1710.

Brown's Imitators

As is already apparent, Capability Brown had several imitators, if not rivals, in his lifetime. Robert Adam's triumph at Kedleston has been mentioned, and this noted architect may also be credited with the far smaller lake and landscape at Belair in Southwark, where he designed the house in 1785. Though diminished by the railway around 1860, and sadly disfigured by modern municipal amenities, the remaining parkland of 24 acres encloses a thin curving lake, fringed by alder and weeping willow, and fed by the River Effra (now otherwise condemned to a subterranean course) – a tarnished jewel in south London.

Among other landscapers following Brown's style was Richard Woods (1716–93), who designed the gardens and landscape at Cannon Hall, near Barnsley in Yorkshire, in 1759 and 1760, including a flower garden within the limit of the ha-ha, close to the house. He also worked at Hartwell House in Buckinghamshire in 1759 (possibly removing some of the hedges depicted by Balthazar Nebot in the 1730s), and later worked on the grounds at Boreham House in 1763 and New Hall around 1767, both in Essex, and at Wardour in Wiltshire in 1764–6.[9]

William Emes or Eames (1730–1803) had an extensive practice in the Midlands and in Wales, and his name has been linked with some 15 different sites. In the mid-1780s, he laid out Hawk Lake at Hawkstone (see page 213), and his work in Wales extended from the 1760s until the 1790s. At Chirk Castle, between 1764 and 1768, his landscaping removed most traces of the earlier formal layout, and constitutes much of the present scheme; but at Erddig, in 1767–89, his work seems not to have affected the large central area (laid out in a formal manner for John Meller in 1718–33, still surviving, and much restored in recent years). At Powis Castle, he proposed destroying the formal terraces, but this did not happen, and his landscaping removed only the formal water garden at their foot, which was replaced with grass.

Other landscape lakes à la Brown were made up and down the country. Though the lakes remain – as at Fonthill in Wiltshire (c.1750) or at Ripley Castle in Yorkshire (sometimes attributed to Brown) – their designers are uncertain. One of the most effective of these lakes is at Castle Howard, where, on the north side of the house, the Great Lake was created in 1795–9.

In Scotland and Ireland fewer artificial lakes were made, almost certainly because natural rivers and lakes, or marine inlets, were so much more frequent. Brown probably never set foot in Scotland or in Ireland, though he designed a stable block for Lord Conyngham at Slane Castle, Co. Meath, and he *may* have suggested improvements to the landscape there at the same time, around 1767. The landscape lake at Slane may, however, be an early work by John Sutherland, who was active in garden and landscape matters in Ireland until the early nineteenth century.[10]

Elsewhere in Ireland, Carton in Co. Kildare should be noted. This property, with a river, the Ryewater, running through it, was landscaped in stages from around 1750 to 1837. Brown was asked to advise, but declined, and the river was first widened around 1758. By 1762, Emily, Lady Kildare, could write:

New river is beautifull. One turn of it is a masterpiece in the art of laying out, and I defy Kent, Brown or Mr Hamilton to excel it: this without flattery.[11]

Lady Kildare probably knew Charles Hamilton and Painshill quite well, since her brother-in-law, Henry Fox, later (1763) the 1st Lord Holland, was a life-long friend of Hamilton, and was advised by him on garden and planting matters at Holland House. She visited Painshill in 1757. Through Henry Fox, she also came to know Peter Collinson, the Quaker naturalist and plant collector.

Two other small but lovely artificial lakes in Ireland are at Lyons, Co. Kildare, created soon after 1805, and at Mount Bellew, Co. Galway, also dating from the early nineteenth century. In Scotland, one far larger lake, given an L-shape and crossed by a bridge with a causeway – reminiscent of Vanbrugh's bridge and Brown's solution at Blenheim – was created at Allanton in Lanarkshire, probably designed by the owner Sir Henry Steuart in 1816, and completed by 1822.[12]

Repton's presentation of a part of his (unadopted) proposals for the Royal Pavilion at Brighton (see pp 243–4). 'Before' is relatively dull, while 'after' shows a prettified and vastly floral garden.

Chambers and Mason

In Brown's lifetime, several writers praised his achievement, some in fulsome terms, like the anonymous author of *The Rise and Progress of the Present Taste in Planting* ... of 1767, who ends his poem with:

For him each Muse enwreathes the Lawrel Crown,
And consecrates to Fame immortal Brown.

Three years later, Thomas Whateley published his *Observations on Modern Gardening* (a work he had written around 1765), with long descriptions of a dozen or more landscape gardens and related scenes, as at Ilam or Piercefield. Brown's work was warmly praised, even when, as seen by Whateley in the 1760s at Blenheim, it was incomplete, since the lake was still far from full. A few months after Whateley's *Observations*, Horace Walpole's essay 'On Modern Gardening' appeared, with continuing but brief praise of Brown.

Then, in 1772, Sir William Chambers published *A Dissertation on Oriental Gardening*. It is an extraordinary work in several ways, not least because it marks the beginning of reaction to the landscape garden as it had evolved through Bridgeman, Pope, Kent and Brown, becoming – we may think – 'purer', 'simpler', less and less 'cluttered'. These are words of approval; but they also have a negative side, implying dull, unimaginative and downright boring, which is the sense Chambers wished to convey. Already in 1757, he had published *Designs of Chinese Buildings* ... (following the appearance of J. D. Attiret's letter on Chinese gardens, written in 1743, published in France in the *Lettres édifiantes* in 1749, and published in English by Joseph Spence in 1752). This book includes a garden section, where Chambers stresses that among the Chinese 'NATURE is their pattern, and their aim is to imitate her in all her beautiful irregularities'. Chinese gardens are divided into three species, the 'pleasing, horrid and enchanted', and Chambers' interest is clearly aroused more by the 'horrid' than the other two.

On the architectural side, Chambers had achieved notoriety, if not fame, with the various 'exotic' buildings which he designed for Princess Augusta at Kew. While two small Chinese buildings, together with the 'Alhambra' and the mosque, have gone, his pagoda, built in 1761, survives, set at the end of a grassy un-Chinese avenue.

In his *A Dissertation on Oriental Gardening* of 1772, Chambers was returning to the matter of variety in gardens. As an extreme statement, it is as pointed as any of the polemical writings of Addison or Pope against topiary and formal gardening some 60 years before, and, like those essays, it marks the beginning of a new attitude. In the *Dissertation*, Chambers expanded on the three categories of Chinese gardens – he now called them 'the pleasing, the terrible, and the surprizing' – and concentrated again on 'their scenes of terror' and 'their surprizing, or supernatural scenes'. While, say, the winding ravine at Corby or the precipices of Hawkstone might offer mild versions of the mildest options Chambers described, it is hard to see any *practical* response among the creators of British gardens to this section on 'scenes of terror':

> The trees are ill formed ... seemingly torn to pieces by the violence of tempests ... the buildings are in ruins; or half consumed by fire, or swept away by the fury of the waters: nothing remains entire but a few miserable huts dispersed in the mountains, which serve at once to indicate the existence and wretchedness of the inhabitants. Bats, owls, vultures, and every bird of prey flutter in the groves; wolves, tigers and jackalls howl in the forests; half-famished animals wander upon the plains; gibbets, crosses, wheels, and the whole apparatus of torture, are seen from the roads.

If this is not sufficient,

> ... they sometimes conceal in cavities, on the summits of the highest mountains, founderies, lime-kilns, and glass-works; which send forth large volumes of flame, and continued columns of thick smoke, that give to these mountains the appearance of volcanoes.

In this Chambers had moved far beyond the hermitages of Caledon, Painshill or Hawkstone. Yet he proposed even more:

> ... to astonish the passenger: from time to time he is surprised with repeated shocks of electrical impulse, with showers of artificial rain, or sudden violent gusts of wind, and instantaneous explosions of fire.[13]

No one in Britain took up this challenge, though on the Continent, at Wörlitz near Dessau, a garden volcano, impressive in size and nocturnal in performance, was built in the 1790s.[14] Dampeningly, I would add that there are no volcanoes in China, and that Chambers' visits there were made, as a midshipman, only to coastal ports.

Within a year, the poet William Mason launched a counter-attack, *An Heroic Epistle to Sir William Chambers*, in which these grotesque sublimities are imagined introduced, by Chambers, within the gardens at Kew:

> ... at our magic call,
> Monkies shall climb our trees, and lizards crawl;
> Huge dogs of Tibet bark in yonder grove,
> Here parrots prate, there cats make cruel love;
>
> Now to our lawns of dalliance and delight,
> Join we the groves of horror and affright;
> This to atchieve no foreign aids we try,
> Thy gibbets, Bagshot! shall our wants supply.

Mason was already engaged on his long poem *The English Garden*. Book I had appeared in 1772, and Book III (1778) contained his praise of landscape lakes, of the sort created by Brown (see page 218). Though loyal to Brown, Mason was nonetheless affected by the wish for greater variety in gardens. While mocking the extremes of the sublime put forward by Chambers, he desired the beautiful, enshrined in flowers and the sentiments they inspired. In 1771–2, he was asked by Lord Nuneham, son of the 1st Earl Harcourt, to design a small garden at Nuneham Courtenay, modelled in part on a fictional garden, the 'Elysée' or 'Julie's garden', described in Rousseau's novel *La Nouvelle Héloïse* (1761).

This area at Nuneham Courtenay, since known as Mason's Garden, covers about 2 acres, and is enclosed by thickets and tall trees. Private, unseen by passers-by, it is in this vastly unlike a landscape by Brown, and was even more unlike in the number of small buildings and memorials it once contained – an orangery, a temple of Flora, a grotto, a well, urns, statues and inscriptions (one by Rousseau) – set among flowering and scented shrubs, and informal flower beds. These flower beds, painted by Paul Sandby in 1777 and described by Mason in Book IV of *The English Garden* in 1781, mark a notable reappearance of flowers *in gardens*, anticipating their reintroduction in Humphry Repton's later work by some 30 years.

It is curious, and mildly ironic, that when Lord Nuneham inherited Nuneham Courtenay in 1777, becoming the 2nd Lord Harcourt, one of his first activities was to call in Capability Brown. In 1778–9, and indeed with some advice from Mason, Brown opened out the wider landscape along the Thames, with grassy sweeps over to the south-west and a vista completed (in 1787, after Brown's death) by the addition of the Carfax Conduit, acquired from Oxford rather as Henry Hoare had acquired the

High Cross at Stourhead from the authorities at Bristol in the 1760s. It was this recent grassy landscaping, up to the very doors of the house, which so discomfited Fanny Burney in 1786 (see page 220).

Flowers and Borders

Mason's Garden at Nuneham Courtenay quickly achieved some fame for its new approach – small, private and flowery. Yet flower gardens, or flowery areas within larger gardens, were by no means unknown in the eighteenth century, though they were uncommon.

I have already mentioned Philip Southcote's flower borders at Wooburn in the late 1730s, and those of Lady Luxborough at Barrells around 1750. Also of this period, the garden notes of Joseph Spence contain proposals for many schemes, mostly for small properties with restricted and usually regular plots, in which flowers and flowering shrubs often figure as lesser features. In 1731, he sketched an 'Idea for a House and Garden' (revised in 1751), with four quarter-circle 'Flowerbeds, and low Flowering Shrubs' within a colonnade close to the house. Another design of 1736, for his own rectory garden at Birchanger in Essex, includes borders of an unspecified kind, but indicating trees and shrubs, and, in 1743 and 1744, he sketched two designs for very small London gardens. The smaller – 50 by 20 feet – has an 'arbor' at the middle, flanked by 'Honeys-suckles, and Jessamin' and a bracketed 'Vine between'. Flowering trees – laburnum, lilac, and almonds at the corners – fill in the remaining central area. The larger garden – 50 by 40 feet – has narrow 'beds for Flowers'. Much use is made of honeysuckle and jessamine, while the house itself is to be covered with 'creepers, filleray [phillyrea], or Vines'. Blue and gold pots by the railings will hold 'myrtles and orange trees, or flowers'.[15]

Honeysuckle and jessamine were favourites with Spence. He included them in a scheme for his own small London garden in Stratton Street in 1744, and in many subsequent plans. Two of these were for people I have mentioned elsewhere – in 1752 for Stephen Duck, who had been the guardian of Merlin's Cave in Kensington Gardens, and in 1753 for Robert Dodsley, the publisher, poet and friend of William Shenstone.

Stephen Duck had been given the living of Byfleet in Surrey, and Spence's proposals for the parsonage grounds include a flower garden (with an alcove) to one side of the house and next to the 'Duckery', which adjoined the 'Great Canal'. Canals and streams were, alas, fatal to both Duck and Spence. Duck was to drown himself four years later, not in the 'Duckery', but in a 'trout stream' close to the Black Lion Inn near Reading, while Spence tumbled into his own garden pool in 1768.

By 1753, Robert Dodsley would have visited Shenstone's *ferme ornée*, and had probably seen Lady Luxborough's flowery walks at Barrells as well. For his garden in Richmond – a terraced site, sloping down to the Thames – Spence recommended 'flowers or Flowrg Shrubs on ye Bank' nearest to the house, with 'Flower Gn. and Kn. Garden' on the next level. Further down, the site, on the plan, is marked 'Close: Grove – Flowering Shrubs?', but the plants are not named, nor do we know of Dodsley's reaction to the scheme.

The 'close grove' is a phrase Spence used several times in relation to flowers or flowering shrubs in his later diagrams. Some of these designs are far less formal, due both to Spence's interest in the irregularities of Chinese gardens (he had translated J. D. Attiret's letter on Chinese gardens into English in 1752), and to the simple fact that they were larger than most of his earlier projects.

Two designs of 1765 are particularly interesting – for Mr and Mrs Rudge at Wheatfield in Oxfordshire, and for 'Dean Paul' at an unnamed site. The first has 'very close grove-work, with the best Flowering Shrubs and Trees and the lowest and best Evergreens', among which are to be planted 'the most pleasing Wild Flowers', named as 'Primroses, Violets, wild strawberries, etc'. The second, for 'Dean Paul', includes details for 'studs' or small beds in the lawn near the house. They are to be planted with

... roses, honeysuckles and jessamins, etc. – here, a damask rose, with a jessamine, there a Provence, with a couple of white miserions [mezereon]: a cabbage rose with two Dutch dwarf honeysuckles, in a third; and a moss-rose, alone, in a fourth, with as much variety as can be.

Spence gives several more combinations, and concludes:

The places for the studs should be dug and kept clean by hoing, either in circles or ovals, from four feet diameter to $1\frac{1}{2}$. And their margins should never come nearer to one another than 10 or 12 feet, to allow for mowing the parts of the lawn between them.[16]

In these 'studs' Spence came, in 1765, to something virtually indistinguishable from the informal beds in Mason's Garden at Nuneham in the 1770s. They were to resurface, in many a form, and with an infinity of different plantings, as 'island beds' throughout the nineteenth and twentieth centuries.

While Spence was designing gardens which might include areas of flowers, the painter Thomas Robins (1716–70) was responding to a parallel interest. His small paintings do not often show gardens with flowers, but their central scenes – house and garden, landscape with a house, summerhouse in a landscape – are set most commonly within a border of twining stems adorned with flowers. There are also occasional butterflies, and sometimes clusters of shells. Within the borders, most of his subjects – for example, Painswick House in Gloucestershire (1747), or Honington Hall in Warwickshire (1759, designed in 1749 by Sanderson Miller) – reveal few flowers, even if they were there. In contrast, two views in the mid-1750s of Woodside at Old Windsor in Berkshire, one of an orangery, the other of a chinoiserie pavilion, both display borders with flowering shrubs, which might be thought comparable with some of Spence's proposals.

Another Berkshire property, painted by Robins before 1748, Grove House at Old Windsor, was ornamented with flowers from the 1730s onwards by the owner Richard (or Dicky) Bateman (d.1773), and his enthusiasm led Horace Walpole, writing to Lady Hervey on 11 June 1765, to call it 'the kingdom of flowers'.[17] Walpole himself boasted that he had 'all kinds of trees and flowering shrubs and flowers' at Strawberry Hill, and that, were it not for the abundance at Dicky Bateman's, he would offer Lady Hervey abundance of his own – 'else, Madam, I could load wagons with acacias, honeysuckles, and syringas'.

By the middle of the century, the summer plenty at Strawberry Hill could be matched at other places – at Lambeth Palace, for example, downstream on the south side of the Thames. Here between 1758 and 1768, in the tenancy of Archbishop Secker, his niece Catherine Talbot remedied the earlier lack of flowers and fruit with much planting. Her residence in the grounds was called 'Jessamine Hall', and by June 1765 the enclosures and gardens of the palace had become

... a town of blooms and perfumes ... The forecourt ... is quite fragrant with lime blossoms. The apartment ... where I now reside ... is sweeter than you can conceive with jessamines that cluster round the windows; the rose walk is to-day in its highest bloom. At every spot ... in the garden is some variety of sweets; here a gale of spicy pinks, there the breath of lillies.

By June 1768, a moment of perfection was achieved, when, as Catherine Talbot wrote,

> ... the garden is sweet and gay, the whole border of the serpentine canal [yes! within the palace grounds] is filled with single pinks, red and white, which perfume the air and look sweet and soft beyond imagination.[18]

In the same period, 1759–60, Richard Woods laid out the landscape at Cannon Hall, near Barnsley in Yorkshire, including a flower garden within the enclosure of the ha-ha. His plan, which shows this as an oval area, states that it was to be 'adorned with clumps of Greens and Shrubs and Beds and Borders of Roses and all sorts of Common and sweet Flowers'.[19]

Intriguing evidence of the love for such 'Common and sweet Flowers' appears at Monreith House in Wigtownshire by the 1770s, when a vast embroidery was prepared by Lady Maxwell, wife of the 3rd Baronet, to record and celebrate the flowers grown in their garden – rather as Thomas Robins had depicted garden flowers in the borders to his garden or landscape scenes a few years earlier. While the garden – round the old castle, now a ruin – has gone, the embroidery, some 12 by 18 feet in size, still hangs in the present Monreith House. It shows a central basket and four cornucopias, one in each corner of the hanging, all loaded with abundant flowers. Sir Herbert Maxwell identified most of them, as follows:

> The madonna lily ... the Isabelline lily, clove carnations, mullein, lupine, hyacinth, red primrose, auricula, polyanthus, guelder rose, anemone, moss rose, scarlet lychnis, pink geranium (its leaves variegated with white), convolvulus, sunflower, sweet-william, scabious, and Canterbury bells, whence one is able to form a good notion of the furniture of a Scottish garden in the eighteenth century. Strange to say, the common daffodil is not among them; the only representative of the family being that double form of *Narcissus incomparabilis* which goes by the homely name of Butter-and-eggs.[20]

Collectors

In this general period – roughly from 1700 to 1770 – those who loved flowers, and collected them, kept them in separate areas – in the kitchen garden or, most often, whether the climate dictated it or not, in hot-houses. Artists who recorded these floral treasures (often newly-discovered and exotic) tended to paint them as single specimens and not in a garden setting. Wholly typical here are the paintings of Georg Dionysius Ehret (1708–70), who first came to England in the early 1730s, and then returned in 1736 to stay for the rest of his life. Ehret's paintings are records of the plants and flowers discovered, introduced and studied in his period, as are, of course, the flowers represented in cut paper ('paper mosaicks') by Mrs Delany, an activity she did not begin until 1772, in her seventy-third year.[21]

The collectors involved were an international confederacy, including John Bartram (in Pennsylvania), Peter Collinson (friend of Lord Petre at Thorndon Hall, of Charles Hamilton and Henry Fox), the great Linné or Linnaeus in Sweden, Lord Bute of Luton Hoo in Bedfordshire, director of the collection at Kew (see page 233), and Philip Miller (1691–1771), Gardener (i.e. director) of the Chelsea Physic Garden from 1722 until a few months before his death.

Miller was the compiler of the great dictionary of garden and plant matters, which first appeared in 1724 as *The Gardeners and Florists Dictionary*, and in 1731, much enlarged, as *The Gardeners Dictionary*. This was published in edition after edition in his lifetime, up to the eighth in 1768. The seventh edition, 1756–59, was 'revised and altered according to the latest system of botany', and accepts Linnaeus' binomial system of plant classification in part, while the eighth edition of 1768 takes most of the binomial system on board.[22] In the binomial system a plant is named by a single generic name plus a single distinguishing name, as in, say, *Morus alba* – the white mulberry, as distinct from *Morus nigra* – the black mulberry. Linnaeus also linked this system with his classification of plants by their sexual characteristics.[23]

The most intriguing by-product of the Linnaean 'revolution' in plant classification was undoubtedly the immense poem *The Botanic Garden* by Erasmus Darwin, published in its entirety in 1791. The second part, *The Loves of the Plants*, has been published earlier, in 1789, and is a clear, poetic and occasionally witty exposition of the sexual characteristics of plants. *En passant*, in his second canto, lines 153–62, Darwin praises Mrs Delany's 'mimic bowers, Her paper foliage, and her silken flowers', all so admirably and accurately achieved that in them 'cold winter' 'eyes with wonder all the blooms of Spring'. In 1800, Erasmus Darwin's prose treatise *Phytologia* was published, which also has a long section related to Linnaeus' system.

While botany is only on the very edge of garden history, the collecting of new, rare, interesting or beautiful plants and flowers impinges more directly on gardens, since, *à la longue*, those plants which are hardy, or will survive out of doors in the summer, even if they must be replaced each year or protected in the winter months, have dramatically changed many aspects of our gardens. Throughout the eighteenth century collectors collected, and often recorded their collections in classified lists, or engaged artists to paint their treasures. At Badminton, Mary Somerset, 1st Duchess of Beaufort, was a famed and intelligent collector, especially of plants from the Cape, and also of auriculas. The more delicate plants she kept in her 'infirmary', and a florilegium was painted of the most lovely specimens by Everhard Kick around 1704, a further selection being painted by D. Frankcom around 1710. Floral enthusiasm at Badminton continued well into the century. In 1750, Thomas Wright produced a plan for an ornate garden with flowery areas; it was, alas, never executed.[24]

In Britain and Ireland, plant collections were amassed, both large small. In the 1730s, at Kilruddery, Co. Meath, one of the great formal gardens in Ireland, the Earl of Meath accumulated some 230 varieties of auricula, and in England, up and down the country, florists' societies grew and flourished, devoted for the most part to auriculas in the spring and carnations in the summer.[25] Among individual plant enthusiasts in Scotland, we might note Andrew Heron (d.1729) at Bargally in Wigtownshire and James Justice at Crichton, near Edinburgh. Andrew Heron was known both for his introduction of foreign trees and shrubs to his part of Scotland, and for his success in the hothouse with 'oranges, lemons, pomegranates, passion flowers, citron trees, oleanders, myrtles, and many others'. Heron was respected for his botanical learning. On going to a noted garden in London, and identifying a rare exotic, the principal gardener there exclaimed to him, 'Then, Sir, you must be either the devil or Andrew Heron of Bargally.' Alas, beyond this anecdote from J. C. Loudon, we know little of this man. Many of his trees, even those set at the corners of his grave, were cut down around 1791, though some were seen and measured by Loudon in 1831.[26] Shortly after Heron's death in 1729, James Justice at Crichton achieved pre-eminence with the first pineapples grown in Scotland.

Enthusiasm in the south was largely centred round Kew, where until his death in 1751, Prince Frederick eagerly encouraged gardening. This royal patronage was continued by his widow, Princess Augusta, with the help of Lord Bute (1713–92), who in 1751 was appointed Director there, a post which passed to Sir Joseph Banks in 1772. Sir William Chambers designed a variety of buildings at Kew from 1757 onwards (the Orangery of 1757 was one of the first and still survives, like the ruined arch of 1759–60 and the Pagoda of 1761), and the botanist William Aiton (who had worked under Philip Miller) was employed there from 1760 to deal

with plant matters. To begin with, in 1759, the botanic garden was small –
some 10 acres – beside the far larger area of lawns, groves, woods and
walks. Aiton adopted the Linnaean system from the start, and a vast
conservatory, the Great Stove, was erected in 1761. This was larger than
Lord Petre's had been at Thorndon, and was possibly, in the 1760s, the
largest in the world.

Amateurs meanwhile developed their own collections. Charles Hamilton's and Henry Fox's collections of rare trees at Painshill and Holland
Park in the 1750s have already been mentioned, and, in the early 1760s,
Lord Bute built a large conservatory at Luton Hoo in Bedfordshire for
his exotics, especially from the Cape, while the hardier specimens were
kept outside in his 'Botanick grounds'. In 1764, Capability Brown also
began a decade's landscaping of the Luton Hoo estate, damming the
River Lee (or Lea) to make two lakes, the larger one being a quarter of a
mile wide.[27] Lord Bute also contributed specimens to the botanic collection of William Curtis in Lambeth. Curtis (1746–99) founded the
Botanical Magazine in 1787, having published the regional list of London's plants, the *Flora Londinensis*, in 1777.

EIGHTEENTH-CENTURY INTRODUCTIONS

1701	Ivy-leaved geranium (*Pelargonium peltatum*)	South Africa
1707	Redhot poker (*Kniphofia uvaria*)	South Africa
1710	Pelargonium (*Pelargonium zonale*)	South Africa
1719	Portuguese laurel (*Prunus lusitanica*)	Portugal
1730	Iceland poppy (*Papaver nudicaule*)	Siberia
1730	Weeping willow) (*Salyx babylonica*)	Euphrates
1730	Indian bean tree (*Catalpa bignonioides*)	North America
c.1730	Magnolia (*Magnolia grandiflora*)	North America
1731	Clematis (*Clematis orientalis*)	Lebanon
1736	Witch hazel (*Hamamelis virginiana*)	North America
1739	Camellia (*Camellia japonica*)	China
1744	Bergamot (*Monarda didyma*)	North America
c.1750	Rhododendron (*Rhododendron ponticum*)	Gibraltar
1751	Tree of Heaven (*Ailanthus altissima*)	China
1752	American Lime (*Tilia americana*)	North America
1754	Ginkgo (*Ginkgo biloba*)	Japan
1758	Lombardy poplar (*Populus italica*)	Italy
1783	Spotted laurel (*Aucuba japonica*)	Japan
1787	Tree paeony (*Paeonia suffruticosa*)	China
1789	Common blush rose (*Rosa semperflorens*)	China
1789	Hydrangea (*Hydrangea macrophylla*)	China
1792	Lupin (*Lupinus arboreus*)*	California
1793	The Pontic azalea (*Azalea pontica*, now *Rhododendron luteum*)	The Caucasus
1793	Chrysanthemum (*Chrysanthemum sinensis* × *indicum*)	China
1795	Monkey puzzle (*Araucaria araucana*)	Chile

1796	Japonica (*Chaenomeles speciosa*)	Japan
1796	Zinnia (*Zinnia elegans*)	Central America
1798	Dahlia (*Dahlia pinnata*)	Central America

---

*Early twentieth-century 'Russell' lupins are a cross between *Lupinus arboreus* and *Lupinus polyphyllus*, introduced to Britain from British Columbia in 1826.

14

LATER LANDSCAPERS

Lancelot Brown died in 1783, liked, admired and successful – his success apparent in the 'capabilities' he had discovered and nurtured in landscape gardens all over England. Yet, as I have said, criticism of his style began in the early 1770s, on the grounds that it was too simple and too plain. The alternatives proposed, and sometimes put into practice, varied from the Chinese horrors of Sir William Chambers to the floral intimacy of Mason's Garden at Nuneham Courtenay.

Something between Mason's Garden and the *ferme ornée* of William Shenstone was elaborated over nearly half a century – from 1780 until the late 1820s – at Plas Newydd, outside Llangollen, by Eleanor Butler and Sarah Ponsonby, who had run away together from their respective homes in Ireland in 1778. Their $2\frac{1}{2}$ acres of land were adorned with lawns, model dairy, shrubbery and flower beds, linked by the gravel path of the 'Home Circuit'. One early scheme for a shrubbery included 'Lilaks, Laburnums, Seringas, White Broom, Weeping Willow, Apple Trees, poplar'. This much was indeed a blend of The Leasowes and the intimacy of Mason's Garden. But their grounds, later somewhat extended, also had a wilder area round the steep banks of a stream, the Cufflymen, and the mountains round about included a glimpse of the medieval ruins of Castell Dinas Bran. The 'sublime', therefore, was – with discretion – on the borders of their domain.[1]

The 'Ladies of Llangollen' were ardent admirers of William Gilpin's 'picturesque tours', the first volume of which – *Observations on the River Wye* – appeared in 1782, a year after William Mason's *The English Garden* was completed. These two works were influential in the creation of Hafod (in the Ystwyth valley in Dyfed) by Thomas Johnes from the early 1780s, both in the many-treed and 'natural' landscape within a wild and barren scene, and in a first flower garden made in the mid-1780s and a second a decade later. While Johnes planted over two million trees to enrich the landscape, and directed his walks to include the natural scenery – cascades and distant vistas – Mason is indeed credited with a great deal, albeit indirectly. On 23 April 1787, William Gilpin wrote to Mason to tell of a meeting with Johnes, in which Johnes had explained that at Hafod

> ... the vales and lawns were laid out by Mr Mason; whose English garden he took in his hand; and wanted no other direction. So if you want to see an exact translation of your book into good Welsh, you must go to Mr Johnes' seat in Cardiganshire ...[2]

Above all Johnes endeavoured to avoid the smoothness of Capability Brown. He said proudly of his treatment of the ground in front of the mansion, 'I have neither shorn or tormented it', a phrase inspired by the poem *The Landscape*, written by his cousin Richard Payne Knight and published in 1794. This poem, as George Johnson wrote in 1829, 'completed the expulsion of the Brunonian system of design'.[3]

Payne Knight had been 'landscaping' his own property at Downton in Herefordshire since 1772, and *The Landscape* is as much a reflection on his own experience as comment on other forms or styles. In it Brown's lack of variety is, however, fiercely attacked, together with the destruction of older gardens which his work involved:

See yon fantastic band,
With charts, pedometers, and rules in hand,
Advance triumphant, and alike lay waste
The forms of nature, and the works of taste!
T'improve, adorn, and polish, they profess;
But shave the goddess, whom they come to dress;
Level each broken bank and shaggy mound,
And fashion all to one unvaried round
... wrapt all o'er in everlasting green
Makes one dull, vapid, smooth, and tranquil scene.

At this point in the poem, two engravings are bound in, from drawings by Thomas Hearne. They are in the 'before' and 'after' manner which was already becoming familiar to experts in landscaping through the Red Books of Humphry Repton, though with a 'message' which Repton would not have accepted (see page 242). Both pictures show the same landscape scene of house, river and surroundings. One, with the scene in Brown's style, has shaven lawns, dotted with a few clumps of trees, a river winding gently between regular banks, and a vaguely Palladian house overlooking the 'dull, vapid, smooth, and tranquil scene'. The other, showing the same scene as Payne Knight would have it, has a house which is adorned with Gothic or Tudor detail, with the land and river as it would be if nature's variety and interest were allowed – and encouraged – to develop. Trees and bushes luxuriate, a fallen trunk and branches stretch into the river, and rocks and ferns give the ground an irregular surface – it is now 'picturesque', much as the valley of the River Teme appeared near to the Gothic structure of Downton Castle, built in the mid-1770s. When Sir Richard Colt Hoare visited Downton and the three-mile river walk in 1799, it afforded:

> . . . a constant succession of natural beauties. Here nature reigns alone; the works of art are scarcely discernible except in the forming of the walks which are done with great judgement and the most picturesque eye.[4]

The Landscape was dedicated to Payne Knight's friend Sir Uvedale Price, who landscaped his own property at Foxley in Herefordshire, and who published *An Essay on the Picturesque* in 1794, the same year as *The Landscape*. Foxley was also visited by Colt Hoare, in 1802. Though not so impressed as he had been at Downton, he still thought that the grounds were 'highly gratifying to the lover of picturesque scenery'.[5]

While Payne Knight and Price differed somewhat in their classifying of the 'picturesque' – a matter which drifts well away from the history of gardens – these two writers were certainly influential in the search for alternatives to the supposed dullness of the 'Brunonian system'. The most impressive garden to survive with the stamp of their 'picturesque' enthusiasm is probably at Belsay in Northumberland. A mid-eighteenth-century landscape had made use of an earlier deer park at Belsay, and contained both a medieval castle and a manor house built in the 1630s. In 1807–17, a new residence in a severe Greek revival style was built for Sir Charles Monck, and the sandstone for this was quarried nearby, leaving a deep and spectacular gorge some 400 yards in length, which Monck, well versed in Gilpin, Payne Knight and Price, used as the framework for a winding garden walk, overhung with yew trees, crossed by a natural rock archway, and with final views out to the tower of the castle and the ruins of the old manor house. This quarry garden was made much more colourful by varied planting in the 1880s.

One of the gardens Sir Uvedale Price greatly admired was Mount Edgcumbe in Cornwall, which had received sporadic landscaping attentions from around the middle of the century (the 'ruin' before 1747, the Zigzags and related seats in the 1750s, and the Amphitheatre and Milton's

Temple in the late eighteenth century). After Mason's *The English Garden* appeared, an 'English Garden' was laid out near to the Orangery, in the area of several small gardens east of the main avenue.

The wilder and most open part of the Mount Edgcumbe landscape – beside the 'ruin' – also impressed the young William Beckford (1760–1844). He had been there in 1779, and visited the house and estate again in the autumn of 1781, accompanied by the *castrato* singer Gasparo Pacchierotti and a bevy of friends. On 17 October he wrote:

> Here am I breathing the soft air of Mount Edgcumbe standing upon the brink of a Cliff overlooking the Sea and singing *Notturnos* with Pacchierotti. Innnumerable Insects are humming about the Myrtles and Arbutus which hang on the steeps and are covered with blossoms ...
>
> I have been up and down and everywhere upon the Rocks ... You would delight in the picturesque fragments – the crooked pines and luxuriant shrubs amongst which I have passed my day.[6]

Just past his twenty-first birthday, Beckford was now in possession of an enormous fortune (Byron later called him 'England's wealthiest son'), since his father had died in 1770. For a variety of reasons, he did not set about gardening his Fonthill estate on a grand scale until the 1790s, but travelled on the Continent, and lived in Portugal for a considerable time. His father, Alderman Beckford (he was twice Lord Mayor of London), had already made a fine lake in the Brown manner on the eastern side of the estate, and in the late 1780s Beckford developed an 'Alpine garden' on the far sloping side of this lake, to which grottoes designed by Josiah Lane were added in the 1790s (Lane had worked for Charles Hamilton of Painshill, who was Beckford's great-uncle).

Beckford returned to England, more or less for good, in 1796. Already in 1793, he had begun to enclose a huge area of the Fonthill estate, westwards from his father's Palladian mansion, 'Fonthill Splendens', within a 12-foot high wall. Eventually, this wall was to enclose some 1,900 acres, and within its enormous and strictly private spaces Beckford created his paradise, round the Gothic treasure house, Fonthill Abbey, designed and built for him by James Wyatt between 1793 and 1813. It is fair, I think, to say that his gardening and landscaping was 'picturesque', but on the grandest scale, which touches the sublime. The 'ride' through the grounds, extending occasionally outside the wall, was 27 miles in length. Within the wall, there was an American garden, with rare conifers, a 'Norwegian Hut', a flower garden, a rosarium, a 'thornery', a herb garden, 'a garden for a favourite dwarf' (his companion Pierre de Grailly) and a range of glasshouses. Well outside the great wall, there was a separate kitchen garden of $7\frac{1}{2}$ acres.

Most to the point, Alderman Beckford had made Fonthill Lake in the gentle manner of Brown, while William Beckford made *his* lake, Bitham Lake, within the enclosure of the wall. Bitham Lake is more or less circular, surrounded on three sides by steep, tree-clad slopes – the Abbey was just visible above, at the highest point. It was seen to have 'the appearance of the crater of an extinct volcano' – not 'Brunonian', but easily sublime.[7]

Beckford's Fonthill paradise has changed and subsided, like the great tower of Fonthill Abbey in 1825. But fragments of the 30-odd years of creation survive – like a single letter, 'Fonthill, 24th July 1799', from Beckford to a garden designer who had offered to landscape the grounds. Beckford returned his thanks for this proposal, and added:

> ... but Nature has been liberal to Fonthill, and some Embellishment it has received from Art, has fortunately gained so much the Approbation of my friends, that my Partiality to it in its present state will not perhaps be thought altogether inexcusable.[8]

In other words, Beckford was saying, 'I don't need your help. I'm doing rather well on my own. Thank you'. His letter was addressed to Humphry Repton, who by 1799 was a landscape designer of some eminence and considerable determination, but whose style was far, far different from Beckford's wild and lavish paradise at Fonthill.

'Capability R-'

Humphry Repton had followed several pursuits for a good few years before he suddenly took up landscape gardening. Born in 1752, he had by his mid-thirties travelled a fair amount – widely in England, and also in Holland and Ireland – developed a pleasing prose style, and a superior competence in sketching and watercolour painting, and established not a few contacts with influential politicians and landowners.

Suddenly, in 1788, he took up landscape gardening, succeeded at once, and continued vigorously almost up to his death in 1818. His decision was made in the course of a night,

> ... when anxiety had driven sleep from his pillow. This scheme ... at first seems to have entered his imagination with almost the vague uncertainty of a dream ... With

his usual quickness of decision, he arose the next morning; and, with fresh energy of purpose, spent the whole of that day in writing letters to his various acquaintances, in all parts of the kingdom, explaining his intention of becoming a 'Landscape Gardener'.[9]

Within a short while he had designed a trade card, headed 'H. REPTON LANDSCAPE-GARDENER' and showing himself at work with a theodolite, overseeing workmen busy with picks, shovels and barrows in a wooded landscape with lawn, lake and a distant Gothic tower. Custom and clients came quickly – his first apparently in 1788, at Catton Hall in Norfolk for Jeremiah Ives. Here he laid out belts and plantations round the 112-acre estate, leaving mainly open parkland in the centre, and separating the house, its immediate lawn and flower beds from the parkland with a ha-ha. Much of this scheme still survives, and might to most observers seem indistinguishable from many another small layout by Capability Brown or one of his imitators. Indeed, by 1792 a somewhat grotchy John Byng met Repton (whom he knew) while staying at the Sun Inn, Biggleswade, and confided to his diary:

> Mr Repton – the now noted landscape gardener – came in, and delay'd me for $\frac{1}{2}$ an hour; he is a gentleman I have long known, and of so many words that he is not easily shaken off.

The next day, he added a further reference to him as '*Capability R-*',[10] a clear enough sign of how and in what context Repton was 'now noted'.

Within a few months of his beginning this new career, in March 1789, Repton produced the first of his Red Books, a distinctive, effective, memorable and often beautiful means of explaining the ideas, outlines and details of his proposals. These books, usually but not always bound in red morocco, were mostly slim quarto volumes, about 8 by 11 inches, though some were much larger. Repton claimed to have prepared some 400 of these Red Books for his clients – an indication also of the approximate number of places for which his advice was sought – though now only some 200 can be traced.

In each of these volumes, with a clear, copperplate manuscript text, Repton explained his views on his client's property. First outlining the situation, he followed with his general and his detailed proposals, which were illustrated by plans and diagrams, and in most instances by Repton's now famous device of one or more combined 'before' and 'after' pictures. In these, a view of the property as it *was* can be turned into a view as it *might be*, by lifting up one or more flaps of paper (Repton called them 'slides') to reveal the parts of the scene which could be 'improved'. We might note, with a smile, that the improved scenes quite often have added attractions missing from the earlier unimproved versions, for example, scruffy labourers are replaced by elegant ladies. The most curious of these changes, which has nothing to do with garden practice but a great deal to do with clever marketing, is in the views of his own cottage property at Hare Street in Romford, Essex. The 'before' view includes a one-legged mendicant with an eye-patch, leaning forward over the fence. In the 'after' view, this sad reminder of misfortune has disappeared completely, hidden by a bed of flowers. Repton has also taken in – or appropriated – a large area of the village green.

From early in his garden career, Repton saw the need for publicity, and saw as well that the Red Books would help to spread the idea – chosen by himself – that he was the successor to Capability Brown. By 1792 or 1793, the Red Book for Tatton Park in Cheshire had been lent to a bookseller to help in the collection of subscriptions for Repton's *Sketches and Hints on Landscape Gardening*, an occurrence which may have provoked one of the first attacks on Repton, as successor to Brown and Brown's style, in Payne Knight's *The Landscape* in 1794.

The Tatton Red Book contained the suggestion that the owner of a distinguished property might increase his fame by having his coat of arms displayed on neighbouring objects – the nearby market house or milestones on the roads leading to the residence. This idea was mocked – and Repton named – in the long footnote to Book I, line 159 of *The Landscape*, and so a relatively gentle combat began. The two illustrations of the 'picturesque' and the 'vapid' Brown-style scene in *The Landscape* have a slight connection with Repton's trade card. Repton's chosen scene is far closer to the view in 'modern style', under attack by the '... fantastic band, With charts, pedometers, and rules in hand', than to the 'undressed' and picturesque view admired by Payne Knight. This disagreement was noted, with delight, by William Mason, who thought that Repton – 'a successor to Mr Brown much in vogue' – had in him 'a little of the coxcomb', but had a useful talent in being able to draw – *à la* William Gilpin – to demonstrate what he proposed to do with a client's grounds. In contrast, Payne Knight and Sir Uvedale Price were 'two greater Coxcombs ... because he writes about what he understands and they do not'.[11]

Repton replied to Payne Knight in his *Sketches and Hints* (which did not appear until 1795), with an 'Appendix' addressed both to Payne Knight and to Price. Most of this is too wordy, too remote from gardens for us to consider, but one brief passage sums up and separates Repton's attitude:

> ... in whatever relates to man, propriety and convenience are not less objects of good taste, than picturesque effect.

'Propriety and convenience' – here are key words for Repton's garden policy, related not so much to the landscape, or to the qualities of beauty, sublimity or the picturesque which might be found there, as to the wishes, status and means of his clients. He had indicated this already in the matter of the milestones at Tatton Park, an unfortunate beginning, but his later commissions show that he was right, since so many of them were for smaller properties whose qualities, or *requirements*, in terms of landscape gardening, were different from those of great estates – we have arrived in the nineteenth century.

Repton was new, and is important and interesting for several reasons. Though his early work often echoes Capability Brown – as at Shardeloes in Buckinghamshire (1793), for example, or at Sufton Court in Hereford-shire (1795), both triumphs of landscape gardening – he quickly developed a style of his own, different in several details from Brown's, and often different in scale, since so many of the properties on which he advised were smaller, and indeed part of an urban rather than a rural environment.

Often enough, Repton would exchange Brown's use of the ha-ha for a terrace, with balustrade and urns, to separate the house and its immediate garden from the ground beyond. The impression of 'grass right up to the house' was therefore changed to one of order, cultivation and propriety nearest to the house, and landscape – or 'nature' – beyond. Within the area of the terrace, Repton often allowed, even encouraged areas of flowers, and many of these were of astonishing formality.

At Valleyfield in Fife, Repton recommended a formal flower garden, with beds along both sides of a long and strictly formal geometrical pool (illustrated in his *Observations on the Theory and Practice of Landscape Gardening*, 1803). For 1801 or thereabouts, it was a proposal of extra-ordinary and indeed of architectural strictness, looking forward even to the neo-Roman fantasy of the Getty Museum at Malibu in California. But this was obviously beyond Repton's knowledge. In his own time, in architectural matters, he worked from around 1795 until 1800 with John Nash, a collaboration which benefitted both for some years, though Repton was clearly exploited at the end.[12] Their collaboration ended at Brighton, where Repton's proposals were deflected by Nash, and replaced by Nash's scheme.

To return to Repton, and to flowers, in his proposals (unexecuted) for the Royal Pavilion at Brighton (1805, and published in 1808 as *Designs for the Pavillon at Brighton*), one view shows a cluster of a dozen wicker-edged baskets of flowers on one side of the lawn, with a further scattering on the other side (the principal bed in his own small garden at Hare Street had a similar wicker framework). Already in 1791, his Red Book for Courteenhall in Northamptonshire had proposed a single but exceptionally large formal flower garden close to the house (separated, it is true, from the park by a screen of trees), and, in his many, and only partially executed, proposals for Ashridge in Hertfordshire in 1813, several flower schemes were put forward, including an astonishing 'rosary', a circular scheme, surrounded by rose-grown arcades, with 18 regular petal-shaped beds of flowers surrounding a central pool and fountain.

In the same year, 1813, he proposed a no less astonishing – in terms of eighteenth-century taste – formal flower garden at Beaudesert in Staffordshire. The Red Book of 1814 has an extraordinary double-page plate showing Repton's idea of a formal flower garden, returning, or so he claimed, to the original Tudor design. Though this would have been odious to eighteenth-century landscapers, the idea of such a recreation had already occurred to the poet William Wordsworth in 1806, when he wrote to Lady Beaumont at Coleorton in Leicestershire, outlining his ideas for a 'winter garden' based on features described in the fifteenth-century poem *The Flower and the Leaf* (see page 38). It was to be enclosed in trellis-work, contain a border with flowers, 'edged with boxwood', and even have a *fountain* – a garden feature banished from 'natural' schemes for most of a century.[13] Though Wordsworth's proposal remained as 'an idea in a letter', Repton's scheme for Beaudesert was carried out, with the aim of matching the new gardens with the Elizabethan features of the house.

The garden at Beaudesert was an extreme example of Repton's return to older models, and has, alas, gone with the house it was to adorn. More important, more characteristic of his work and still surviving is the complex Repton landscape at Endsleigh in Devon. Repton had already prepared a Red Book for Woburn Abbey, Bedfordshire, for the Duke of Bedford in 1804, including designs for the dairy in Chinese style, and some years later he was asked for proposals for the Bedford estate at Endsleigh, which overlooks the River Tamar on the border of Devon and Cornwall. In 1809, he made suggestions for a 'Swiss cottage', which is indicated on the 1-inch Ordnance Survey map of the same year, and his Red Book was presented in 1814, presumably illustrating several features which had already been executed.

At Endsleigh, Repton worked with the architect Jeffry Wyatt, who designed the 'Swiss cottage', the main residence, the 'pond cottage' and the dairy. Repton's landscaping is testimony to his debt to Brown – the superlative vistas from the main house, out over the Tamar – to the lovers of the picturesque, with the 'Swiss cottage', set high over the wooded river, and to his acceptance of new, more intimate and formal garden ideas in the regions near the house. In the Red Book, two of his watercolour views are particularly instructive, the 'Terrace Walk' and the 'Children's Cottage and Garden'. In each of these, the distant land-scape forms part of the background, in each case with a white cliff or gleaming cascade to give 'picturesque' emphasis. But in each, the main subject is resolutely Repton.

In the 'Terrace Walk', the terrace lawn is strictly rectangular, with a long, raised edge supporting flower beds, backed by a conservatory and tonsured hedges, and with a fountain enclosed at the clipped arcaded end. The 'Children's Cottage and Garden' is even more formal. Close to the 'cottage' – the modern Endsleigh Lodge – a segment of a circle is enclosed by a wall with a parapet, in fact with a miniature canal in which the children's boats may float. Outside lies the landscape, with the River Tamar, woods and cascade, while within is a geometrically divided flower garden, centering on a fountain. At this point, Repton's garden design has returned to the age of Louis XIV.

One further remark on Repton is necessary, to show how far he moved away from the Arcadian imaginings of Kent at Rousham or of Shenstone at The Leasowes. After a visit to The Leasowes, Repton perceived there only 'many beautiful small fields, connected with each other by walks and gates'. He failed to mention the monuments, tablets and poetic illusions in Latin, French and English. True, this was long after Shen-stone's death in 1764, and a rapid succession of owners. But Shenstone's Arcadian ideal was still known, and Repton ignored it.

Repton wrote several books on garden design – unlike his predecessors Kent and Brown. These are listed in the following table, together with a list of his most important commissions.

IMPORTANT WORKS BY HUMPHRY REPTON

Main books:

1795	*Sketches and Hints on Landscape Gardening*
1803	*Observations on the Theory and Practice of Landscape Gardening*
1806	*An Enquiry into the Changes in Taste in Landscape Gardening*
1808	*Designs for the Pavilion at Brighton*
1816	*Fragments on the Theory and Practice of Landscape Gardening* (with J. Adey Repton)

Main commissions: ('R' = Red Book)

1780s	1786	Hare Street Cottage, Romford, Essex (for himself)
		Catton Hall, Norfolk
	1788–90, 1791	Holkham Hall, Norfolk
	1789 ('R')	Welbeck Abbey, Nottinghamshire
	1789 ('R' in 3 vols, 1790, 1793, 1803)	Bulstrode Park, Buckinghamshire
	1789–c.1802	
1790s	1790–c.1805 ('R' 1790)	Rode Hall, Cheshire
	1790–1811 ('R' 1790)	Cobham Hall, Kent
	1791 ('R' 1791)	Tatton Park, Cheshire
	1791–1807	Garnons, Herefordshire
	1791	Thoresby Park, Nottinghamshire
	1791 ('R' 1791)	Glemham Hall, Little Glemham, Suffolk
	1792 ('R' 1792)	Antony House, Cornwall
	1792 ('R' 1792)	Port Eliot, Cornwall
	1792 ('R' 1793)	Stoneaston Park, Somerset
	1793	Gayhurst, Buckinghamshire
	1793	Rug Hall, Merionethshire
	1793 ('R' 1794)	Shardeloes, Buckinghamshire
	1793	Kenwood, London
	pre-1794–6	Tyringham, Buckinghamshire
	c.1794	Brocklesby Park, Lincolnshire
	1795 ('R' 1796)	Blaise Castle, Gloucestershire
	1795 ('R' 1795)	Sufton Court, Herefordshire
	1795 ('R' 1795)	Burley-on-the-Hill, Rutland
	pre-1796–1800	West Wycombe Park, Buckinghamshire
	pre-1796	Barrells, Warwickshire
	1796–1801	Corsham Court, Wiltshire
	1797	Grovelands, Middlesex
	1797 ('R' 1798)	Attingham Park, Shropshire
	1798–9	Plas Newydd, Anglesey
	c.1798	Moccas Court, Herefordshire
	1799	Adlestrop Park, Gloucestershire
1800s	1800	Dyrham Park, Gloucestershire
	1800 ('R' 1800)	Bayham Abbey, Kent
	1801-c.1809 ('R' 1801)	Wimpole Hall, Cambridgeshire
	c.1801 ('R' c.1801)	Valleyfield, Fife
	1803–11 ('R' 1804)	Longleat, Wiltshire
	1803 ('R' 1803)	Stanage Park, Radnorshire, Powys
	1804–5	Sezincote, Gloucestershire
	1804–10 ('R' 1805)	Woburn Abbey, Bedfordshire
	1805 ('R' 1806)	Royal Pavilion, Brighton, Sussex
	1806	Bulgaden (or Bulgadeen), Kilmallock, Co. Limerick
	1808 ('R' 1809)	Stoneleigh Abbey, Warwickshire
	1809 ('R' 1809)	Tregothnan, Cornwall
	1809–14 ('R' 1814)	Endsleigh, Devon

1810s	1810 ('R' 1810)	Uppark, Sussex
	1812–19 ('R' 1812)	Sheringham Hall, Norfolk
	1813–15 ('R')	Ashridge Park, Hertfordshire
	1813 ('R' 1814)	Beaudesert, Staffordshire

15

'THE SUBURBAN GARDENER'

J. C. Loudon

When Humphry Repton died in 1818, John Claudius Loudon was already well established as a writer on plant and garden matters. Born in Scotland in 1783, his writings – books, pamphlets and articles – began to appear in 1803, and continued until his death in 1843. His widow, Jane Webb Loudon (1807–58), continued to edit her late husband's works, and to produce her own, well into the Victorian era. One of Loudon's last publications, in 1840, was a compendious edition of Repton's five published volumes, entitled *The Landscape Gardening and Landscape Architecture of the Late Humphry Repton Esq.*

Loudon's publications were copious, varied, serious and learned, and indeed encyclopaedic. They extended round gardens to hothouses, botany, arboriculture, agriculture, architecture, cemeteries and education. Some, like his *Encyclopaedia of Gardening*, were many times reissued, and among his periodicals, *The Gardener's Magazine* was immensely successful.

Among the most important of his many titles, we should note:

1812   *Hints on the Formation of Gardens and Pleasure Grounds*
1822   *An Encyclopaedia of Gardening* – 8th edition, 1835
1833   *Encyclopaedia of Cottage, Farm and Villa Architecture and Furniture*
1835–8 *Arboretum et Fruticetum Britannicum* (8 vols)
1838   *The Suburban Gardener and Villa Companion*
1842   *The Suburban Horticulturist*

Loudon also edited, and largely wrote, the following periodicals:

1826–43 *The Gardener's Magazine*

1828   *The Magazine of Natural History*
1834–38 *The Architectural Magazine*[1]

Loudon's garden concerns were extensive. They included both planting and design, generally in a more formal style than even the later work
of Repton; choice of plants and their cultivation, both as regards fruit
and vegetables and flowers native or exotic; the technical side, whether
concerning hothouses, on which he wrote many times, or new
implements and equipment, such as the lawn mower; and a deep and
life-long awareness of the *social* importance of gardens, whether as the
small but cherished property of the growing middle class, with 'suburban
villas' to enjoy, or as far larger public parks, offering facilities for recreation to the gardenless working class, or as the setting for public
cemeteries, or as the essence of town and city squares. His earliest
published article, in the *Literary Journal* of 31 December 1803, was headed
'Hints respecting the manner of laying out the grounds of the Public
Squares in London', and proposed in particular a more thoughtful choice
of trees, shrubs and flowers to achieve more variety in different seasons
and in different parts of the ground.[2] Loudon returned to the question
of public parks in 1829 in an educational pamphlet, mainly to do with
the need for universal primary education, where he proposed the pro-
vision of bands or belts of ground round the capital to absorb the smoke
and reinvigorate the air – 'breathing zones or unoccupied places, half a
mile broad, at different intervals around London' – an idea which had
been put forward more poetically but with equally little success in John
Evelyn's *Fumifugium* in 1661.

Last but not least in his writings, he described gardens. In *The Gardener's Magazine* there are numerous 'tours', probably all but a few by
Loudon himself (and signed 'the conductor'), mainly in England with
some in Scotland or on the Continent. These accounts range from the
grandest of properties – Blenheim, Chatsworth, Alton Towers in
Staffordshire, or Beckford's Fonthill – to the 'villa gardens' of the middle
class, and to the nursery gardens which supplied the plants and trees for
them all.[3]

Loudon also designed gardens – not many, but some of significance in
the nineteenth century. Early on, he designed the landscape at Barnbar-
roch in Wigtownshire (*c*. 1805–7), and supplied plans for the palace
garden at Scone in Perthshire in 1804. In 1805, he redesigned parts of a
landscape at Llanarth Court in Gwent, where Samuel Lapidge had
worked in 1792, and in the late 1820s he designed St Peter's Square
in Hammersmith, an early and important contribution to London's
nineteenth-century squares.

He invented a term for a new category in garden design – the 'gardenesque' – first used in his *Gardener's Magazine* in December 1832. This, according to Loudon, was a style which would enable each plant in a garden to thrive and to display itself to best advantage, in contrast with the irregular, competitive and unpredictable conditions to be found in nature. With this principle, he advised, for example, the planting of trees so that their growth upwards, from roots to trunk, could be perceived. So, in the 1830s, he advised on the development of the arboretum at Bicton in Devon (though the great araucaria or monkey puzzle avenue was not laid out until 1842 by James Barnes, the head gardener, it was on Loudon's advice that each tree was raised on a mound). He designed the Birmingham Botanical Gardens in 1830–31 and the Derby Arboretum in 1839–40. This last commission, probably his most important design, is of interest not just because he had 'directed all the trees to be planted on little hills ... so that the junction of the main roots with the base of the trunk will appear above ground',[4] but because this scheme involved the complementary ideas of an *arboretum*, a place for collection and study of trees, and of a *public park*, in which recreation and education for the public were combined.

'We Were Much Gratified'

While the sense of his term 'gardenesque' was quite quickly modified – by Edward Kemp in 1850, in his *How to Lay out a Small Garden*, and by (James) Shirley Hibberd in 1856, in his *Rustic Adornments for Homes of Taste* – to mean a middle style of gardening between the strictly geometrical and the picturesquely wild, Loudon's concern with public parks was to be taken up and magnified, as was his fascination with technical developments and their advantage to horticulture, to the 'suburban' owners of 'villas', and to the labourers whose work was in gardens. Not a little of this concern was continued in the writings of his wife, Jane Loudon. It was apparent to an extraordinary degree, first, in Loudon's comments in 1831–2 on the newly-invented lawn mower, and, second, in Jane Loudon's comments a decade later.

The mower was invented by Edwin Beard Budding (c.1796–1846), being an adaptation of a cloth-shearing machine used in textile manufacture. Budding signed 'articles of agreement' with John Ferrabee for the manufacture of the machine in May 1830, and obtained a patent for this 'machine for mowing lawns' on 31 August that year. Not long after, the manufacture was taken over by Ransome's of Ipswich, and their advertisements were among the earliest documents to illustrate Budding's invention. Loudon's first comments were in *The Gardener's Magazine* for October 1831, when he reported enthusiastically on the machine's performance in the grounds of the Zoological Society at Regent's Park over 'nearly four months'. 'We were much gratified,' he wrote, partly because 'the foreman of the gardens there, Mr Curtis, informed us (Sept.23) that he is entirely satisfied with it', and partly because

... what is particularly gratifying ... the grass is required to be perfectly dry; so that, where it is used ... men can neither be set to work at it very early in the morning nor late in the evening ... Even if a corresponding period of rest be allowed to men thus set to work at unseasonable hours, we still think such a mode of labouring has a tendency to oppression; and we rejoice to see the means by which gardeners may in future be emancipated from it.

Loudon reported again in *The Gardener's Magazine* for February 1832, with detailed explanations of how the mower worked, how the grass cuttings were collected in a box, and how the blades were sharpened. There were three pictures. Later in the same journal (October 1832), he commented on the poor condition of many Scottish lawns, and hoped that the 'recently invented mowing machine' would soon 'become general in Scotland' as well.

'Become general' it did. Budding's mower conquered the lawns of the world. First pushed or pulled, by a man or a boy, a horse- or pony-drawn mower was patented in 1842, and a steam-powered mower in 1893. A petrol-powered mower appeared in 1899, followed by electric mowers in 1919, and on and on. But Loudon could not see that far. What he did see was that it cut the lawn better than any scythe (let alone a nibbling sheep), that it could improve a gardener's working conditions, and that it enabled a proprietor of modest means to cut his grass for himself. In his article in February 1832, he quoted from Budding's own description in the patent document – 'Country gentlemen may find, in using my machine themselves, an amusing, useful, and healthy exercise.' Loudon then added a comment by another correspondent on the two available sizes of the machine, stating that while 'wide' mowers 'are preferable for workmen who have much to cut', the 'narrow machine ... is best for a gentleman who wishes to use it himself'.

Jane Loudon

This interest in the well-being of the 'suburban horticulturist' leads, still in Loudon's lifetime, to the writings of his wife Jane, many of whose 18 garden books have the word 'ladies' in their title. So, in 1840, her *Instructions in Gardening for Ladies* stated that a lawn must be regularly cut, but 'this is an operation which a lady cannot very well perform for herself: unless indeed, she have strength enough to use one of Budding's mowing machines'. The following year, in her *Ladies' Companion to the Flower Garden*, she gave qualified approval – 'it is particularly adapted for amateurs, offering an excellent exercise to the arms and every part of the body ...'

The fourth edition of *The Ladies' Companion* appeared in 1846, and included quite a few articles which had been written wholly or in part by J. C. Loudon before his death in 1843, an 'Appendix' on the design and planting of flower gardens, and a further section on rock-work. Whether written by Jane Loudon or by her husband, the book as a whole with its wide choice of topics – earwigs, grottoes, implements (with newly-developed tools which ladies may use, such as special pruning shears), entomology, and a great deal on aspects of bedding, borders, flower gardens and parterres – indicates firmly that the subject is largely formal, often exceptionally so, and that it is of interest not merely to the grand and great, laying out new parterres at Wrest Park or at Trentham, but to those with gardens of only two, or one, or even less than one acre.

Formality is almost taken for granted. In a garden of two acres or so, one might indeed have 'winding walks', like the paths of sheep, or 'wild animals on commons'. But this 'would be to copy vulgar nature, and therefore art refines on these lines ... Nature requires to be copied ... to show art'. What matters is to choose the kind or kinds of formality one desires, best indicated in the section on 'Flower-gardens':

> All flower-gardens, to have a good effect, ought to be symmetrical ... [with] one general character of form and outline; that is, either curved, straight, or composite lines ought to prevail.

The explanation then specifies several kinds of 'flower-gardens': the 'French garden, or parterre'; the 'ancient English flower-garden' (approximately a 'knot', bordered by box edging); the 'modern English flower-garden', set in lawn with a pattern or patterns of symmetrical beds; and the 'architectural flower-garden or Italian garden', involving balustrades, terraces and statues.

With such emphasis on symmetry, geometry and 'art', often of a clearly architectural kind, it is not surprising that this volume, like many others in the period, says little or nothing about wilder, natural or landscape gardening, as is also the case, say, in Shirley Hibberd's *Rustic Adornments for Homes of Taste* (1856), or Edward Kemp's *How to Lay out a Small Garden* (1850). Jane Loudon's *Ladies' Companion* has really only one brief excursion into the wild, in the section on 'Rock-work', where a firm division of two kinds is made: 'that which is intended to imitate natural scenery ... and that which is intended to serve merely as a receptacle for plants'. While the latter could often be extremely small (going back only a short way in garden history, to the heap of volcanic lava from Iceland brought back by Sir Joseph Banks in 1772, and piled near the centre of the Chelsea Physic Garden), a rockery 'to imitate natural scenery' presented problems of verisimilitude and taste. The 'stratification' had to be convincing, and the rockery could not be set up with propriety near to the house, or indeed in any really small garden.

The forms of formal flower garden Jane Loudon described in *The Ladies' Companion* were to continue for the rest of the century – symmetrical, architectural and usually immensely bright. Though their floral content was sometimes thought to be crude, and was vehemently attacked in the 1880s, Jane Loudon stressed that 'the laying out and planting of parterres should always be attended to by the ladies of the place', since many gardeners lacked the necessary 'degree of taste and artistical feeling'. In the 'Appendix' on flower gardens, there is a first plan of immense intricacy, accompanied by numbered lists of plants. The first list, to cope with 60 different beds, 'will keep the beds full of flowers from June till October'; the second offers a simplification of the beds – now only 38 – with three separate lists of flowers, for spring, for summer and for autumn, and a separate list of standard roses. The 'Appendix' continues with further plans, for an 'American garden' to be planted with azaleas, kalmias, rhododendrons and magnolias, and for a 'dahlia and hollyhock garden'.

Compared with this lengthy section on an impressively time-consuming garden feature, there is only one page on 'Borders' and 'Border Flowers', reflecting an attitude which continued through the middle decades of the century. 'Borders', which were beloved of Philip South-cote, Lady Luxborough and Dicky Bateman, were still mentioned with approval by William Cobbett in *The English Gardener* in 1829. He prefered them to *beds*, 'where the whole bed consists of a mass of one sort of flower'. In *borders*,

... an infinite variety of them are mingled together, but arranged so that they may blend with one another in colour as well as in stature ... to form a regular series higher and higher as they approach the back part, or the middle of the border; and so selected as to insure a succession of blossom from the earliest months of the spring until the coming of the frosts.[5]

Though Cobbett's *The English Gardener* was reprinted several times, up to 1860, his particular liking for borders was not generally shared, and was not revived until the 1870s, when they were 'discovered' as a charming and informal element in cottage gardens of a supposedly old-fashioned kind (see page 274).

Palaces for Plants

The bedding schemes described by Jane Loudon, changed three times each season, would have been impossible in earlier periods of garden history, unless one had the resources and determination of, say, Louis XIV at Trianon or Sarah, Duchess of Marlborough at Blenheim. For people who lived merely in a 'suburban villa', such displays of annuals became possible only in the early decades of the nineteenth century, with the development of bigger, better and less costly glasshouses in which the tender seedlings could be raised prior to bedding out. (Though there are occasional differences in sense, the terms 'hothouse', 'greenhouse', 'palm house' and 'conservatory' were also used through most of the century, like the earlier 'stove' and 'orangery').

Though J. C. Loudon had written several items on the construction of glasshouses, and though various experiments in novel forms of design and construction were made in his lifetime, the decisive advances came shortly after his death in 1843. In 1845 and 1850, the cost of materials was lowered through the abolition of the glass tax and the brick tax, and in.1847 James Hartley patented an improved method for producing sheet glass, far clearer and larger in size than the panes previously available. In roughly the same period, new techniques for glazing bars, either in cast-iron or in wood, were developed.

Sufficient examples of these buildings survive for their remarkable development over some 30 years to be seen and wondered at. At Bicton in Devon the late eighteenth-century Orangery still stands at the head of the main garden axis, in its essential classical form little different from Sir William Chambers' Orangery at Kew, being a building related essentially to the needs and interests of human beings, not to plants. Not far away is the Palm House, a domed glasshouse built around 1820, which is instantly comprehended as a place for plants, providing protection, warmth, space and maximum light. Again, we may think of the large and elegant Orangery at Sezincote in Gloucestershire, built around 1805 by Samuel Pepys Cockerell in an elegant 'Indian' style, or the small Gothic conservatory at Abbotsford in Selkirkshire, built around 1820 and probably designed by Sir Walter Scott himself, as examples of the old-style orangery, and contrast them with the 12-sided conservatory at Dalkeith Palace near Edinburgh, designed by William Burn in 1827 and built by 1832, and the amazing glass and cast-iron Great Conservatory at Syon Park, designed by Charles Fowler and built in 1827–30. Though parts of the Great Conservatory doorway still hark back to the orangeries, the glass roof and soaring dome show, as at Bicton, that this is a building for plants, a message even more strongly conveyed in Joseph Paxton's Great Stove at Chatsworth, built in 1836–40 (demolished 1920), and most of all in the Palm House at Kew.

The Palm House at Kew, designed by Decimus Burton and Richard Turner and built in 1844–8, was completed in parallel with the remodelling of much of the grounds in the late 1840s to designs by William Andrews Nesfield, including areas of parterres and a formal pond beside the Palm House. Queen Victoria had sanctioned the establishment of the Royal Botanic Gardens at Kew in 1840, consolidating the slow development which had begun with Princess Augusta in 1759. In 1841, Sir William Hooker was appointed first Director.

Decimus Burton's Palm House has the purity of form and singleness of purpose of an igloo and the size of a cathedral. Within its soaring glassy framework, it serves as a home, a habitat for plants (most obviously palms!) needing a combination of light, warmth and space which cannot be found in Britain out of doors with certainty, and which smaller and less glassy conservatories cannot provide either. Human beings, however, might find it as unsatisfactory to live in as a goldfish bowl. Comparable in size and purity of form is the Temperate Palm House in the Royal Botanic Garden, Edinburgh, built in 1858. At Kew, the much smaller Water Lily House (1852) has, more or less, the same functional qualities, but the Temperate House (also designed by Decimus Burton, built 1859–62 and extended in 1898–9), has returned to an architecture of human as well as botanic concern. It is certainly beautiful, but it is the beauty of a fairy palace, not of a home for plants.

Another conservatory-palace – to my mind, the finest private example of its type in England – was added to the remodelled house at Flintham Hall in Nottinghamshire in the 1850s. With a Byzantine exterior, an interior balcony connecting with the first floor of the house, a fountain and sculpture, it was designed for people to take delight in plants, as a considered part of human enjoyment.

Also in the 1850s, another greenhouse-palace was built for Thomas Bewley (1810–75) at Rockville, near Blackrock in Co. Dublin. Rockville was famous in Western Europe for its collections of tree ferns and orchids, and their elaborate and extravagant settings were a part of the attraction. Both the plants and their surroundings were repeatedly described in gardening magazines of the period; William Robinson alone wrote four times in their praise in the *Gardeners' Chronicle* of 1864.

Botanic Gardens

The excitements at Kew ran parallel to the enthusiasm for botanic gardens – gardens for the reception, growth, study and dissemination of any and all botanic specimens – throughout the century. It is proper to list the more notable botanic gardens of that period in order of foundation:

1795	GLASNEVIN, DUBLIN, for the Dublin Society, later the Royal Dublin Society, later the National Botanic Gardens
1802	LIVERPOOL BOTANIC GARDEN; catalogue of plants, 1808
1803	CORK (until 1829); re-established in the 1850s
1804	THE HORTICULTURAL SOCIETY AT CHISWICK, later (1861) at Kensington
1806	TRINITY COLLEGE, DUBLIN, AT BALLSBRIDGE (until the 1960s)
1812	HULL, YORKSHIRE (until 1883)
1817	GLASGOW UNIVERSITY AT SANDYFORD; catalogue of plants 1825; resited in 1839–41 at Kelvinside as the Glasgow Botanic Gardens (a small physic garden was founded within the university in 1704, but this expired in the early 1800s)
1819	BURY ST EDMUNDS, SUFFOLK
1820–3	ROYAL BOTANIC GARDEN, EDINBURGH (founded 1670) moved to its present site at Inverleith, Edinburgh in 1820
1829	BELFAST
1832	UNIVERSITY OF BIRMINGHAM (designed by J. C. Loudon 1830, land acquired 1831); catalogue of 9,000 species, 1834
1833	SHEFFIELD BOTANIC GARDEN (designed by Robert Marnock, first curator)
1846	UNIVERSITY OF CAMBRIDGE (land acquired 1831)
1840	REGENT'S PARK, LONDON (Royal Botanic Society acquired the Inner Circle 1835, Robert Marnock designed the grounds and became curator 1840)
1861	THE ROYAL HORTICULTURAL SOCIETY, KENSINGTON (gardens designed by W. A. Nesfield)
1874	CHURCHTOWN BOTANIC GARDEN, SOUTHPORT, LANCASHIRE (opened 1875)

Beside botanic gardens there were also *arboreta*, collections of living trees, laid out with similar enthusiasm for botany, study, and also for public benefit or private pleasure. The Derby Arboretum has already been mentioned, but it was by no means the only foundation of its kind created in this period:

1805	GLAZENWOOD, ESSEX (copious plantings of fruit trees and other species by Samuel Curtis (1779–1860), who continued the *Botanic Magazine*, founded by his father in 1787); 1,200 varieties of roses by 1843
c.1805–10	ST ROCHE'S ARBORETUM, WEST DEAN, WEST SUSSEX
1829	WESTONBIRT ARBORETUM, GLOUCESTERSHIRE (begun by R. S. Holford as an extension to the park of Westonbirt House)
c.1830	BICTON, DEVON; pinetum, 1839
1840	DERBY ARBORETUM (designed by J.C. Loudon)
1846	SANDLING PARK, KENT (woodland, 1846 onwards, rhododendrons, 1854); further development from 1897 and in present century
1848	BOWOOD PINETUM, WILTSHIRE; rhododendron gardens, 1854
c.1845–50	ABERCAIRNY, PERTHSHIRE (mainly conifers)
1852	SCONE PALACE, PERTHSHIRE; pinetum begun 1848
1852	NOTTINGHAM ARBORETUM (designed 1850 by Samuel Curtis)

Conservatories, botanic gardens, arb   plants, whether in private or public hands, wei   growing enthusiasm. The manifestations extended   t limits of gardens, yet were so intimately rela   not be ignored.

The new plants came to Britain thanks to the plant hunters, and thanks to the intermediaries, eminent botanists on the one hand and enthusiastic nurserymen on the other, who encouraged the plant hunters and helped to finance their expeditions. Among the most famous in this period were David Douglas (1798–1834), the Scottish explorer who worked for William Hooker of the Glasgow Botanic Garden, moved to the Horticultural Society in London, travelled through many parts of northern America, and died in Hawaii; William Lobb (1809–63), who travelled through North and South America on behalf of the Veitch nurseries in London and Exeter; his brother Thomas Lobb (1811–94), who also worked for the Veitch concern, going to Burma and the East Indies; George Forrest (1837–1922), another Scot, who was connected with the Royal Botanic Garden at Edinburgh, and whose journeys to China, Tibet and Burma were made for several sponsors, including the Edinburgh Botanic Garden, Bees Seeds and private collectors in Cornwall; E. H. Wilson (1876–1930), who worked at Kew, but in 1909 joined the staff of the Arnold Arboretum near Boston, and whose travels in China and Japan were made on behalf of the Veitch nurseries and later for the Arnold Arboretum; Reginald Farrer (1880–1920), who travelled in Burma and, like Wilson, in the little-known parts of China; and Frank Kingdon-Ward (1885–1958), as noted for his geographical explorations in remoter China and Tibet as for his plant hunting successes, undertaken also for Bees Seeds.[6]

Another intrepid voyager, more world-wide than the previous collectors, was Marianne North (1830–90). She was not so much a plant hunter as a plant delineator; she painted the plants, flowers and trees which she observed in each of the continents she visited, often with an appropriate landscape or architectural background. Her paintings were given to the Royal Botanic Gardens, Kew, and the building to house them, the Marianne North Gallery, was opened in 1882 (to my mind one of the most fascinating parts of a great institution). Miss North also gardened in England in her last years, from 1886, at The Mount House, Alderley, Gloucestershire.[7]

development of sealed case for transport of plants → The Wardian case, 1830s

One more nursery in the early ninetee[...] tioned – the firm of Loddiges, in Hackney. [...] in 1771, his sons William and George Lod[...] 1840s. Their firm was noted for the rariti[...] plants, palms and orchids – and for its pe[...] (1817–33), illustrating these treasures. T[...] for their subsequent interest in an inve[...] importance in the introduction of new pla[...] case.

The Wardian case was named after its inventor, Dr Nathaniel Bagshaw Ward, whose hobbies included the growing of ferns, and the study of moths and butterflies. His keenness for ferns had, however, become blunted, since the smoky London air prevented them from growing. By chance, in 1829, he had left (and forgotten about) the chrysalis of a Hawk Moth, buried in moist soil inside a glass jar, with a lid over the top. Eventually, he spotted that moisture from the soil rose up to the lid and condensed there each day, falling down again into the jar. After a while (we may forget about the moth), a small fern and a blade of grass appeared, having germinated in the moist soil. They continued to grow.

Puzzling over this – they would have died, had they been out in the sooty London air – Ward saw that they were in effect in a *sealed* environment, with continuing and adequate moisture, light and warmth. He made further trials (at first with the aim of growing ferns more successfully), and produced a 'Tintern Abbey House', the clear and unique ancestor of the innumerable fern cases to be found in Victorian houses, sealed and relatively trouble-free miniature gardens.

A while later, Ward decided that another use might be made of his discovery – to provide sealed containers for the transport of little plants and seedlings from overseas, since their shipment in *open* cases was desperately inefficient. He sent two of his cases with a con-signment of ferns and grasses to Australia, where they arrived a year and a half later in flourishing condition. The same cases were shipped back to him from Sydney with some Australian seedlings, passing through snow and sweltering sun. When the ship reached London on 24 November 1834, Ward went to collect these much travelled cases, accompanied by a professional nurseryman. He wrote:

I shall not forget the delight of Mr George Loddiges, who accompanied me on board, at the beautiful appearance of the fronds of *Gleichenia microphylla*, a plant never before introduced alive into this country.[8]

NINETEENTH- AND TWENTIETH-CENTURY INTRODUCTIONS

1804	Tiger lily (*Lilium tigrinum*)	China
1805	Kerria (*Kerria japonica*)	Japan
1816	Wistaria (*Wistaria sinensis*)	China
1817	Snowberry (*Symphoricarpus rivularis*)	North America
1818	Mahonia (*Mahonia pinnata*)	North America
1820	Maple or Acer (*Acer japonica*)	Japan
1820	Camellia (*Camellia reticulata*)	China
1825	Choysia (*Choysia ternata*)	Central America
1827	Douglas fir (*Pseudotsuga menziesii*)	North America
1831	Sitka spruce (*Picea sitchensis*)	N.W. American coast
1831	Clematis (*Clematis montana*)	The Himalayas
1831	Deodar (*Cedrus deodara*)	Western Himalayas
1831	Petunia (*Petunia nyctagniflia*)	Brazil
1834	Tassel bush (*Garrya elliptica*)	North America
1835	Dogwood (*Cornus nuttallii*)	Western N. America
1837	California lilac (*Ceanothus thyrsiflorus*)	California
1837	Fuchsia (*Fuchsia fulgens*)	Mexico
1838	Monterey cypress (*Cupressus macrocarpa*)	California
c.1840	Atlas cedar (*Cedrus atlantica*)	Atlas mountains
1840	Eucalyptus (*Eucalyptus gunnii*)	Tasmania
1841	Parrotia (*Parrotia persica*)	Northern Persia
1843	Rhododendron (*Rhododendron fortunei*)	China
1844	Winter jasmine (*Jasminum nudiflorum*)	China
1844	Forsythia (*Forsythia viridissima*)	China
1844	Japanese anemone (*Anemone japonica*)	China
1845	Weigela (*Weigela rosea*)	China
1849	Barberry (*Berberis darwinii*)	South America
1850	Forsythia (*Forsythia suspensa*)	Japan
1853	Wellingtonia (*Sequoiadendron giganteum*)	California
1853	Western red cedar (*Thuja plicata*)	North America
1853	Lawson cypress (*Chamaecyparis lawsoniana*)	N.W. California, S.W. Oregon
1854	Hydrangea (*Hydrangea paniculata*)	Japan
1862	Crab (*Malus floribunda*)	Japan
1878	Magnolia (*Magnolia stellata*)	Japan
1879	Cotoneaster (*Cotoneaster horizontalis*)	China
1879	Wych Hazel (*Hamamelis mollis*)	China
1885	Double China rose (*Rosa chinensis*)	China
c.1890	Russian vine (*Polygonum baldschuanicum*)	Siberia
1892	Crab (*Malus sargentii*)	Japan
1893	Vine (*Vitis coignetiae*)	Japan
1896	Buddleja (*Buddleja davidii*)	China
1897	Brewer's spruce (*Picea breweriana*)	California
1901	Paper bark maple (*Acer griseum*)	S.W. China
1903	Handkerchief tree (*Davidia involucrata*)	China
1904	Lily (*Lilium regale*)	China
1914	Buddleja (*Buddleja alternifolia*)	China
1914	Viburnum (*Viburnum fragrans*)	China
1917	Common hydrangea (*Hydrangea macrophylla*)	Japan
1924	Blue poppy (*Meconopsis betonifolica*)	Southern Tibet
1948	Dawn Redwood (*Metasequoia glyptostroboides*)	China

The 'new' plants, discovered, depicted, introduced and pro-pagated, were not kept in public institutions alone, but grown eagerly and widely in private properties where conditions of climate and soil permitted. Some scores of these collections, often (but not always) concentrating on recently acquired rhododendrons, camellias and azaleas, were established, particularly in the south-western tip of England, in the west of Ireland and on sheltered parts of the west coast of Scotland, where frost is extremely rare and the rainfall copious. A small number are listed below, together with another group in Sussex (though these are by no means the only examples):

CORNWALL AND THE SCILLIES

1820s	GLENDURGAN, for Alfred Fox.
1824–68	CARCLEW, for Sir Charles Lemon.
1826	TREBAH, for Charles Fox, brother of Alfred Fox of Glendurgan. Planting extended in twentieth century.
1830	TREGREHAN, for members of the Carlyon family, beginning with conifers, much extended, and further extensions post-1945.
1830s	PENCARROW, for Sir William Molesworth, beginning with conifers. Development on into twentieth century.
1834	TRESCO ABBEY, for Augustus Smith, who began the gardens round the ruins of the priory of St Nicholas. Shelter belts were established – holm oak, Monterey pine, Monterey cypress – to counter Atlantic gales. The most consistently warm and moist garden setting in either Britain or Ireland, noted for its exuberant sub-tropical plantings. Given coherence by a firm, architectural terraced layout, made more apparent by immmense protective hedges of holm oak. Continuous development and addition of species into the 1990s.
1860–80	LAMELLEN. Further development 1901 onwards for E.J.P. Magor.
1896	CAERHAYS CASTLE, for John Charles Williams.
1906	TREWITHEN, for G.H. Johnstone.

WEST COAST OF SCOTLAND

c.1820	BENMORE (YOUNGER BOTANIC GARDEN), ARGYLLSHIRE, planting of conifers. 1865, Wellingtonia avenue for Piers Patrick. Further development, early 1900s, for H.G. Younger.
1862	INVEREWE, ROSS-SHIRE. Shelter belts begun in 1862, for Osgood Mackenzie, author of *Gardening in the Western Highlands*, 1908. Development from later 1870s.
1870s	LOGAN, WIGTOWNSHIRE, now Logan Botanic Garden. Much development into the twentieth century, with contributions from Forrest, Wilson and Kingdon-Ward.
1890s	ARDTORNISH, ARGYLLSHIRE, for Valentine Smith. Much further development from 1930s until 1990s, latterly for John Raven, and then for Mrs Faith Raven.

IRELAND

1840s	FOTA, CO. CORK. Established by Hugh Smith Barry (later Lord Barrymore) on the island of Fota in the River Lee. Begun with a formal garden, a walled garden and an arboretum of some 15 acres, and continually enriched with rare specimens until 1975. The arboretum is now maintained by the University of Cork. Fota is comparable in its history and development with the gardens at Tresco Abbey.

SUSSEX

1889	LEONARDSLEE, for Sir Edmund Loder.*
1892	BORDE HILL, for Colonel Stephenson Clarke – pinetum, arboretum, exotic shrubs.
1903–36	WAKEHURST PLACE, for Gerald W.E. Loder, subsequently an annexe to the Royal Botanic Gardens, Kew.*
1906	THE HIGH BEECHES, for Giles Loder.*
1909–34	SHEFFIELD PARK, for A.G. Soames, following initial landscaping by Capability Brown in 1776, and further landscape development in later nineteenth century.

* These three properties, all related to the Loder family, are especially noted for plantings of rhododendrons, camellias and azaleas.

'The Evidence of Artistic Taste'

The greatest conservatory of them all was the Crystal Palace, originally sited in Hyde Park to house the Great Exhibition of 1851. Designed by Joseph Paxton, following his success with the Great Stove and other glasshouses at Chatsworth, it was dismantled after the exhibition, and reassembled at Sydenham in 1852–4 in grounds designed by Sir Joseph (he was knighted in 1851) and laid out by Edward Milner.

The landscape of gardens and park which Paxton and Milner devised was both extravagant, extraordinary, and to some extent characteristic of grand layouts at this time. Set on formal terraces, and with a great central axis running out for half a mile, the Crystal Palace overlooked many formal elements, with balustrades, bedding, classical pavilions and a variety of fountains in balanced yet exuberant groups which out-spouted Versailles – so much f̲ ... ̲ eastern tip of the main axis there was ... scattered trees, 'natural' in outline, on ... 27 life-sized models of prehistoric a̲ ... today, though the Crystal Palace itsel ... ation of a wild and pre-human landsca ... 4 when this area was completed, an ... al con-fidence, as if to say 'see how fa̲ ... Crystal Palace and its marvels, since t... it was but a step away from Charles Darwin's On the Origin of Species (1859), albeit a step we might take less surely today. In 1854, the Illustrated London News pub-lished a view of one of these concrete animals – an iguanodon – with its vast body opened up, and with a crowd of Fellows of the Royal Society dining inside – the image, I think, of Homo sapiens britannicus in control of the evolutionary process.

Such a mixture of features, often including a conservatory, occurred many times in the more extravagant gardens of the nineteenth century. At Alton Towers in Staffordshire, the 15th and 16th Earls of Shrewsbury laid out the valley of the Churnet below the mansion (by Augustus Pugin, in Gothic style) with an unmatched miscellany of features, designed mainly by J. B. Papworth and Robert Abraham, and mostly completed by around 1830. The conservatory, by Abraham, was modelled in part on the eastern or Indian style of the Brighton Pavilion. The pagoda, also by Abraham, was supposedly modelled on an original in Canton, but had a cast-iron frame and a fountain jet at the top (a world apart from Sir William Chambers' Pagoda at Kew!). There was a 'Stonehenge', a 'Swiss Cottage' for a blind harper, and much, much more. J. C. Loudon was there in 1831, and wrote, after describing a fair number of features:

> The remainder of the valley ... displays such a labyrinth of terraces, curious architectural walls, trellis-work arbours, vases, statues, stairs, pavements, gravel and grass walks, ornamental buildings, bridges, porticoes, temples, pagodas, gates, iron railings, parterres, jets, ponds, streams, fountains, caves, flower baskets, waterfalls, rocks, cottages, trees, shrubs, beds of flowers, ivied walls, rock-work, shell-work, root-work, moss houses, old trunks of trees, entire dead trees, etc., that it is utterly impossible for words to give any idea of the effect.[9]

Loudon's tour of 1831 also took him on to Chatsworth, where he admired some of the early work of Joseph Paxton, who had been head gardener there since 1826. Paxton was active at Chatsworth, working for the 6th Duke of Devonshire, until the Duke's death in 1858. By then the Great Stove and other glasshouses had been created, together with a wealth of other features – pinetum, arboretum, various elaborate rockwork constructions, and a waterfall-cum-aqueduct sited above the head of Grillet's cascade.

In the formal area to the south, the Canal Pond of 1702–3 was adorned with Paxton's soaring Emperor fountain, completed in 1844. Three or four years earlier, a much smaller waterwork was recreated by Paxton, modelled on the 1693 'willow fountain', a hollow, artificial tree which sprayed out water from its branches and twigs. In 1693, it was a hydraulic curiosity in keeping with joke-fountains of Renaissance origin, but in the 1840s it was a strange and intriguing return to a forgotten feature from the past.

Biddulph Grange in Staffordshire had, and still has, elements and features which were quite as numerous as those at Alton Towers. The house was built in the 1840s for James Bateman and his wife Maria, both passionate plant lovers, and they began to lay out the gardens and grounds in 1842. From 1849, their friend E. W. Cooke, the marine painter, helped and advised. By 1862, the *Gardeners' Chronicle* could devote five articles by Edward Kemp to their achievements.

The grounds, covering 22 acres within park and woodland, were divided with rare skill to allow a score of different areas to exist close together, but without conflict. Most impressive is the division achieved at 'Egypt', where carved sphinxes flank the approach to an Egyptian tomb, surmounted by huge pyramidal yews. Entering the 'pyramid', the tunnel leads to the inside of a Cheshire cottage and then out to the pinetum. The most carefully concealed area is 'China', largely sheltered behind high piled-up banks of stone. A tunnel leads to a pavilion, a joss-house, a lake with bridge, part of the 'Great Wall', and accurate and appropriate planting of Chinese and Far Eastern species. Elsewhere, there is a 'stumpery', a rhododendron ground, an arboretum, and, of course, an Italian garden with terrace and balustrade near the house. Attached to the house was a glassy 'fern house', a variant on the conservatory.[10]

While some gardens were able to make use of natural rock formations, large or small (as at Stancliffe Hall in Derbyshire in the 1870s), this was not always possible, and the inadequacies and incongruities of some fabricated rocky scenes led to criticism. A solution was found in the composite material Pulhamite, formed from Portland cement and clinker, and manufactured from the 1830s onward by the Pulhams, father and son. Their first big contract was at Hoddesdon Hall in Hertfordshire in 1838. The younger James Pulham (c. 1820–98) then continued with several massive rockeries at Highnam Court in Gloucestershire in around 1847–84, at Battersea Park in London in 1866–70, at Sandringham in Norfolk in the early 1870s, and at Bearwood in Berkshire in 1879–83. At Bearwood the winding course of a stream (or possibly an old clay-pit) was dug out for 150 yards to form an artificial ravine, with 'rock, cascade and rivulet', lined with Pulhamite blocks, and then lavishly planted.[11]

'Another Feature in the Park'

Another feature in the Park is the Rockwork. This is entirely artificial . . . yet . . . the huge boulder-like masses, with their many fissures and rifts, so closely resemble natural rocks that many visitors are deceived by them. The rocks represent a mountain side, as if it had been rent asunder by some volcanic eruption . . .

So wrote Nathan Cole in 1877 in *The Royal Parks and Gardens of London*, describing the Pulhamite erections in Battersea Park. They are still there, overlooking the equally artificial lake.

Battersea Park was one of many public parks established in the mid-nineteenth century. The extent to which they were 'public' varied, some being royal properties, some being given by private individuals, some being purchased by local authorities, and some being attached to a group of houses whose residents might have special privileges. Many of the London squares, for example, were laid out for the use of those who lived in the surrounding houses, and some still maintain this practice.

A handful of these parks are named here to indicate their dates and their variety:

1825–30	PITTVILLE PARK, CHELTENHAM, GLOUCESTERSHIRE. The Pump Room was built by John Forbes 1825–30, and the adjacent park, with lake, twin bridges by Forbes and areas of bedding, was laid out by 1830.
1828–40	CALVERLEY PARK AND GARDENS, TUNBRIDGE WELLS, KENT. Designed by Decimus Burton as an amenity for the adjacent houses.
1830	ROYAL VICTORIA PARK, BATH. Fully described by the head gardener, Frederick Hanham, in *A Manual for the Park*, 1857.
1841–5	VICTORIA PARK, HACKNEY, LONDON. Designed by James Pennethorne in 1841, opened 1845.
1842–4	PRINCE'S PARK, LIVERPOOL. Designed by Joseph Paxton, laid out 1842–4.
1843–7	BIRKENHEAD PARK, MERSEYSIDE. Designed by Joseph Paxton 1843, laid out by Edward Kemp 1843–7. The first park in England to be established at public expense, and for this reason influencing the American F. L. Olmsted, who later designed New York's Central Park.[12]
1851–8	BATTERSEA PARK, LONDON. Site acquired 1851, laid out 1854–7 by James Pennethorne and John Gibson, opened 1858.
1867–72	SEFTON PARK, LIVERPOOL Designed by the Frenchman Edouard André 1867, opened 1872, its curving paths thought to be reminiscent of the Bois de Vincennes and the contemporary Buttes Chaumont.
1868	DERBY SQUARE, DOUGLAS, ISLE OF MAN. A town square laid out as a garden and overlooked by houses.
c.1870–5	VICTORIA EMBANKMENT GARDENS, LONDON. The site was created in 1864–70, as a result of the embankment of the Thames. The gardens are in four sections, curving round a part of the north bank of the river, and were opened between 1870 and 1875. All have displays of bedding, a variety of monuments, and notable mature planes.
1884–9	ST GEORGE'S GARDENS, CAMDEN, LONDON. Made in a disused burial ground, with a variety of table tombs, obelisks and urns as ornaments, the enclosing walls lined with tombstones. A secret and beautiful garden, recalling the *via dei Sepolcri* at Pompeii, with meandering paths, lawns, mature trees and small bedding displays.
1887	ST LUKE'S GARDENS, CHELSEA, LONDON. Made in the area of the churchyard south of St. Luke's Church. Lawns, walks, rose beds and annuals, with mature trees.
1889–95	ISLAND GARDENS, ISLE OF DOGS, LONDON. Formed from neglected riverside ground on the north bank of the Thames, facing Greenwich Hospital. Opened 'amid great enthusiasm' on 3 August 1895. A narrow strip of garden, with lawn, bedding, a few trees and superb river views.

The design and features of these parks also varied, depending on size, funding and intended use, but in the nineteenth century one feature was common to virtually every one – the display of *bedding*. Nathan Cole was himself head gardener at Kensington Gardens, and his inclination was clearly in the direction of intricate bedding designs. His book contains many planting plans, some of his own devising, some noted from other gardens, such as those at the Crystal Palace, Hampton Court and Victoria Park. At the latter, he wrote, they have 'last but not least, a magnificent display of flowers that is equal to anything seen in and about London ... examples of good taste, which afford delight to all beholders'.[13]

While Victoria Park today still boasts remarkable areas of massed bedding, this is no longer true of all public parks, though in the 1870s, and until the First World War, many of their head gardeners vied with each other to produce more and more spectacular displays. One form, carpet bedding, appears to have been invented in the 1860s, using combinations of small plants of uniform size, which were set close together to present a level and uniform surface. This in John Fleming, head gardener at Cliveden, and i taken up in both private and public gardens. only 20 years or so in private gardens, many using it competitively until around 1914 – and course, still be seen.[14]

[handwritten: 1856]

[handwritten: a continuation of the house (see next page)]

'The Garden is an Artificial Contrivance'

Though Shirley Hibberd, who wrote this phrase in 1856, was thinking mainly of the smaller gardens of the middle classes, it applied every bit as much to the gardens of the great, which were seen and admired by many visitors, and described and illustrated in the copious garden literature of the time. Again and again, these gardens were laid out with massive terraces close to the house, with balustrades, flights of steps, urns and sculpture, and with complex parterre designs set in lawn or gravel. We may think of the Italian garden at Wilton, designed in 1820–1 by Sir Richard Westmacott; of Drummond Castle in Perthshire, where Lewis Kennedy and his son George Kennedy designed and laid out the gigantic formal garden, with the plan of St Andrew's cross on the lowest of the three terraces, from the 1820s onwards; of Clumber Park in Nottinghamshire, where William Sawrey Gilpin devised a formal lakeside in front of the house, with terraces, balustrades and parterres to remedy earlier 'natural' landscaping; of Osborne House in the Isle of Wight, where in 1847–53 the Italianate terraces were built out for some 80 yards beyond the house, the design, directed by Prince Albert, recalling examples he had seen in northern and central Italy; and of Powerscourt in Co. Wicklow, south of Dublin (I think the most impressive of all these), where a long series of developments from 1841 into the 1870s achieved a majestic sequence of terraces and steps in front of the house, in a landscape backed by the Wicklow mountains. The parterres at Powerscourt were designed by Edward Milner. Notable formal bedding designs in this period were laid out at Wemyss Castle in Fife, with 'ribbon' bedding much praised in 1862; at Castle Ashby in Northamptonshire, where the Marquis of Northampton is credited with the design of the parterres; and at The Hirsel in Berwickshire in the 1880s. Such 'artifice' in the design cannot be seen better than at Terling Place in Essex, where a garden of utmost formality was created on the southern side of the house in the mid-nineteenth century. Within a semi-circular ha-ha, terraced areas of perfect symmetry extend to the left and right of the centre of the house, and downwards towards the landscape, outlined by balustrades, urns and a central flight of steps. Rectangular parterres to left and right are matched by circular bedding below. Order and geometry reign supreme.

So many were the designers (as often architects as garden designers) and their works, that it should be helpful to view a chronological list of these people, indicating the main gardens with which they were connected (many of these, such as Cliveden, the Crystal Palace and Chatsworth, have already been mentioned):

1789–c.1840 **Lewis Kennedy**: Abercairney, Tayside, c.1813; Drummond Castle, with his son George Kennedy, who redesigned the formal garden at Bowood, Wiltshire, 1851.

1793–1881 **William Andrews Nesfield**: One of the most prolific of Victorian garden designers, some of his later work was in partnership with his sons, William Eden Nesfield (1835–88), and Markham Nesfield (c.1842–74). He was noted, first with praise, and then in the 1880s with growing disapproval, for his frequent use of inert materials – crushed brick, slate, fragments of glass or spar – to provide constant and contrasting colours between the box edging and scrollwork of his parterres. Flowers were of course added in summer, but these inert substances gave needed brilliance in winter.

In 1844, his plans for the Royal Botanic Gardens, Kew, were elaborated in co-operation with Decimus Burton; in 1848, he made the parterres at Balcaskie in Fife more formal; in 1849–57, he worked with William Burn on the broad terraces and parterres at Holkham Hall, and in the same period at Somerleyton Park in Suffolk, where his work included a maze.

In the early 1850s, he remodelled the parterre to the south of Vanbrugh's house at Castle Howard, adding the Atlas Fountain from the Great Exhibition. The fountain remains, though the parterre was refashioned in the 1890s by the 9th Countess of Carlisle, and given the lawns and massive yew hedges which survive today. Another Nesfield parterre noted for its use of box and coloured gravels was at Broughton Hall in Yorkshire, laid out in 1855–7, to be compared with the parterre at Oxon Hoath in Kent. In 1858, he was commissioned to design the new gardens for the Royal Horticultural Society at Kensington. These were opened in 1861, praised at the time, but soon attacked as excessively artificial. In the 1860s, he worked with his son, W. E. Nesfield, at Witley Court, Herefordshire, on the great semi-circular parterre, and at Combe Abbey, Warwickshire, recreating terraces, a moat and parterres, in a sense restoring the formality close to the house which Capability Brown had removed in the 1770s.

At Blickling Hall in Norfolk, he and his younger son, Markham Nesfield, submitted a design for the terrace and parterre in 1870, but by 1872 the actual planting of the parterre had been replanned by the Marchioness of Lothian, who combined hedges, ribbon borders and a copious scattering of beds with herbaceous plants, a scheme much altered in 1932 by Norah Lindsay. In Wales, he worked with his son W. E. Nesfield at Kinmel Park in 1871–4, and in 1873–4 at Bodrhyddan in Clwyd, where the formal layouts both survive.

1795–1860   **Sir Charles Barry**: Trentham, Staffordshire, in 1834–42; Barry set two broad Italianate terraces between the house and Capability Brown's lake, and George Fleming (1809–76) laid out the formal parterres. Around 1848, Barry designed remarkable parterres for Dunrobin Castle in Sutherland, and in 1850 designed the terraced formal garden at Kiddington in Oxfordshire, thus 'distancing' Brown's small lake and parkland from the house. In 1850–2, Barry enclosed much of Gawthorpe Hall in Lancashire within a narrow balustraded walk, with parterres on two sides of the house. At Shrubland in Suffolk, from around 1850 until 1854, Barry laid out and completed an elaborate scheme of gardens, with an exceptionally impressive sequence of terraces and staircase. Areas to each side of the staircase were treated as a 'wild' garden in 1888 by William Robinson. At Cliveden, Barry was principally involved in rebuilding the house, in 1850–1, but the main terrace overlooking the parterre is his work (with a later balustrade), and the parterre itself remains essentially his design; John Fleming (d. 1883, and son of George Fleming at Trentham) was head gardener.

1799–1879   **Ninian Niven**: Curator of the Royal Dublin Society's botanic garden, 1834–9; designed the Winter Garden for the Dublin Industrial Exhibition of 1852; redesigned the garden of the Viceregal Lodge in Phoenix Park, Dublin with a parterre and yew walk in 1861, altering Decimus

Burton's earlier plan; designed the gardens for the Dublin International Exhibition of 1863.

1800–81 **Decimus Burton**: Formal garden of the Viceregal Lodge in Phoenix Park, Dublin, 1820s; 1844–8, built the Palm House at Kew, with Richard Turner, and co-operated with W. A. Nesfield in the layout of the gardens; 1855 onwards, built the Temperate House at Kew.

1800–89 **Robert Marnock**: Sheffield Botanic Garden, 1834; Regent's Park – gardens of the Royal Botanic Society in the inner circle, 1840 (Marnock was curator from 1841 to 1869); 1869, the flower garden at Warwick Castle – noted for its modest return to a less formal layout.

1803–65 **Joseph Paxton**: Head gardener at Chatsworth from 1826; Prince's Park, Liverpool, 1842–4; Birkenhead Park, 1843–7; Crystal Palace erected in Hyde Park, 1851 (Paxton was knighted in consequence); re-erected at Sydenham 1852–4, gardens laid out with Edward Milner (1819–84) by 1854; Mentmore Towers, Buckinghamshire, mid-1850s.

1817–91 **Edward Kemp**: Worked at Chatsworth under Paxton, and assisted Paxton in laying out Birkenhead Park. His designs for public parks included Stanley Park, Liverpool in 1867 and possibly Hesketh Park, Southport, Lancashire, in the mid-1860s.

In 1850, Edward Kemp, the last designer on the list above, published *How to Lay Out a Small Garden*. It was just one among scores of books and tens of periodicals on gardening practice which were produced in the Victorian period, most of them directed at least in part at the owners of smaller properties (termed by J. C. Loudon 'suburban villas'). The books ranged from serious Scottish tomes, such as *The Planter's Guide* by Sir Henry Steuart of Allanton (1828), Nathaniel Patterson's *The Manse Garden* (1838) and *The Book of the Garden* (2 volumes, 1853–5) by Charles M'Intosh, to the relatively lightweight *Gardener's Receipt Book* by William Jones (1858), H. Allnutt's *Our Flower Garden, How We Made the Most of It* (c.1872) and the minute and delightful *Rus in urbe: or Flowers that Thrive in London Gardens and Smoky Towns* by Mrs Haweis (1886). Immensely popular, and running through many editions, were *The Beeton Book of Garden Management* (1862 onwards) and *Beeton's Dictionary of Every-Day Gardening* (1870s onwards).

Periodicals likewise ranged from the publications of learned societies, like the *Journal of the Horticultural Society of London* (1846 to the present, since 1975 *The Garden*), or serious and educative works such as J. C. Loudon's *Gardener's Magazine* (1826–44) to the much more discursive *Gardener's Chronicle* (1841 to the present) or *Amateur Gardening* (1884 to the present). Somewhere in between was *The Garden*, founded by

William Robinson in 1871, and in his time (until 1900) frequently polemical in tone, though less combative in its later years, until its demise in 1927.[15]

One of the most successful and characteristic writers of the time was (James) Shirley Hibberd (1825–90), who produced some 15 books on garden matters, many of them specifically directed to owners of smaller gardens, for example, *The Town Garden* (1855), *Rustic Adornments for Homes of Taste* (1856), *The Fern Garden* (1869), *The Amateur's Flower Garden* (1871) and *The Amateur's Kitchen Garden* (1877).

Hibberd's own garden, at Stoke Newington, was small – a long but narrow strip, 280 by 36 feet at the widest, down to 8 feet at the tip. Again and again, he insisted on the essential formality of the garden:

> ... the garden is an *artificial* contrivance ... a continuance of the house. Since it is a creation of art, not a patch of wild nature; a part of the house or the town ... so it should everywhere show the evidence of artistic taste, in every one of its gradations from the vase on the terrace, to the 'Lovers' walk in the distant shrubbery ... Nature is to be robed, dressed, and beautified, and made to conform to our own ideas of form and colour ...[16]

In *Rustic Adornments*, from which these lines are taken, the chapter 'The Flower Garden' stresses that 'the geometrical garden is most appropriate'. It 'must have a symmetrical arrangement' with 'a distinct and decided pattern', and if the garden is small – 'in suburban gardens' – the borders 'often present the most attractive features, owing to the limited capacity of the garden precluding geometric arrangements ...' – in other words, the geometry must be accommodated to the small rectangular area available. 'Let us take even the smallest of suburban or town gardens,' Hibberd wrote, 'measuring say from sixty to ninety feet in length, by from twenty to thirty in breadth. The garden is bounded on three sides by walls, and on the fourth by the house.'[17] While this rectangle may have a small central and symmetrical scheme of beds, the borders are crucial. 'The style of planting known as *ribbon gardening*, so finely carried out at Trentham, is usually most appropriate.' '*Ribbonism*', as he called it, is 'the arrangement of plants in lines, each line being of one colour or one set of blended tints', and a few pages later the recommended plants are listed. They are virtually all annuals and tender bedding plants – lobelia, geranium, calceolaria, salvia, fuchsia. In the bedding, 'the colours are to blaze like the variegated lamps at Vauxhall'.[18]

In *Rustic Adornments*, so concerned with the small garden, Hibberd included two whole chapters on the Wardian Case. Though he praised 'Dr. Ward' for his invention and its use in bringing tender seedlings back to this country, Hibberd's interest was in the attractiveness of the Wardian Case as the container for an indoor miniature greenhouse in which small tender evergreens, particularly ferns, might be grown. The garden could hardly become smaller. Later in his book, he devoted some 40 pages to the larger 'fernery', an indoor garden, and in 1869 published *The Fern Garden*, with sections on growing ferns outdoors, indoors in a fernery, and in the minute space of the Wardian case, which by then had been produced in a multitude of highly ornamental forms, suitable for display in Victorian interiors.

It is ironic that the literature describing and advising the design and planting of Victorian gardens survives in its entirety, while the gardens, 60–90 by 20–30 feet, thousands upon thousands of them, survive for the most part only as brick-walled enclosures, with no more than an outline or skeleton of their plan. Rope-edged tiles may sometimes be found along the paths together with the outlines of beds, but the borders, bedding and rockery which were once there are largely gone. Such is the nature of gardens.

Two somewhat larger examples, happily surviving, may be noted – Bridge End Gardens in Saffron Walden, Essex and the Plantation Garden, Norwich. Bridge End Gardens, first laid out in the 1790s, have always been separate from the owner's house, and were developed from 1839 onwards with several distinct areas – a walled garden for fruit and vegetables, with a cruciform plan centred on a fountain, and a main ornamental garden with topiary, box bedding and another central fountain. A balustraded parapet gives views over the open ground on one side, while a separate walled rose garden contains a circular layout with slender iron arches. A hedge maze, approached by wrought iron gates, also dates from around 1840. These gardens were opened to the public by the owners in the 1890s, and taken over as a public park in 1918 – hence their survival.

In Norwich, the Plantation Garden was developed in the sloping and enclosed area of a disused chalk quarry, downhill from the house built for Henry Trevor in 1856. The vaguely oval site included a conservatory or palm house, a central lawn with formal beds, a water garden with pools and cascades, and a complete belt of serpentine walks, rockery, shrubs and trees around the enclosing slopes. The encircling trees and shrubbery served to enhance the artifice of alternating circular and rectangular beds in the central lawn.

16

REBELLION

Seeking Alternatives

Such intensely geometrical garden schemes as those I have just mentioned were to continue until the end of the nineteenth century, indeed until the period of the First World War, constituting the most distinctive feature of mid-nineteenth-century gardening. We may see them to this day, less numerous to be sure, and often on a smaller scale than they would have been in the 1860s, but still resolutely formal and planted with exactly spaced blocks of annuals, referred to as 'carpet bedding', 'massed bedding', 'ribbon bedding' or 'mosaic bedding', to indicate their contrived part in an overall design; and as 'municipal bedding', to indicate their frequent and characteristic appearance in public parks.

Other approaches to garden design and to planting were of course proposed, and sometimes practised, notably the development of the herbaceous border, which has already been mentioned. But other suggestions were made, and must be discussed. Just as Wordsworth in 1806 had proposed a small, enclosed and flowery garden, based on that in the Chaucerian poem *The Flower and the Leaf* (see pages 38 and 244), as an alternative to the excessive wildness of the landscape garden, so Sir Walter Scott in 1823 and 1828 urged a return to formality of a possibly old-fashioned kind near the house, claiming that 'nothing is more completely the child of art than a garden', and attacking the bare landscapes of William Kent, Capability Brown and their successors.[1]

Scott's own property at Abbotsford near Melrose, Borders, developed from 1811 onwards, had landscaped parkland and plantations in the outer areas, but the enclosures near the house were formal. They included geometrical flower beds and clipped pillars of yew, whose design and layout is thought to have been by Scott.[2]

By 1839, an unsigned essay, 'The Poetry of Gardening' in *The Carthusian*[3] took up the attack on 'the vain assumptions of these coxcomical times', condemning not the absurdities of the later landscapers – 'the picturesquians have fortunately had their day' – but those of the 1830s, two in particular: first, the excesses of the plant fanciers, pursuing 'rarity, strangeness, and variety', and second, the follies of garden designers, producing 'scores of unmeaning flower-beds, disfiguring the lawn in the shapes of kidneys, and tadpoles, and sausages, and leeches, and commas'. Against these evils, two remedies are suggested. One is to take up old-fashioned topiary (discussed on page 276), and the other is a return to the flowers of the cottage garden, particularly the sunflower and the hollyhock, in place of the '500 choice varieties of the dahlia' with 'odious distinctive names'.[4]

An extraordinary deviation from the early Victorian garden was created from the 1840s onwards by James Mellor (1797–1891), in an area of some 3 acres, set in 50 acres of farmland. Mellor's Gardens, as they have long been called, at Hough Hole House, near Rainow in Cheshire, present the main incidents of Christian's journey, as told in John Bunyan's *Pilgrim's Progress*. Along the paths, past pool, stream and sloping banks, there are, for example, the Wicket Gate, the Slough of Despond, the Delectable Mountains, a distant view of Doubting Castle and the Land of Beulah. Sundry Christian memorials were added and a curious extra – Uncle Tom's Cabin.[5] Mellor's Gardens are one of the tiny group of gardens in England which have an 'itinerary'; two or three others, like the vicarage garden at Claydon in Sussex of about 1870, present a Via Dolorosa.

The Cottage Garden

Cottage gardens must now be briefly discussed, since they – or rather, the public's imaginings about them – were mentioned with increasing approval as the century moved on. Until the 1830s little notice had been taken of them, but the overlapping images of the small farmhouse, the labourer's cottage and the rural 'villa' retreat (as in J. C. Loudon's *Encyclopaedia of Cottage, Farm, and Villa Architecture* of 1836) led to the growth of a glowing, romanticised idea of the rural labourer's garden, rich with a medley of herbs, vegetables, fruit and flowers (usually 'old-fashioned'). This reached a pictorial climax in the watercolours of the 1890s and early 1900s, often overlapping with views of similarly luxuriant herbaceous borders – notably in the paintings of Helen Allingham (1848–1926), summed up in her illustrations for *The Happy England of Helen Allingham* in 1903, with text by Marcus Huish. Nonetheless, there was some truth in the idea – to become an ideal – of the small rural garden, as seen in Samuel Palmer's painting *In a Shoreham Garden* (c.1825–35), and as described by Samuel Felton in 1829, referring to cottage gardens in south Wales in the 1820s.[6]

The author of 'The Poetry of Gardening', in 1839, trumpeted the excellence of 'the cottager', who alone appreciated, unlike wealthier city gardeners, 'the rich mulberry colour of the foliage of the pear-tree in September', and 'the scarlet runner ... this beautiful plant' (we should remember William Turner's phrase 'arber beans', in 1548.) Many writers later in the century were to echo these sentiments. Sometimes the setting was raised up from the rural cottager's sphere to become the small enclosed garden of a wealthy person, like Lady Corisande's garden, described at the end of Disraeli's novel *Lothair*, crowded with 'cabbage-roses, sweetpeas, and wallflowers ... It is very old-fashioned'.[7] Other writers, like Richard Jefferies in *Bevis* (1882), told more of the truth, seeing both the gooseberries, the hollyhocks, *and* the ignorance, a view not dissimilar to Gertrude Jekyll's in a brief, sensible chapter 'Cottage Gardens' in *Old West Surrey* (1904), illustrated with her own photographs. Others, like Ouida in her essay 'Gardens', in 1895, plunged into a welter of fantasy:

An English cottage ... with roses clambering to the eaves, and bees humming in the southern-wood and sweetbriar, and red and white carnations growing beside the balsam and the dragon's mouth, is a delicious rural study still linked, in memory, with foaming syllabub and ruddy cherries, and honey-comb yellow as amber, and with the plaintive bleating of new-born lambs sounding beyond the garden Coppice.[8]

In the next paragraph, Ouida linked these images with the flowers named by Shakespeare, Milton and Ben Jonson, and then maintained that 'such cottage gardens as these are still extant', as an example to set against the 'squalor, famine, crime, drunkenness and envy' of the industrial poor. Ouida's remarks may now seem embarrassingly naïve, but the ideal, as hard to pin down as 'the good old days' or 'Merrie England', survives to this day, not least in the crowded colourful pictures on packets of 'cottage garden mixture'.

Topiary

Coming back to 1839 and 'The Poetry of Gardening', we find that the author had another remedy for the 'scores of unmeaning flower-beds'. It was another return, not to the humble cottage garden, but, on a grander scale, to

> ... the good old system of terraces and angled walks, and clipt yew-hedges, against whose dark and rich verdure the bright old-fashioned flowers glittered in the sun.

At this point he added, 'I love the topiary art, with its trimness and primness, and its open avowal of its artificial character'.[9] We have, therefore, in a few lines the linked admiration for 'the good old system', 'old-fashioned flowers', and the artifice of topiary.

By 1839, there was precious little left in Britain of the topiary so common in 1700, and so vigorously criticised by Addison and Pope in 1712 and 1713. If it had not been destroyed, it was neglected, and had grown out and away from whatever formal shape it had once been given. We may remember Thomas Jefferson's summing-up of Hampton Court in 1786 – 'Old fashioned. Clipt yews grown wild'. In the mid-nineteenth century, therefore, entirely new topiary schemes were undertaken, as at Elvaston Castle in Derbyshire, between 1830 and the mid-1840s, modelled on the curving topiary tunnels of the 'Queen's Cabinet' in the gardens of Het Loo in the Netherlands,[10] and notice was taken of such yew hedges and topiary work as might be thought to survive from old formal gardens.

This was especially true of the topiary at Levens Hall in Westmoreland, which by 1900 had become the type of the old-world topiary garden. As we in the 1990s know, this garden was laid out in 1689, and an early plan indicates that the trees, clipped to simple cones or obelisks, were part of a highly formal design. There was then virtual silence about these trees until J. C. Loudon passed by in 1831 and admired 'this genuine specimen ... of garden antiquities', but he did not elaborate – and earlier visitors, William Gilpin in 1772 and John Britton in 1814 or earlier, say as little (Gilpin 'did not ride up to it', and Britton states that 'its lawn still preserves the formal character of that age' without more detail).[11] The first mention of topiary at Levens might well be in 1851, when 'eagles of holly and peacocks of yew' were praised, and the earliest picture seems to have been published in 1869.[12] By this time old topiary in other gardens has been trimmed and reshaped. In 1866, for example, the poet

Dante Gabriel Rossetti visited Brickwall, at Northiam in Sussex, praising the 'garden full of walks of quaintly cut fir-trees, the best thing of the sort I ever saw', and ordered copies of photographs 'which already exist of Northiam house and garden'.[13] Hedges in the garden at Brickwall may well date from the late seventeenth century or early eighteenth century, but their condition before the 1860s is uncertain. The same applies to the topiary works at Packwood House in Warwickshire, where some of the yews were planted in the early or mid-eighteenth century, and others not until the 1850s, after which the grouping of the trees came to be known as a representation of the Sermon on the Mount, with attendant Apostles and Multitude.

William Robinson and Forbes Watson

Almost always in this period, gardens of any size were deliberately planned with a varied set of areas and features. So, the author of 'The Poetry of Gardening' may praise old-fashioned flowers and topiary work, but when he comes to sketch out his garden 'as it is, or is to be' it contains much more, running from the 'upper terrace . . . strictly architectural' to the distant 'lover's walk', and 'the endless winding tracks in the distant wood'. In between are 'trimly cut parterres', planted with annuals, a topiary garden with a maze and a 'sun-dial of flowers, arranged according to the time of day at which they open and close'.[14]

The kitchen garden has both fruit and flowers; there is a rock garden, and another scented garden which, I think, might be considered 'herbaceous'; further away is a shrubby garden, underplanted both with 'bold broad strips' of spring bulbs, and others set randomly 'under the dark underwood of the adjoining coppice'. There are other areas besides, but I have quoted enough to show the wide-ranging elements of such an imaginary garden scheme. It was repeated pretty closely by Lord Lytton in 1863,[15] who was very possibly thinking of the variety of his own gardens and grounds at Knebworth in Hertfordshire. The most sumptuous, and I think the most successful, of such 'mixed' garden schemes is at Manderston in Berwickshire, largely laid out between the 1880s and 1906 (see page 290).

Less sumptuous, but possibly more convincing to contemporaries was the 'old-fashioned' garden of the gardener-writer 'E.V.B.' (Mrs Evelyn Boyle) at Huntercombe in Buckinghamshire. She was active there from 1871, reshaping the earlier gardens with varied yew hedges or topiary items, and 'old-fashioned' plants in the borders.

These alternatives to massed bedding schemes were put forward many times over many decades, and with degrees of enthusiasm and understanding. They are however mild in the extreme in comparison with the drastic proposals published by two writers in the early 1870s, William Robinson and Forbes Watson.

In 1861, William Robinson (1838–1935) came to work at the Royal Botanic Society's garden in Regent's Park, under its curator Robert Marnock, and rapidly made a name for himself both as a horticulturist and as a gardening correspondent. In 1867, he spent most of the year in France visiting gardens, studying horticultural techniques, and covering the garden aspects of the International Exhibition in Paris. By 1868, his many newspaper articles and related thoughts had coalesced into a book, *Gleanings from French Gardens*, and by 1869 into another, *The Parks, Promenades and Gardens of Paris*. While he admired the horticultural expertise of the French, and the excellence of some of their tools, like the *sécateur*, invented in 1836 but still hardly known in Britain,[16] and made lasting friendships with French plant enthusiasts, such as the Vilmorins, he was repelled by the formal vastness of Versailles, by the 'indescribable emptiness and ugliness of the scene' – 'To me,' he wrote, 'there is nothing more appalling than the walls, fountain basins, clipped trees, and long canals, etc. of such a place as Versailles.'[17]

After his main French visit in 1867, Robinson went to Switzerland, where the mountain flowers and their setting gave him a wholly different prospect, described in *Alpine Flowers for English Gardens* (1870), and from which *The Wild Garden* of 1870 launched out into a violent statement of how a garden to his, William Robinson's, taste should be made. An even more violent attack on massed bedding and florist's flowers was made by the botanist Forbes Watson in *Flowers and Gardens*, published in 1872, three years after the author's death. In 1882, William Morris included a section in his *Hopes and Fears for Art* which reinforced Forbes Watson on the (supposed) perversion of 'over-artificiality in flowers'. Between them, Robinson, Watson and Morris, in the texts I have named, set out the sternest principles for 'natural' as opposed to 'artificial' gardening which had been enunciated since the eighteenth century.

The *theory* is most clear-cut in Forbes Watson's *Flowers and Gardens*. He starts with the individual plant, and ends with God, its creator. Gardens and gardeners, he claims, show too little respect for either. 'Gardeners are teaching us to think too little about the plants individually', and failing to follow 'the natural course', which is that of 'loving and cherishing plants from their earliest youth ... into age'. Properly considered, a garden should be 'the home of plants, where all ages, the young, the mature, and the decayed, mix freely and in easy dress'. When this occurs – in the true 'old-fashioned garden', for example – we see 'that look of happy rest among the plants, each of which seems to say, "All plant life is sacred when admitted here." '[17]

Such respect for 'the individual plant' means also that we (or those of us who are 'florists') should not tamper with, or try to improve on, the original creation. Essentially the wild plant is superior to the cultivated form, the superiority showing in the true beauty of the 'Dog rose' compared with the – to Forbes Watson – falsity and presumption of double, cultivated roses. For one to like 'the double flower' proves 'that your taste is most seriously injured. You cannot believe that the work of God is faulty here, and that the Wild Rose is an imperfect creation.' Look again at wild roses and their like – 'the pure works of God will give you the best criterion for judging the works of man'.[19]

These ideas go back, of course, to Rousseau, advocate of a early form of 'wild' gardening in his novel *La Nouvelle Héloïse* (1761), and, in the *Rêveries* (1782), of 'herborising' – we might call it 'nature study' – not in gardens, but in the countryside, as a means of leaving the social world and entering the world of nature and its Creator.[20] For Rousseau, such views had led by 1767 to a rejection of the man-made garden, as something which disfigured the natural beauty of the vegetable world, and Forbes Watson's attitude was essentially the same – the true 'old-fashioned garden' which he praised was hardly to be found.

William Robinson was far more violent in his language than Forbes Watson, though allowing occasional forms of compromise here and there. He revolted against 'the death-note of the pastry-cook's garden' (that is to say, the system of massed bedding of annuals, called elsewhere 'garden-graveyards'), but accepted that wild and cultivated roses both have their value and their beauty, and their respective places in our gardens.[21] His view was more positive (at least in garden terms) than Forbes Watson's, since he described how an *acceptable* form of garden, the 'Wild Garden', should be made:

My object ... is to show how we may have more of the varied beauty of hardy flowers than the most ardent admirer of the old style of garden [i.e. 'old-fashioned' or 'cottage' gardens] ever dreams of, by naturalising many beautiful plants of many regions of the earth in our fields, woods and copses, outer parts of pleasure grounds, and in neglected places in almost every kind of garden.[22]

'Wild gardening', in Robinson's eyes, is therefore best practised in certain areas – along woodland walks, beside shrubberies, in meadows beside streams and ponds – which tend most often to be at a distance from the house – 'such beauty may be realised in every wood and copse and shrubbery that screens our "trim gardens" '. He saw them as being a *part*, the most important part, of the garden, and not necessarily the whole. One merit of the wild garden's outlying position is that it doesn't interfere 'with the flower-beds near the house'.

So, the wild garden should be sited 'on the fringes of shrubberies and plantations', and contain *hardy* plants (which will be allowed their full cycle of growth, flowering and decay, as Forbes Watson insisted). These are, however, not simply the native flora, but *any* plants hardy enough to survive in the British climate. In a redefinition Robinson talked of 'wild gardening, pure and simple – that is to say, the naturalisation of foreign hardy plants'.

The 'wildness' of Robinson's system involves giving plants full freedom of growth at all stages of their life-cycle. With quite a few, such as spring bulbs, this necessitates leaving them alone after they have flowered, and so Robinson urges again and again that they are planted close to, or in, the shelter of shrubs, or in meadow grass which is left unmown until they have died down entirely – '*not* to mow is almost a necessity in the wild garden'.[23]

In line with much of *Flowers and Gardens* and *The Wild Garden* is a brief section in William Morris' *Hopes and Fears for Art* (1882), where he urges town gardeners to cultivate flowers 'that are free and interesting in their growth, leaving nature to do the desired complexity'. This will succeed, so long as we do not 'desert her [nature] for the florist'. Morris saw two evils in garden matters – the florists, who ruined many a flower by breeding for excess rather than delicacy, whether in size, scent or colour; and 'carpet-gardening', which he considered 'an aberration of the human mind'. So far, Robinson and Watson would have agreed. But Morris continued, 'to sum up as to a garden':

> Large or small, it should look both orderly and rich. It should be well fenced from the outside world. It should by no means imitate either the wilfulness or the wildness of Nature, but should look like a thing never to be seen except near a house. It should, in fact, look like a part of the house.[24]

Here, by 1882 (Morris had given the matter of this book in lectures in 1878–81), compromise had set in, harking back to Sir Walter Scott's words 'nothing is more completely the child of art than a garden'. Forbes Watson died before his book, *Flowers and Gardens*, was published, but

Robinson and Morris were both to live on and to dilute (or change) their message. In 1883, Robinson published his most important work, *The English Flower Garden*, and in 1885 he acquired the house and grounds of Gravetye Manor in Sussex. The book would be reissued and re-edited many times, and the house and grounds would be enlarged and much extended – and both book and house would end far away from the truculent assertive views of *The Wild Garden*.

By 1883, when *The English Flower Garden* was first published, Robinson was prepared to include several plans of a formal kind, and in his own garden and grounds at Gravetye there were from the start both formal and 'natural' parts. Close to the house, on the southern and western sides, were two geometrical areas. That to the south was enclosed, and its paved paths surrounded a dozen rectangular beds, planted mainly with roses and carnations. To the west, the larger 'flower garden' was at first a long rectangle of lawn with beds at the corners and along the sides, planted again with roses and with some carnations and pansies. Though this west lawn was level, the ground rose up to the north, and was thickly planted with flowering shrubs. To the south it was bounded by a long straight terrace wall, with a mixed border on the outer lower side. In 1902, Robinson eliminated the lawn from the west or 'flower garden' entirely, dividing the whole into a host of rectangular beds, rigidly separated by paving stones, a scheme which has been maintained with only slight change to the present day. As an exercise in strictly formal subdivision of a regular area it is both simple and resolutely geometrical, a fact which is easy to overlook as one admires the free shapes of the plants and shrubs. Robinson saw the apparent paradox clearly enough, and resolved it happily with the words 'formality is often essential to the plan of a garden but never to the arrangement of its flowers or shrubs'.[25] His sensitivity to the contradiction is revealed in his article on Gravetye published in *Country Life* in 1912. 'I am a flower gardener,' he wrote, 'and not a mere spreader about of bad carpets done in reluctant flowers.' Explaining how he had divided his 'flower garden' into stone-edged beds in order 'to contain the greatest number of favourite plants in the simplest way', he complained about 'a young lady' who, 'instead of warming her eyes at my Roses and Carnations, said, "Oh, you, too, have a formal garden!"' She was 'a silly person', to make such a remark 'instead of looking at the flowers'.[26]

The *Country Life* article includes the 'garden plan at Gravetye' with its 46 rectangular beds. Downhill, below the long terrace – and therefore separated both visually and physically from 'the flower garden proper' (Robinson's words) – he planted some 30,000 bulbs to create the 'Alpine meadow', a sloping, grassy area left unmown for much of the year, and one of the forms of 'wild garden' he most favoured. At the bottom of the slope is a lake, enlarged from an existing hammer pond, and this he planted round with lavish drifts of daffodils beside the trees along the bank – the setting for a 'wild' water garden. North of the house and the 'flower garden' is a large area of woodland, planted by Robinson with an astonishing variety of trees and shrubs – another 'wild' area – and in it, north-west from the house, he built in 1898–1900 the massive oval walled 'fruit garden' – a formal architectural feature of powerful originality. Standing on sloping ground, the walls are stepped to follow the contour, and have a strangely 'battlemented' air.

The Plantsman's Garden

Robinson's garden achievement at Gravetye is therefore *mixed* in its use of formal and natural features, and in this respect not impossibly different from the schemes proposed by more traditional writers such as Lord Lytton (see page 277). The same may be said of the garden of Robinson's friend and admirer, Samuel Reynolds Hole (1819–1904) at the Deanery, Rochester in Kent, depicted by George S. Elgood in the frontispiece to Hole's *Our Gardens* in 1899. While the plants grow exuberant and free, the borders in which they are set are perfectly regular.

But with Dean Hole, as with Robinson and Forbes Watson, the theorist of *Flowers and Gardens*, the emphasis was always on the plants. The words 'plantsman's garden' came later, but their sense is derived from the understanding and energy of Robinson and Watson long before, and they fit better than 'wild garden' to the ideals of Robinson, wishing to grow, care for and appreciate individual plants in the most thoughtful manner. 'Wild garden', to my mind, is not a helpful term, being tainted with the ideas of the sublime from the late eighteenth century, and, for modern readers, with diverse jungly concepts from our own epoch.

Sir Herbert Maxwell (1845–1937) was an early and proper disciple of William Robinson. His long essay 'Gardens' in *Post Meridiana* (1895) is eloquent in discussion of what should or should not be in a garden, and his greatest praise is given to 'Mr George Wilson's grounds at Oakwood, near Weybridge' – that is to say, the 60 acres of 'wild' garden at Wisley developed between 1878 and 1902 by G. F. Wilson (1822–1902), acquired in 1903 by the Royal Horticultural Society, and subsequently extended to some 200 acres (and indeed much developed). Maxwell wrote before the term 'plantsman's garden' had been coined, and so he used other phrases to define 'the owner and maker of this paradise' and to outline his creation:

> [He] may best be described as a decorative botanist: deeply versed in all plant-lore, yet with a constant eye to what consists with beauty, he has enclosed several acres on the slope and crest of a hill, including a wood at the foot and a piece of water. Here he has assembled a vast collection of plants, carefully arranged, but with all trace of design studiously concealed. A lady lately visiting it expressed the effect in a single sentence. 'I hardly know,' she said, 'what this place should be called; it is not a garden, it is a place where plants from all over the world grow wild.'[27]

Oakwood, or Wisley as it is now called, was in its time one of the very few purely 'wild' gardens in Britain, as opposed to the many created as part of a larger scheme, indeed as at Gravetye, or as developed later at Wisley by the Royal Horticultural Society after Wilson's death. Sir Herbert Maxwell, ardent plantsman as he was, himself designed an intensely formal terrace garden beside his residence at Monreith in Wigtownshire, with a long phrase from Psalm 103 laid out in clipped box (see page 102); but in 1894–1904 his son-in-law, Sir John Stirling-Maxwell, seems to have made a uniquely 'wild' garden at Corrour in Inverness, a remote and mountainous site beside the winding shores of Loch Ossian, a spot singularly favourable for alpine plants.[28]

Another garden in or close to the 'wild' category in this period was at Bitton in Gloucestershire, where a 1½-acre rectory garden had been adapted in the 1830s from an earlier formal scheme by the Revd Henry T. Ellacombe (1790–1885, and rector 1835–1850), and much developed by his son, Canon Henry Nicholson Ellacombe (1822–1916, and curate at Bitton 1848–50, rector 1851–1916). Canon Ellacombe was a noted lover of plants, having many rarities in his garden, and was warmly praised by William Robinson, Dean Hole and Sir Herbert Maxwell. Several editions of Robinson's *The English Flower Garden* include the plan of the Bitton garden, which shows its curving paths, and the areas devoted to different kinds of plants – 'ornamental brambles', 'bog garden', 'large leaved perennials' and so forth – and the accompanying text adds that Ellacombe 'thinks more of seeing his plants happy and healthy than he does of any unnecessary trimness'.[29]

Ellacombe's two books describing his garden – *In a Gloucestershire Garden* (1895) and *In My Vicarage Garden and Elsewhere* (1902) – are resolutely to do with plants rather than plan. His earlier volume, *The Plant-Lore and Garden-Craft of Shakespeare* (1878), while giving an encyclopaedic survey of the subject, nowhere suggests that we should endeavour to create old-world 'Shakepearean' gardens for ourselves. Indeed, it states firmly that 'the whole fashion of the Elizabethan garden has passed away, and will probably never be revived'.[30] This attitude is very different from that of enthusiasts in the 1890s and later, such as Sir Frank Crisp at Friar Park in Oxfordshire, Diana, Countess of Warwick at Easton Lodge in Essex, and Ernest Law at New Place in Stratford, Warwickshire, who all created noted 'Shakespearean' and other period gardens, which were imitated again and again until the present day.[31]

Beside Ellacombe's garden at Bitton, four others of a 'wild' nature deserve mention – Lamorran in Cornwall, Mount Usher in Co. Wicklow, Garinish Island in Co. Kerry, and Annes Grove in Co. Cork. The Rev. J. T. Boscawen's rectory garden at Lamorran was laid out in the later 1860s, and much praised by Dean Hole in A Book about the Garden. It was, Hole wrote, 'the most perfect example of a wild garden ... to be found in England', with 'trees, evergreen and deciduous, notably the Sikkim rhododendrons ... graceful palms ... also Paulownias and Bambusas; conifers in their full grandeur ... flowers of all denominations ... bulbs, vernal, aestival, autumnal, and hibernal, lilies from minimum to maximum ... this charming site ... this genial climate ... all things bright and beautiful'.[32] The garden at Lamorran has since declined, but those at Mount Usher, Garinish Island and Annes Grove still flourish.

Mount Usher began in 1875 as a 1-acre riverside plot, intensively gardened by the Walpole family to hold a collection of rare plants. It was visited and much praised by William Robinson, and considerably enlarged in 1888, and again in 1905. By that time, it included (and still includes) flower, woodland and water gardens and a famous tree collection, the eucalyptus collection, begun in that year. The extensions to the original site make full use of the gentle slopes beside the river, crossed by several small bridges. Opened by lawns and bordered by shrubs and individual trees, the scenery is strikingly like that at Ninfa, south of Rome, where the most convincingly 'Robinsonian' garden on the Continent was begun in 1922.

Garinish (not to be confused with Garinish Island in Co. Cork, which is also called Ilnacullin; see page 296) was developed from around 1901 by the 4th Earl of Dunraven as a home for exotic and subtropical trees and shrubs. These introductions were spaced widely in the several small valleys or glens which cross the island, to give them full scope for their natural growth – as Robinson would have wanted, and as he no doubt said on his several visits to the island. Annes Grove, some distance inland, was enlarged as a woodland and water garden from 1907 by Richard Grove Annesley, a dedicated plantsman, helping to fund plant hunting expeditions, and enriching his grounds with exotic discoveries.[33]

The Formal Garden

'Wild' gardens continued (and so did 'Shakespeare' gardens, though they were of less importance). Their development, equally part of the reaction against geometrical layouts of ribbon or carpet bedding, coincided with a broader attack against the artificiality of massed bedding, the grassy emptiness of eighteenth-century landscape gardens, and also the supposed hostility of William Robinson and his supporters to formal and architectural gardens. This movement was led by writers and garden designers with a strong architectural inclination – architects, historians of architecture, artists with a preference for architectural subjects, or amateurs with related interests. The table on page 286 lists, in chronological order, designers and writers in this category, though they would not have thought of themselves as forming a 'group' or 'school'.

These people are by no means equal in importance. The architect John James Joass is notable for a single article in *The Studio* in 1897, signalling the interest of old 'architectural' gardens in Scotland, such as Barncluith; he designed no gardens. Achille Duchêne, who designed several features at Blenheim for the 9th Duke of Marlborough, did no other work in Britain. Likewise, John Kinross is noted for only one important garden, at Manderston. But others – Blomfield, Mawson, Peto and Lutyens – designed gardens of great significance and continuing beauty. Their work is with us now, and their enthusiasms are still for us to share.

Sir Reginald Blomfield was standard-bearer, with *The Formal Garden in England* (1892), illustrated by Inigo Thomas. This work, following on John D. Sedding's *Garden Craft Old and New* of 1891, is steeped in the details of older formal gardens. While Sedding could write in his Preface that the 'old gardens' were 'beautiful yesterday, beautiful to-day, and beautiful always', Blomfield could agree, and say, against *natural* gardens, that, in a garden context, 'the building cannot resemble anything in nature, unless you are content with a mud-hut and cover it with grass'.[34] And – here is the vital point – the building and the garden must be united and in harmony. William Morris – possibly to the chagrin of William Robinson – had stated in 1882 that the garden should 'look like a part of the house' (see page 280), and Blomfield and his allies were emphatic that this was so, and that the architect should therefore have a say, indeed a controlling part, in the designing of the garden. 'The horticulturist and the gardener are indispensable, but they should work under control' – the control coming, of course, from the architect.[35] Though his book was both controversial and well-received, Blomfield was not rapidly successful as a garden designer, and his two most important commissions came a decade later – Godinton in Kent, in 1902–06, and Mellerstain in Berwickshire, from 1909.

GARDEN DESIGNERS AND WRITERS WITH AN ARCHITECTURAL BIAS ACTIVE FROM THE 1890s

Name	Dates	Garden writing	Garden designs
Harold Ainsworth Peto	1854–1933	'A Boke of Iford' (manuscript, 1917)	Iford, Wiltshire; Buscot, Oxfordshire; Heale, Wiltshire; Garinish, Co. Cork
John Kinross	1855–1931	—	Manderston, Berwickshire
Sir Reginald Blomfield	1856–1942	*The Formal Garden in England* (1892)	Godinton, Kent; Mellerstain, Borders; Brocklesby, Lincolnshire; Caythorpe, Lincolnshire and others
Robert Weir Schultz	1860–1951	—	West Green, Hampshire; Old Place of Mochrum, Wigtownshire; Tylney Hall, Hampshire
Sir George Reresby Sitwell	1860–1943	*An Essay on the Making of Gardens* (1909)	Renishaw, Derbyshire; Montegufoni, near Florence, Italy
Thomas Hayton Mawson	1861–1933	*The Art and Craft of Garden-Making* (1900)	In all over 200 designs, including Mount Stuart, Isle of Bute; Rivington Pike/Lever Park, Lancashire; The Hill, Hampstead; Madresfield, Herefordshire
Sir Robert Stodart Lorimer	1864–1929	Article 'On Scottish Gardens' (1899)	Kellie, Fifeshire; Earlshall, Fifeshire
Achille Duchêne	1866–1947	—	Blenheim, Oxfordshire
(Francis) Inigo Thomas	1866–1950	Illustrator for Blomfield's *The Formal Garden in England* (1892)	Athelhampton, Dorset; Chantmarle, Dorset; possibly Parnham, Dorset
John James Joass	1868–1952	Article 'On Gardening: Formal Gardens in Scotland' (1897)	—
Sir Edwin Landseer Lutyens	1869–1944	—	See table on page 303
Philip Tilden	1887–1956	—	Port Lympne, Kent, for and in cooperation with Sir Philip Sassoon

At Godinton – which is in my estimate one of the most beautiful gardens in the country – Blomfield designed a sequence of garden areas to the north, east and south of the old house, which he had restored in 1902. These areas, some 12 acres in all, are enclosed by massive hedges of clipped yew, separating the gardens from the outer parkland, and lesser hedges or changes in level divide the different areas one from another. Notable are the topiary corner to the north, the water garden in the south-eastern corner, and the Italian garden (a later addition by

Blomfield in 1916, and modified again in the 1920s) to the south-west. This last feature, adjoining the walled kitchen garden, has a loggia with statues at one end, a narrow cruciform pool running the length of the garden, and, at the southern end, an open colonnade with statues, giving onto a 4-acre plot of mature woodland, underplanted with spring bulbs, and allowing further glimpses out to the countryside. The water garden to the south-east is not immediately perceived, since it is sunk several feet lower than the surrounding areas, and its large pool, shaded by weeping willows, is not seen until the edges of the garden are reached. At the far end, steps lead up to viewing points, looking out to the park.

Mellerstain is a garden on a larger scale than Godinton, and was laid out by Blomfield on the southern side of Mellerstain House, built by William and Robert Adam in 1725–38 and 1770–78. It is also an 'open' garden in the grand, balanced manner – like Versailles or Hampton Court – in which the main lines of the layout can be seen at a glance from the house, and are best seen from the *piano nobile*, revealing a magnificent sequence of terrace, balustraded steps, parterre (with patterning principally in roses and lavender), balustrade and further steps, and a vast sweep of lawn leading down to a distant lake, its nearer end balustraded to complete the formal scheme. Though Blomfield's plan was not realised in full detail, it is nonetheless the most ambitious design to be carried out in the formal architectural manner in the British Isles in this century.

The many illustrations to Blomfield's *The Formal Garden in England* were prepared by the artist (Francis) Inigo Thomas, who designed in 1891–3 the linked groups of formal gardens beside the old house at Athelhampton in Dorset. These garden areas are each complete in themselves, but connected with each other, and with the courtyard, house and grounds, by gateways in walls and hedges; with the advantage of varying levels, and gateways which are sometimes central, sometimes set slightly to one side of the main axis, there is a continuing process of enticement, urging the visitor to visit and enjoy one area after another – a device which was perfected at Sissinghurst in the 1930s (see page 310). The 'great court' with its pyramidal yews and central fountain is large and square; the 'corona' is smaller and circular, with lesser areas on either side; and the 'private garden' is rectangular, with a rectangular pool, and firmly enclosed by walls, surrounding trees, and the house itself at one end. The idea of these separate, but linked areas, is essential to Blomfield's work at Godinton, and was employed, with variations, at Great Dixter, Hidcote, Sissinghurst and beyond. It was not new – the Elizabethans and the Jacobeans had thought long before that their garden areas should be divided for a variety of reasons – but Athelhampton set it off again with particular vigour.

Inigo Thomas designed other fine gardens in Dorset and Somerset. In the mid-1890s, he laid out Barrow Court in Somerset, and, in 1910 and later, Chantmarle in Dorset, with splendid formal areas defined by balustrades, steps, and Irish yews, and with a long flanking canal. He may have been involved in the design for Parnham in Dorset, in 1911–14, with a sequence of terraces including a double stair and double water-channels, clearly inspired by Italian Renaissance models.[36]

By the early 1900s, a strong 'Italian' theme was apparent in new garden designs. While Blomfield had at first said that the Italian Renaissance garden needed a warmer and sunnier climate than we could expect in England, his later gardens show a distinct change of attitude. Two books – Edith Wharton's *Italian Villas and their Gardens* (1904) and Sir George Sitwell's *An Essay on the Making of Gardens* (1909) – brought Italian gardens to the attention of the public, Sir George's volume adding many pointers towards their adaptation in this country. Already around 1897, Sir George had begun to remodel the gardens at his residence in Derbyshire, Renishaw Hall, and Inigo Thomas was consulted, though he may not have had much influence on Sir George's decisions. At Renishaw, the terraces lead away and downwards from the house towards a lake, but with a far more heavily accented descent than at Mellerstain, because each level is marked not only by steps, statues and balustrades, but by tall clipped hedges. Sir George Sitwell's enthusiasm for Italian gardens was triumphantly extended from 1909 onwards, when he acquired the Castello di Montegufoni, near Florence. Here he spent much of his time restoring the building, the gardens and the grotto, and in 1925 he left England to live permanently at Montegufoni, remaining there until his death in 1943.

Sir George Sitwell had no interest in 'wild' gardening. Indeed, he was not enthusiastic for flowers of a brilliant kind at all, whether displayed as single rare specimens or massed in bedding schemes. But at Bodnant in Denbighshire, both 'wild' woodland and water gardens, and formal Italianate terraces were created in the same period. Henry Pochin bought the steeply sloping estate at Bodnant in 1875, and engaged Edward Milner to plant conifers in the gorge south-west of the house, the Dell. By the 1890s, a scheme of terraces was begun to the west, and, in 1904–14, these were extended and completed, to the design of Pochin's grandson, Henry Duncan McLaren (1879–1953), who was to become the 2nd Lord Aberconway. The terraces, five in all, are a superbly varied formal scheme in the Italian style, enhanced both by intriguing sculpture, magnificent trees (cedar of Lebanon) and rampant wistaria, and by the distant view towards the River Conway and Snowdonia. In 1909, the Dell was further developed as a Robinsonian woodland and water garden – two years

In 1879–85 this gorge or ravine was created in the grounds at Bearwood in Berkshire The rockwork was made from Pulhamite, *the artificial stone much favoured in late-Victorian gardens.*

Dating from 1829, the Botanic Garden at Belfast is one of the many important nineteenth-century foundations. The conservatory may fairly be compared with those at Kew or Edinburgh.
© N Ireland Tourist Board

after Richard Grove Annesley began work on the 'wild' garden at Annes Grove in Co. Cork (see page 284). Annesley's wife was a cousin of Lady Aberconway.

A 'mixed' garden scheme, as ambitious as the single design at Mellerstain, but with all the variety of features which many proprietors desired, was laid out in this same period – from 1890 until around 1906. While the lake, with 'Chinese' footbridge, at Manderston in Berwickshire may have been landscaped in the late eighteenth century to go with the original mansion, the other elements of the gardens are the work of John Kinross, who was also engaged by the owner, Sir James Miller (1863–1906), to design several buildings on the estate, and from 1901 to remodel the house itself. In 1890, Kinross began the four formal terraces south of the house, with topiary, bedding, fountains and sculptured urns, and in 1894 he designed the boathouse (resembling a Swiss chalet). Informal woodland, underplanted with hybrid rhododendrons, was developed on the further side of the lake, away from the house, and, in opulent contrast, the walled gardens, set on the far northern side of the house, contain several areas divided by paths and pergola – a fountain garden with sculpture and formal bedding, a sunken garden with borders and rockery, a 'lily court' with sculpture, and glasshouses, including a fernery section with splendidly preserved tufa panels. It is likely, I would suggest, that the rich variety of the gardens at Manderston formed the inspiration for John Buchan's description, in his romance *John Macnab* (1925), of the gardens at 'Haripol' in the Highlands. There were three enthusiasts, 'the head gardener . . . Lady Claybody . . . and an expert from Kew', who had between them formed a lavish assemblage of

> . . . fantastically shaped beds and geometrical patterns, and geraniums and lobelias and calceolarias . . . lawns . . . a pleasaunce (with) crazy-paving and sundials and broad borders . . . a lily pond and a rosery and many pergolas, and what promised in twenty years to be a fine yew-walk.

At a distance was the original walled garden, 'now relegated to fruit and vegetables', and then

> . . . the rhododendron thickets . . . a rustic bridge . . . a pleasant wilderness [with] a wonderful wild garden.[37]

Interest in old Scottish gardens had gone on parallel with that in old gardens in England in the nineteenth century. Alicia Amherst had published her *History of Gardening in England* in 1895, a milestone in the writing of garden history. Now articles by John James Joass (1897) and

Sir Robert Stodart Lorimer (1899), each with plans and views by Joass, pointed out the particular interest and quality of these Scottish sites,[38] while Lorimer had already planned and laid out a formal garden beside the walls of Kellie Castle in Fife, acquired in a derelict state by his father in 1877. This garden was more or less complete by 1888,[39] and in 1892 he began the restoration of Earlshall in Fife, which included the laying out of appropriate gardens – walled, and with lesser walled or hedged divisions separating orchard from croquet lawn from flower walks, parterre or pleasaunce, and kitchen garden. By 1900, the original scheme had been somewhat modified, particularly in the change to the pleasaunce, which was ornamented with topiary figures, illustrated in 1902 in H. Inigo Triggs' *Formal Gardens in England and Scotland*, and in 1925 in Nathaniel Lloyd's *Garden Craftsmanship in Yew and Box*. A century after Lorimer's work began, this part of the garden at Earlshall has acquired the monumental character of the topiary at Packwood, and something of the strangeness of that at Levens (see page 276). As in all gardens, generally and in particular, topiary will not wait. Lorimer's other garden work in Scotland includes Wemyss Hall (now named Hill of Tarvit) in Fife (1906–7), and Balmanno in Perthshire (1916–21).

Robert Weir Schultz's work is mainly in England, but he was employed in 1903 to refit the interior and to lay out gardens at the Old Place of Mochrum in Wigtownshire. Just as Lorimer did at Kellie, Schultz designed a strictly formal layout for the garden, a square plot backed by the tower and adjacent buildings, walled for the remainder, but with spacious views out.[40] Schultz had already designed several gardens in England – for himself at the Barn, Hartley Wintney in Hampshire from 1900 onwards, after work at West Green nearby, and in 1901–5 at Tylney Hall in Hampshire, where he was employed by Lionel Phillips to add to the existing garden scheme. Tylney Hall already had an eighteenth-century park and avenue, and to this, close to the house, Schultz added feature after feature – borders, summerhouse, rose garden, aviary and more. It may be that John Buchan, spending his honeymoon here in 1907, acquired a touch or two for the gardens at 'Haripol' in his novel *John Macnab*.

Another Scottish garden or landscape project is linked with Thomas Hayton Mawson, author of *The Art and Craft of Garden-Making* (1900), a work reprinted and enlarged several times in Mawson's lifetime. In the years 1893–98, Mawson had laid out a 'rock garden' at Mount Stuart in the Isle of Bute for the 3rd Marquess of Bute, and then, in 1898, he was engaged to help create a separate woodland feature – a 'Via Dolorosa' including the Stations of the Cross, the Cross of Calvary, Church of the Sepulchre, and a tall Crucifix. His colleague, Dan Gibson, designed the

A fine example of a 'mixed' garden, Manderston in Berwickshire. The formal terraces, designed by John Kinross in 1890, overlook the lawns, landscape lake, and rhododendron thickets beyond.

A superb example of the 'topiary revival' in the later nineteenth century – the chess-board garden, laid out in the 1890s, at Haseley Court in Oxfordshire.

architectural features, while Mawson laid out the paths and supervised planting and the elaboration of waterfalls. The 3rd Marquess died in 1900, and the scheme was not completed, though much of Mawson's landscaping was carried out.[41] For a private property, such a project is singularly uncommon, and harks back to the mid-nineteenth-century garden at Claydon in Sussex, illustrating the events of Christ's passion, and James Mellor's garden at Hough Hole in Cheshire, with Christian's itinerary in the *Pilgrim's Progress* (see page 274).

Mawson coined the term 'landscape architect' to describe the profession he followed. It was a deliberate snub to Robinson and his plant-loving followers, indicating that architects were the proper people to design landscapes as well as buildings, and a rejection too of Shenstone's much earlier term 'landscape gardener', which urged the association of gardens and gardeners with painters of landscapes. Mawson's garden commissions – well over 200 by the end of his career – were mainly in the British Isles, and a great many of these were either in the north-west of England or in the Home Counties. He enjoyed the patronage of W. H. Lever (later Lord Leverhulme), for whom he made gardens and wider landscapes at the Lever home at Thornton Manor in Cheshire (1905–12 and later), at Rivington Pike and Roynton Cottage in Lancashire (1906 onwards), and at the Hill, Hampstead (1905–6, 1912, and 1917–20).

The work at Rivington Pike (also named Lever Park) and Roynton Cottage spread over some 450 acres, beside the Lower Rivington Reservoir, which had been built in 1852–57. After vicissitudes, the park was opened in 1904, and Mawson, employed as landscape designer, laid out avenues through the park, several converging on a monumental castle-folly beside the reservoir. On higher ground to the north-east, Lever's private gardens were built round Roynton Cottage, first built in 1901 and demolished in 1947. The steeply sloping site allowed Mawson to design a varied layout with terraces and steps, and, in 1922, a 'Japanese' garden with lake, tea-houses and lanterns.

Though much of the Roynton Cottage garden scheme has been re-absorbed into the woodland, Mawson's work for W. H. Lever at Hampstead survives as a most impressive early twentieth-century architectural layout. The Hill (also called Inverforth House) was rebuilt and extended from 1905 onwards, the architects including James Lomax-Simpson (1882–1976), who worked with Mawson on several other projects, notably the castle-folly in Lever Park. Terraces westward from the house were first laid out, with steps down to a paved area with a pool. Beyond this, aligned on the pool and the house, Mawson built a pergola which stretches out towards – and indeed *over* – Hampstead Heath, being raised upon massive rubble and brickwork foundations. The pergola is heroic in its extent and proportions, with cross-walks parallel to the house terrace, a further arm to the south, and an extension built around 1912 on into the Heath. Viewing points and summerhouses punctuate the scheme, and the western end is completed with a public garden (likewise Mawson's work) with pool, lawn and pavilion.

The pergola at the Hill is, I would think, Mawson's most important garden work. It is superb, and, in its way, comparable with Blomfield's terraces and landscaping at Mellerstain as an expression of architectural and aesthetic confidence. Two smaller works by Mawson should also be noted – around 1903, his redevelopment and extension of the formal rose garden at Madresfield Court in Herefordshire (he worked on an earlier layout of around 1865), and around 1909, his building of a rose garden and a double terrace beside the mansion at Rydal Hall in Cumbria, so restoring formality to the vicinity of the house after earlier 'land-scaping'[42] – somewhat in Humphry Repton's manner a century before.

So far as I know, the only wholly non-British garden designer active in Britain in this period was Achille Duchêne (1866–1947), who is noted for work, often with his father, Henri Duchêne, on the restoration of formal gardens in France. His success in this led to his engagement by the 9th Duke of Marlborough to add several formal areas to the gardens at Blenheim. Beginning in 1908, Duchêne designed the Italian garden east of the palace, an exercise in formal scrollwork *broderie* which has changed little in its outline since it was first laid out. Some years later, in 1925–30, he returned to lay out the much more architectural terraces and water gardens between the west front of the palace and Capability Brown's lake. The upper part, with fountains set in a swirling stone-edged pattern backed by box *broderies*, is patently reminiscent of the *parterre d'eau* at Versailles; the lower terrace, with twin obelisks in pools, imitates Berni-ni's 'Four Rivers' fountain in the Piazza Navona in Rome. Both terraces far more openly follow continental examples than any of the garden work of Duchêne's British contemporaries.

Of the several architects involved in garden design in this period, the most successful in uniting elements of an Italian Renaissance kind with sites and landscapes in the British Isles was Harold Peto (1854–1933). At Iford Manor in Wiltshire, a property which he acquired in 1899, and where he lived for the rest of his life, he developed a sequence of three main terraces on steep ground beside the house. Though grassy terraces may already have been made in the eighteenth century, Peto's achieve-ment is essentially a magnificent combination of his architectural ingen-uity and the quality of the site – his genius *and* the genius of the place.

Peto had worked as an architect, in partnership with Ernest George, from 1876 to 1892, when the partnership was dissolved. He then spent a considerable time on the Riviera, making periodic visits to Italy, studying architecture, interior design and gardens, and acquiring items of architectural interest – columns either entire or partial, urns, plinths, statues, sections of arch or doorway, panels with carved figures or inscriptions. This collection – part treasure, part ancient bric-à-brac – was brought back to Iford after 1899, and incorporated into the fabric of the garden, adorning steps, terraces and diverse buildings.

Like the busts, capitals, well-heads, marble lions and coats of arms, the buildings are varied – loggia, conservatory, casita, tea-house, cloisters – but so skilfully spaced that they do not in any way clash with one another. The upper slopes of the garden are backed by woodland, the terraces themselves given an Italian feeling by accompanying yew, cypress, juniper and bay, and the viewpoints from seats and balustraded walkways look out to orchard, garden lawn and rockery, and beyond to the Wiltshire countryside. At times, the carved fragments by one's side and the further rural scene are reminiscent of Kent's 'elegant and antique ... philosophic retirement' at Rousham, but the richness of the evergreens makes Iford also into a version of Pompeii – with trees. A curious parallel exists between Peto's garden at Iford and the 5 acres of 'Italian garden' at Hever Castle in Kent, designed by Frank Pearson for William Waldorf Astor (created Baron Astor in 1916, Viscount Astor in 1917), and laid out in 1904–8 by Joseph Cheal & Son. Part of a far larger scheme of gardens, lake and parkland (some 95 acres, and comparable as a 'mixed' layout with Manderston), the enclosed 'Italian garden' was intended as a garden framework for Astor's superb collection of classical sculpture – the northern wall of the garden is named the 'Pompeian Wall', and is divided by a series of buttresses to provide distinct settings for the display of statues, sarcophagi and other stony treasures. The southern wall, with an arched colonnade and many water jets and springs, running down over moss and ferns, recalls the 'avenue of the hundred fountains' at the Villa d'Este.

Beside his own garden at Iford, Peto created notable gardens in an Italian manner on the Riviera at Cap S. Jean Ferrat – Villa Sylvia (1902), Villa Maryland (c.1904) and Villa Rosemary (c.1908)[43] – and others in England and in Ireland. In 1905–10, at Buscot in Oxfordshire, Peto devised a long and narrow woodland avenue and water garden – 150 yards of sloping avenue, flanked by box hedges, with 80 yards of water garden at the lower end – extending between the house and the upper lake. It is a *tour de force* of variety and maintained expectation with strictly limited materials – water, stone, grass and evergreen hedges – in a rigorously limited and unusual space. The views are strictly forwards (to the lake), or back up the avenue towards the house, or inwards, to admire the few sculptured figures lining the avenue, the water jets from the boy-and-dolphin fountain, and the gentle falls of the step cascade. Compared with the spendthrift abundance of sculpture and the diversity of outward view at Iford, this composition at Buscot is a masterly exercise in calmness and restraint.

Other garden work by Peto in England includes a formal design, the west garden, at Heale House in Wiltshire (1906 onwards); a pergola with pillars and central pavilion at West Dean in Sussex (1910); and a range of pergola and pavilions with a hint of Mawson's influence (from the Hill, Hampstead) at High Wall, Headington, near Oxford (c.1912).[44]

In this same period, in 1910, Peto began work on a commission in Co. Cork – the 37-acre island of Ilnacullin (also called Garinish Island), which had been bought that year by Annan Bryce. Bryce was enthusiastically aware that the gentle climate at Ilnacullin was favourable to plant introductions, and so he shipped quantities of good soil from the mainland to make beds for his exotic trees and shrubs. Meanwhile Peto was engaged to design a co-ordinated scheme of pavilions, pools and pathways, to give an architectural centre or 'backbone' to the design. Bryce and Peto worked well together, and their association produced an eminently intriguing combination of 'wild' and formal elements. Peto's 'Italian garden' at Ilnacullin, with central pool, casita, temple, and aligned steps and paths, is a model of formal garden design, with the axes leading to contrasting features (walled garden, flower borders, different 'wild' areas) and varied views over the island and Bantry Bay. There is a striking similarity of purpose – and equal success – in this combination of 'wild' and formal gardens at Ilnacullin and at Bodnant (see page 288), both given distinctive formal features in this period. One should note also that the 'wild' gardens created in Ireland shortly before – Garinish in Co. Kerry and Annes Grove in Co. Cork – do not have any such notable formal elements.[45]

17

'PARTLY FORMAL, PARTLY CONTROLLED WILD'

Gertrude Jekyll

Gertrude Jekyll (1843–1932) acquired a 15-acre plot close to her mother's house at Munstead in Surrey in 1883. At first, she referred to it as 'OS' – the *other side* of the road from Munstead House – but by the early 1890s it was known as Munstead Wood, her most famous garden, created and elaborated over the course of half a century.

She is now assured of her place among Britain's famous garden writers, makers and designers. But until around 1880 (and not decisively until 1891), her manifold interests and activities extended into matters apparently far removed from gardens. She travelled widely in France, Switzerland, Italy, Algeria and the Levant. She was musical. Painting particularly fascinated her – both study and practice – and she was one of the early women students at the School of Art in South Kensington. She then met Ruskin, followed by acquaintance with several of the Pre-Raphaelites and founders of the Arts and Crafts movement, notably William Morris. Her interests here spread to aspects of design – furniture, metalwork, inlay, embroidery – both in theory and in practice, and numerous examples of her handiwork survive, in private ownership or in museums.[1]

Plants and gardens were then a part, but only a small part, of her interests. As a child, she had owned and used to the uttermost a copy of C. A. Johns' *Flowers of the Field*[2] – 'the most precious gift I ever received' – and, aged nine, she was 'steadily collecting garden plants . . . mostly from cottage gardens'. Cottage gardens, plants and embroidery – these were allied with her interest in the local architecture and crafts of Surrey to be celebrated in her book *Old West Surrey* (1904), recorded in her photographs of cottage and garden scenes (she took up photography round 1885), and preserved in her collection of old Surrey artefacts, mostly of a farm, household or kitchen nature, now in the Guildford Museum.

By 1880, plants and embroidery came together in two designs which she supplied for Miss L. Higgin's *A Handbook of Embroidery* – 'designs for chair-seats or cushions', plate 9 'Periwinkle' and plate 10 'Iris'. She was in good company; other designs in this small book are by Edward Burne-Jones, William Morris and Walter Crane. In the following year, 1881, she gave advice to G. F. Wilson at his garden, Oaklands (now better known as Wisley), celebrated by Dean Hole and Sir Herbert Maxwell as a fine 'wild garden' and by herself as 'about the most instructive it is possible to see'.[3] Her help was to do with the ordering or planning of a slightly sloping site, and was one of her earliest attempts at garden design – 'making a flat Alpine garden'.[4] She had already met William Robinson, in 1875, had become a contributor to his magazine *The Garden*, founded in 1871, and was necessarily involved in the campaigns surrounding Robinson's *Wild Garden* of 1870 and *The English Flower Garden* of 1883.

1883 was the year she acquired Munstead Wood, and we should note that Robinson, who did not acquire Gravetye Manor until 1885, may have been influenced in his layout there by what he had seen in the new work at Munstead Wood and by her earlier gardening at her mother's property, Munstead House. Robinson may indeed have given advice at Munstead House, as he first visited the place in the company of Dean Hole in 1880, not many years after the Jekylls had moved there, and was 'a frequent visitor'.[5]

Gertrude Jekyll occupies an important place in this history, bridging the gap of argument and recrimination which had divided 'wild' from 'formal', 'natural' from 'architectural' garden theorists. In practice, they were often capable of compromise (or inconsistency, if one looked at them unkindly), and Jekyll's keen intelligence and her exceptional diversity of interests allowed her a measure of understanding, which could perceive elements of excellence on both sides. Her development of the 15 acres at Munstead Wood included areas in distinctly different styles, ranging from 'wild' areas in woodland and the 'natural' treatment of a 'hidden garden' to areas with a firmly formal plan – the courtyard, pergola and main flower border – even if the planting of those areas was exuberant and, apparently, 'free'.[6] In her first books, *Wood and Garden* (1899) and *Home and Garden* (1900), which were prompted above all by her experience at Munstead Wood, there is much which is derived from the writings of William Robinson, and in 1900–01, she was to take over as joint editor, with E. T. Cook, the direction of William Robinson's most celebrated periodical, *The Garden*. Yet by 1927, she could write of the woodland at Munstead Wood, and then add 'there is little else of wild gardening except for a shady region [the 'hidden garden'] where there are hardy Ferns, Trillium and Solomon's Seal ... I do not want more, for I think that of all kinds of planting for pleasure, wild gardening needs the greatest caution and the most restraint'.[7]

Even in 1900 or soon after, a new visitor to Munstead Wood, the architect Harold Falkner, could state that 'it was partly formal, partly controlled wild'. Falkner had worked for a while under Reginald Blomfield, and was therefore fully aware of the debate over 'formal' and 'wild'. He recalled Gertrude Jekyll's delight over the apparent inconsistencies of Robinson and Blomfield in the design of their own gardens, Robinson at Gravetye and Blomfield at Point Hill, near Rye in Sussex: 'Robinson designed himself a garden all squares, and Reggy a garden on a cliff with not a straight line in it.'[8]

Jekyll's importance in this perennial dispute – for it is not settled, nor will it ever be – is that she could appreciate, and use, the merits of both sides. To 'see' them would be an ironic phrase, as she had been plagued since childhood by ever-worsening short-sightedness. Her sight was never good, and in 1891 (when she was 48, and eight years after she acquired Munstead Wood) an oculist ordered her to cease painting and embroidery, as being harmful to her remaining sight. Garden lovers should be grateful, since at this point she turned decisively to gardens and away from the practice of painting. Others, such as Helen Allingham (1848–1926) and George S. Elgood (1851–1943), her friends and collaborators, were to paint, in watercolours, the glories of her borders. Jekyll now used her camera, her many surviving photographs providing a fine record of her wide-ranging interests.

The artist in her survived this sentence. From *Wood and Garden* in 1899 she had proclaimed that the flower border – give or take a little, the *herbaceous border* – was not so difficult to create: '... the trained eye sees what is wanted ... It is painting a picture with living plants.' In this 'painting' of a garden picture, she recommended 'graduated harmonies, culminating into gorgeousness',[9] and the need for a painter's eye and a painter's sensibility was repeated again and again – in *Colour in the Flower Garden* of 1908 and much later, in 1924, in a firm and coherent section:

> Herbaceous borders ... are arranged, not as of old, with single plants in a haphazard way, but with definite intention directed to the forming of a picture of garden beauty and glory. Flowers of delicate cool tints strengthen gradually into warmer, and these lead to a gorgeous mass of richly related colour; after this, again returning to the cooler and quieter.[10]

Many today will think of the Jekyll influence as being above all to do with the perfection of single-colour gardens, with a predominance of white, grey or blue in the overall effect. Certainly this was said in *Colour in the Flower Garden* (1908, republished as *Colour Schemes for the Flower Garden*), and was repeated many times in later writing.[11] In 1924, she recommended 'a whole double border' to be devoted to 'grey foliage with pink and purple flowers', and in 1929, she outlined 'the satisfaction of a desire for a special colour such as blue', and again praised 'grey and silvery foliage in the arrangement of flower borders for the late summer'.[12]

In 1929, when her garden at Munstead and her long border, 200 feet long and 14 feet wide, had been established for some 40 years, she could write with absolute confidence, contrasting 'the crudest and most garish effects' of the old mid-nineteenth-century system of bedding with 'an example of the better arrangement':

> It begins with flowers of tender and cool colouring – palest pink – blue, white and palest yellow – followed by stronger yellow, and passing on to deep orange and rich mahogany ... to ... the strongest scarlet ...
>
> The progression of colour then recedes in the same general order ... to quiet harmony of lavender and purple and tender pink, with a whole setting of grey and silvery foliage ...[13]

Edwin Lutyens

When, in 1929, Gertrude Jekyll wrote this last passage, she had known Edwin Landseer Lutyens (1869–1944; he was knighted in 1918) for 40 years, and an enormous number of her garden designs, for parts or for the whole of gardens, had been prepared in collaboration with him, to do with houses and gardens on which he was working. She met Lutyens in 1889, two years after he had begun work with the firm of Ernest George and Peto. Though that engagement was brief, he had secured other commissions, and by 1891 he and Gertrude Jekyll were involved in a joint project, Crooksbury in Surrey. In 1892, they began to work on a cottage, 'The Hut', to be built in the Munstead Wood site, which was put up in 1894–5, and in 1896 the main house at Munstead Wood was begun; it was complete by October 1897 – a triumph of co-operation between the two.

By this time, 1897, their association was well established. Their first big joint commission had been at Woodside, Chenies, in Buck-

The woodland collection and water gardens at Mount Usher in Co. Wicklow began in 1875,
and now present one of Ireland's greatest and most genuine 'wild' gardens.
Courtesy Irish Tourish Board
Photo Paddy Tutty

inghamshire, and their co-operation clearly continued until 1928, at Plumpton Court in Sussex, and possibly afterwards, though the evidence for later work is slight. In all, it has been calculated that she and Lutyens worked together on some 112 gardens,[14] and that she was consulted (a vague word, extending from a brief discussion, without further work, to numerous visits and the preparation of detailed plans, the whole stretching over several years) on some 350 different garden projects altogether. As often as not, she was in direct contact with the owners of the garden, working without an architect, since no building was needed; and her 112 or so commissions in co-operation with Lutyens by no means prevented her from working with other architects, such as M. H. Baillie-Scott, Sidney Barnsley, Robert Lorimer, Robert Weir Schultz, Hugh Thackeray Turner and Charles Voysey.

Details of her work – dates, places, owners – are to be found in the appendix to Francis Jekyll's A Memoir of 1934, and a treasure-store of site and planting plans may be consulted in the Reef Point collection of her papers, held at the University of California, Berkeley, of which a microfilm copy is held in the National Monuments Record in London. For one who produced so many proposals and plans for gardens, the distribution of her work is somewhat limited, being for the most part in the Home Counties and especially in Surrey, Sussex and Hampshire. After 1900 or 1901, she preferred to stay regularly near her home, confining her personal visits 'to places within a driving radius of Munstead'.[15] Rare excursions occurred, to France in 1902, and to Lindisfarne in 1906. For her many and continuing commissions beyond the 'radius of Munstead', she worked on descriptions and plans which were supplied by owners and architects.

The table below lists Gertrude Jekyll's main publications and the main garden designs which she prepared, either with Edwin Lutyens, or with other architects, or on her own; the short table below it lists a group of gardens designs by Lutyens in which, most probably, she did not

---

IMPORTANT WORKS BY GERTRUDE JEKYLL

Main publications

1899	*Wood and Garden*
1900	*Home and Garden*
1900–1	Joint editor, with E.T. Cook, of *The Garden* (Vols. 57–60)
1904	*Old West Surrey*
1904	*Some English Gardens* (with illustrations by George S. Elgood)
1908	*Colour in the Flower Garden*
1912	*Gardens for Small Country Houses* (with Lawrence Weaver)

| 1937 | A *Gardener's Testament*, edited by Francis Jekyll and G. C. Taylor (a collection of articles by Gertrude Jekyll published from 1896 onwards) |

Main garden designs, working with Edwin Lutyens[16]

1893	Woodside, Chenies, Buckinghamshire
1896	Munstead Wood, Surrey
1899	Goddards, nr. Abinger, Surrey
1899	Orchards, nr. Godalming, Surrey
1899–1901	The Deanery, Sonning, Berkshire
1901–4	Marsh Court, Hampshire (architectural work by Lutyens); garden advice by Jekyll, 1905–15
1901, 1912	Folly Farm, Sulhamstead, Berkshire (architectural works by Lutyens); garden advice by Jekyll, 1906, 1916
1902–3	Papillon Hall, Leicestershire
1903–12	Lindisfarne Castle, Holy Island, Northumberland (architectural work by Lutyens); garden advice by Jekyll, 1906, 1911
1904	Bois des Moutiers, Varangeville, nr. Dieppe, France
1904–8	Hestercombe, Somerset
1907/8–12	Lambay Castle, Co. Dublin
1909	Nashdom, Buckinghamshire
1910	100 Cheyne Walk, London
1928	Plumpton Place, Sussex

Garden designs, working with other architects or directly with owners

1881	Oaklands, Wisley, Surrey
1906	Tylney Hall, Hampshire (after architectural work, 1901–5, by R. Weir Schultz)
1908	Old Manor House, Upton Grey, Hampshire (after architectural work by Charles Newton, with Wallis and Smith)
1917	Barrington Court, Somerset
1920	Mount Stewart, Co. Down

Gardens designed by Edwin Lutyens (without direct consultation with Gertrude Jekyll)

1901–3	Ammerdown, Somerset
1910	Great Dixter, Sussex
1911/12	The Salutation, Sandwich, Kent
1926	Tyringham, Buckinghamshire

participate. Garden plans with which Lutyens was involved were of course frequently linked with his work on houses, new or old, and were therefore closely and deliberately allied to an underlying, often imposing, architectural scheme. Insofar as these gardens survive today, most of them appear far more strongly structured, with aligned geometrical terraces, steps, paths and pools, than they would have done in the early twentieth century. When we look at the contemporary plans, it is easy for us to misread these architectural diagrams, by forgetting the exuberant, softening and painterly effects of the Jekyll planting in, over and around the Lutyens framework. The element of change in gardens – declared at the very start of this history – is nowhere more apparent than in the fate of gardens made by Jekyll and Lutyens. Most have gone. Some have been replanted in ways one might regret. A handful have been restored, or, more truthfully, remade from scratch, while others remain as architectural skeletons, excellent and admirable as witnesses to Lutyens' genius, but somewhat misleading as examples of how a garden made by these collaborators would have appeared in its glory.

Woodside, at Chenies in Hertfordshire, was Jekyll and Lutyens' first important joint commission. Though the property is now divided, the garden has retained most of its original plan, and is still remarkable for the firm geometry of paths, formal pools and steps spread over the sloping site. At the Deanery, Sonning, in Berkshire, we should note the wonderful complexity of the architectural scheme. First, there is a slow angled approach round the house, and then a choice of ways – a garden at two levels, with one axis leading away from the house to an orchard, crossing over another at right angles, running beside the house, with a long canal or stream (here called a rill) leading to a circular pool, backed by steps and a paved viewing platform. This water feature – a narrow channel between paving, with occasional pools at key points – is characteristic of many Lutyens designs, surviving in its most celebrated form at Hestercombe in Somerset.

At Marsh Court in Hampshire, the architecture is even more dominant, with capriciously contrasting styles within the house. Outside, a sunken pool garden and related pools and pergola display exceptional complexity. You need to watch your step. At Papillon Hall in Leicestershire, designed soon after, Lutyens' ingenuity with garden steps, leading out from the butterfly-wing sections of the house, down to, round and beyond the different garden areas, reached its most elaborate expression. Papillon Hall has gone, levelled in 1950. But at Hestercombe we may still see Lutyens' steps and rills, the central planting by Jekyll and – not to be forgotten – the views of the countryside beyond the walls and pergola which enfold the garden.

Folly Farm in Berkshire was worked on by Lutyens and Jekyll twice, first from 1901 and then from 1912, after a change in ownership. Lutyens' solid and distinctive architecture has survived better than Gertrude Jekyll's planting. Today the best testimony to their partnership is the sunken pool garden there, with lilies, roses and characteristic steps. Miss Jekyll's 'solo' work can be signalled at Tylney Hall in Hampshire, where the main building development was completed by 1905. In 1906, she was asked to design a 'wild garden' at a little distance from the house, which she did, basing her design and suggestions on a plan supplied by Robert Weir Schultz. A year later, John Buchan spent his honeymoon at Tylney Hall, and we may wonder whether his and his bride's steps took them to the new Jekyll garden.

Not far distant, at Upton Grey, Charles Newton had enlarged the Manor, or Old Manor House, and Gertrude Jekyll was again called in to design the gardens after building was complete. Today the importance of this site is that the 4-acre garden has been restored, since the mid-1980s, with singular fidelity to plan and to planting. Areas and features include a formal garden and borders, rose garden, nuttery and a wild garden with a pond.

The garden designs which Lutyens prepared without direct co-operation with Gertrude Jekyll have been remarked on as being more openly monumental than the rest, and this is amply true of his work at Tyringham in Buckinghamshire in 1926. Here, the gigantic pool, stretching 170 yards away from the house, with twin columns surmounted by leopards, and the sumptuous flanking pavilions are a statement of magnificence in building, not of delicacy in the composition of a mixed border. But two other Lutyens garden plans are significantly different – Ammerdown in Somerset and Great Dixter in Sussex.

Ammerdown is without doubt monumental. But it is principally monumental not in stone or stone-edged pools, but in walls and bastions of clipped yew, altogether more mysterious and more alive. And – a vital point – it is a scheme of hedges which offers *enticement* – the possibility of 'something else', a different view to be discovered when one has walked to the next division in the enclosing hedge. At Great Dixter, where Lutyens worked with the owner, Nathaniel Lloyd, from 1910, enlarging the old house with another old building brought from Benenden in Kent and with a new wing designed by Lutyens himself, a garden was created, again applying the enticement principle, round the irregular plan of the house. It extended in a series of areas, some divided by walls and archways, but principally by topiary hedges, and given variety by changes in level and distinct differences in extent. No other garden in this history has such satisfying variations from part to part. I have already mentioned the enticement principle at Athelhampton in Dorset and at Godinton in Kent (see pages 286 and 287). It was employed again as a vital part of the design at Hidcote in Gloucestershire, and later at Sissinghurst in Kent (see pages 116 and 287), and was most properly and necessarily used and developed in many later British gardens.

At Great Dixter, Nathaniel Lloyd worked first with the Lutyens plan, and later, in 1925, extended it by adding a sunken garden with an octagonal pool, replacing an area of lawn. The essence of the scheme has since been preserved and immensely enriched by Christopher Lloyd, Nathaniel's son, so that the garden has been consistently developed from 1910 until the present day. Lutyens' characteristic steps are well represented, and the topiary, as clipped hedges to divide areas (as at Ammerdown) and as individual items (as in Sir Robert Stodart Lorimer's garden at Earlshall in Fifeshire), is wholly typical of the period. Nathaniel Lloyd's *Garden Craftsmanship in Yew and Box* of 1925 has not only photographs of the topiary work at Great Dixter, taken at early and later stages of growth, but comparable views of the topiary at Earlshall and at Brickwall, at Northiam in Sussex (admired by Rossetti in 1866).

Great Dixter's sequence of garden enclosures is excellently varied – a rose garden, hidden behind a converted cowshed, wide spaces with orchard trees and bulbs, areas of free-standing topiary, a 'wild' area round a horsepond and vegetable and nursery gardens. The sunken garden of 1925 is to my mind notable not only in summer, for the juxtaposition of low-growing plants, but also in the depth of winter, when dry stems and seedheads make striking patterns against the water, stonework and enclosing hedges and buildings. But most celebrated is the 'long border' to the south of the house, which begins beside the Lutyens steps and extends for some 70 yards to the east. Originally a herbaceous border, it is now famed for the mixed planting of shrubs, herbaceous and other plants, and recorded, for example, in Christopher Lloyd's *The Mixed Border* (1957, 1985) and *The Well-Tempered Garden* (1970, 1985).

The Enticement Principle

With Lawrence Johnston's creation at Hidcote in Gloucestershire we encounter two different and vital aspects of the modern garden in Britain. We learn that a growing number of important British gardens came from designers who produced only one or two gardens (usually their own!), and we experience the characteristic design which this garden so excellently embodies.

The first point is not hard to convey – Lawrence Johnston (1871–1958) was his own designer. No doubt, over the years, he was offered, and maybe accepted, advice from others; names have been suggested, but there is no certainty. The central intelligence, however, remains his own. The property at Hidcote Bartrim was his from 1907, and he decided to make a garden beside his Cotswold house. It came to cover some 11 acres within a larger farming estate. Much later, in 1924, he acquired a hillside property near Menton in the Riviera, and here he made a second, and in many respects comparable garden, La Serre de la Madone.[17] Though many lovers of gardens have said they were inspired by Johnston and by his work at Hidcote, he himself designed no other garden in Britain. Though the partnership of Jekyll and Lutyens was far from over, and though a few other designers, for example Percy Cane, Russell Page, Sir Clough Williams-Ellis and Sir Geoffrey Jellicoe, have continued to stamp distinctive styles on their clients' ground, it has not been done with the expansiveness or the frequency of earlier masters. Instead, we may imagine a catalogue, no less distinguished, of isolated creations, one or two at a time – Mapperton, Charleston, Garsington, Sissinghurst, Abbots Ripton, Haseley, East Lambrook and Stonypath – which impress and inspire other garden makers, leading again to further single designs – the principal material of this chapter.

The design of Hidcote has been so often and so highly praised, that it is often summarised (and therefore in a sense dismissed) with an 'Ah yes, garden rooms'. But its importance in the history of gardens, – its achievement of 'infinite variety' (and therefore of continuing interest and delight) within a relatively limited area – must not be diminished. Johnston followed a long-known and occasionally practised principle of dividing the areas of his garden so that they did not impinge one upon the other, but rather *led* the visitor from one part to the next (as at Biddulph in the 1860s or at Athelhampton in the 1890s). The same idea was to be essayed, roughly in parallel with Johnston at Hidcote, at Godinton (by Blomfield in 1902) and at Great Dixter (by Lutyens and Nathaniel Lloyd in 1910), and a half of the idea was expressed, in 1925, by Nathaniel Lloyd when he wrote:

> The word 'garden' ... signifies an enclosure: indeed ... the actual sense ... is not experienced (whatever the cultivation) except when there is also a feeling of enclosure.[18]

'Enclosure' – this is truly the essence of Hidcote, but it is given a liberty by means of the magisterial framework, a spacious T-shaped scheme from which a multitude of smaller garden schemes depend. From the house, westwards, Johnston drew out an avenue along rising ground, ending at the highest point with gates looking out over a ha-ha onto the countryside. This long avenue, divided by steps and flanking summer-houses at the centre, provides the 'top' of the T-shaped scheme, its eastern side adorned with 'red' borders, the western with lines of pleached hornbeams. From the middle of this avenue, beside the steps and summerhouses, another hedged avenue, the Long Walk (the 'stem' of the 'T'), leads south, first falling gently, and then rising up (an echo possibly of St Paul's Walden Bury). Each of these avenues is, in itself, complete. For many gardens, in the seventeenth- and early eighteenth-century tradition, this would have been enough – covering the space, with controlling views out. But at Hidcote Johnston gave himself many distinct and different gardens or garden areas on either side of these avenues, principally to left and right of the Long Walk.

Some of these areas, like the sequence of circular gardens on the eastern side of the 'T', are strongly formal and architectural, with topiary and stonework and a distinct geometrical plan. To the west, the terrace and topiary pillar gardens are more open, while the southern areas on each side of the Long Walk – a woodland area to the south-east and a stream garden to the south-west – are informal in the Robinsonian tradition. Johnston was a passionate plantsman, and each and every part of the gardens at Hidcote has its own scheme of planting and colour qualities, fully in the tradition of Gertrude Jekyll's Munstead Wood.

'Garden Rooms'

Harold Nicolson (later Sir Harold) and Lady Vita Sackville-West were married in 1913. In 1915, they acquired Long Barn in Kent, adding a further old building in 1916 (in a process closely resembling that at Great Dixter). They lived, wrote and gardened there until 1930. In 1925, Sir Edwin Lutyens designed a 'Dutch garden' on a part of the terraced site. The garden still exists, as indeed does the far older garden at Knole, also in Kent, where Vita Sackville-West grew up.

In 1930, the Nicolsons acquired the dilapidated property of Sissinghurst Castle, with some 10 acres of walled or moated ground, within an agricultural property of some 250 acres. These 10 acres were then planned, planted and perfected to become one of Britain's most famous garden creations. Most parts had been undertaken by 1939, though the 'white garden', one of the more renowned areas, dates from 1946. In this year, Vita Sackville-West published her long poem, *The Garden*, 20 years after a comparable poetic work, *The Land*.

The much-used term 'garden rooms' is applicable with real truth only at Sissinghurst, thanks to the sixteenth-century tower. At Sissinghurst the garden (or gardens, since there are so many different parts) may be surveyed, or rather overlooked, at almost every point from the top of the tower, which stands relatively central to the scheme. From here the

The water garden at Godinton – designed by Blomfield as part of a sequence of different areas round the houses.

Lutyens and Jekyll were engaged with the layout and planting at Hestercombe between 1904 and 1910. Here, a terraced 'rill' flanks the 'Great Plat'. Beyond, the countryside of Somerset.

parts of the garden may be viewed *from above*, and are seen again and again as enclosures, framed in most instances by the old and often slightly irregular walls of the sixteenth-century buildings. At Sissinghurst, thanks to the tower, we see down into these enclosures as if they were rooms from which the roof had just been lifted up, rooms with their distinct and different contents, and with doors or windows leading into or looking through to other rooms and areas – the main courtyard, the tower lawn, the rondel, the white garden, the south cottage and its garden, the nuttery, the orchard, the moat and countryside beyond.

One must add that the linking doors or archways, or gaps in clipped wall-like hedges, are often ever so slightly off-centre. While this may well have been an initial accident, resulting from the piecemeal nature of the older wall structures, it has at Sissinghurst been used to achieve an exceptional felicity of enticement – to glance, to wander, to explore on either side and beyond, among the marvels of a superlative garden.

Harold Nicolson is generally credited with the design of the gardens, while Vita Sackville-West saw to the planting. The division is simple, yet true, as she herself said in 1946:

> Gardens should be romantic, but severe.
> Strike your strong lines, and take no further care
> Of such extravagance as pours the rose
> In wind-blown fountains down the broken walls,
> In gouts of blood, in dripping flower-falls,
> Or flings the jasmine where the walls enclose,
> Separate garths, a miniature surprise.[19]

Today most visitors to Sissinghurst will wonder at the planting, and, I hope, appreciate the differences in colour, texture and seasonal effect between the courtyard – mainly reds and purples – the pale greens of the nuttery, the roses climbing in the orchard trees, the glowing yellow-orange of the south cottage and the long-continuing and delicate variety of the white garden. Much at Sissinghurst looks back to William Robinson and Gertrude Jekyll – both visited by Vita Sackville-West – but much is original, prompted by a passion for plants and by an equally vital love of the site and the surrounding scene.

An Eastern Interlude

I have remarked (see page 264) that until James Bateman and E. W. Cooke created 'China' at Biddulph Grange in Staffordshire in the 1840s no serious attempt to make an authentic garden in Chinese style had been undertaken in Britain or Ireland. Interest in Japan came afterwards, stimulated first by the plant introductions (seeds and conifers) achieved by J. G. Veitch (1839–70) in the early 1860s, and seen, for example, at Batsford Park in Gloucestershire, where in 1890 A. B. Freeman-Mitford (later the 1st Lord Redesdale) began a garden and arboretum with many trees and plants from China and Japan, including an outstanding collection of bamboos, together with acers and flowering cherries, and various garden buildings of a Chinese or Japanese character. Lord Redesdale later published *The Bamboo Garden* (1896), recording his particular enthusiasm and achievement.

A curious Anglo-Indian garden, the Larmer Tree Grounds at Tollard Royal in Wiltshire, created in the 1880s, should not be overlooked. The 11-acre site, mainly wooded ground, was laid out by Lt.-Gen. Pitt-Rivers 'for the recreation of the people in the neighbouring towns and villages', and contained an octagonal temple, beside a small pool, with a further six 'quarters' in Indian style. Several of these buildings survive, notably the Theatre (1895) and the Lower Indian Room (c.1880).

Gardens aiming to achieve a distinct and genuine Japanese manner came later, and in rather a rush, from around 1900 onwards. Although a variety of causes for British fascination with Japan have been proposed, easily the most important in garden terms was the publication in 1893 of Josiah Conder's *Landscape Gardening in Japan*, following his *Flowers of Japan and the Art of Floral Arrangement* of 1891. These volumes revealed both the difference between the flowers available in Japan and the West, and the hitherto wholly unknown significance of different parts, features and aspects of the layout of Japanese gardens.[20] Soon after 1893, a water garden with pond, island and rough stone bridges in 'Japanese style' was laid out at Cliveden in Buckinghamshire, and in 1900 a Japanese pagoda, which had been exhibited in 1867 at the Paris exhibition (the very exhibition William Robinson had covered for *The Times*) was installed as a brilliant 'eye-catcher'.

This garden at Cliveden was, I suspect, the earliest to follow Conder's publications, and it was quickly followed and indeed overtaken in terms of serious emulation of Japanese models. At Heale House in Wiltshire, which had been much enlarged by Detmar Blow in the mid-1890s, the owner, Louis Greville, employed Japanese gardeners from 1901 to create an area with appropriate plants and buildings, such as a tea house, a lacquer bridge, stone lanterns and so forth, in an irregularly contoured space crossed by two branches of a stream. In 1901–5, Japanese advice and direction were obtained at Fanhams Hall in Hertfordshire, and garden ornaments were imported from Japan in the elaboration of a

3-acre garden. In 1905, a 6-acre garden at Cottered in Hertfordshire was begun by Herbert Goode (1865–1937), after a visit he had made to Japan in that year. At Cottered, appropriate ornaments were again imported, and the 'landscape', in Japanese style, was elaborated over the next 30 years. For three years, in 1923–6, a Japanese expert, Seyemon Kusumoto, was engaged to complete the design, incorporating lake, streams, cascades, miniature mountains, with several buildings, gateways and arches, and appropriate planting of acers, azaleas, wistaria, bamboo, iris and dwarf conifers.[21]

In Wales, at Shirenewton Hall in Gwent, another such garden was made by Charles Liddell in the early 1900s, prompted by the owner's experience of Japan,[22] while in Ireland, Colonel Hall-Walker directed the creation of a $1\frac{1}{2}$-acre Japanese garden at Tully in Co. Kildare. The work lasted from 1906 to 1910, with a resident Japanese gardener, Tassa Eida, and was backed by a shipload of artefacts, trees and shrubs, and, of course, specimens of bonsai.[23] Not only did individual elements of this garden have a symbolic meaning, but the winding paths provided a symbolic itinerary – the ways of life. As a frequent visitor to this garden in the 1960s, I was again and again delighted by the variations of this theme offered by the guides who led parties of strangers along the paths – it could be the 'journey through life' of a single person, from childhood to old age; or of three brothers, one good, one middling, and the third a real shocker; or of a young man and his beloved, separated at some point where the path divided, reunited after perilous passage over river and mountain.

Not all 'Japanese' gardens were endowed with imported ornaments. By the early 1900s, stone lanterns and the like could be obtained from British suppliers. V.N. Gauntlett's catalogue of 1901 illustrates both stone lanterns and bronze cranes, and the Gauntlett nursery (at Chiddingfold in Surrey) laid out the nearby Japanese garden at Ramster with a variety of these items, backed by acers, bamboos, azaleas and rhododendrons in a wider woodland setting.

The enthusiasm continued, helped by *The Flowers and Gardens of Japan* by Florence and Ella Du Cane (1908). From the Japanese-British exhibition of 1910, a replica of the 'Gateway of the Imperial Messenger' (the original, Chokushi-Mon, is in Kyoto) was erected in the grounds at Kew, though, as if to make a parallel with Chambers' pagoda, 150 yards away, the planting round about of Japanese azaleas is in Western style.

At Great Dixter this sunken garden was designed in 1923 by Nathaniel Lloyd, replacing an earlier lawn, and becoming an essential part of the sequence of garden areas round the house.

In my opinion, the most convincingly authentic of the 'Japanese' gardens created in the British Isles is the Japanese Garden at Bitchet Wood in Kent, laid out in 1919–21 on an enclosed rectangular site of about two-thirds of an acre. Here one of the detailed plans in Conder's *Landscape Gardening in Japan* (plate XXV, 'Hill Garden – Finished Style') provides the essential list of features – five different miniature 'hills', ten 'stones', seven principal trees and nine artefacts, ranging from the 'garden well' to three different bridges, a lantern and a shrine – and these features, each with its purpose and symbolism, reappear in the garden at Bitchet Wood, though by no means copying the layout in Conder's plan. The features, and their interconnection, may have been inspired by the plan of 1893, but their layout is thoughtfully related to the nature of the site, which allows an additional area of bog garden, with iris and waterside plants, and an extra wooden bridge formed of planks in a zig-zag pattern. From the 'Distant Mountain Hill' the view leads out, not to the 'borrowed scenery' of Mount Fuji, but to a sandy Kentish cliff a mile distant. This Japan-in-England is an astonishing and deeply beautiful creation.

In Britain and Ireland in this century, the Japanese garden forms a slight but continuing element. The thoughtful grace of the garden at Bitchet Wood has few equals, though in the most recent time (1992) a fine Japanese garden, designed by experts from Japan, has been created in Holland Park in London, with lake, rocky cascade, islands, lanterns and sinuous paths with stepping stones. Like the nearly contemporary Japanese garden in Boston, Massachusetts (1988), it is a foreign creation on British (or American) soil, an admirable yet still unfamiliar garden form.

18

MODERN MASTERS

In the second half of the twentieth century, British and Irish gardens have been designed, augmented, changed and restored by many people. Some half a dozen designers have had a fair share of the commissions, and the books written by several of them have extended their influence. In the amateur tradition, more gardens have been designed and developed by the owners themselves, following particular inspirations, enthusiasms and interests, leading to further books which have influenced yet other gardeners.

The garden enthusiasms of the nineteenth century have continued, reflected in a prolific output of books and periodicals, in ever more varied garden shows and exhibitions, in an extension of the earlier 'picturesque tour' to cover not hundreds but thousands of possible gardens which may be visited and viewed in the summer season, and in the proliferation of activities concerned with the recording, protection and restoration of other gardens. In this last group, the National Trust, English Heritage and the Historic Houses Association are especially important.

Noted Designers

Percy Cane (1881–1976) was connected with many gardens in Britain and Ireland and further afield, though his work in other countries, like that of Russell Page or of Sir Geoffrey Jellicoe, is not our business here. In England, one of his public commissions was at King George's Park, Wandsworth in 1921–3, with several formal areas beside the main pathway, and later, in 1945, he remodelled the ancient site at Dartington Hall in Devon (after proposals by Avray Tipping in 1927 and Beatrix

Farrand in 1933), being responsible for the terraced shaping of the Tour-nament Ground and the great sequence of steps up to the Glade, now focused on Henry Moore's sculpture of the 'Reclining Woman'.[1] Two important gardens by Cane are in Scotland – the terraces at Falkland Palace, Fife, where Cane worked in 1946–52 to add interest to the six-teenth-century framework, and the bastion and terrace area at Monteviot House, Roxburghshire, dating originally from the 1860s, and remodelled by Cane in 1961–8. In each of these gardens, as at Llanerch Park in Wales in the late 1920s, his work is essentially in the Blomfield/Lutyens/Peto tradition, extending the 'order' of the house (or castle) out over terraces and walks to enhance the further view. At Llanerch, we might think that his terraces and paved walks have redeemed the 'landscaping' of the eighteenth century, which destroyed an earlier terraced scheme, 'frittered into an errant villa' when Thomas Pennant passed by in 1773.[2]

Wales contains most of the surviving work of Sir Clough Williams-Ellis (1883–1978), notably at Plas Brondanw in Gwynnedd, his own house, and at the nearby coastal site at Portmeirion. At the former, which he developed from 1908 onwards, the garden radiates from the house to a surrounding glory of mountains, whose shapes and summits complete the vistas of walk and terrace. The sublime is linked to the comic, with the tiny fireman who commemorates a disastrous fire there in 1950. At Portmeirion, Clough Williams-Ellis worked from 1926 for some 50 years, creating an entire village-port-sea-garden composition, formed from the existing landscape, hamlet and woodland and enriched with a multitude of imported architectural fragments, planted round with flowering shrubs. It was my fortune to meet him in 1973, on his ninetieth birthday, when he was complaining, with a certain pride, that when he had tried to remodel one of his creations at Portmeirion, the 'authorities' had forbidden him to touch the building; it had been listed, and could not be altered. Gardens change and we cannot stop them. We may wish to change a building, but we may not be allowed to do so.

In Wales, Williams-Ellis also designed Nantclwyd Hall in Clwyd from 1956 onwards. Here the architectural element is again predominant, with an encircling landscape of hill and field. The main, but by no means the only, garden area is an arcaded, hedged and pavilioned enclosure stretching away from the house towards wrought-iron gates, which open to further delights in the park – bridges, a temple and a grotto.

Less prolific, but not to be overlooked was John Codrington (1898–1991), garden designer and watercolourist. One should note a delightful 'silver' garden which he designed for Lord de L'Isle at Penshurst in Kent, and the outstanding herb garden which he planned for a quadrangle (or 'pentangle') in Emmanuel College, Cambridge, around 1970. The latter

The White Garden at Sissinghurst was created in 1946. While marvelling at the associated tones of silver, grey and white, we should also appreciate the subtle formality of the plan.

The gardens of Holland House in London began in 1605, with the plant-lover Sir Walter Cope; their varied development is signally extended with this fine Japanese garden, created by Japanese experts in 1991–2.

is a triumph of imaginative design, coping with an irregular enclosed area by means of different-sized triangular or wedge-shaped beds, outlined with hedges of stepped box, set in cleverly patterned paving.

Schemes of a much wider and more expansive nature, but still acknowledging the principle of formal control, are characteristic of the work of Sir Geoffrey Jellicoe (b.1900). At Ditchley in Oxfordshire, early in his career, he designed a formal sequence of parterres for an area which should have received a formal garden designed by James Gibbs two centuries before, and at Shute House in Wiltshire in the 1970s, working again for the same family, he elaborated a complex and extensive water garden with canal, cascades, bridges and sculpture, a scheme which is indeed geometrical, but animated by lavish planting, directed by Lady Anne Tree. At Sutton Place in Surrey, a large and rambling area of gardens round the Elizabethan house had been given shape and order by Gertrude Jekyll at the beginning of this century and had subsequently deteriorated, to be reshaped by Jellicoe in the early 1980s with formal enclosures, much topiary, pools and lawn. In its turn, alas, this scheme also declines.

The most memorable British garden designer since the 1930s was Russell Page (1906–85), who worked in partnership with Jellicoe until 1939. While his commissions, over four hundred, were spread all over the gardening world, enough were achieved in the British Isles to be mentioned with respect. His earliest important work was at Longleat in Wiltshire, beginning in 1932, with repeated contact until the mid-1950s. Here, he was involved both in the broad landscape of the park, laid out by Capability Brown in 1757–62, and in redesigning areas of Victorian flower garden between the house and the orangery. Though much of Page's work shows a deep sense of order (as, indeed, in his remodelling of the approach avenue at Longleat and in the several garden areas beside the Dower House at Badminton in Gloucestershire), his genius extended to luxuriant planting schemes, like the minute 'silver' garden within a stable courtyard at West Wycombe in Buckinghamshire, executed around 1975, and the superb shrub and herbaceous borders, 130 yards long, at Port Lympne in Kent. In the formal line, Page also remodelled a part of Tilden's terraces at Port Lympne in the same period, around 1974, creating the chessboard garden with its squares of lawn and seasonal bedding plants. A series of commissions at Leeds Castle in Kent extended (as at Longleat) from before the Second World War until around 1980, and with a similar range of style. In the main landscape, he broadened the course of the River Len, to create the Great Water, a lake to south and south-east of the medieval moat, while he also designed the Culpeper Garden between the stables and the Great Water. This garden was partly replanted in the early 1990s, but still retains much of Page's formal framework.

Another designer in a mainly formal style was Lanning Roper (1912–83), an American who worked on several gardens in Britain and Ireland, particularly at Abbots Ripton in Cambridgeshire for Lord de Ramsey in the 1950s and 1960s, co-operating at times with Humphrey Waterfield (d.1971). Roper was also responsible for development of the complex gardens at Glenveagh Castle in Co. Donegal. Begun around 1860, beside Loch Veagh and looking across to the Derryveagh mountains, it was reshaped by Roper in the 1960s round the castle with several areas in different formal manners, a 'pleasure garden' of sweeping lawn amid shrubs and borders, a walled kitchen and flower garden and woodland areas beyond.[3]

Lanning Roper, like several of the designers who have just been mentioned, was also a writer, for some years garden correspondent of *The Sunday Times* and author of *Town Gardening* (1957). Percy Cane was active as contributor to, and eventually editor of *My Garden Illustrated* (1918–20). He also edited *Garden Design*, from 1930 to 1939, and produced his autobiographical *The Earth is My Canvas* in 1956. Sir Clough Williams-Ellis's books are predominantly to do with architecture, but Sir Geoffrey Jellicoe wrote several of importance both to garden history and to garden design – with J. G. Shepherd, the acute and invaluable *Italian Gardens of the Renaissance* (1925); on his own, *Gardens and Design* (1927); and with Susan Jellicoe, his wife, *The Landscape of Man* (1975), drawing to some extent on the two earlier works to relate the history of town, garden and landscape planning. Russell Page's autobiography, *The Education of a Gardener*, was published in 1962, a masterly account of his life and gardening up to that point. Rather like the more copious writings of Gertrude Jekyll, Page brought together the values of the formal and the natural, plants and architecture – an example for us to admire and to follow.

'They Made a Garden'

Beside this group of noted designers and writers, there are many other recent and active gardeners who may have created only one or a couple of gardens, sometimes writing about their work as well.

At East Lambrook Manor in Somerset, Margery Fish and her husband Walter began to develop a 2-acre site into a garden of infinite floral and herbal variety in 1938–9. By the time of her death in 1969, she had laid out and stocked ten or a dozen happily different areas, white garden, silver garden, terrace garden, rock garden, green garden and so on (not to forget the vegetable garden), and written seven books about her experience, beginning with *We Made a Garden* in 1956. After a period of decline, the garden was rescued by new owners in 1985. To my mind, its variety and its closely crowded order make it one of the most lovely small plantsman's gardens there are, though one which demands heroic resolution to maintain.

At Docwra's Manor, Shepreth, near Cambridge is a garden with similar love of plant variety, augmented by an enthusiasm for rarities. These were described by the owner, John Raven, in *A Botanist's Garden* (1971), together with plants in the garden at Ardtornish, at the head of Loch Aline in Argyllshire. This second garden, inherited by Mrs Raven, was begun by her ancestor Valentine Smith in the 1890s with considerable plantings of both conifers and rhododendron hybrids. Further informal development took place in the 1930s and again from the 1970s, with particular areas or small gardens concentrating on limited groups of plants. Somewhat further to the south, but still on the western side of Scotland, several other gardens were established to take advantage of the exceptionally mild climate. Arduaine Gardens in Argyllshire was begun by the 1920s, and developed with a notable rhododendron collection by J. A. Campbell and his descendants. Crarae, likewise in Argyllshire, was begun in 1912 by Lady Campbell, who was the aunt of Reginald Farrer, the celebrated traveller and plant collector. Her son, Sir George Campbell, continued the gardens from 1925, with astonishing additions of both conifers and rhododendrons, planted in a distinctly 'natural' manner. At Brodick Castle on the Isle of Arran, where the gardens are set beside the medieval castle, the walled garden dating from 1710 with other areas laid out in the mid-nineteenth century, the woodland garden was begun by the Duchess of Montrose around 1920, and includes rhododendrons brought back by George Forrest and Frank Kingdon-Ward. At Achamore, on the island of Gigha in Argyllshire, Sir James Horlick began his garden in 1944, enriching it with a wealth of rhododendron hybrids, as well as azaleas, hydrangeas and sorbus.

Other gardens with notable collections of plants and shrubs were of course established further south, in England, in this century. Exbury in Hampshire was begun by Lionel de Rothschild in 1919, with a renowned rhododendron collection, many being hybrids bred at Exbury. At Nymans in Sussex, Ludwig Messel laid out garden areas – indeed a formal garden – in the 1890s, with advice from William Robinson on the planting of the walled garden, and from the 1920s the surrounding grounds were given a 'rhododendron wood' and many rare ornamental trees and shrubs. The garden at Trengwainton in Cornwall was laid out from 1925 to 1969, under the guidance of E. H. W. Bolitho, who received rhododendron seed from Frank Kingdon-Ward in the late 1920s, and had links with J. C. Williams of Caerhays and other Cornish plant experts. The Savill Garden in Surrey, on the edge of Windsor Park, was begun in 1932–9 by Sir Eric Savill and continued in the 1950s and 1970s. This began as a woodland garden, dubbed at first the 'Bog Garden' because of the pervasive moisture – several pond gardens make brilliant use of the available element – but the overall 35 acres of the site now contain one of the widest ranges of trees and shrubs to be found in the British Isles. I would single out the moss garden, set beneath spreading beech trees, which recalls Kokedera, at Saiho-ji in Kyoto, Japan.

In Ireland, in the same adventurous botanic tradition, there are the 100-odd acres of garden and grounds at Mount Congreve in Co. Waterford, beside the River Suir. Here the house was first built in 1725, and the large walled garden and conservatory date from the same period. The modern gardens were, however, begun only in the mid-1960s by Mr Ambrose Congreve, a descendant of the original owners. In the walled garden, there are now some of the best herbaceous borders in Ireland and areas of hybrid hydrangeas, while outside, the woodland encloses a rare collection of trees, accompanied by masses of flowering shrubs, including fine cedars, many and varied magnolias, rhododendrons, embothriums and azaleas.[4]

It is also important to mention the Hillier Arboretum, begun in 1963 by the Hilliers nursery in Hampshire as an adjunct to their nursery concern, founded a century before. The arboretum was given to the Hampshire County Council in 1977, with its encyclopaedic – no less – collection of trees, shrubs and plants. Hilliers have since 1972 published the *Hilliers' Manual of Trees and Shrubs*.

Gardeners – and Writers

Returning to smaller gardens – yet with gardeners every bit as important – we come to people who have gardened for themselves, sometimes inheriting an earlier scheme, sometimes starting from scratch. Among these, some of the more distinguished have both gardened and then written about it, or lectured and pontificated. May this continue.

From his father's Lutyens-based garden at Great Dixter, Christopher Lloyd has elaborated one of the most varied and entrancing sets of 'garden rooms' in England, together with a 'long border' celebrated in

The water garden at Stanton Harcourt Manor in Oxfordshire, created from old fish ponds since the 1960s, has a medieval background. In Pope's Tower, Alexander Pope translated a part of the Illiad.

The author's garden in Berkshire, made since 1980: formality, fruit and flowers.

several of his published volumes. His lectures are as welcome as those of Rosemary Verey, who, at Barnsley House in Gloucestershire, has laid out a knot garden with a convincingly interlaced pattern, and, just as important, made a laburnum walk and a vegetable garden of rare delight. Rosemary Verey's garden writings may be compared with those of Penelope Hobhouse, who in recent years has cared for and developed the gardens of Tintinhull House in Somerset. These were first laid out by Phyllis Reiss in the early 1930s.

There are many gardeners and many designers, and I fear that some of them, still alive and gardening, may grudge my silence on their behalf. I'm sorry. We must, however, mention John Brookes, designer, writer and teacher, whose garden creation at Denmans, Fontwell, in Sussex, in collaboration with Mrs J. H. Robinson, is the setting for his school of garden design; Anthony du Gard Pasley, designer of the garden at The Postern, near Tonbridge in Kent, and lecturer at the English Garden School, at the Chelsea Physic Garden; Michael Balston, who restored the eighteenth-century landscape (with a formal Y-shaped canal) at Purley Hall in Berkshire in 1986–7, and whose book, *The Well-Furnished Garden*, a study of garden buildings, furniture and ornaments, was published in 1986; and, in the younger generation of designers, Tom Stuart-Smith, whose own courtyard garden at Serge Hill in Hertfordshire is a triumph of trim hedges and well-balanced flowers.

And still they – the gardens and their creators – must be named. At Little Haseley in Oxfordshire, Nancy Lancaster acquired Haseley Court in 1955, with a remarkable 1890s topiary 'chessmen' garden and other areas, such as the large walled kitchen garden, in a near-to-derelict state. These she has restored, and, in the last decade, has moved to the adjoining Coach House to concentrate on the walled garden area, which is divided into four quarters by box-edged paths, each quarter with a distinctive character – one with lawns and borders, one with a topiary 'wheel' in contrasting golden yew and box, and elsewhere roses in abundance, fruit trees, vegetables and herbs. Outside is a fine laburnum walk, like that at Rosemary Verey's Barnsley House.

Another old walled garden was brilliantly adapted in the 1920s in Sussex, at Charleston Farmhouse, when it was lived in by Vanessa and Clive Bell and Duncan Grant and their friends. This garden has been restored in the early 1990s, making thoughtful use of old fruit trees, their shapes contrasting with occasional pieces of sculpture and with the patches of colour in adjacent borders. Being on sloping ground, there are vast views out over the Downs.

At Chenies Manor House in Buckinghamshire, a garden with Tudor origins has been restored and extensively elaborated since the 1950s by

Lt.-Col. and Mrs MacLeod Matthews. The original sunken garden is now joined by a white garden, a topiary garden and other areas, including a circular turf maze laid out in 1982 and, at a little distance, a hedge maze of somewhat 'mathematical' character, planted in 1992.

In contrast with these three gardens, the many different areas at Compton Acres, near Poole in Dorset, are a well-linked scheme of eight or ten varied gardens in styles ranging from Roman to Italian to Japanese, with colonnades, statuary, pools and fountains, a heather garden, a sub-tropical area and a rose garden. A peripheral path connects them all. Compton Acres was first laid out in 1914–20 by T. W. Simpson in a deliberately eclectic manner, and restored in the 1950s.

It is also important to mention some of the people whose love of plants, and enthusiasm in their collection and propagation, has contributed to the more recent gardens. At the Dower House, Boughton, North-amptonshire, (and therefore beside the great formal garden laid out in the 1680s) Valerie Finnis (Lady Scott) has since 1947 established a garden replete with rarities yet pleasing in its design – the two do not always coincide; and the same may be said of Lionel Fortescue's Garden House, at Buckland Monachorum in Devon, begun in 1945.[5]

Other enthusiasts have coupled their love of plants with a nursery or garden centre, as has Beth Chatto, acclaimed as a writer on garden practice, as a gardener and as a distinguished provider of excellent plants. Much the same applies to John Treasure, gardening for himself at Burford House in Shropshire from 1954, and establishing the remarkable Trea-sures of Tenbury clematis nursery beside his own garden. Two other nurseries – among hundreds – to single out are Blooms of Bressingham, at Diss in Norfolk, and the Hollington nursery, near Newbury in Berkshire, which specialises in herbs, but, like many other nurseries, has gardens of high merit, with good borders, exemplary topiary and a small but delightful knot.

Pastime – and Passion

The garden feeling of the last 30 years has been reflected in a bewildering profusion of books, magazines, columns in newspapers and radio and television programmes. Beside the thoughtful writings of Arthur Hellyer, doyen of the columnists who died in 1993, there are the much-listened to or watched 'Gardener's Question Time' and 'Gardener's World', both followed, so we are told, by millions, some of whom do nothing, some of whom apply the advice in their own garden and some of whom – a gently diminishing number – go off to cultivate their allotment.

The allotment movement developed slowly from the early nineteeth century onwards, with the aim of providing small areas of land for gardenless workers to use for growing vegetables. From 1887, with the Allotments Act, this was firmly assured, and $\frac{1}{2}$ million allotments were in cultivation by 1900. The number grew to $1\frac{1}{2}$ million during the First World War, declined with the peace and grew again to almost $1\frac{1}{2}$ million by 1942. Since the 1950s, there has been a steady decline, a sad but peripheral part of the history of British gardens.

The passion for gardens – sometimes indeed an obsession – has, however, been a part of British and Irish life in the last two decades. The growth of garden centres has catered for a generation of garden owners, eager to cope with their property. Those who are 'plant lovers' will consult the *Plant Finder*, devised and compiled by Chris Philip, edited by Tony Lord and first published in 1987. Those who want to see what is what will go to the flower shows, principally the Royal Horticultural Society's annual show at Chelsea and their seasonal shows in Vincent Square, and the shows at Wembley and at Hampton Court, or they will go a-visiting (a habit contracted in the eighteenth century, though we may not remember the fact). The 'Yellow Book', *Gardens of England and Wales*, lists in 1993 'over 3,000 private gardens' open for viewing, while many hundreds more are open via the Historic Houses Association, the National Trust and English Heritage.

To add to the feeling of the period, we have in the last 20 or 30 years seen many *recreations* of gardens in earlier styles (as already recorded in the nineteenth century) and – a new development – many *restorations* of gardens made in earlier times. Of the period recreations, we should note that at Edzell Castle in Angus, laid out in the 1930s within the castle enclosure; the medieval garden – 'Queen Eleanor's Garden' – by the Great Hall in Winchester and the knot garden at the Tudor Museum, Southampton, both laid out in the 1980s by Dr Sylvia Landsberg; and knot gardens laid out at Barnsley House by Rosemary Verey, at Hatfield House in Hertfordshire by Lady Salisbury, and also at the Museum of Garden History in London; and a further knot garden at Helmingham in Suffolk. At Little Moreton Hall in Cheshire a knot garden was laid out in 1972, based on a 1670 pattern; it now serves as a superb example of such attempts to recreate gardens from the past.

Beside these recreations, the many restorations of gardens are linked with the current concern to record and, if possible, to protect the important gardens of the past. This protection has been undertaken principally by the National Trust, with its superlative garden directors, Graham

Stuart Thomas and John Sales, and at a slightly less extensive level by English Heritage (who nonetheless used me as their Garden Historian to 'list' the historic gardens of England in 1984–8). Other groups – the Historic Houses Association, the NCPPG. (National Council for the Protection of Plants and Gardens) and several county garden trusts (they arise, flourish and subside, only to rise again) – all thrive and spread, like comfrey or buttercups.

Most significant are the restorations of earlier gardens, an activity which had not been attempted seriously before the 1970s. I must mention, from among a larger number and in roughly chronological order of their original creation, the following:

Ham House, London (National Trust), c.1640
Kirby Hall, Northamptonshire (English Heritage), c.1680
Westbury Court, Gloucestershire (National Trust), c.1690
Castle Bromwich, West Midlands, c.1700
Chatelherault, Lanarkshire, c.1735
Painswick, Gloucestershire, c.1740
Painshill, Surrey, c.1750
Purley Hall, Berkshire, c.1750
Upton Grey, Hampshire, 1908

Not a bad list.

A Final Choice

I think it is fair to conclude this history with a few examples of widely different gardens made in the last few years. Each one is highly individual, each is creative, each is in its own way a statement of what is important for its creator, yet all look back to, and continue, the diverse traditions which this book discusses. I would suggest, that while such varied, exciting and original gardens continue to be made, the British and Irish 'genius of gardening' is alive and well.

I begin with Thomas Shearer, at Beechgrove, near Broughton, not far from Biggar in Lanarkshire. Here, since 1960, Mr Shearer has developed several acres in a highly original way. While I, driving by, was first attracted by the fields of meconopsis, the ornamental garden on the other side of the house was no less fascinating. Backed on sloping ground, with a bank glowing with orange-yellow rhododendrons and stands of lupins nearby, the hourglass-shaped lawn is flanked by as precise a formal

A secluded part of Ian Hamilton Finlay's garden at Little Sparta: an archway for Rousseau's lovers, Julie and Saint-Preux, and a memorial to the young Rousseau – the episode of the cherries.

bedding layout as I have ever seen, dominated on the upper side by a large – and accurate – floral clock. Mr Shearer raises some 5,500 bedding plants every year, which are used for different patterns and designs each season, all triumphs of careful, controlled and colourful planning.

In immense contrast are the gardens of Corpus Christi College at Oxford. Here the architectural framework of the quadrangle is strictly rectilinear, and the outer garden area, enclosed by the city wall, was planted formally from the sixteenth century onwards. In the last decade or so, however, the present gardener, David Leake, has set both the beds lining the walls of the quad and much of the outer garden with free-growing and luxuriant plants of a distinctly *un*formal kind. They are, simply and reasonably, grown in the tradition of William Robinson's wild garden, and chosen for their qualities as plants, not as a medium for a pictorial or architectural composition. So among the roses and hollyhocks grow leggy fennel and sprawling thyme, and beneath the secular trees dry teazle-heads rear up, gaunt sentries along the city wall.

Related to the spirit of the planting at Corpus, but on an expansive scale and without the geometry of college buildings, are the 5 acres of woodland garden, with broad lawns, borders and winding paths which lead to the bog and lake garden below, all developed since 1960 by Mr and Mrs John Phillips at Home Covert, near Devizes in Wiltshire. Here William Robinson would rejoice again to see the rarities, the carefully chosen and diligently hunted trees and shrubs, the wealth of bog primulas in the water garden and, indeed, the herbaceous borders beside the upper lawn. Above all, Home Covert is a magnificent woodland creation – not an arboretum, but a garden glorious with trees.

Begun later – in the 1980s – and within a farmland estate of some 180 acres, Hazelbury Manor, near Box in Wiltshire, has been developed by the architect Ian Pollard with two garden creations of astonishingly different characters. Round the Elizabethan manor house are 8 acres of gardens in largely formal style, notably the spacious rectangular lawn to the east of the house, surrounded by clipped hedges of yew and box and with long terraced walks on each side, connected with the central lawn by steps, sculpture and urns. These walks lead past a variety of different gardens, with borders both herbaceous and annual, areas of topiary, fountains and a foliage garden. Nearby there is a rockery, and on the western side of the house are more lawns, a terraced walk and the walled kitchen garden. All are delightful, indeed, partly because the planting has not followed the 'fashionable' order of the last few years.

But beyond, to the west and south, the scene changes, and opens out to the rolling Wiltshire countryside. Not far from the house, a grassy hollow contains a circle of massive stones – Pollard's version of

Avebury – and further away are two grassy 'mounts' with ascending spiral paths, echoes of the tumuli on Salisbury plain. Nearby, a turf maze coils over the rising ground, and off to the east there is a nascent topiary Stonehenge. We are back in the 'wish'd *Elyzium*' of the Druids, as imagined by Henry Rowlands in the 1720s.

A last example, far to the north of Hazelbury and its memories of the remotest past, is a garden with many more monuments, devised by the poet-writer-gardener Ian Hamilton Finlay, conceiver of sculptural or multi-dimensional poems. These are set in his 9-acre garden at Little Sparta (Stonypath), near Dunsyre in Lanarkshire. It is a secluded site, on the edge of the Pentland Hills, which he has developed since 1967 from a small farm building, its walled garden and the adjacent moorland. Water was diverted from a nearby burn to create several ponds, and these are often the background to the monuments, or even a crucial element in their composition. Finlay's 'visual poems' – or poetic monuments – are less primitive than Pollard's 'Avebury', but more lyrical; some enigmatic, some teasing, perplexing or suddenly stern.

Making use of walls, hedges and small groves of trees (all grown, with few exceptions, since 1967), the garden areas contain and separate these 'visual poems', related to a dozen or more sometimes overlapping themes – the classical 'Arcadia'; the beauty of fishing smacks, their sails and their names; warfare, with allusions to submarines, aircraft carriers (one posing as a bird-table), tanks, hand grenades and the debris of war. A secluded area celebrates the lyrical side of Rousseau, while elsewhere a small island and tomb remember his death at Ermenonville, and out on the moorland, overlooking the largest pond, Lochan Eck, gigantic incised stones spell out Saint-Just's unrelenting message: 'The present order is the disorder of the future.'

Behind the house is another pool, overlooked by a building decorated with a portico and pillars, and bearing the dedication 'To Apollo – His Music – His Muses – His Missiles' – a sense of paradox, or ambivalence, which appears in many of these poetic yet prickly monuments.

Finlay's garden creation is a rare and demanding achievement, as far away from Nesfield's vast parterres as it is from Shirley Hibberd's suburban villa gardens. Yet it is just as much a part of British garden tradition, linked to the thoughtful, allusive scenes of Rousham, Stourhead and Painshill. May such variety long continue.

Now, gentle reader, back to your garden. It will have changed.

NOTES

CHAPTER 1
Druids, Romans and Anglo-Saxons

1) See Oliver Rackham, *Trees and Woodland in the British Landscape*, 1978, pp. 34–8, 123–6.
2) See Christopher Taylor, *The Archaeology of Gardens*, 1983, pp. 25–6.
3) See Charles Squire, *Celtic Myth and Legend*, n.d., pp. 189, 219.
4) Caesar, *De Bello Gallico*, VI, 13.
5) Pliny the Elder, *Natural History*, XVI, 249–51.
6) Tacitus, *Annals*, XIV, xxix-xxx.
7) Cf. Caesar, *De Bello Gallico*, V, 14.
8) *Ibid.*, V, 14.
9) Strabo, *Geography*, IV, 5.
10) Tacitus, *Agricola*, XIII.
11) C. Taylor, *op. cit.*, pp. 30–2.
12) See B. Cunliffe, *Fishbourne*, 1971, pp. 134–8, 143–6.
13) Tacitus, *Agricola*, XIV.
14) Pliny the Elder, *Natural History*, XII, 13.
15) Pliny the Younger, *Letters*, V, 6.
16) See Webster, D., *et al.*, 'A Possible Vineyard at North Thoresby', *Lincolnshire History and Archaeology*, 2, 1967, 55–61.
17) André Simon, *The History of the Wine Trade in England*, 1906, I, 2–3.
18) Attr. to Magnobodus, c. 620, in *Monumenta Germaniae Historica: auctorum antiq.*, IV, ii, 1885, ed. Bruno Krusch, 93–4 (tr. C. T.).
19) Cf. Christopher Thacker, *The History of Gardens*, 1985, ch. 5.
20) For example, those quoted in Thomas Wright, ed., *A Volume of Vocabularies*, 1857.
21) *Ibid.*, pp. 30, 32, 33.
22) See Alicia Amherst, *A History of Gardening in England*, 1895, p. 19.
23) Bede, *The Ecclesiastical History*, ed. and tr. A. M. Sellar, 1907, pp. 5, 9.
24) Quoted in Sir H. Ellis, *General Introduction to Domesday Book*, 2v., 1833, I, 119.
25) A. Simon, *op. cit.*, p. 10.
26) Reproduced in A. Amherst, *op. cit.*, p. 21, and F. A. Roach, *Cultivated Fruits of Britain: Their Origin and History*, 1986, p. 249.
27) Rolls Series, 28, iv, 1, 1867, 21.
28) *Liber Eliensis*, ed. E. O. Blake, Camden Society Third Series, XCII, 1962, 124.
29) *The Anglo-Saxon Chronicle*, tr. J. Ingram [1823], 1934, p. 114.
30) See C. Squire, *op. cit.*, pp. 135–6.

CHAPTER 2
From the Conquest to 1200

1) *Anglo-Saxon Chronicle*, year 1085, p. 163.
2) Sir H. Ellis, *op. cit.*, I, 116, says 'at least eight and thirty', but I would reckon over 45.
3) Eadmer, in J.-P. Migne, *Patrologia Latina*, 159, 2 (1854), 428a-429.
4) Cited in John Stow, *A Survey of London*, ed. C. L. Kingsford, 2v., 1908, II, 220, 226.
5) Virgil, *Aeneid*, V, 585–91, 674.
6) Roger de Hoveden, *Chronica*, ed. W. Stubbs, Rolls Series, 1869, II, 32.
7) Giraldus Cambrensis, *The Itinerary through Wales* and *Description of Wales*, tr. R. C. Hoare [1806], 1944, p. 184.
8) *Ibid.*, pp. 106, 85.
9) Pipe Roll for 3 Henry II, quoted in W. H. St John Hope, *Windsor Castle*, 2v., 1913, I, 69 and n.
10) *Pipe Roll Society*, I, 1884, 37.
11) Hope, *op. cit.*, I, 18 n.26, 24 n.12, 35 nn 28, 29, 31.
12) *Ibid.*, 'treylicium', I, 37 nn 52–3, 41 n 96, 58 n 116.
13) T. E. Harwood, *Windsor Old and New*, 1929, p. 111.
14) H. M. Colvin *et al.*, *The History of the King's Works: the Middle Ages*, 2v., 1963, I, 910; *Pipe Roll Society*, I, 1884, 38; XII, 1890, 157.
15) See my *History of Gardens*, ch. 5.
16) H. M. Colvin, *op. cit.*, pp. 1009–10; William of Malmesbury, *Chronicle of the Kings of England*, tr. G. A. Giles, 1847, p. 443.
17) H. M. Colvin, *op. cit.*, pp. 1010–6 and pl. 52.
18) John Brompton, *Chronicon*, in Roger Twysden, *Historiae Anglicanae Scriptores*, X, 1652, I, col.1151, 43. Brompton, fl. 1436, may have derived much material from Higden and other mid-fourteenth-century sources.
19) See Bishop Percy's *Reliques of Ancient British Poetry*, 4v., 1794, II, 143–55; also

W. H. Matthews, *Mazes and Labyrinths*, 1922, 1970, 164–9.

20) Lambertus Ardensis, *Hist. Comitum Ardensium*, in P. de Ludwig, *Reliquiae Manuscriptorum*, 1727, IV, 127, 549.

21) *Pipe Roll Society*, 22 Henry II, p. 122.

22) William of Malmesbury, *De Gestis Pontificum Anglorum*, R. S., III, 1870, 259.

23) Giraldus Cambrensis, 'De Menevensi ecclesia dialogus', in *Opera*, R. S., XXI, iii, ed. J. S. Brewer, 1863, 342–3.

24) Cf. *Sussex Archaeological Collections*, I, 1848, 179 n.; G. Bunyard and G. Thomas, *The Fruit Garden*, 1904, pp. 51–3; E. V. Lucas, *Highways and Byways in Sussex*, 1904, p. 156; *The Garden*, Oct. 19, 1901, 267 8.

25) See John Harvey, *Mediaeval Gardens*, 1981, p. 54, and Daines Barrington, 'On the Trees . . . Indigenous in Great Britain', *Philosophical Transactions of the Royal Society*, LIX (1769), 596.

26) Giraldus Cambrensis, *The Autobiography*, tr. J. E. Butler, 1937, p. 71.

27) J. P. Migne, *Patrologia Latina*, 207 (1855), 15.

28) J. Harvey, *op. cit.*, ill. 28.

29) In T. Wright, *op. cit.*, pp. 110–1.

30) Giraldus Cambrensis, in *Opera*, VI, 201.

CHAPTER 3

'Hortulus Angliae'

1) Leo of Rozmital, *Travels*, tr. M. Letts, 1955, p. 53.

2) A. Amherst, *op. cit.*, pp. 40–1.

3) J. Harvey, *op. cit.*, pp. 155–6.

4) C. Thacker, *Historic Garden Tools*, 1990, p. 33.

5) H. M. Colvin, *op. cit.*, p. 381 n 3.

6) See Dorothy Gardiner, *The Story of Lambeth Palace*, 1930, pp. 19–20, quoting from Lambeth Court Roll no. 1193.

7) D. Gardiner, *op. cit.*, p. 32.

8) James Bentham, *History . . . of the Cathedral Church of Ely*, 1771, pp. 147–8.

9) *Calendar of Liberate Rolls*, 1240–45, 58.

10) W. Fordyce, *History and Antiquities of . . . Durham*, 2v., 1855, I, 550.

11) *Pipe Roll of the Bishopric of Winchester: 1210–11*, ed. N. R. Holt, 1964, pp. 95–6.

12) *Accounts of the Obedientar of Abingdon Abbey*, ed. R. E. G. Kirk, Camden Society, LI, 1892, 57–8.

13) See A. Amherst, 'A Fifteenth Century Treatise on Gardening', *Archaeologia*, LIV, I, 1894, 157–72.

14) Richard Hakluyt, The *Principal Navigations . . .* [1589], V, 1904, 241.

15) Alice M. Coats, *Flowers and Their Histories*, 1968, p. 64.

16) J. F. Roach, *op. cit.*, p. 23.

17) See J. Harvey, *op. cit.*, pp. 122–3, 163.

18) F. A. Roach, *op. cit.*, p. 312.

19) See J. Harvey, in *Garden History*, I, 1 (1972), 14–21; IV, 1, (1976), 46–57.

20) See J. Sparke, *Historiae Coenobii Scriptores*, 1723, pp. 155, 163, 164.

21) See C. Taylor, *op. cit.*, pp. 34–7.

22) See M. W. Thompson's translation, in *Mediaeval Archaeology*, 1964, p. 223.

23) John Leland, *The Itinerary in . . . 1535–1543*, ed. L. T. Smith, 1907–8, V, 109.

24) J. Harvey, *op. cit.*, pp. 156–7.

25) See J. Harvey, *op. cit.*, p. 112. No reference is given.

26) James I, King of Scotland, *The Kingis Quair*, ed. A. Lawson, 1910, pp. 16–8, with modern spelling.

27) Illustrating the *Livre du Cuer d'Amours Espris*, in the Österreichische Nationalbibliothek, Vienna.

28) *Lancelot of the Laik*, ed. W. Skeat, E.E.T.S., 1865, 11. 46–50.

29) Geoffrey Chaucer, *Complete Works*, ed. W. W. Skeat, 1915, p. 354.

30) *The Flower and the Leaf*, stanzas 7–16, in *Chaucerian and Other Pieces*, ed. W. W. Skeat, 1897, pp. 362–6.

31) See my *History of Gardens*, ch. 5, pp. 89–93.

32) Stephen Hawes, *The Pastime of Pleasure*, ed. W. E. Mead, E.E.T.S., 1928, pp. 77–80, 11. 2008–30.

33) C. S. Lewis, *The Allegory of Love*, 1971, p. 281.

34) H. M. Colvin, *op. cit.*, pp. 995, 998.

35) In F. Grose, and T. Astle, *Antiquarian Repertory*, 4v., 1808, II, 316.

36) Between 1512 and 1527 the duties of the Earl of Northumberland's gardener included 'Setting of Erbis and Clipping of Knottis', though for which of his gardens it is not clear. See T. Percy, ed., *The Earl of Northumberland's Household Book*, 1770, p. 45.

37) George Cavendish, *The Life of Cardinal Wolsey*, ed. S. W. Singer, 2nd. ed., 1827, pp. 299–301.

38) Edward Hall, *Chronicle . . . from Henry the Fourth . . . Henry the Eighth* [1548, 1550], 1809, p. 516. The roses were the red and white 'Tudor rose', combining the roses of Lancaster and York, while the pomegranates were the device of Catherine of Aragon, whom Henry VIII married in 1509.

39) *Ibid.*, p. 517.

40) *Ibid.*, p. 519.
41) *Ibid.*, p. 611.
42) *Ibid.*, p. 639.
43) H. M. Colvin, *op. cit.*, p. 949.
44) Edward Hall, *op. cit.*, 722–3.
45) Leon Battista Alberti, *De Re Aedificatoria*, IX, iv. Completed 1432, first printed 1485.
46) Quoted in Mollie Sands, *The Gardens of Hampton Court*, 1950, pp. 13–4.
47) 'Le Historye Cardinalis Eboracensis', in George Cavendish, *op. cit.*, p. 532.
48) Sir Thomas More, *Utopia*, tr. Ralph Robynson, 1551, ed. J. H. Lupton, 1895, p. 29. Cf. p. 114.
49) Quoted in A. Amherst, *op. cit.*, p. 84.
50) See *ibid.*, p. 81, and E. S. Rohde, *The Story of the Garden*, 1936, pp. 69–70.
51) See A. Amherst, *op. cit.*, pp. 88–90; also Roy Strong, *The Renaissance Garden in England*, 1979, pp. 25–8.
52) See R. Strong, *op. cit.*, pp. 64–66.
53) A. Amherst, *op. cit.*, pp. 78–9, 90.
54) John Leland, *The Itinerary . . . in or about the Years 1535–43*, ed. L. T. Smith, 1907–8, I, 52.
55) Cavendish, *op. cit.*, pp. 128–9.
56) Leland, *op. cit.*, I, 114, III, 43.
57) Leland, quoted, in Latin, in William Camden, *Britannia*, [1586], 1590, p. 212. Tr. Bentley.
58) John Dent, *The Quest for Nonsuch*, 1962, pp. 123–30.
59) In John Nichols, *The Progresses . . . of Queen Elisabeth*, 3v., 1823, I, 17–8.
60) Alberti, *op. cit.*, IX, iv.
61) Jacques Androuet Du Cerceau, *Les Plus excellents bastiments de France*, 1576–9. Several glimpses of mazes, e.g. at Gaillon or Montargis, may well be of patterns laid out much earlier in the century.
62) See E. Trollope, 'Ancient and Mediaeval Labyrinths', *Archaeological Journal*, XV, 1858, and W. H. Matthews, *op. cit.*
63) W. H. Matthews, *op. cit.*, p. 78.
64) Fitzherbert, *The Book of Husbandry*, ed. W. W. Skeat, E.E.T.S., 1882.
65) See Agnes Arber, *Herbals: Their Origin & Evolution*, ed. W. T. Stearn, 1986, pp. 41–51, 119–24. The *Libellus* is in facsimile, ed. B. D. Jackson, 1877, likewise *The Names of Herbes*, ed. J. Britten, E.E.T.S., 1881.
66) William Turner, *Names of Herbes*, pp. 36, 41, 77.
67) See O. Rackham, *op. cit.*, p. 4; Ralph Dutton, *The English Garden*, [1937], 1945, p. 40; F. A. Roach, *op. cit.*, pp. 35, 201; J. Harvey, *Early Nurserymen*, 1974, p. 28; William Lambarde, *A Perambulation of Kent*, [1576], ed. R. Church, 1970, pp. 222–3.

CHAPTER 4
The Reign of Elizabeth

1) William Harrison, *The Description of England* [1587], ed. G. Edelen, 1968, p. 265. Harrison's remarks are naive, but understandable. In later times similar claims would be made by Temple, Defoe and others, some with far less justification.
2) Sir Philip Sidney, *The Countess of Pembroke's Arcadia*, ed. E. A. Baker, n.d. (1908), pp. 11–2, 70–1.
3) Michel de Montaigne, *Journal de Voyage en Italie*, ed. C. Dédéyan, 1946, p. 413 – 'di grandissimo grido'. He also noted, p. 415, a grotto with remarkable water effects, reproducing both the sight and sound of falling rain.
4) See D. Coffin, *The Villa d'Este at Tivoli*, 1961, pp. 15–6, n 3, for the 1571 report; and John Buxton, *Sir Philip Sidney and the English Renaissance*, 1954, for Sidney's contacts in Paris and Vienna.
5) Thomas Nashe, *The Unfortunate Traveller*, [1594], in *Shorter Novels: Elizabethan*, intr. G. Sainsbury, 1929, 1966, pp. 322–4.
6) Bernard Palissy, *Oeuvres*, edd. B. Fillon and L. Audiat, 2v., 1888, I, 69–95.
7) Saluste Du Bartas, *Works*, edd. U. T. Holmes and J. C. Lyons, 3v., 1935–40, III, 1–25. Lines 473–9 and 489–502 clearly come from Palissy. Both writers show that they have read Vitruvius, *De Architectura*, X, vii and viii, on water-powered devices.
8) W. Harrison, *op. cit.*, p. 270.
9) *Ibid.*, p. 265.
10) *Ibid.*, p. 268.
11) Thomas Hill, *The Gardener's Labyrinth*, 1577, ch. ii.
12) See Mavis Batey, *Oxford Gardens*, 1982, p. 25.
13) John Stow, *Survey of London*, ed. C. L. Kingsford, 2v., 1908, II, 80.
14) *Ibid.*, I, 165; II, 78. Cf. I, 129, 301.
15) Phillip Stubbes, *The Anatomie of Abuses* [1583], ed. F. J. Furnivall, 1877–9, p. 88.
16) *Ibid.*, p. 279. Cf. the later reference, c.1625, in Philip Massinger, *The Bondman*, I, iii.
17) See, for example, John Harvey, *Early Nurserymen*, 1974, p. 30, on John Chapman, gardener at Hampton Court, and purveyor of plants and tools, and Barbara Winchester, *Tudor Family*

Portrait, 1955, pp. 116–7, on despatches of seeds from London to a manor in Northamptonshire in the 1540s.

CHAPTER 5

Gardens of the Great

1) W. Turner, *The Names of Herbes* [1548], ed. J. Britten, 1881, pp. 76, 88.
2) C. Heresbach, tr. B. Googe, *Foure Bookes of Husbandry*, 1577, 'The Epistle to the Reader'.
3) R. Holinshed, *Chronicles*, 1587, p. 1512.
4) See Sir Walter Raleigh *et al.*, *Shakespeare's England*, 2v., 1917, II, 165–6.
5) Cf. A. Amherst, *op. cit.*, pp. 24–5.
6) Similar claims are made for the grand unified plan of house and garden at Wollaton in Nottinghamshire, built in 1580–88. See R. Strong, *op. cit.*, pp. 56–7, and John Dixon Hunt, *Garden and Grove*, 1986, p. 107.
7) In John Dent, *The Quest for Nonsuch*, 1962, pp. 113–23.
8) Paul Hentzner, *Travels in England*, tr. H. Walpole [1757], 1792, pp. 58–9; Thomas Platter, *Englandfahrt im Jahre 1599*, ed. H. Hecht, 1929, pp. 77–87; *The Diary of Baron Waldstein*, tr. and ed. G. W. Groos, 1981, pp. 155–63.
9) William Lawson, *The Country House-Wife's Garden* [1617] ... and selections from *A New Orchard and Garden* [1618], intr. Rosemary Verey, 1983, p. 62.
10) See R. Strong, *op. cit.*, pp. 38–9, 63–9, and J. D. Hunt, *op. cit.*, pp. 103–4.
11) See Elizabeth H. Whittle, 'The Renaissance Gardens of Raglan Castle', *Garden History*, XVII, 1, Spring 1989, 83–94.
12) John Aubrey, *Brief Lives*, ed. Andrew Clark, 2v., 1898, I, 311.
13) See C. Thacker, 'A Note on Wilton, and Adrian Gilbert', *Wiltshire Gardens Trust Journal*, 24, Autumn 1991, pp. 13–5.
14) John Taylor, *A New Discovery by Sea ...* 1623, in C. Hindley, ed., *The Old Book Collector's Miscellany*, 1873, III, 36–9.
15) Joshua Sylvester, *The Complete Works*, ed. A. B. Grosart, 2v., 1880, *Eden. The First Part of the First Day of the II Week*, 11. 560–3.
16) See Prudence Leith-Ross, *The John Tradescants*, 1984, p. 46.
17) Cf. Agnes Arber, *op. cit.*, pp. 89–91.
18) See Vendeuheym in W. B. Rye, *England as Seen by Foreigners*, 1885, p. 62; *The Diary of Baron Waldstein*, pp. 163–5; Thomas Coryate, *Crudities*, [1611], 2v., 1905, II, 36.
19) J. Nichols, *Progresses*, III, 441, 513.
20) See A. Amherst, *op. cit.*, pp. 152–4.
21) John Evelyn, *Diary*, ed. E. S. de Beer, 1952, pp. 393, 1059–60.
22) J. Gibson, 'A Short Account of Several Gardens near London ... in December 1691', *Archaeologia*, XII, 1796, 182.
23) Sir Hugh Platt, *The Jewel House of Art and Nature* [1608], 1653, p. 5.
24) John Gerard, *A Catalogue of Plants ... 1596–1599*, ed. B. D. Jackson, 1876. See p. xiii, where two earlier, and similar continental works, by Conrad Gesner and Johann Franke, are mentioned.
25) See B. D. Jackson, 'On a Draft of a Letter ... by John Gerard', *Cambridge Antiquarian Communications*, IV, 1881, 7–8.
26) Richard Hakluyt, *The Principal Navigations* [1589, and 1598–1600], 1904, V, 229. Cf. 230–9.
27) *Ibid.*, V, 241–2. For the dates of these introductions, cf. Alice M. Coats, *Flowers and Their Histories*, and F. A. Roach, *op. cit.* For the 'Tulipas' see particularly *The Turkish Letters of Ogier Ghiselin de Busbecq*, tr. E. S. Forster, 1927, pp. 24–5.
28) From 'an anonymous contemporary manuscript', in Francis Peck, *Desiderata curiosa*, 1779, I, 26, ch. xviii, para. 13.
29) P. Hentzner, *Travels*, p. 38.
30) Waldstein, *op. cit.*, pp. 82, 87.
31) In Rye, *op. cit.*, p. 44, and Waldstein, *op. cit.*, p. 82.
32) Orazio Busino, quoted in the *Quarterly Review*, CII, no. 204, Oct. 1857, 435. This heraldic bedding, or something closely comparable, survived until 1650, when a Parliamentary survey was made.
33) Quoted, without source, in E. S. Rohde, *op. cit.*, p. 81.
34) See A. Amherst, *op. cit.*, pp. 312–22.
35) From Ben Jonson, *The Forrest*, II, 'To Penshurst', in Alexander Chalmers, ed., *The Works of the English Poets*, 21 v., 1810, V, 515.
36) See J. Nichols, *op. cit.*, *passim*; see *ibid.*, III, 101 for the 'Engraving of the Great Pond' at Elvetham; and Jean Wilson, *Entertainments for Elizabeth I*, 1980.
37) For Norden and Rathgeb, see Rye, *op. cit.*, pp. 207, 19; P. Hentzner, *op. cit.*, p. 58; T. Platter, *op. cit.*, pp. 90–1; Waldstein, *op. cit.*, p. 147.
38) In J. Nichols, *op. cit.*, 420–523. The garden description is on pp. 472–7.
39) *Ibid.*, p. 427.
40) In Nichols, *ibid.*, I, 553–5, II, 94–103. Cf. J. Wilson, *op. cit.*, pp. 57–8 and nn.
41) See J. Nichols, *op. cit.*, III, 75, 241–5; George Peele, *Works*, ed. A. H. Bullen, 2 v., 1888, II, 304–14.

42) Related in J. Nichols, *op. cit.*, III, 101–21.

43) See *Antiquity*, LVI, 216, (1982), 46–7 and pl.III on the aerial view of the probable site.

CHAPTER 6

Of Gardens and Grottoes

1) See P. Leith-Ross, *op. cit.*, pp. 28–30.

2) *Ibid.*, pp. 28–42.

3) A. Amherst, *op. cit.*, p. 155.

4) Gladys Taylor, *Old London Gardens*, 1977, pp. 161–4; Peter Coats, *The Gardens of Buckingham Palace*, 1978, pp. 14–24.

5) H. M. Colvin, *History of the King's Works*, IV, 213–4.

6) P. Leith-Ross, *op. cit.*, pp. 93, 106, 114.

7) J. W. Neumayr, *Reise in Frankreich, Engelland und Niederland*, 1620, 2v., I, 184–5.

8) See R. Strong, *op. cit.*, pp. 87–101, for dates and details of de Caus' work in England – a period of his life about which relatively little is known.

9) See P. Leith-Ross, *op. cit.*, pp. 37–8, 41–2.

10) B. Palissy, *op. cit.*, I, liii-liv.

11) J. W. Neumayr, *op. cit.*, I, 211–12.

12) P. Hentzner, *op. cit.*, p. 37. The old tower may be seen in an anonymous painting of Greenwich, c.1580–90, reproduced in John Harris, *The Artist and the Country House*, 1979, ill. 18.

13) The name 'Mirefleur' is also taken up around 1590 by Sir Arthur Gorges, in 'A pastorall unfynyshed', when the glorious 'Eglantyne' – Elizabeth herself – is said to live 'in plesaunte Meryfleur'. Sir Arthur Gorges, *Poems*, ed. H. E. Sandison, 1953, pp. 124–5.

14) John Donne, *Complete Poetry and Selected Prose*, ed. J. Hayward, 1949, p. 20.

15) See David Jacques, 'The Chief Ornament of Gray's Inn', *Garden History*, XVII, 1, Spring 1989, 41–67.

16) J. Aubrey, *op. cit.*, I, 83.

17) British Museum ADD MSS 27, 278, 24–5.

18) J. Aubrey, *op. cit.*, I, 78–81.

19) Charlotte Grimston, *The History of Gorhambury*, n.d., (1821 or later), p. 56.

20) Francis Bacon, *Sylva sylvarum*, in *Works*, ed. J. Spedding, 1886, II, 475–527.

21) T. Coryate, *op. cit.*, I, 176.

22) From J. Aubrey, *loc. cit.*, and Lt. Hammond, 'Relation of a short Survey of The Western Counties', ed. L. G. Wickham Legg, *Camden Miscellany*, XVI, 1936, 81–3. These and other matters on Bushell are discussed in C. Thacker 'An

Extraordinary Solitude', in *Of Oxfordshire Gardens*, by S. Raphael, C. Thacker *et al.*, 1982, pp. 25–48.

23) Thomas Bushell, 'Post-Script to the Judicious Reader', in *An Extract by Mr Bushell of . . . Bacons Philosophical Theory in Mineral Prosecutions*, 1660, pp. 21–2.

24) Robert Burton, *The Anatomy of Melancholy* [1621], ed. H. Jackson, 3 v., 1948, II, 74–5.

25) James Howell, *Epistolae Ho-Elianae*, ed. J. Jacobs, 2 v., 1892, I, 106–7.

26) Daniel Defoe, *A Tour thro' the Whole Island of Great Britain*, 2nd. ed., 3 v., 1738, III, 270.

27) Fynes Morison, 'Description of Ireland', in *Ireland under Elizabeth and James the First*, ed. Henry Morley, 1890, pp. 419, 421.

28) Sir John Davies, 'A Discovery of the True Causes Why Ireland . . .' in *ibid.*, p. 289.

29) Sir John Harington, *Nugae antiquae*, ed. Thomas Park, 2 v., 1804, I, 275–7.

30) Sir William Brereton, *Travels in Holland . . . and Ireland*, ed. Edward Hawkins, Chetham Soc., 1844, I, 135.

31) Psalm 103, v. 15–16. See Sir Herbert Maxwell, *Scottish Gardens*, 1908, p. 39. Cf. Gavin Maxwell, *The House of Elrig*, 1965, p. 5.

32) John Chamberlain, *Letters*, ed. N. E. McClure, 2 v., 1939, I, 227, 234–5.

33) J. Aubrey, *op. cit.*, I, 312.

34) Sir Henry Wotton, *The Elements of Architecture* [1624], in *Reliquiae Wottonianae*, ed. Isaac Walton, 1685, pp. 64–5.

35) J. Chamberlain, *op. cit.*, I, 290.

36) *Ibid.*, I, 468.

37) H. Wotton, *op. cit.*, p. 64.

38) *Ibid.*, p. 8.

39) John Aubrey, *The Natural History of Wiltshire*, ed. J. Britton, 1847, p. 93.

40) There is a long description by Aubrey in 1691, adding to his comments in *Brief Lives*, held in the Bodleian Library, Oxford, Aubrey MS 2, f. 53–6, with a sketch, f. 59. The description is reproduced in A. M. Charles, *A Life of George Herbert*, 1977, pp. 61–5.

41) R. Strong, *op. cit.*, pp. 176–9; J. D. Hunt, *op. cit.*, pp. 126–30.

42) A. M. Charles, *op. cit.*, pp. 63–4.

43) J. Aubrey, *Brief Lives*, ed. Richard Barber, 1975, p. 96.

44) In John Aubrey, *Monumenta Britannica* [c. 1690], ed. John Fowles, 1980, p. 312.

45) J. Leland, *op. cit.*, III, 102.

46) William Stukeley, *Itinerarium curiosum*, 2nd. ed., 2 v., 1776, *Iter* iv, September 1721, p. 67.

47) J. Evelyn, *Diary*, p. 464. The next day, Evelyn went on to see Bushell's 'extraordinary solitude' at Enstone.

48) Nicholas Stone, *The Note-Book and Account Book of*, ed. W. L. Spiers, Walpole Society, 1919, pp. 70–1.

49) P. Leith-Ross, *op. cit.*, pp. 97–8; Sandra Raphael, 'The Oxford Botanic Garden', in *Of Oxfordshire Gardens*, pp. 1–24.

50) The painting is in the Queen's House, Greenwich (National Maritime Museum).

51) Quoted in Sir R. Rait, *Five Stuart Princesses*, 1902, pp. 54–5.

52) See Giacomo Castelvetro, *The Fruit, Herbs and Vegetables of Italy*, tr. and intr. G. Riley, 1989.

53) See John Summerson, *Architecture in Britain 1530 to 1830*, 1963, pp. 77, 351.

54) See my *History of Gardens*, ch. 10.

CHAPTER 7

'The Best Figure of a Garden'

1) W. Lawson, *op. cit.*, pp. 59–62.

2) R. T. Gunther, 'The Garden of the Rev. Walter Stonehouse . . . 1640', *The Gardeners' Chronicle*, 15 May 1920.

3) Sir Thomas Hanmer, *The Garden Book*, intr. E. S. Rohde, 1933, 1991, p. xix.

4) See W. G. Hiscock, *John Evelyn and His Family*, 1955, pp. 28–32. Hiscock however misunderstands Evelyn's words, taking the area of the whole property as the area of the garden.

5) Sir William Temple, 'Upon the Gardens of *Epicurus*; or of Gardening in the Year 1685', [1685], in Temple, *Miscellanea*, 2 pts., 1697, II, 109.

6) *Ibid.*, II, 126–7.

7) Thomas Dineley, 'Extracts from the Journal . . . to Ireland', *Journal of the Kilkenny . . . Archaeological Society*, N.S, IV, 1862–3, 41.

8) Sir W. Temple, *op. cit.*, pp. 131–3.

9) See C. Taylor, *op. cit.*, pp. 16–8.

10) See *Country Life*, 26 Jan. and 2 Feb. 1961, 5 Mar. 1992.

11) Sir W. Brereton, *op. cit.*, p. 127.

12) See *The Coltness Collections*, ed. James Dennistoun (Maitland Club), 1842, pp. 55–6.

13) My information comes from Mr Donovan Hadley, of Dromin House, Listowel, Co. Kerry, to whom I am deeply obliged.

14) Thomas Dineley, *The Account of the Official Progress of His Grace the First Duke of Beaufort . . . through Wales in 1684*, pref.

Richard W. Banks, 1888, pp. 246, 358, 375.

15) Reproduced in J. Harris, *op. cit.*, pl. III.

16) Cf. J. D. Hunt, *op. cit.*, pp. 131–2.

17) See J. Harris, *op. cit.*, p. 130.

18) J. Aubrey, *Natural History of Wiltshire*, ed. John Britton, 1847, p. 119.

19) Aubrey MS 17, in the Bodleian Library. Cf. J. D. Hunt, *op. cit.*, pp. 153–7, for several of Aubrey's sketches.

CHAPTER 8

'The Noblest in All England'

1) See John Bold, with John Reeves, *Wilton House and English Palladianism*, 1988, pp. 33–43; also Timothy Mowl and Brian Earnshaw, 'Inigo Jones Restored', *Country Life*, 30 Jan. 1992, pp. 46–9.

2) J. Bold and J. Reeves, *op. cit.*, pp. 43, 91.

3) *Ibid.*, p. 25 and n. 7.

4) See the northward view of the garden, with the proposed south front of the house, extending across the garden to match the garden scheme, in *ibid.*, p. 37.

5) J. Evelyn, *Diary*, p. 73.

6) See my *History of Gardens*, ch. 9, and T. Coryate, *op. cit.*, I, 175–6, 188.

7) By Henry Winstanley, reproduced in J. Harris, *op. cit.*, as fig. 88a.

8) From the 'Survey of Wimbledon' undertaken in 1649, reproduced in A. Amherst, *op. cit.*, p. 310.

9) Cf. A. Amherst, *op. cit.*, pp. 307–9.

10) See H. M. Colvin, *History of the King's Works*, IV, 215; P. Leith-Ross, *op. cit.*, p. 96.

11) *Ibid.*, pp. 73–7.

12) 'Ground Plan of ye old house', in Pearl Finch, *The History of Burley-on-the-Hill*, 2 v., 1901, I, 6.

13) In J. Harris, *op. cit.*, pl. 92a.

14) In *ibid.*, pl. 66a, b.

15) See P. Leith-Ross, *op. cit.*, pp. 44–6.

16) Lt. Hammond, *op. cit.*, pp. 18–9.

17) In P. Leith-Ross, *op. cit.*, pl. 3.

18) See Larch S. Garrad, *A History of Manx Gardens*, 1985, pp. 21–2.

19) See R. T. Gunther, *op. cit.*, in *Gardeners' Chronicle*, 15, 22, 29 May and 12 June 1920.

20) J. Evelyn, *Diary*, p. 337.

21) In J. Harris, *op. cit.*, pl. 27.

22) See Daines Barrington, 'On the Progress of Gardening', *Archaeologia*, VII, 1785, 128; M. R. Gloag, *A Book of English Gardens*, 1906, pp. 19–34; Nikolaus Pevsner, *Berkshire*, 1966, p. 216.

23) Henry G. de Bunsen, *Boscobel*, 1878, p. 15.

24) John Buxton, *New College, Oxford: a Note on the Garden*, 1976, and Mavis Batey, *op. cit.*, pp. 42–3.

25) Gervase Markham, *Cheape and Good Husbandry*, 3rd. ed., 1623, p. 174. The following section, 'Of Fishing', pp. 175 ff., was printed in the 1st. ed. of 1614, pp. 158 ff., but without the illustration. At no point does Markham refer to Tackley.

26) J. Evelyn, *Diary*, pp. 47 and n., 318.

27) *Ibid.*, p. 317.

28) Ian Nairn and N. Pevsner, *Surrey*, 1962, p. 453.

29) The plan, which is held in the Library of Christ Church, Oxford, is reproduced in W. G. Hiscock, *op. cit.*, pp. 28–32, with a full and clear commentary.

30) It is reproduced in John Prest, *The Garden of Eden*, 1981, ill. 34.

31) J. Evelyn, *Diary*, 9 June 1698, p. 1025.

32) J. Evelyn, *Sylva*, 4th. ed., 1706, ed. John Nisbet, 2 v., n.d., c.1908, II, 176–7.

33) In J. Harris, *op. cit.*, ill. 23a-e. The views were engraved by Hollar in 1645, but may have been drawn in the 1630s.

34) J. Evelyn, *Fumifugium*, 1661, pp. 46–9.

35) Thomas Johnson, *Botanical Journeys in Kent and Hampstead*, ed. J. S. L. Gilmour, 1972, pp. 1–4.

36) Joseph C. Walker, 'Essay on the Rise and Progress of Gardening in Ireland', *Transactions of the Royal Irish Academy*, 1790, IV, 14.

CHAPTER 9

'So Mightily Improved'

1) In A. Chalmers, *Works of the English Poets*, VIII, 62.

2) J. Evelyn, *Diary*, 9 June 1662, p. 439.

3) Celia Fiennes, *The Journeys*, ed. Christopher Morris, 1967, p. 356.

4) See my *History of Gardens*, ch. 10.

5) Martin Lister, *A Journey to Paris in the Year 1698*, 1699, pp. 198, 203.

6) See David Green, *Gardener to Queen Anne: Henry Wise*, 1956, pp. 87–8.

7) See Donald Mallett, 'Le Nôtre jardinier de l'Europe', *Medecine de France*, 219, 1971, 28–31. Cf. D. Green, *op. cit.*, pp. 15–6.

8) Béat Louis de Muralt, *Lettres sur les Anglois* ... [1725], 2nd. ed., 1727, p. 87, tr. C. T.

9) Anthony Ashley Cooper, 3rd Earl of Shaftesbury, *The Moralists*, 1709, III, ii, 125.

10) Marot's drawing is held by the Boymans-van Beuningen Museum, Rotterdam. Cf. the etching, 'Parterre d'Anton-court inventé par D. Marot' in Daniel Marot, *Oeuvres*, 1703. Knyff's painting is at Hampton Court.

11) See *Garden History*, Autumn 1974, III, 4, 66–78.

12) *Vitruvius Britannicus* was reprinted in 1967. See also: John Slezer, *Theatrum Scotiae*, 1693; Sir Henry Chauncy, *Historical Antiquities of Hertfordshire*, 1700; Sir Robert Atkyns, *The Ancient and Present State of Glostershire*, 1712; Dr John Harris, *The History of Kent*, 1719. Some fifty views by these artists are reproduced in *English Houses and Gardens*, ed. Mervyn Macartney, 1908. See also the copious reproductions, and commentary, in J. Harris, *The Artist and the Country House*, 1979.

13) John Evelyn, *Diary*, 17–18 October 1664.

14) See J. Harvey, *Early Nurserymen*, pp. 51–6.

15) In Beeverell, *Les Délices de la Grande Bretagne*, 1707, and reproduced in A. Amherst, *op. cit.*, p. 229.

16) E. Malins and the Knight of Glin, *op. cit.*, pp. 6–7.

17) T. Dineley, 'Extracts from the Journal ... to Ireland', 104–6.

18) H. M. Colvin, *Biographical Dictionary of British Architects 1600–1840*, 1978.

19) Samuel Pepys, *Diary*, ed. Henry B. Wheatley, 8 v., 1924, V, 348.

20) Sir W. Temple, *op. cit.*, p. 110.

21) J. Aubrey, *Natural History of Wiltshire*, p. 93.

22) J. W. (John Worlidge or Woolridge), *Systema Horti-Culturae*, 1677, p. 19.

23) T. Dineley, *Account of the ... Progress*, pp. 85–6.

24) See D. Green, *op. cit.*, p. 111.

25) R. C. H. M., *Inventory of Historic Sites: Central Northants*, 1979, pp. 60–1.

26) Saint-Évremond, *Letters*, ed. and tr. John Hayward, 1930, p. 356.

27) John Morton, *The Natural History of Northamptonshire*, 1712, p. 491. Detailed analysis of the gardens at Boughton is in R.C.H.M., ... *Central Northants*, pp. 156–62.

28) Quoted in Elisabeth Whittle, *op. cit.*, p. 25.

29) *Ibid.*, p. 32.

30) John Byng, *The Torrington Diaries*, ed. C. Bruyn Andrews, 4 v., 1934, I, 137.

31) For Kilruddery and Carton, see E. Malins and the Knight of Glin, *op. cit.*, pp. 9–12.

32) *Ibid.*, pp. 19–20.

33) Quoted from Thomas Morer, *A Short Account of Scotland*, (1689), in E.H.M. Cox, *A History of Gardens in Scotland*, 1935, p. 44.

34) John Reid, *The Scots Gard'ner*, 1683, pp. 22, 107, 112–4. This text was reprinted in facsimile, intr. Annette Hope, in 1988.

35) James Macky, *A Journey through Scotland* [1723], 2nd. ed., 1732, pp. 31–2.

36) Samuel Boyse, 'Retirement', in A. Chalmers, *op. cit.*, XIV, 577–8.

37) J. Macky, *op. cit.*, pp. 202–3.

38) D. Defoe, *op. cit.*, III, 285–6; J. Macky, *op. cit.*, pp. 50–1.

39) Reproduced in E.H.M. Cox, *op. cit.*, pl. 7.

40) J. Macky, *op. cit.*, p. 281.

41) *The Spectator*, no. 477, 6 Sep. 1712.

42) See D. Green, *op. cit.*, p. 31.

43) D. Defoe, *op. cit.*, III, 55–6.

44) C. Fiennes, *op. cit.*, p. 236.

45) See Christopher Hussey, *English Gardens and Landscapes 1700–1750*, 1967, pp. 119–25.

CHAPTER 10

All Change

1) D. Defoe, *op. cit.*, I, 166.

2) Treasury Papers, cclxiii (Public Records Office), quoted in D. Green, *op. cit.*, pp. 148–50.

3) Thomas Jefferson, *Garden Book*, ed. Edwin Morris Betts, 1944, p. 111.

4) *Architectural History*, VII, 1964, 70.

5) James Thomson, *Complete Poetical Works*, ed. J. Logie Robertson, 1908, p. 156. The full passage on Eastbury in the 1748 edition of *Autumn* covers 11. 654–82.

6) For Bilton, see S. Ireland, *Picturesque Views on the . . . Avon*, 1795, pp. 69–71. The main developments at Wimborne St Giles are the work of the 4th Earl of Shaftesbury in the 1750s.

7) *The Letters of Sir Thomas Browne*, ed. Geoffrey Keynes, 1945, p. 301.

8) Shaftesbury, *The Moralists* [1709], in *Characteristics*, ed. J. M. Robertson, 1964, III, ii, 125. Cf. Thacker, *The Wildness Pleases: the Origins of Romanticism*, 1983, ch. 2.

9) Shaftesbury, *The Life, Unpublished Letters and Philosophical Regimen*, ed. Benjamin Rand, 1900, pp. 247–51.

10) See Thacker, *The Wildness Pleases*, p. 32.

11) Batty Langley, *New Principles of Gardening*, 1723, pl. 14.

12) Cf. Mrs Calderwood's comments in 1756, *The Coltness Collections*, pp. 152–4; and Joseph Cradock's strictures in the 1780s, in his *Literary and Miscellaneous Memoirs*, 4 v., 1828, I, 270, II, 312–3.

13) Cf. Peter Willis, *Charles Bridgeman and the English Landscape Garden*, 1977, *passim*.

14) C. Fiennes, *op. cit.*, p. 30; C. Hussey, *op. cit.*, pl. 114.

15) In C. Hussey, *op. cit.*, pp. 95–6.

16) See Mavis Batey, *op. cit.*, pp. 106–8.

17) See Sir George Clutton and Colin Mackay, 'Old Thorndon Hall, Essex', Garden History Society, *Occasional Paper*, no. 2, 1970, 27–40.

18) *The World*, no. 118, 3 April 1755.

19) *The Spectator*, no. 477, 6 Sep. 1712.

20) Horace Walpole, 'Of Modern Gardening' [1771], in *Anecdotes of Painting in England*, ed. Ralph N. Wornum, 3 v., 1876, III, 80.

21) See my *History of Gardens* for general comment on the ha-ha. An oddity in its career is that the ah-ah first mentioned in French in 1709 should be excessively rare in France. *Vive la différence!*

22) William Stukeley, *Itinerarium curiosum*, 1724, Iter II, p. 44.

23) In C. Hussey, *op. cit.*, pp. 95–6.

24) Quoted by J. C. Loudon, without further reference, in *The Gardener's Magazine*, III, 12, 1828, 480.

25) In Ragnar Josephson, 'Le Grand Trianon sous Louis XIV', *La Gazette des Beaux-Arts*, 1927, p. 21; cf. my *History of Gardens*, p. 156.

26) Daines Barrington, *op. cit.*, p. 127.

27) In J. Harris, *op. cit.*, ill. 187g.

28) D. Green, *op. cit.*, p. 77 and pl. 25.

29) In William Shenstone, *Works*, 2 v., 1764, II, 384–5.

30) *The World*, no. 15, 12 April 1753.

31) In Joseph Addison, *Works*, ed. Richard Hurd, 6 v., 1856, I, 29.

32) Note that Horace's poem ends with the speaker changing his mind and returning to the cares of business – he is a usurer. The classical theme of rural retirement, as seen in British life between 1600 and 1760, is fully studied in Maren-Sophie Røstvig, *The Happy Man*, 2 v., 1954–8.

33) 'Down-Hall: A Ballad', in Matthew Prior, *Literary Works*, edd. H. Bunker Wright and Monroe K. Spears, 2 v., 1971, I, 550–7.

34) Hist. MSS Comm., *Calendar of the MSS of the Marquis of Bath*, 3 v., 1908, III, 504, 488–9, 492. Cf. P. Willis, *op. cit.*, pp. 73–5 and pl. 67.

35) 28 July 1721, in Jonathan Swift, *Works*, ed. J. Hawkesworth, 18 v., 1778, XV, 291–3.

36) See Kenneth Woodbridge, 'Bolingbroke's château of La Source', *Garden History*, IV, 3, 1976, 50–64.

37) 28 June 1728, in J. Swift, *Works*, XVI, 128.

38) 28 April 1748, in Lady Luxborough, *Letters*, 1775, p. 22.

39) Stephen Switzer, *Ichnographia rustica*, 'Appendix' to v. III (1742), pp. 8–9.

40) Joseph Spence, *Observations, Anecdotes, and Characters of Books and Men*, ed. James M. Osborn, 2 v., 1966, 1125, 1126.

41) See my *History of Gardens*, ch. 6.

42) Vincenzo Scamozzi, *L'Idea dell'architettura universale*, 1615. Tr. as *Oeuvres d'architecture*, 1713. J. F. Félibien des Avaux, *Les Plans et les descriptions de deux des plus belles maisons de campagne de Pline le Jeune*, 1699. Further editions, some included in larger works, in 1705, 1706, 1707, 1725, 1736.

43) See H. M. Colvin, *A Biographical Dictionary*.

44) It is then discussed by other, continental commentators on Pliny. See Helen H. Tanzer, *The Villas of Pliny the Younger*, 1924.

45) Robert Castell, *The Villas of the Ancients Illustrated*, 1728, p. 32.

CHAPTER 11

Burlington, Kent, Pope – and Paradise

1) Pub. 1720. See John Gay, *Poetry and Prose*, edd. Vinton A. Dearing and Charles E. Beckwith, 2 v., 1974, I, 203.

2) See J. Harris, *op. cit.*, ill. 187a, c, e, g.

3) See J. D. Hunt, *op. cit.*, p. 199.

4) G. Falda, *Fontane di Roma*, 1675.

5) H. Walpole, 'On Modern Gardening', pp. 81–5.

6) See John Harris, 'Esher Place, Surrey', *Country Life*, 2 April 1987, 94–7.

7) C. Hussey, *op. cit.*, p. 80.

8) 'Epistle to Lord Burlington', *Moral Essays*, IV.

9) 15 Sep. 1721, to Lady Mary Wortley Montagu, in Alexander Pope, *Correspondence*, ed. G. Sherburn, 5 v., 1956, II, 82.

10) George Lord Lyttleton, *Works*, 3 v., 1776, III, 309.

11) In J. Swift, *Works*, XVII, 87.

12) 3 Feb 1722/3, in John Gay, *Letters*, ed. C. F. Burgess, 1966, p. 43.

13) Imitations of Horace, Ode IV, 1, 21–4, in Alexander Pope, *Poetical Works*, 10 v., 1938–67, IV, 151–2.

14) 'Inventory of Pope's Goods Taken after his Death', *Notes and Queries*, series 6, v. 5, 13 May 1882, 363–5.

15) See John Serle (or Searle), *A Plan of Mr Pope's Garden . . . with a . . . View of the Grotto . . . with an Account of the Gems, Minerals, Spars, and Ores . . .*, 1745.

16) 'To Mr Pope. Nov 7, 1733', in Aaron Hill, *Works*, 2v., 1754, I, 239–40.

17) A. Hill, *Ibid.*, I, 251–65. Hill had Huguenot connections, which may explain a knowledge of Palissy.

18) Cf. Morrice R. Brownell, *Alexander Pope's Villa* (exhibition catalogue, Greater London Council), 1980, pp. 9, 57–65.

19) Quoted in C. Hussey, *op. cit.*, p. 45.

20) In J. Spence, *op. cit.*, 606.

21) *Ibid.*, 1129.

22) Cf. R. W. King, 'Joseph Spence of Byfleet', in *Garden History*, VI, 3 (Winter 1978), VII, 3 (Winter 1979), VIII, 2 (Summer 1980), VIII, 3 (Winter 1980).

23) See Thacker, *The Wildness Pleases*, pp. 34–6, and Margaret Jourdain, *The Work of William Kent*, 1948, p. 76.

24) Joseph Spence, *op. cit.*, 603, post-1751; 1122, c.1752.

25) See my article 'The Temple of the Sibyl' in *Park und Garten im 18ten Jahrhundert* (Carl Winter, Heidelberg, 1978), pp. 29–35.

26) Horace Walpole, 'Journals of Visits to Country Seats', *Walpole Society*, XVI, 1928, 26–7; 'On Modern Gardening', p. 84.

27) Edward Young, *Correspondence, 1683–1765*, ed. Henry Pettit, 1971, p. 54.

28) In *The World*, no. 6, 1753 – written probably by Francis Coventry. For Richmond, Kent's buildings and Stephen Duck, see B. Sprague Allen, *Tides in English Taste*, 2v., 1937, II, 135–8, and C. Thacker, *The Wildness Pleases*, pp. 67–8.

29) Henry Hoare, letter of 23 Oct. 1762, quoted in Kenneth Woodbridge, *Landscape and Antiquity*, 1970, pp. 52–3.

30) In William Shenstone, *Works*, 2v., 1744, 125, 129.

31) Gilpin to Mason, 15 Jan 1782, quoted in Carl Paul Barbier, *William Gilpin*, 1963, p. 120.

32) Reynolds in 1791. Quoted in C. R. Leslie and T. Taylor, *Life of Sir Joshua Reynolds*, 2v., 1865, II, 607.

33) Quoted in J. Spence, *op. cit.*, 1129–33.

34) *Ibid.*, 1127.

35) R. Pococke, *Travels through England*, ed. James Joel Cartwright, 2v., 1888, II, 260.

36) See J. Spence, *op. cit.*, ill facing p. 424, and detailed comment in R. W. King, 'The

"Ferme Ornée": Philip Southcote and Wooburn Farm', *Garden History*, II, 3, Summer 1974, 27–60. Mr King suggests, p. 41, that the 'fence' may at some points have been a ha-ha.

37) From a Renaissance, not a Roman text. See Kenneth Woodbridge, *The Stourhead Landscape*, 1986, p. 47.

38) Quoted in Kenneth Woodbridge, *Landscape and Antiquity*, 1970, p. 53.

39) In *Ibid.*, p. 62.

40) See also my *Enchanting Paths: the Gardens of Painshill, Stourhead and Fonthill*, due to appear in 1994.

CHAPTER 12

'Divini Gloria Ruris'

1) Reported in Richard Graves, *Columella; or the Distressed Anchoret*, 2 v., 1779, I, 128.

2) And on for three more stanzas. In 'A Description of the Leasowes', by Robert Dodsley, in W. Shenstone, *op. cit.*, II, 335–6.

3) Samuel Johnson, *Works*, 12 v., 1796, XI, 278.

4) In W. Shenstone, *op. cit.*, II, 360.

5) From Lady Luxborough *op. cit.*, pp. 38, 163, 224, 97, 126; the flowers on pp. 126–7.

6) See Thacker, *The Wildness Pleases*, pp. 36–7, 193.

7) Lady Luxborough, *op. cit.*, pp. 31, 298, 382; 232–3, 31.

8) Cf. Thacker, *The Wildness Pleases*, pp. 48–9.

9) William Shenstone, *Letters*, ed. Marjorie Williams, 1939, pp. 147–8.

10) R. Pococke, *op. cit.*, I, 225.

11) Joseph Heely, *Letters on the Beauties of Hagley, Envil and the Leasowes*, 2 v., 1777, I, 152–3.

12) Letter of 10 Sep. 1731, in Mary Granville, Mrs Delany, *Autobiography and Correspondence*, ed. Lady Llanover, 6v., 1861–2, I, 287.

13) 13 Aug. 1732, in *ibid.*, I, 372. Cf. I, 382–3.

14) 30 March 1732, in *ibid.*, I, 344–5.

15) 2 Sep. 1736, in J. Swift, *Works*, XVIII, 30.

16) 19 July 1744, to Mrs Dewes, in Mrs Delany, *op. cit.*, II, 314–6.

17) *Ibid.*, I, 405–6.

18) Letters of 5 April 1733, in *ibid.*, I, 405–6, and 5 Aug. 1748, II, 501–3.

19) E. Malins and the Knight of Glin, *op. cit.*, p. 41.

20) *Ibid.*, p. 45, ill. 51.

21) Letter of 2 Aug. 1748, in Mrs Delany, *op. cit.*, II, 492–3.

22) Republished by Eileen Harris, as Thomas Wright, *Arbours and Grottos*, 1979.

23) See E. Malins and the Knight of Glin, *op. cit.*, pp. 85–7.

24) Quoted in William Spink, 'Sir John Clerk of Penicuik', in *Furor hortensis*, ed. Peter Willis, 1974, p. 32.

25) Sir John Clerk, *Memoirs . . . 1676–1755*, ed. John M. Gray, Scottish History Society, XIII, 1892; R. Pococke, *op. cit.*, I, 26–7.

26) From Sir John Clerk, 'The Country Seat', printed in part in J. D. Hunt and P. Willis, *The Genius of the Place: the English Landscape Garden 1620–1820*, 1975, p. 201. Clerk's poem has never been printed in full.

27) See Priscilla Minay, 'Early Improvements in the Eighteenth-Century Lothians', *Bulletin of the Scottish Georgian Society*, 2, 1973, 3–46; P. Minay, 'James Justice (1698–1763)', *Garden History*, I, 2, 1973, 41–62, II, 2, 1974, 51–74, III, 2, 1975, 37–67, and IV, 2, 1976, 53–91. For the 'Pine Apple Stove' see II, 2, 55–6.

28) Sir J. Clerk, *Memoirs*, pp. 164–5.

29) R. Pococke, *op. cit.*, I, 215; Samuel Johnson, 'A Journey into North Wales in the Year 1774', in James Boswell, *Life of Johnson*, edd. G. B. Hill and C. F. Powell, 5 v., 1964, V, 434; *Torrington Diaries*, II, 54.

30) For Piercefield, see E. Whittle, *op. cit.*, pp. 50–1; for Thicknesse, see Philip Gosse, *Dr Viper*, 1952, pp. 145–6.

31) *Torrington Diaries*, I, 28.

32) William Gilpin, *Observations on the River Wye, 1770*, 1782, pp. 42–3.

33) Sir Richard Colt Hoare, *The Journeys of . . .*, ed. M. W. Thompson, 1983, pp. 149–9.

34) See Catherine Thompson-McCausland, 'Separated by Nature', *Country Life*, 13 Feb. 1992, 30–3.

35) In Boswell, *Life of Johnson*, V, 433–4.

36) Sir R. C. Hoare, *Journeys*, pp. 192–5; for the hermit, see Thacker, *The Wildness Pleases*, pp. 128–9.

CHAPTER 13

'One Brown'

1) Letter of 22 July 1751, in H. Walpole, *Correspondence*, ed. W. S. Lewis *et al.*, 48 v., 1937–83, IX, 121.

2) See Dorothy Stroud, *Capability Brown*, 1975, pp. 122–5.
3) See D. Stroud *ibid.*, p. 101.
4) Quoted in D. Stroud, *ibid.*, pp. 156–7.
5) Mrs Delany, *Autobiography and Correspondence*, III, 435.
6) In A. Chalmers, *op. cit.*, XVIII, 291.
7) See Thacker, *Masters of the Grotto*, 1976, p. 22.
8) Mme d'Arblay (née Fanny Burney), *Diary and Letters*, 3v., 1842, III, 79.
9) See Fiona Cowell, 'Richard Woods', *Garden History*, XIV, 2 (Autumn 1986), 91–4, 105–9, 114–5.
10) See D. Stroud, *op. cit.*, pp. 202–246, and E. Malins and the Knight of Glin, *op. cit.*, p. 89.
11) *Correspondence of the Duchess of Leinster*, ed. Brian FitzGerald, 2v., 1949–57, I, 150.
12) See A. A. Tait, *The Landscape Garden in Scotland, 1735–1835*, 1980; pp. 215–6, 220.
13) Sir William Chambers, *Dissertation on Oriental Gardening*, 1772, pp. 35–9.
14) See Thacker, *The Wildness Pleases*, pp. 184–7.
15) Quoted and illustrated in R. W. King, 'Joseph Spence of Byfleet', *Garden History*, VI, 3 (Winter 1978), 40, 42, 44, 45.
16) R. W. King, *op. cit.*, *Garden History*, VI, 3, 47–9. VII, 3 (Winter 1979), 40, 45; VIII, 3 (Winter 1980), 96, 99, 102.
17) See John Harris, 'Father of the Gardenesque', *Country Life*, 7 June 1979, 1838, 40; H. Walpole, *Correspondence*, XXXI, 35–6.
18) From *A Series of Letters between Mrs Elizabeth Carter and Miss Catherine Talbot* [1808], 4v., 1809, III, 116–7, 162.
19) Quoted in George Sheeran, *Landscape Gardens in West Yorkshire*, 1990, p. 193.
20) See H. Maxwell, *op. cit.*, p. 38.
21) See Ruth Hayden, *Mrs Delany: her Life and Her Flowers*, 1980, ch. 7.
22) See Hazel Le Rougetel, *The Chelsea Gardener*, 1990, pp. 170, 176–7.
23) For a lucid explanation of botanical classification, see William T. Stearn, 'What's in a name?', in *The Making of the English Garden*, ed. Richard Girling, 1988, pp. 116–8.
24) See Ruth Duthie, *Florists' Flowers and Societies*, 1988, fig, 23, 41, and p. 40.
25) See R. Duthie, *op. cit.*, *passim*.
26) J. C. Loudon, *Arboretum et Fruticetum Britannicum*, 8v., 1838, I, 95–9.
27) See Alice M. Coats, *Lord Bute*, 1975, p. 38.

CHAPTER 14

Later Landscapers

1) See Elizabeth Mavor, *The Ladies of Llangollen*, 1971, *passim*.
2) Quoted in C. P. Barbier, *op. cit.*, p. 72.
3) G. W. Johnson, *op. cit.*, p. 268.
4) Sir R. C. Hoare, *op cit.*, p. 109.
5) *Ibid.*, p. 201.
6) Quoted in Lewis Melville, *The Life and Letters of William Beckford*, 1910, p. 123.
7) See my *Enchanting Paths: the Gardens of Painshill, Stourhead and Fonthill*, to be published in 1994.
8) W. B. to Humphry Repton, in L. Melville, *op. cit.*, p. 256.
9) Quoted by J. C. Loudon from unpublished and now lost 'Memoirs' in *The Landscape Gardening . . . of the late Humphry Repton*, 1840, p. 15.
10) *Torrington Diaries*, III, 9, 12.
11) Mason to Gilpin, 26 December 1794, quoted in Mavis Batey, 'William Mason, English Gardener', *Garden History* I, 2 (February 1973), 23.
12) See George Carter, Patrick Goode, Kedrun Laurie, *Humphry Repton: Landscape Gardener*, 1982, p. 73, and Edward Hyams, *Capability Brown and Humphry Repton*, 1971, pp. 165–74.
13) Letter of 23 December 1806, in William and Dorothy Wordsworth, *Letters – The Middle Years*, ed. E. de Selincourt, 2v., 1937, I, 90–7.

CHAPTER 15

'The Suburban Gardener'

1) For a longer, but still incomplete list, see John Gloag, *Mr Loudon's England*, 1970, pp. 179–81.
2) The article is reprinted, and discussed, in Laurence Fricker, 'John Claudius Loudon: The plane truth?', in *Furor Hortensis*, ed. P. Willis, pp. 76–88.
3) See the full and well-illustrated selection from his tours in Priscilla Boniface, ed., *In Search of English Gardens: the Travels of John Claudius Loudon and His Wife Jane*, 1987.
4) *Gardener's Magazine*, XVI, (1840), 534.
5) William Cobbett, *The English Gardener* (1829), intr. Anthony Huxley, 1980, p. 257.
6) See Alice M. Coats, *The Quest for Plants*, 1969; and Kenneth Lemmon, *The Golden Age of Plant Hunters*, 1968.

7) See Marianne North, *Recollections of a Happy Life*, 2v., 1892.

8) From N. B. Ward, *On the Growth of Plants in Closely Glazed Cases*, 1842, p. 47. Cf. C. Thacker, *The History of Gardens* pp. 236–8.

9) In *The Gardener's Magazine*, VII, August 1831, 392.

10) See Peter Hayden, *Biddulph Grange*, 1989.

11) See Sally Festing, 'Pulham has done his work well', *Garden History*, XII, 2, Autumn 1984, 136–56. For Bearwood, cf. *Country Life*, 15 March 1902, 336–43 and *Gardeners' Chronicle*, 20 Jan 1885, 797–9.

12) See F. L. Olmsted, *Walks and Talks of an American Farmer in England*, 1852, pp. 74–83.

13) Nathan Cole, *The Royal Parks and Gardens of London*, 1877, p. 27.

14) See Brent Elliott, *Victorian Gardens*, 1986, pp. 154–8; and *idem.*, 'The Vagaries of Carpet Bedding', *The Garden*, February 1993, pp. 62–5.

15) See R. G. C. Desmond, 'Victorian Horticulture: a Guide to the Literature', *Garden History*, V, 2, Summer 1977.

16) S. Hibberd, *Rustic Adornments*, 2nd. ed., pp. 330–1.

17) *Ibid.*, pp. 348. 353, 407.

18) *Ibid.*, pp. 354, 370–1.

CHAPTER 16

Rebellion

1) Scott's first remarks are in the 'Introduction' to *Quentin Durward*, (1823), much enlarged in his essay 'On Ornamental Plantations and Landscape Gardening', *The Quarterly Review*, v. 37, no. 74, 1828, 303–44. See esp. 303–17.

2) See A. A. Tait, *op. cit.*, pp. 203–9.

3) 2v., 1839, II, 465–91. The Librarian at Charterhouse School, Mrs A. C. Wheeler, has kindly informed me that the author was most probably Thomas James (1809–63), assistant master at Charterhouse 1832–36.

4) *Ibid.*, II, 466–7, 472–3. In his scorn for the named dahlias – 'The Quakeress', 'Jim Crow', 'King Boy' and a dozen more – he quotes a rapturous section of George Crabbe's verses, from *The Borough* (1810) letter viii – on the *auricula*! An intriguing deception, obligingly pointed out to me by Thomasina Beck.

5) See R. C. Turner, *Mellor's Gardens* (guide book), 1989.

6) Samuel Felton, *Gleanings on Gardens* [1829], 1897, pp. 73–7. See also Brent Elliott, *op. cit.*, pp. 63–4, on aesthetic and political attitudes to the cottages of the rural labourers in the first half of the century.

7) Benjamin Disraeli, Lord Beaconsfield, *Lothair*, 1870, pp. 480–2.

8) Ouida, 'Gardens', in *Views and Opinions*, 1895, p. 48.

9) 'The Poetry of Gardening', II, 467.

10) Compare the engraving by Romein de Hooghe, in his *Short Description of the King's Loo*, 1698, pl. 3, with E. Adveno Brooke's view of the area named 'Mon Plaisir' in *The Gardens of England*, 1856, pl. 16.

11) See Annette Bagot, 'Monsieur Beaumont and Col. Grahme . . .', *Garden History*, III, 4, 1975, 66–78; J. C. Loudon, *The Gardener's Magazine*, VII, October 1831, 550; William Gilpin, *Observations on . . . Westmoreland . . . 1772*, 3rd. ed., 2v. in 1, 1805, I, 84; John Britton *et al.*, *The Beauties of England and Wales*, XV, ii, 1814, 225.

12) Philip Henry Stanhope, *History of England from the Peace of Utrecht*, 7v., 1836–54, VI, (1851), 500; G. F. Weston, 'Levens Hall, Westmoreland', *The Archaeological Journal*, XXVI, June 1869, 97–120.

13) Dante Gabriel Rossetti, *Letters*, ed. Oswald Doughty and John Robert Wahl, 2 v., 1965, II, 609.

14) 'The Poetry of Gardening', II, 482–8. The idea of the flower-dial had been suggested long before, by Linnaeus, and was taken up again by J. C. Loudon – cf. E. S. Rohde, *op. cit.*, p. 227.

15) E. G. E. L. Bulwer-Lytton, 'Motive Power', in *Caxtoniana* [1863], 1875, pp. 241–4.

16) William Robinson, *The Parks . . . of Paris*, 1869, pp. 574–6. Cf. C. Thacker, *Historic Garden Tools*, 1990, pp. 10, 35.

17) William Robinson, *op. cit.*, pp. 247, 2 42.

18) Forbes Watson, *Flowers and Gardens*, 1872, pp. 131, 138, 136, 168.

19) *Ibid.*, pp. 178, 203.

20) See C. Thacker, 'Voltaire and Rousseau: eighteenth-century gardeners', in *Studies on Voltaire in the Eighteenth Century*, XC, 1972, 1596–1614; also Thacker, *The Wildness Pleases*, pp. 225–9.

21) William Robinson, *The Wild Garden*, [1870], 'Foreword' to 1894 edition, and pp. 122–4.

22) *Ibid.*, pp. 2–3.

23) *Ibid.*, pp. 4, 9, 75, 86, 137.

24) William Morris, 'Making the Best of It' in *Hopes and Fears for Art*, 1882, pp. 123–8.

25) William Robinson, *The English Flower Garden*, 8th ed., 1902, p. 20.

26) *Country Life*, 28 Sep. 1912, 409–11.
27) Sir Herbert Maxwell, 'Gardens' in *Post Meridiana*, 1895, p. 286. A few years later, G. F. Wilson himself described his grounds 'as a place where plants from all over the world grow wild' – in *The Garden*, vol. 57, 1900, 17.
28) Sir Herbert Maxwell, *Scottish Gardens*, pp. 39, 85–90.
29) W. Robinson, *The English Flower Garden*, 8th ed., 1902, pp. 299–301. There is nothing in the 1st ed. of 1883. The commentary is part Ellacombe, and part F. W. Burbidge.
30) H. N. Ellacombe, *The Plant-Lore and Garden-Craft of Shakespeare*, [1878], 'new edition', c. 1896, p. 369.
31) See Brent Elliott, *op. cit.*, pp. 228–30, 240; Alastair Forsyth, *Yesterday's Gardens*, 1983, pl. 67, 69, 70; David Ottewill, *The Edwardian Garden*, 1989, p. 151–2.
32) S. Reynolds Hole, *A Book about the Garden and the Gardener*, n.d., (1892), pp. 220–1.
33) For these Irish gardens see Edward Malins and Patrick Bowe, *Irish Gardens and Demesnes*, pp. 115–6, 119–22, 123–7.
34) Reginald Blomfield, *The Formal Garden in England*, 1892, p. 2.
35) *Ibid.*, p. 20.
36) See Brent Elliott, *op. cit.*, p. 228; David Ottewill, *op. cit.*, p. 18.
37) John Buchan, *John Macnab*, 1925, ch. xiii, 'Haripol – Auxiliary Troops', pp. 267–8.
38) J. J. Joass, 'On Gardening: with some description of formal gardens in Scotland', *The Studio*, II, 1897, 165–176; R. S. Lorimer, 'On Scottish Gardens', *The Archaeological Review*, VI, November 1899, 194–205.
39) Sir Herbert Maxwell, *Scottish Gardens*, pp. 91–5; D. Ottewill, *op. cit.*, p. 42.
40) See *Country Life*, 3 Aug. 1912, 162–7; D. Ottewill, *op. cit.*, pp. 47–8.
41) Illustrations of the 'woodland walks' for this scheme appear in the first and second editions of *The Art and Craft of Garden Making*. See also Geoffrey Beard, *Thomas H. Mawson: a Northern Landscape Architect*, 1976, p. 59.
42) See the illustrations in Charles Holme, *Gardens of the Northern Counties*, 1911, pl. 109–10.
43) See Charles Quest-Ritson, *The English Garden Abroad*, 1992, pp. 34–43.
44) For High Wall, see Percy S. Cane, *Modern Gardens British and Foreign*, (The Studio) 1926–7, pp. 26–8.
45) See Edward Malins and Patrick Bowe, *Irish Gardens and Demesnes*, pp. 97–100; D. Ottewill, *op. cit.*, pp. 155–6.

CHAPTER 17

'Partly Formal, Partly Controlled Wild'

1) Cf. Francis Jekyll, *Gertrude Jekyll: a Memoir*, 1934, pp. 87–8, 134.
2) The Rev C. A. Johns, *Flowers of the Field* (1853), republished many times. See Gertrude Jekyll, *Wood and Garden* (1899), pp. 192–3.
3) Gertrude Jekyll, *Wood and Garden*, p. 184.
4) Quoted without reference in Francis Jekyll, *op. cit.*, p. 108.
5) *Ibid.*, pp. 105–9.
6) For a thoughtful description and 'reconstruction' of Munstead Wood in Jekyll's time, see Jane Brown, *Gardens of a Golden Afternoon*, 1982, pp. 33–46.
7) From an article in *Gardening Illustrated*, 27 Aug. 1927, reproduced in Gertrude Jekyll, *A Gardener's Testament*, edd. Francis Jekyll and G. C. Taylor, [1937], 1984, p. 14.
8) Undated recollections by Harold Falkner quoted in Betty Massingham, *Miss Jekyll*, 1966, p. 83.
9) Gertrude Jekyll, *Wood and Garden*, pp. 212, 207.
10) Gertrude Jekyll, article in *Empire Review*, 1924, quoted in *A Gardener's Testament* p. 63. Cf. *ibid.*, p. 164.
11) There is a fine summary in Betty Massingham, *op. cit.*, pp. 122–7. See also Gertrude Jekyll, *A Gardener's Testament*, ch. vi, 'Colour in the Garden'.
12) *Ibid.*, pp. 166, 171, 178.
13) *Ibid.*, p. 168, from *Journal of the Royal Horticultural Society*, LIV, 2, 1929.
14) See Jane Brown, *op. cit.*, p. 159.
15) Francis Jekyll, *op. cit.*, p. 208. Cf. pp. 141–2.
16) Practically all the gardens mentioned in this table are described and illustrated in either or both of the following: Lawrence Weaver, *Houses and Gardens by Sir Edwin Lutyens, R. A.*, 1925; Gertrude Jekyll and Lawrence Weaver, *Gardens for Small Country Houses*, 1912. See also David Ottewill, *The Edwardian Garden*.
17) Cf. Charles Quest-Ritson, *op. cit.*, pp. 50–2.
18) Nathaniel Lloyd, *op. cit.*, p. 9.
19) Vita Sackville-West, *The Garden*, 1946, 'Summer', p. 112.
20) See my *History of Gardens*, ch. 4.
21) See Herbert Goode, *The Japanese Garden at Cottered, Herts 1905–1933*, 1933.
22) See Elisabeth Whittle, *op. cit.*, pp. 74–5.
23) See Edward Malins and Patrick Bowe, *op. cit.*, pp. 150–2.

CHAPTER 18
Modern Masters

1) See Percy Cane, *The Earth is My Canvas*, 1956, pp. 79–83, 153–6.
2) See Ronald Webber, *Percy Cane*, 1974, pp. 62–3.
3) See Edward Hyams, *Irish Gardens*, 1967, pp. 51–7.
4) Cf. E. Malins and P. Bowe, *op. cit.*, pp. 166–8.
5) For these two gardens, cf. George Plumptre, *The Latest Country Gardens*, 1988, pp. 121–5.

A SHORT BIBLIOGRAPHY

Since details of all works consulted are given in the notes to each chapter, it is both unnecessary and misleading to list here more than the essential texts.

Periodicals

Three periodicals must be included: *Country Life* (1897–), for its unequalled photographic record; *Garden History* (1972–); and *The Journal of Garden History* (1981–).

General

Amherst, Alicia M. T., *A History of Gardening in England*, 1895
Coats, Alice M., *Flowers and Their Histories*, 1968
Coats, Alice M., *Garden Shrubs and Their Histories*, 1963
Coats, Alice M., *The Quest for Plants*, 1969
Desmond, Ray, *Bibliography of British Gardens*, 1984
English Heritage (Historic Buildings and Monuments Commission for England), *Register of Parks and Gardens of Special Historic Interest in England* (46 v., in 44 parts), 1984–8
Hadfield, Miles, *A History of British Gardening*, 1969 (originally *Gardening in Britain*, 1960)
Henrey, Blanche, *British Botanical and Horticultural Literature before 1800* (3 v.), 1975
Hunt, Peter, ed., *The Shell Gardens Book*, 1964
Johnson, George W., *A History of English Gardening*, 1829 (reissued in facsimile *c.*1978)
Jones, Barbara, *Follies and Grottoes*, enlarged ed., 1974
Matthews, W. H., *Mazes and Labyrinths*, 1970
Roach, F. A., *Cultivated Fruits of Britain: Their Origin and History*, 1986
Scott-James, Anne and Lancaster, Osbert, *The Pleasure Garden*, 1979
Taylor, Christopher, *The Archaeology of Gardens*, 1983
Thacker, Christopher, *The History of Gardens*, 1985
Thomas, Graham Stuart, *Gardens of the National Trust*, 1979

Middle Ages

Harvey, John H., *Mediaeval Gardens*, 1981

Seventeenth and Eighteenth Centuries

Green, David, *Gardener to Queen Anne: Henry Wise*, 1956
Hunt, John Dixon and Willis, Peter, *The Genius of the Place*, 1975
Hussey, Christopher, *English Gardens and Landscapes, 1700–1750*, 1967
Malins, Edward, *English Landscaping and Literature, 1660–1840*, 1965
Stroud, Dorothy, *Capability Brown*, enlarged ed., 1975

Nineteenth Century

Boniface, Priscilla, *The Garden Room*, 1982
Elliott, Brent, *Victorian Gardens*, 1986
Forsyth, Alastair, *Yesterday's Gardens*, 1983

Twentieth Century

Ottewill, David, *The Edwardian Garden*, 1989
Plumptre, George, *The Latest Country Gardens*, 1988

Ireland

Malins, Edward and the Knight of Glin, *Lost Demesnes, Irish Landscape Gardening, 1660–1845*, 1976
Malins, Edward and Bowe, Patrick, *Irish Gardens and Demesnes from 1830*, 1980
Nelson, E. C. and Brady, A., eds., *Irish Gardening and Horticulture*, 1976

Isle of Man

Garrad, Larch S., *A History of Manx Gardens*, 1985

Scotland

Land Use Consultants, Glasgow, *An Inventory of Gardens and Designed Landscapes in Scotland* (5 v.), 1987
Tait, A. A., *The Landscape Garden in Scotland, 1735–1835*, 1980

Wales

Whittle, Elisabeth, *The Historic Gardens of Wales*, 1992

INDEX